TITIRANGI

TITIRANGI
Fringe of Heaven

MARC BONNY

Edited by Bruce and Trixie Harvey

West Auckland
Historical Society INC

To the pioneers and residents who have made Titirangi what it is today.

Published with the assistance of the Portage Licensing Trust, the Waitakere City Council and Wallie Titchener.

Published for the West Auckland Historical Society, Inc. P.O. Box 21-416, Henderson, Auckland, New Zealand by Oratia Media, 783 West Coast Road, Oratia, Auckland 0604; www.oratiamedia.com

Copyright © 2011 West Auckland Historical Society Inc.
Copyright in this edition © 2011 West Auckland Historical Society

The copyright holders assert their moral rights in the work. The right of Marc Bonny to be identified as the author of this work and Bruce and Trixie Harvey to be identified as the editors of this work in terms of section 96 of the Copyright Act 1994 is hereby asserted. All rights reserved.

This book is copyright. Except for the purposes of fair reviewing, no part of this publication may be reproduced or transmitted in any form or by any means, whether electronic, digital or mechanical, including photocopying, recording, any digital or computerised format, or any information storage and retrieval system, including by any means via the Internet, without permission in writing from the publisher. Infringers of copyright render themselves liable to prosecution.

ISBN 978-1-877514-13-5
First published 2011

Project editor: Carolyn Lagahetau
Design: Katsura

Cover image: Frederick Rice Stack *View from Titirangi looking towards Little Muddy Creek and the Manukau Harbour* 1862. (Alexander Turnbull Library, Wellington, NZ, c-060-023)

Typeset in Sabon
Printed in China by Nordica

Contents

Preface — Trevor Pollard 6
Acknowledgements 7
Introduction 8

Part 1 The Chronicle

1   The beginning 13
2   The Bishops — an early settler family 24
3   Early vigour 41
4   The Atkinson story 55
5   Exhibition Drive 59
6   Improved communications 65
7   Prominent buildings in Titirangi 71
8   Community gatherings 81
9   Sports and services in growing Titirangi 93
10 Early days in Titirangi arts: a recollection by Lois McIvor 100
11 At home among the trees 105
12 Performing and literary arts in Titirangi: 1950s to the present .. 114
13 Rangiwai and the Geddes family 122
14 Nature and nurture 124

Part 2 The Memoirs

Essie Hodge 136 • The Burberys and the Thursbys 147 • Thayer Fairburn 149
Alwynne Broady 157 • The Bright family 161 • The Gordon family 163
W.N. (Bill) Bishop 166 • Bernard Holibar 170 • Estelle Bray 178 • Ken Hanson 191
Hendrina Sluiters 197 • Dr Mary Hamilton 200 • David Kennedy 202
Dr David Blaiklock 205 • Wallie Titchener 208 • Graham and Vivienne Shaw 212
H. Morgan Lewis 215 • Marc Bonny 220 • Trevor Pollard 223

Appendices

1   The Bishop family 226
2   Crown grants and landholders in Titirangi 228
3   Map of lots 231
4   Electoral roll for Northern Division 1855 232
5   Waitemata Electoral Roll, 1881 234
6   Titirangi women enrolled to vote in the Eden electorate, 1893 235
7   The Titirangi Post Office 235
8   The Titirangi Drama Group 236

Further reading 237
Index 238

Preface

My personal interest in the history of Titirangi comes from my 60 years of living in Titirangi, firstly with my parents and then building my own house and raising my family and working in the surrounding area.

The West Auckland Historical Society's interests span the whole of West Auckland, but in Titirangi, my interest in the history is compounded by observations and memories of the village and surrounding area over a period of change, from a rather poor hideaway for artists and potters to a bustling, prosperous suburb noted for the beauty of its regenerating forest and spectacular views of the surrounding hills and the Manukau Harbour.

In my work I have visited an enormous number of homes in the area and have come to know many people and their backgrounds. My interest and work for the Volunteer Fire Brigade has further enhanced my deep interest and understanding of the area.

Historical Society member, Marc Bonny, has collected memoirs and information from Titirangi residents for many years and, with the help of editors Bruce and Trixie Harvey and other Society members, has tackled the huge task of presenting this information to the public in a readable and interesting form.

Since 1990 the Society has published several books, beginning with the two volumes of *West Auckland Remembers* and followed by *Rail Tracks and Chimney Stacks, Whatipu, A Brief History of Henderson Creek* and smaller pamphlets on Henderson Mill and early Henderson. The Society now puts out *West of Eden*, a journal published several times a year that contains interesting articles and photographs on topics researched by its members. The Society is committed to preserving and recording local history in the West Auckland area, and this book is a further addition to its list of publications. We intend it to be a worthy companion to our other local histories and hope it will be popular with present residents and those whose roots lie in Titirangi.

Trevor Pollard
President of West Auckland Historical Society Inc.
2011

Acknowledgements

It is always difficult to isolate the help that has been obtained in creating a book such as this, where there have been so many people contributing to not only the information contained in it but also the photographs, maps and other inputs that make up the whole.

Marc Bonny has collected the major part of the information over many years of research. He has also collected or tracked down most of the illustrations. In the task of collating and sorting the illustrations he has been greatly helped by West Auckland Historical Society colleague Vivien Burgess. We are greatly indebted to those who have written articles on special topics such as Arnold Turner and Fiona Drummond, whose research into the history of Exhibition Drive was done originally for *Waitakere Ranges* and is reprinted and updated here; Megan Edwards and Jacqueline Bell, two local architects who have made a special study of Titirangi architecture; Alison O'Grady, who has written a more detailed history of West Lynn Gardens; Kate Wells, who brought our knowledge of Lopdell House Gallery's events and functions up to date; and Lois McIvor, whose delightful book *Memoir of the Sixties* records the arts scene in Auckland during that decade of change and innovation. Trevor Moreland and Randolph Covich wrote the history of the Fire Brigade, Peter Van Rooyen the article on the Coast Guard, Martin Northcott wrote the history of the French Bay Yacht Club and Dave Lawrence updated the history of the Returned Serviceman's Association (RSA). Others who gave assistance from their personal knowledge and have allowed us to use existing articles and reproduce paintings, photographs and maps are: Beverley Buffett, Pim van der Voort, Edith Diggle, Bill Bishop, Lisa Truttman, Gilbert and Doreen Shaw, Wallie Titchener, Graeme Murdoch, Fane Kearney, John and Claire Geddes, Andrew and Janet Geddes, Peter and Jean Blaiklock, Dr David Blaiklock, Len Castle, Sandy Matheson, Angela McKnight, Mia Stein, Helen Dammer, Simon Devitt, Brigid Ursula Bisley, Harvey Waite, Mary Woodward, Dorothy Ann Whiteoak and the late Cyril Whiteoak. We also thank the many old identities of Titirangi who contributed to the oral and written histories on which we depended for this book.

We also thank Louise Pether of the Colin McCahon Trust; Kyle Balderston, Planning, Waitakere City; David Verran, Auckland City Library; Keith Giles, Sir George Grey Special Collections, Auckland Central Library; George Wadsworth, The Huia Museum; Auckland War Memorial Museum; the Waitakere Library and Information Services; and Nick Keenleyside, cartographer.

Without the sponsors, Waitakere City Council, Portage Licensing Trust and Mr Wallie Titchener and our team, with the overview of Peter Dowling and Carolyn Lagahetau of Oratia Media, Lesley Smith, designer, and the help of Trevor Pollard, Gai Bishop, Vivien Burgess and Lisa Truttman, proofreaders and the West Auckland Historical Society, we would not have won the day. Thank you one and all.

Marc Bonny, Bruce Harvey, Trixie Harvey
2011

Introduction

Over many years Marc Bonny has interviewed many older residents of Titirangi for their recollections and insights about the past. He has also collected photographs and articles about the Titirangi area from newspapers, magazines and other publications both past and present, and assembled information from the West Auckland Historical Society Inc. (WAHS), other similar societies and the libraries and institutions of Auckland.

In 2008, the editors, Bruce and Trixie Harvey, were invited to help with a publication about Titirangi, sponsored by the West Auckland Historical Society. Because there were many memoirs and experiences that had emotional appeal as well as historical information, it was decided to divide the book into two parts: 'The Chronicle', which presents the history as a sequence from Maori beginnings to the present day; followed by 'The Memoirs', which show a more personal view. The memories and writings of the people that were in the area at the time form the major narrative throughout both parts.

The Titirangi area had a dramatic Maori history before the settlement of Pakeha. The area was the scene of the defeat of Waiohua, who had controlled most of the Tamaki isthmus until the mid-1750s. This battle occurred on the Titirangi slopes, towards the present Arataki Centre.

The timber getters, cutters and sawing stations pre-dated bush burning and farming, which at that time helped to feed growing Auckland. The lives of the first settlers reflect the pioneer times of nineteenth century New Zealand, leading to the gradual settling of the village and its conversion into the attractive bush outer-suburb it is today.

This book gives an insight into the settlers, their hardships and their achievements, the roads and communications and the growing community that required buildings for education and other public needs. After the New Zealand Land Wars during the 1860s, Auckland's needs were increasingly met by products from the Waikato, which was being opened up for intensive farming. As a result, land west of Auckland became less important for farming. The land was always marginal for food production and farm labour was increasingly hard to find as workers were attracted to jobs in the city. After the First World

Huia Road with view towards Titirangi c.1885. Waitakere Library and Information Services

War, land around Titirangi slowly recovered much of its former forest beauty, with thousands of small kauri rickers reaching for the sky.

Today, Titirangi is a beautiful village. The beaches of the Manukau and the returning forest attracted, at first, holidaymakers, then new residents with their makeshift housing. In the 1950s, 1960s and 1970s, higher quality and innovative residential buildings were constructed and an artistic element came to Titirangi that included painters, potters, wood carvers, designers, writers and architects. The performing arts were not forgotten during the settler period and this facet of the community continued to develop into drama and music societies from the 1930s on. Many community organisations evolved in the early twentieth century including the Titirangi Beautifying Society, the RSA and the Titirangi Residents and Ratepayers Association, all contributing to making a vibrant society.

In recent years a redevelopment plan for the village has seen power lines moved underground and a major upgrade, making it a focal point for visitors to the west. We do not want to forget our history or our beginnings and this publication is an endeavour to make a record for ourselves and future citizens. Unless we know the past, we cannot fully understand the present.

Bruce and Trixie Harvey
Editors
May 2010

In this part of the book the editors have tried to record the history of Titirangi as extracted from written articles, some interviews and the research of members of the West Auckland Historical Society, principally Marc Bonny.

We have also included pieces written specifically for this volume; Lois McIvor writes about the arts and artists in Titirangi during the 1950s, and Megan Edwards and Jacqueline Bell explore the architecture that was such a feature of Titirangi during the period 1950–70.

We have tried to give a picture of the village's growth from a Maori battlefield to a timber workers' camp, which was followed by a farming period, became an artists' hideaway and eventually changed into a sophisticated urban village on the outskirts of Auckland.

Maori canoe in bush, Huia Road area (detail). Chappie Bishop is on the left.
Waitakere Library & Information Services, Bishop Collection

Part 1
The Chronicle

Maori canoe in bush, Huia Road area. Chappie Bishop is on the left.
Waitakere Library & Information Services, Bishop Collection

1

The beginning

Titirangi is a village and a district on the outskirts of Auckland, gateway to the Waitakere Ranges and the west coast's dark dramatic beaches; a village with a character all its own. The area was named by the Maori chief Rakataura in the fourteenth century, a name given at that time to the whole range of hills that run along the edge of the Manukau Harbour at right angles to the main Waitakere Range, which at that time was known to the Maori as Hikurangi.[1]

Rangi is the Sky God of Maori legend and Titirangi is sometimes translated as 'the edge of Rangi's realm', or more poetically 'the fringe of heaven'. It is a name that suits the area perfectly.

The steep ranges to the west of the Tamaki isthmus are the eroded remains of a large volcano that was active in the western sea about 20 million years ago.[2] Titirangi is situated on the eastern and southern flank of the dumped remains of a cataclysmic eruption and is where the Waitemata sandstone that covers most of the Auckland isthmus meets the volcanic remains.

To the south and west Titirangi looks out to the Manukau Harbour that was formed from a faultline of the original volcano. A navigable channel runs close to the Titirangi side, from the harbour mouth to Onehunga, and this was used extensively by Maori and early Pakeha settlers. The shores of the Manukau and the slopes leading up to Titirangi have been settled and traversed since humans first came to New Zealand. Ridges crowned with tall kauri forest, and stream-fed gullies with tree ferns and nikau were the environment encountered by early Maori and the first European settlers.

The muddy estuaries, down the hill from Titirangi, were important food gathering places for Maori, who also used the flatter areas for growing kumara. Remains of pa and food stores can be found all along the Manukau coast at Little Muddy Creek (Laingholm), Tokoroa Point (the point at the end of South Titirangi Road), Green Bay and Blockhouse Bay.[3] Extensive middens can be found all along the coast, echoes of long-ago feasts consisting of the sea bounty of the harbour. Maori also used the forest, cutting down trees for canoes. The unfinished remains of some of these have been found in Alice Glen between Titirangi and Little Muddy Creek.[4] A tributary of the Whau is known as Kotuitanga, or the 'dovetailing of canoes'.

The Whau River (the eastern boundary of Titirangi district) is named after a native tree, *Entelea arborescens*, which has large, heart-shaped leaves, white flowers and a spiny seed case. During ancient times, the tree was common on the banks of the rivers. The wood of the whau is exceedingly light and Maori used it to make rafts and floats for fishing nets. Of particular importance to Maori in this area was the Whau portage. One of the shortest and easiest routes between the eastern and western coasts of New Zealand was by canoe, from the Waitemata Harbour up the Whau River as far as was possible, and then to drag the canoe over land the short distance to the Manukau Harbour at Green Bay.

The Whau portage was protected by two pa; one at Te Whau Point (Blockhouse Bay), protected by a large ditch,[5] and the other, known as Karaka Pa, on the high cliff tops west of Green Bay. On the low-lying flats alongside the tidal reaches of the Whau are middens, indicating the temporary camping sites of Maori parties.[6] At New Lynn, on Great North Road by the shopping centre, the Portage Sculpture of a waka being carried on the shoulders of warriors[7] symbolises the historic importance of this area[8] as the main connecting route. It was used by northern Maori to reach the Manukau from where they could then reach the Waikato River via the Waiuku portage. In pre-European times this was the equivalent of a main highway south, and it is the route followed by Hongi Hika in 1824 on one of his expeditions to the Auckland and Waikato areas.[9]

To the north, the link from north of the Kaipara via that harbour to a portage at Riverhead led into the Waitemata. From there the Whau provided access to the Manukau and the highway of the Waikato and Waipa rivers. Associated with the portage were tracks leading to the summit of the Titirangi ridge (roughly following present day Godley Road) and along the harbour's edge to Cornwallis, Whatipu, then following the ocean northwards to Te Henga. Another walkway skirted the foothills of the Waitakere Ranges and headed north via present day Henderson, and another track followed the Whau Stream to its headwaters and then on to Maungakiekie, the site of an important pa.

The earliest inhabitants of the area were the legendary turehu or patupaiarehe ('fairies' or 'forest people'), who lived in the great forest of Tiriwa (the Waitakere Ranges). From them are descended Te Kawerau and Waiohua. Titirangi is on the edge of the ranges and has been a sphere of influence for tribes of the great forest and the isthmus, Tamaki Makau-Rau (Auckland). Both areas had resources, the trees and food of the forest, the fishing in the harbour, and on the wild coast, and kumara growing on the volcanic flats

Extract from the diary of Rev. Richard Laishley, 1860

The natives not infrequently visit Little Muddy Creek (Laingholm) and cut their canoes in the neighbouring forest. I myself saw one of these in an unfinished state, probably 40 or 50 feet in length. As the tree, a large kauri, fell, it was cut off immediately below the branches and at once shaped where it fell. Perhaps as many as 100 natives assemble from a distance to launch the canoe when it is ready for sea. They bring a large supply of provisions with them and when the canoe is launched they feast, while the proprietor of the canoe walks up and down and in a speech returns thanks to his friends who have aided him to convey it to the sea. The pigs are roasted in holes in the ground heated for the purpose and the women serve potatoes in little baskets on the occasion. The Maori dance on these occasions but are careful to observe their morning and evening devotions. The women make a gay appearance adorning their heads tastefully with feathers. About seven of these launches took place last year. The settlers speak in the highest terms of the Maori justice and intelligence.

> **In his memoir, Thayer Fairburn recalls the track from Green Bay to the area of 'Godleys'.**
> We thought it to be the original Maori track from the Blockhouse [pa] out to Huia — we believed it went through Haresnape's* place in Titirangi because he could still see the remains of an old road coming out from the Toby Jug and going down South Titirangi Road.
>
> Thayer Fairburn, oral history, West Auckland Historical Society
>
> *(Bill Haresnape's home was in upper Otitori Road.)
>
> **Professor Blaiklock[10] remembers:**
> An ancient track running south from the eastern border [of their property] ran straight as natural obstacles allowed to its harbourside destination. Perhaps it was the last remnant of a trail that may have begun on the other side of the isthmus, Auckland's Karangahape Road, the line of a ridge track of the Orakei tribesmen. They would make for the Western Springs, then with a line on some Titirangi summit come on along the line of the Great North Road, circle the top end on the Whau Estuary and join the other East West track which is Godley Road.

and in the valleys of the west coast. Various tribal groupings at times occupied the isthmus: Nga Oho in the thirteenth century, and Ngati Awa in the fifteenth and sixteenth centuries. These groups built the great pa at Maungakiekie, and probably also built the pa called Te Karaka at Green Bay and another at Te Whau Point.[11] During the seventeenth century two main tribes on the isthmus were Nga Iwi and Waiohua; from 1700 Waiohua dominated from the Tamaki River to the Whau.[12]

The area known as the Whau portage or just 'the Whau' is the area encompassing the upper reaches of the Whau stream, its tributary and the land over which Maori dragged their canoes to the Manukau Harbour. Beyond the Whau, tribal boundaries were more fluid, but a mixed people called Te Kawerau a Maki came to dominate. Maki was a leader of Ngati Awa, who migrated from Taranaki. He defeated the Waiohua and Kawerau and eventually settled with the latter at South Kaipara and along the west coast. Also originating from the Kaipara were Ngati Whatua, who invaded the Tamaki isthmus between 1680 and 1730, taking many Waiohua pa.[13] Friction also occurred between Ngati Whatua and Te Kawerau a Maki, notably when Kawharu, a famous Waikato warrior chief allied to Ngati Whatua, exacted revenge on Te Kawerau for the killing of two Ngati Whatua chiefs in the Kaipara. This was known as the 'stripping conquest' and many Te Kawerau people were trapped and killed at Destruction Gully, near Whatipu. Later, in a famous battle with Waiohua leader Kiwi Tamaki, Ngati Whatua defeated Waiohua at Titirangi and proceeded across the Manukau to attack pa at Awhitu and Papakura. Returning across the harbour, they assembled at Paruroa (Big Muddy Creek, now Parau) and were attacked by Kiwi Tamaki, who was eager for revenge. As Ngati Whatua retreated up the slopes towards Titirangi, their eagerness led Waiohua to put themselves at a tactical disadvantage and Ngati Whatua regrouped and attacked, killing Kiwi Tamaki and many of his warriors. From then on Ngati Whatua were masters of the Tamaki isthmus and controlled the Manukau shore up to Huia Valley, including the Titirangi area and the Whau portage. The Waiohua, however, were not completely wiped out and continued to live on the isthmus and marry into families of Ngati Whatua and Te Kawerau people.

Beyond Huia and up the coast to South Kaipara was the principal domain of Te Kawerau a Maki. In the eastern area of the isthmus Ngati Ata and Akitai of Waikato occupied some areas. This was the situation when Europeans first visited the Waitemata Harbour.

During the 1820s and early 1830s, Hongi Hika and Ngapuhi from the north obtained muskets and war parties invaded the area. Inhabitants of the isthmus and the ranges fled their pa and gardens to take refuge in the Waikato. When Europeans first came to settle rather than just visit, the isthmus and the Manukau were only sparsely populated. It was not until 1835 that Maori began to return from the Waikato to their traditional homelands in the Waitakeres and the north Manukau shore. In 1836 the Karangahape pa was constructed on Puponga peninsula (Cornwallis) and Ngati Whatua, Te Kawerau and other Waikato people occupied it for a short while. In 1838 many of these people shifted to Mangere, where they rebuilt their gardens. Some Te Kawerau people drifted back to the Waitakere coast. At this time Europeans, missionaries, timber cutters and would-be farmers and settlers were becoming interested in acquiring land around the Manukau and Waitemata harbours.

In the 1830s and early 1840s, Europeans noted the resources in the area, particularly timber along the Manukau shore and the easy access by water to the bays and creeks. Initially, few looked to settle and farm; most were interested in cutting the timber. The landing at Little Muddy Creek was used by visiting boats, and pit sawing was carried out in minor settlements in the bays between Huia and Blockhouse Bay. The Woodsman's Rest Inn at Swanson Bay on Big Muddy Creek was set up to cater to bushmen and pit sawyers. Some attempts to buy land were made. Missionary William White and timberman John Mitchell 'bought' a huge amount of land from Maori at Karangahape pa in 1835. This land was later sold to the Manukau Company in the ill-fated Cornwallis settlement. The amount of land bought in this purchase was severely reduced with the advent of Crown control, but final settlement was a long time coming for the migrants at Cornwallis.

After 1840 the population of Auckland burgeoned, but incoming immigrants were unable to access land to the south of Auckland. This created pressure on areas that were accessible, such as the west, and a road was pushed through to Titirangi. The road or track passed through Blockhouse Bay, across the upper reaches of the Whau and up to the ridge at approximately the position of the present Golf Road. From there it passed over the ridge and into the valley following the present Atkinson Road and up again to the Titirangi ridge

---

Our research into the names of geographical features in the Titirangi area included stories about the naming of Opou Point, a headland between Wood Bay and French Bay on the Manukau harbour.

Graeme Murdoch, a Maori historian, explained the name as follows. The proper name of the place is Te Kai o Poutukeka, The Food of Poutukeka. Poutukeka lived several hundred years before the tribe called Te Kawerau came to the area, although they descend from him through marriage with Te Waiohua. Poutukeka was a leading chief of the Tainui canoe and stopped at the point for a meal when first exploring the Manukau Harbour. Poutukeka later settled on Puketutu Island, where his dwelling place is also known as Opou. He was a founding ancestor of Ngati Poutukeka, who later became known as Waiohua. His descendants still live at marae around the Manukau.

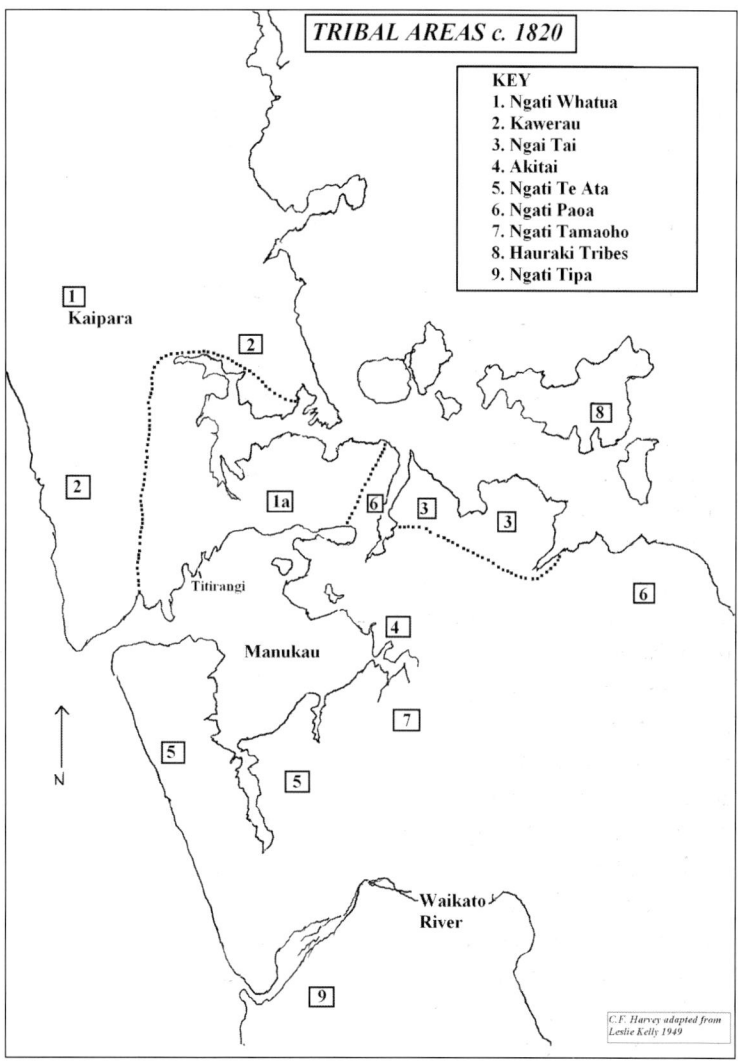

Tribal district map, c.1820. These areas were roughly the same in 1750, except in area 1a where Waiohua were in control of the Tamaki isthmus before the invasion of Ngati Whatua. Ngati Whatua (1a), Akitai (4) and Ngati Te Ata (5) were the Maori vendors when the Crown made the Hikurangi Purchase (Deed 280) in 1853.

C.F. Harvey, adapted from map of L.G. Kelly c.1949

at the position of the village. From there it ran down South Titirangi Road and turned down the hill to Little Muddy Landing (now Landing Road).

In a letter to Governor Hobson in 1841, the Surveyor General Felton Mathew[14] said,

> ... there is an excellent line of road from the portage at the *Wahu* (Whau) to Auckland; but from the *Wahu* to Karangahape (Cornwallis) no practicable line can be found except along the shore at low water, with the disadvantage of two or three considerable streams and a great deal of soft mud to traverse between the two places ...

In the first years of Crown control, private buyers were prevented from acquiring Maori land. All sales were supposed to be 'pre-emption sales', that is the Crown bought land to resell to settlers. However, during Governor Fitzroy's term (1843–45) the ban on private buyers was waived, causing some confusion.

In 1845 Governor Grey reinstated 'pre-emption sales' and continued to review all previous sales. All of the Titirangi area was included in a sale in 1853 called the 'Hikurangi

The beginning 17

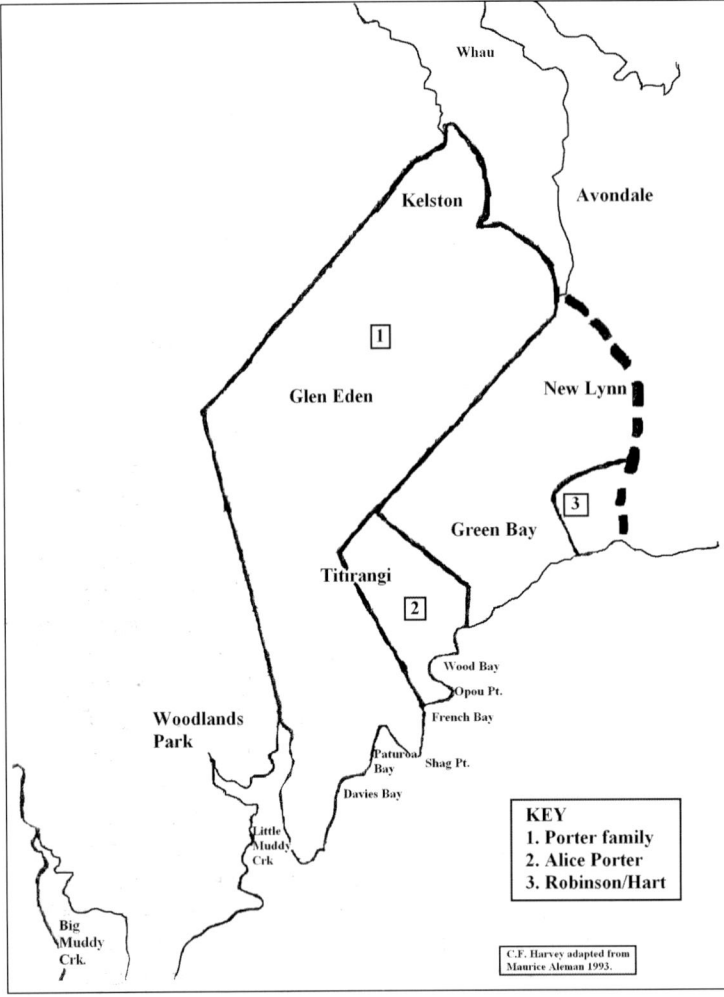

The Porter 'Purchase'. This map shows the extent of the land purchase by the Porter family (600 + 4300 acres), stretching from the Whau to Little Muddy Creek in 1845. The Maori vendors were chiefs Te Keene and Te Kawau of Ngati Whatua. In 1848 these claims were disallowed.

C.F. Harvey, adapted from an illustration in 'Earliest Land Transactions', a talk given to the West Auckland Historical Society by Maurice Alemann, 1992

purchase', which repurchased the land extending from the Whau portage along the Manukau coast to Whatipu, along the coast to Te Ahu (a point between Karekare and Piha), back to the Waitemata Harbour to a point north of the Te Atatu Peninsula and along that coast back to the Whau estuary. Three tribal groups signed the deed of sale; Ngati Whatua, Ngati Ata, and Akitai of Waikato.[15] Te Kawerau a Maki were conspicuously absent.

In the early 1840s, records show Captain William Field Porter 'bought' 1200 acres from Maori extending from the Whau to the headwaters of Little Muddy Creek.[16] Other records show that Alice Porter (Deed 101) 'bought' 600 acres of land from the Maori chief Te Keene, consisting of land on the eastern slopes of Rangiwai hill, Titirangi. Other records show the Porter family purchased 3488 acres of land from chief Te Kawau that covered almost all the land between Titirangi and New Lynn to the Whau. The purchase price paid by the Porters for this land was one cutter (the *Oripia*), two cloaks, one gold watch, one double-barreled pistol, one bag of flour, one bag of sugar, six shirts, six pairs of trousers,

New Zealander, Volume 4, Issue 240, 16 September 1848, page 1

TO SAWYERS, BUILDERS, AND OTHERS.
HYAM JOSEPH*
Has received instructions to sell without reserve at his mart, on Monday, the 25th instant, at 11 o'clock — the RIGHT TO CUT TIMBER over a very large tract of Land in Little Muddy Creek, for the period of three years. The above land is very heavily Timbered, and no Timber has yet been cut or felled upon the Land.

*Hyam Joseph was a trader/merchant in Auckland

In 'An Overland Trip to the Manukau Heads', a letter to the *New Zealander*, 7 January 1860.

Sir,

I have taken advantage of the Christmas holidays to explore a district which is pretty much a terra incognita to our Auckland seekers after the picturesque, and yet is a district almost at their doors. I beg therefore to give a few 'Pencillings by the Way', that others may enjoy the same treat that I have enjoyed.

Passing from Auckland to Newtown, along the North Road, and so by the Northern Hotel, kept by Mr. Edgecombe (3 and a half miles from Town), and on to the Whau Bridge, 7 miles, about a mile beyond the bridge, I left the North Road, turning to the left. Striking due South, I came to the Ranges, about 10 miles from Auckland. Here I entered the bush, or rather what was bush, but is now a grass paddock, belonging to Mr Bishop. Passing on through the paddock to the top of the hill, how striking was the contrast in the scenery! Looking back over the road I had traversed, the eye roved wearily over the dull sterile district extending from Auckland to Henderson's Mill, with hardly a tree or patch of cultivated field to rest upon. In the distance were Auckland, Mount Eden, the Waitemata, and the views so well known at Auckland: before me, the Manukau, at my feet, with a foreground of dense forest. Papakura, Hunua, and Waikato Hills in the distance. A noble kauri — a relic saved from destruction — marks and seems to guard the spot. The road continues through what was forest, but is now burnt shrubs and grass to the bottom of the hill — affording the most delicious peeps of Little Muddy Creek and the valley through which it runs, dotted with small houses and pretty enclosures. The road leads to a landing place at the head of the tideway, where the creek is easily crossed either on foot or horseback.

A steep hill, partly cleared and partly covered with bush, juts out as a spur from the ranges above, dividing the creek, which flows upon either side. Crossing the hill, I descended the second branch of this creek, and crossing that I entered upon the property of Mr Thomas Russell Snr., who has built a house, in which he resides, on a spot commanding a view magnificent in the extreme, extending far over the waters of the Manukau.

five coats, ten blankets and £50 pounds cash: total value £230.[17] In 1848 and 1849 the Crown disallowed these purchases and awarded the Porters 325 acres in the Green Bay/Titirangi area and compensation of £270, later spent on purchases of land in the Howick area.

As an example of an early European migrant family, the Porters have an interesting history. In 1838 Captain William Field Porter set off from Liverpool for Adelaide in a 250-ton brig, the *Porter*, with his family and possessions. A smaller boat, the *Dorset*, accompanied them 90 tons, which carried tradesmen. These men worked for Porter in Australia until their fare was paid. After 18 months in Australia and having sold the

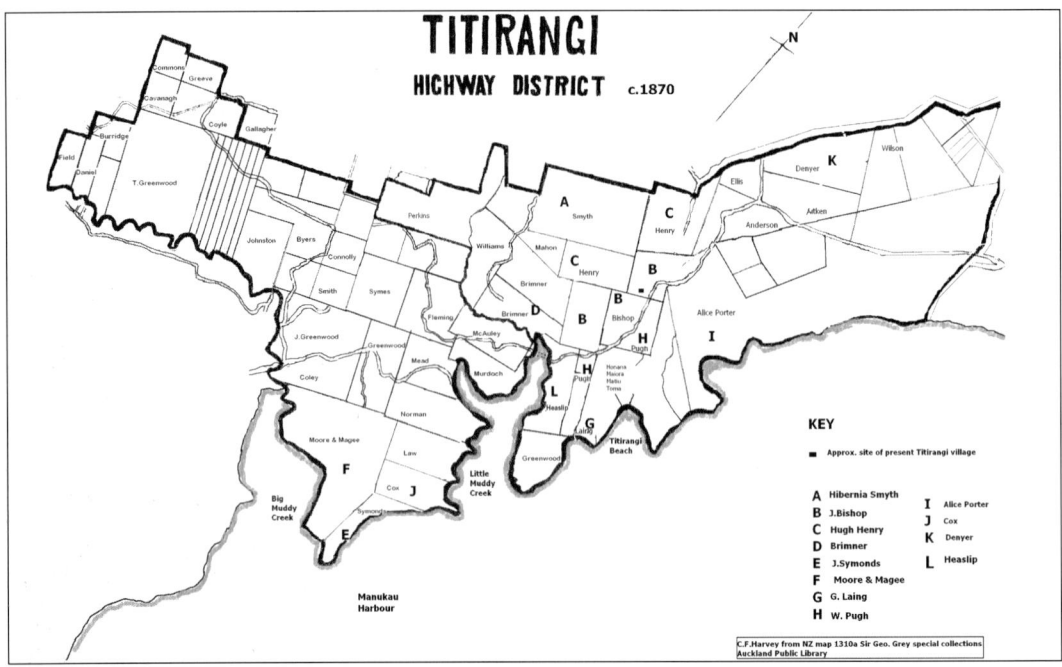

Titirangi Highway District map, c.1870, showing the major landholders in the district. In 1870 the Highway Board defined Titirangi District as being from the Whau to beyond Big Muddy Creek.
C.F. Harvey, adapted from NZ Map 1310a, Sir George Grey Special Collections, Auckland City Libraries

Dorset, the family sailed to Auckland in the *Porter*. They found accommodation scarce so lived on board for three months, eventually landing with their chattels in August 1841. Young W.F. Porter, son of Captain Porter, was initially educated at a German-owned school in Victoria Street East, but soon after went to Nelson for three years to continue his education. A diary of their adventures was kept by the Porters.[18]

It is said that the first plough, which had a mould board made of wood, was used in the Auckland district at Waipareira, Titirangi, by a friend and neighbour of the Porters, Mr William Atkin, who had two working bullocks. At the time there was no road cleared from Auckland to 'West Tamaki' (Titirangi), only an old Maori track that was visible part of the way. Captain Porter went down to his farm in his boat, probably via the Whau. On one occasion it is recorded that he went overland and lost his way.

In 1848 the first legal sale of 103 acres in the Titirangi area was made to John Kelly. During the 1850s, the difficulties of resolving the purchases of the Cornwallis land and the Porter claims were still being unwound.

After the Hikurangi purchase, more land was sold. These early sales were to Thomas Bray, 73 acres at Titirangi in 1853; John McGee and James Moore, 319 acres at Big Muddy Creek in 1854; William Brimner, 110 acres between Titirangi and Little Muddy Creek and a similar area in the valley in 1855; Hibernia Smyth, 550 acres on the slopes below Mt Atkinson between 1854 and 1857; and Hugh Henry, 84 acres surrounding Mt Atkinson.[19]

During the next two decades sales increased and land changed hands so that by the

1880s Titirangi had a population of 140 and the area along the Manukau coast to Whatipu (including Pararaha) had a population of 194, most of whom worked in the timber mills.[20]

As time passed, tracts of the land lots bought by the early settlers and speculators changed hands due to many factors, but by the late 1860s land ownership was becoming stable. Growing Auckland had to be fed so many plots became self sufficient and surplus produce was sold in the town. At this time land near Auckland was at a premium as Maori in the Waikato were unwilling to sell. In due course this led to the Land Wars in the Waikato where the much richer agricultural land was, and as this land came into farming the more meagre productivity of Titirangi and the Waitakere foothills became less relevant.

Before the land wars Waikato Maori brought large quantities of food by canoe up the Waikato River and across the Waiuku portage and the Manukau Harbour to sell in Auckland; without this supply the town's food requirements would not have been met. In the Titirangi and Waitakere areas, trees were felled and the timber sold, then grass seed was sown, after the scrub had been burned, to form rough farms with a cow or two, some chickens and gardens. Many settlers on small plots worked in various jobs, if available, outside of their plot to increase their economic viability. It is seen in the variety of job descriptions in the electoral roll of 1855 (see p. 230). Small holders were obliged to work as labourers, sawyers, splitters, and boat builders and so on to augment the income from their farmlet.

Some of the settlers whose names are on the electoral roll in 1855 obtained Crown grants in the Titirangi area and are mentioned in historical records such as newspaper articles and Road Board maps. The names of Porter, Denyer, Henry, Bishop, Pugh, Brimner, Moore, Smyth and Symonds frequently appear. In his historical article on the early history of Big and Little Muddy creeks,[21] Jack Diamond mentions William Brimner as having two blocks of land below Titirangi at the head of Little Muddy Creek. Two others were Hazlett and Charlie Moore, both of Little Muddy Creek. In the electoral roll they are described as Charlie Moore, carpenter and Reuben Haslep (spelling is considered a mistake in the original), a sawyer. In the 1870 Titirangi Road district map the name is rendered Heaslip, but it probably refers to the same person.

> **BALL AT LITTLE MUDDY CREEK**
>
> THE 17th March being St. Patrick's Day, it was celebrated here by a grand ball, given by the members of the Titirangi Quadrille-class, in the large barn belonging to Mr. Thomas Brimner, Little Muddy Creek, which was kindly lent for the occasion, and was very tastefully decorated. The class has been formed about three months, and its meetings are usually held in a large building belonging to H. Smith, Esq., under an excellent master, Mr. Edward Clifton, who acted as M.C. at the ball on the 17th instant. The party assembled about 7 o'clock, when a large number of the fair sex, from the Whau and surrounding neighbourhood, made their appearance; and, when the lights were lit, the building looked quite gay. Dancing commenced at 8 o'clock, and was kept up with great spirit until daylight. Mrs. Poppleton and another lady favoured the company with some excellent singing during the intervals. The refreshments and music were really all that could be desired; and all present expressed themselves highly delighted with the evening's entertainment.
> —[Correspondent.]

Ball at Little Muddy Creek, 1871.
Daily Southern Cross, 4 April 1871, p. 3

The beginning

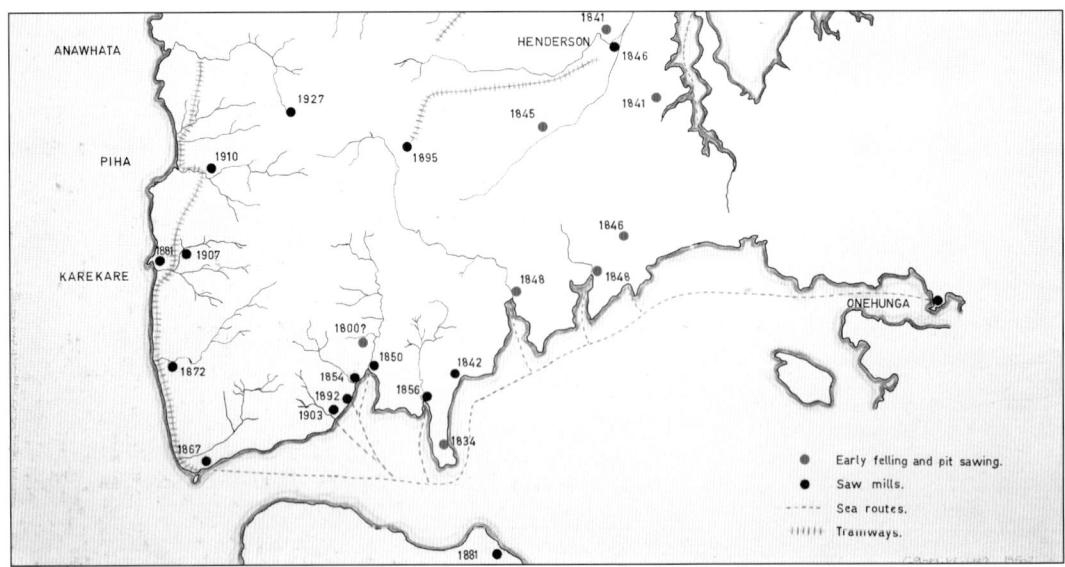

Early sawing station map, c.1820–50. Note sawing stations at Little Muddy Creek and near the top of Godley Road. Auckland War Memorial Museum Collections (drawn in 1950)

One of the very early personalities of Titirangi was Captain Hibernicus Scott Smyth, or Hibernia Smyth. He was born in 1803 and died in 1883 and buried in the Grafton Gully cemetery. Smyth arrived in New Zealand from Ireland, via Adelaide, with his wife Sarah and son. The family settled in the Waitakeres in 1842. They had six children, son Hibernicus Richard Smyth (1837–1920) being the one most notable for his connection to Titirangi.

Captain H.S. Smyth bought land between 1854 and 1857, which amounted to nearly 550 acres, on the northern slopes of Mt Atkinson and across the present Atkinson Valley[22] (now Kaurilands). He established a cattle run and house and timber mill. Captain Smyth's daughter Maria married her cousin, and they operated a timber mill in the Waitakeres, the remains of which could at one time be seen along Smyth's track. Captain Smyth was a colourful character, listed as a mariner (in the Shipping Log of the *Navarina*, which arrived in Adelaide 16 December 1837). He lived near where Kopiko and Konini roads converge today. During his time, travellers got to the property following a route approximately along the present Glendale and Withers roads, crossing a swamp before getting to the house. Cattle and sheep ran wild and there was little fencing.

The Smyths bullock team was for hire; at the age of 18 it would have been Hibernicus

Notice of the marriage of the daughter of Hibernia Smyth, 1863.

Daily Southern Cross, 31 January 1863, p. 13

> On the 20th instant, by the Rev. J. F. Lloyd, of Auckland, by special license, at the residence of the bride's father, Esther, eldest daughter of Hibernia Smyth, Esq, of Woodbine House, Titirangi, third son of the late Richard Smyth, Esq, Castledowneen, Rosscarberry, County Cork, to Henry Smyth, Esq, Kauri Grove, Waitakeri, youngest son of the late Isaac Smyth, Esq, Denamore, Newry.

Richard Smyth (often known as Hibernia or Hybie) who brought the Bishop family and all their belongings to Titirangi. He would also bring loads of posts, shingles and firewood to Karangahape Road for sale as part of his income. Hibernicus Richard Smyth was a large man, careful and thrifty with his money and a tough pioneer of Titirangi.[23] He is recorded as among the trustees of the original Titirangi school, and is remembered by T.A. Bishop as a crusty old fellow in his eighties. Smyth married later in life but had no children.

Another of Captain Smyth's daughters, Esther, is recorded as marrying Henry Smyth (possibly another cousin) from Ireland, at Kauri Grove, Waitakere, on 20 January 1863.[24]

John Bishop, often considered the 'Father of Titirangi', arrived in Kororareka (Russell) from Australia in 1839. The story of the Bishop family and their Titirangi connection is expanded in the next chapter.

1. Harvey, Bruce and Trixie (eds). *Waitakere Ranges*. Waitakere Ranges Protection Society Inc., 2006, p. 26.
2. Ibid, p. 36.
3. Hayward, B.W. and Diamond, J.T. *Prehistoric Archaeological Sites of the Waitakere Ranges*. Parks Department, Auckland Regional Authority, 1978, p. 121, maps 8 and 9.
4. Ibid, p. 89.
5. *Blockhouse Bay Settlers Handbook*. With Rona Walker, Annette Brown and Lorraine Wilson, Blockhouse Bay Committee, 1990, p. 4.
6. Hayward, B.W. and Diamond, J.T. *Prehistoric Archaeological Sites of the Waitakere Ranges*. Parks Department, Auckland Regional Authority, 1978, p. 107.
7. Commissioned 2002, West Auckland Sculpture Trust, designed and made by Bill McKay and Warren Viscoe.
8. McLaren, Bruce and Michele Slade. *History of New Lynn*. New Lynn Borough Council, 1981.
9. Cloher, Dorothy Urlich. *Hongi Hika*. Viking (Penguin Books), Albany, Auckland, 2003, p. 181.
10. Blaiklock, E.M. *Between the Valley and the Sea*. Dunmore Press, Palmerston North, 1979, p. 37.
11. Hayward, B.W. and Diamond, J.T. *Prehistoric Archaeological Sites of the Waitakere Ranges*. Parks Department, Auckland Regional Authority, 1978, p. 9.
12. Stone, Russell. *Tamaki Makarau to Auckland*. Auckland University Press, Auckland, 2001, pp. 19–20.
13. Hayward, B.W. and Diamond, J.T. *Prehistoric Archaeological Sites of the Waitakere Ranges*. Parks Department, Auckland Regional Authority, 1978, p. 10.
14. Auckland City Library, MSS 82, Felton Mathew letter book. 15 June 1840–3 January 1842: Sir George Grey Special Collections, p. 58.
15. Aleman, Maurice. *Earliest Land Transactions in West Auckland*. Unpublished thesis, Library of West Auckland Historical Soc. Inc., Auckland, 1993, p. 20.
16. Diamond, J.T. 'The Early history of Big and Little Muddy Creeks (2)'. *West Auckland Historical Society Newsletter* 101, May 1988, p. 3.
17. Aleman, Maurice. *Earliest Land Transactions in West Auckland*. Unpublished thesis, Library of West Auckland Historical Soc. Inc., Auckland, 1993, p. 16.
18. Brett, Sir Henry. *White Wings*. Brett Publishing Co. Ltd, Auckland 1928, pp. 120–22.
19. Diamond, J.T. *Once the Wilderness*. J.T. Diamond, Auckland, 3rd edition, 1977, p. 133.
20. Census of the colony of New Zealand, 1881. Auckland City Library, George Didsbury, Government Printer, Wellington.
21. Diamond, J.T. 'Early history of Big and Little Muddy Creeks (1)'. West Auckland Historical Society Newsletter 100, April 1988.
22. Diamond, J.T. *Once the Wilderness*. J.T. Diamond, Auckland, 3rd edition, 1977, p. 33.
23. Sinkinson, Carol (ed.). *Titirangi Primary School 1872–1997. 125 years.* Titirangi Primary School, Auckland, 1997.
24. *Daily Southern Cross*, 31 January 1863. Auckland City Library, p. 13.

2

The Bishops — an early settler family

The settler family who has had an impact on Titirangi for several generations is the Bishop family. John Bishop and his future father-in-law John McLeod arrived at the Bay of Islands in 1839 aboard the *Jess*. The McLeod family are all recorded as leaving Scotland together in August 1838 on the *Portland* and arriving in Sydney in December. John McLeod then left Sydney in May 1839 on the *Jess*. John Bishop is believed to have been working as a carpenter on this ship as three other passengers on this ship became his partners in a later unsuccessful land purchase. During the next year John McLeod returned to Sydney and brought his family out on the *Diana* under Captain Robert Milne. John Bishop and Elizabeth McLeod married in 1841 at Christ Church, Kororareka.

John Bishop.
McLeod Family History, courtesy W. Titchener

Elizabeth Bishop.
Mia Stein Collection

For a while the McLeods and the Bishops lived in the Bay of Islands. In 1839 Elizabeth's father, John, had purchased land that was, 'in all five hundred acres, more or less… it joins James R Clendon's purchase leading to Man-a-War Bay, situated up the Waikari River about seven miles from the port of Russell'[1]. John Bishop had bought, in partnership with three others, some adjoining land. The purchases were made before 1840, so they had to be submitted to the Commissioner of Lands for approval, which in the case of the Bishop claim was rejected for unknown reasons. The McLeod claim was approved, but before it could be of much use to the family John McLeod unexpectedly died. His death is recorded in the journal of Charles Baker on 10 December 1841. He was buried somewhere on the Waikare land, but the exact place has been lost. During the time they lived in the Bay of Islands two children Christiana and Hannah were born to John and Elizabeth Bishop.

Another tragedy soon overwhelmed the family. Shortly before the sacking of Kororareka (Russell) on 11 March 1845, their house was burned down by hostile Maori. The loss of all their possessions forced the family to move to Kororareka for protection.

When Kororareka was sacked the women and children (including Mrs McLeod and Mrs Bishop and her two children) gathered in Polack's stockade and were taken aboard the United States warship *St Louis* and evacuated to Auckland. John Bishop and his two brothers-in-law, John and James McLeod, served with the Volunteers and later also came to Auckland.

The family lived in tents until they could get proper housing and the men were given work roadmaking. On 21 July 1845 Mrs McLeod died; the cause of her death was not recorded. She was buried in the Symonds Street Cemetery. Her grave was among those removed for the motorway and her name is recorded on the Memorial Wall as Christiana McLeod.

Shortly after in 1845, John Bishop entered into partnership in a timber mill in Freemans Bay with Thomas Canty. During this time two more children were born to John and Elizabeth but both died as infants. While engaged in the timber industry, John Bishop took at least one shipload of sawn timber to Sydney. In order to obtain a supply of timber for their mill Canty and Bishop bought land at Henderson and later at Titirangi.

In 1851 the Bishop family moved to the Henderson property, which was situated on Canty's Creek, now called Oratia Stream. Elizabeth Bishop always claimed that she was the first European woman at Henderson. We do not know how long the family lived at Henderson, but the partnership was later dissolved and the Bishop family moved to Titirangi and the Canty family to Henderson. The property at Titirangi, Lots 44, 45 and 46, comprising 227 acres, was the subject of a Crown Grant to John Alfred Langford at the price of £102-11. John Bishop and Thomas Canty purchased the property in December 1855 for £324. In November 1858, Canty transferred his interest in the property to John Bishop for £500. This would have been offset by a similar transfer of John Bishop's interest in the Henderson property. In 1856, John Bishop and Thomas Canty had also purchased Lot 25, comprising 111 acres, from William Brimner, for £95 plus a mortgage of £50. This allotment had been the subject of a Crown Grant dated 19 April 1855 to William Brimner. The mortgage was repaid and, in 1858, for £100 Thomas Canty transferred this property to John Bishop. The move to Titirangi was made by bullock wagon driven by Hibernia Smyth, then a youth of 18, already living in Titirangi in the Kaurilands area. A nikau whare served as the family home until a house could be built.

John Bishop, who was a carpenter by trade and had been a ship's carpenter on the voyage to New Zealand, set about the task with his usual zeal. The timber was pit-sawn on

> WANTED by the undersigned Six pairs of Sawyers to proceed to Titirangi, the best wages will be given, and constant employment.
> For particulars apply to CANTY & BISHOP at Titirangi, or for the next fourteen days to
> THOMAS CANTY,
> Victoria-street.
> Sept. 12, 1857.

Daily Southern Cross, 6 October 1857, p. 1

Dunvegan, the Bishop family's first house, circa early 1880s. The windows are in their original position.
Mia Stein Collection

the property and a two-storeyed house was built. The house was named 'Dunvegan' as a reminder of Dunvegan Castle, the seat of the McLeod clan in the Isle of Skye. Later, family members visiting Scotland realised that it should have been 'Dunvagan' but the New Zealand spelling was not changed.

At first there was no chimney and the cooking was done in a semi-detached building. A large open fireplace, which was large enough to burn whole logs, was a feature and the family sat on the long benches in the winter evenings. Frequently, when the family awoke there would be one or more travellers who had sought the comfort of a warm place to sleep during the night. They were always welcomed as the Bishop home was an open house for passers-by.

Much hard work went into the property and it was not long before a flourishing farm had been established. At that period the road from Titirangi onward ran along what is now known as South Titirangi Road to as far as the former school. It then traversed Mr McEldowney's property (Lot 39, Crown Grant to R. Haslip and J. McPike in April 1854, 88 acres for £40, (see appendices 2 and 3) and crossed Little Muddy Creek at Landing Road. The road to Auckland was via Blockhouse Bay and on to Surrey Crescent.

A gate known as Bishop's Gate, between the present Lopdell House and The Hardware Café marked the entrance to the Bishop property. During the period 1858–80, Auckland was under threat of attack by Maori and later there was also a fear of attack from Russia. A quantity of arms and ammunition was stored at Dunvegan and the men of the district paraded in an adjacent paddock for instruction under Sergeant Duane. On one occasion a scare induced the women and children to move to Auckland for safety. The next day the eldest daughter, Christiana, then in her early teens, walked home to be with her father.

Provisions for the family had to be bought in Auckland. This meant a three-day trip about every three months in the bullock dray. The bullocks were let loose in Surrey

Crescent; shopping took up the following day and the third day was spent finding the bullocks and getting home.

John Bishop and his wife did not neglect the education of their children. With eight children to educate they engaged a tutor, Mr Patterson, and converted the large room upstairs at Dunvegan into a schoolroom. The services of the tutor were also made available to the neighbours' children. When Patterson died his place was taken by Ben Carrol, who then became the first teacher at Titirangi School when it opened in William Pugh's shed in 1872. Mrs Bishop donated the desks and equipment to the new school and had offered to give land, but the one-acre site was eventually bought from the chairman of the School Committee, Mr Pugh, for £100. The Bishops helped in every way with the 'soirees' held to raise money to build the school.

Tragedy again struck the family on 21 June 1865, when John Bishop died. He and the other settlers were engaged in building a new road leading from Titirangi through what was then Porter's Bush (from Titirangi township along what is now Park Road). John Bishop had contracted a chill and died of pneumonia. The following obituary was published in the *New Zealand Herald* on Monday 26 June 1865.

> *Funeral of the late John Bishop*
>
> *Another of our old settlers has passed away from our midst. John Bishop of Titirangi died on the 21st inst. He was well known formerly as one of the firm of Canty and Bishop, carrying on business as sawyers in Freeman's Bay. During the time of Heke's war at the Bay of Islands where he was residing, he lost everything he possessed in the world. About nine years ago he went to reside at Titirangi where he has made a very comfortable residence and farm, and where he lived up to the time of his death which occurred on Wednesday last. He has been in the Colony altogether about 25 years. His remains were brought in from Titirangi on Friday evening to the residence of his brother-in-law, Mr James McLeod of Freeman's Bay, from which place he was taken on Saturday to his last resting place in the Church of England Cemetery. The coffin was covered with black cloth and handsomely mounted, and the hearse was provided by Mr Dickinson of Victoria Street. The funeral cortege left Mr McLeod's about two o'clock and was followed by Mr McLeod and two sons of the deceased as chief mourners. A large concourse of people followed, among whom we noticed several settlers from the Whau and the neighbourhood of Titirangi, who had assembled to pay their last tribute of respect to an old and esteemed neighbour.*

John Bishop was only 52 years of age and at that time had only one son, William Thomas. At her husband's death, Elizabeth Bishop was pregnant with their second son, John Joseph, who was born on 2 July, nearly two weeks after his father had died. The other 'son' referred to in the obituary notice would have been James McLeod (Junior), who lived with the Bishop family after his mother's death in 1854, and who was often known as Jimmy Bishop. He was the son of Elizabeth's second brother James, and would have been 11 years old at the time.

John Bishop was buried in the Church of England Cemetery in Symonds Street. When the motorway access road was constructed in 1968 it was necessary to remove some of the graves, including the Bishop plot in which John and his wife Elizabeth and their two children Harriet and John (who had died in infancy), were buried. With the other remains from the cemetery, their remains were cremated and the ashes buried in a common consecrated plot. Their names are recorded on a Memorial Wall surrounding the plot.

John Bishop died intestate, although an unsigned will dated 19 June (two days before his death) was found. It stated that, 'In case of my death, my wife to take charge of the place and the stock until the youngest child comes of age, then the place and stock to be sold, one third to go to the widow, the rest to be fairly divided among the children'. It has been suggested that he had not signed it because his wife wished to include James McLeod (Jimmy Bishop) as one of the children. Under the law at that time his widow received one third of the estate and the elder son, William Thomas, the remainder. There were two houses in Auckland as well as the property at Titirangi.

Elizabeth Bishop carried on the farm with hired labour and with the help of her daughters, who were as capable as any of the men on the farm. When her two sons William and John were old enough they took over the farm work. There was some difficulty getting suitable labour so she leased two portions of the property, one to Jack Parr, who built a small house and farmed his portion, and the other to Jack Nelson, who also built a house and an orchard.

John and Elizabeth's children were Christiana (1842–1937), Hannah (1844–1931), Harriet (1847–1849), John (April 1850–June 1850), Sarah (1851–1923), Eliza Jane (1853–1933), Elizabeth Euphemia (1856–1911), Henrietta (1858–1941), William Thomas (1860–1943) and John Joseph (1865–1933). (See pp. 226–27) for Bishop family tree.)

Christiana, the eldest daughter, was married three times (see appendix 1). Her first husband, John Porter, drowned in the Manukau Harbour. He was probably the first postmaster in the district; in the *Gazette* of 19 August 1861, John Porter was Postmaster of 'Little Muddy Creek' Post Office from 1 October 1861. Porter owned a property of about 10 acres overlooking Little Muddy Creek, near what is now McEldowney Road. The post office closed in June 1862, after Porter's drowning. The Porters had two children, Joseph and John (Jock). Jock was a legendary member of the family. He left home when he was a young man, without telling anyone where he was going. There was always speculation as to whether he was dead or whether he would return. However, about 1934 Marshall Laing, the local member of the Auckland Hospital Board, discovered Jock at the Blind Institute in Dunedin. Assuming his family would be interested to know of his whereabouts, Laing arranged for Jock to be transferred to the Auckland Blind Institute. However, Jock's mother, who was then in her nineties, was not interested in him because, she said, for so many years he had taken no interest in her or his family. Jock died shortly after his transfer to Auckland. Christiana married her second husband Archibald Wilson at Dunvegan and lived at Titirangi. Later with her third husband Adam Winder and her children she continued to live in the area.

John and Elizabeth's second daughter, Hannah, married another early Titirangi settler, William Pugh, on 12 December 1860. Within the family it has always been said that John Bishop had given Hannah 56 acres, however, a Deed of Conveyance shows that in fact the land had been bought by William Pugh in 1861. In later times the Titirangi War Memorial Hall, the library, the Titirangi Returned Serviceman's Association (RSA) and the Titirangi Soldiers Memorial Church were all located on this parcel of land. William Pugh was the first chairman of the School Committee and he was also the first postmaster of the Titirangi Post

Office, which opened in his house in March 1873. The Pugh property was later sold to Henry Atkinson and the Pugh family went to live in Mt Roskill. Hannah lived for a while in Auckland and Wellington, but eventually returned to live in the Titirangi area.

As a young girl, Sarah, the fourth daughter, was a favourite of her uncle John McLeod and his wife Rebecca, who lived in Wellington. The couple had no children and wished to adopt Sarah. At first Sarah's mother seemed agreeable, but later she would not give her consent as she said Sarah would have no opportunity of being married in Wellington as she would not know anyone in Wellington. Sarah's mother also said that Sarah's other sisters could not marry until she had married. Such were the social customs of the time! Sarah married William Speer, and their daughter, Bertha, married her first cousin, Frank Oscar Peat, the son of Euphemia Bishop. Descendants from this union remained in Titirangi for several generations and became prominent citizens.

The next daughter, Eliza Jane, married John Armstrong, whose father had served in the New Zealand Wars with the British troops. John Armstrong's father had bought a property in Titirangi that was previously owned by the McPike brothers. He and his wife lived there for a short time; when they moved to Auckland, they divided the property between their two sons, John and Thomas, who was schoolmaster at Titirangi School from 1884 to 1890. John Armstrong carried the mail to the Titirangi, Brooklyn (Parau) and Huia post offices for many years until he retired and left Titirangi to live in Auckland, but their children were Titirangi residents for some time.

Elizabeth Euphemia (called by her second christian name), the next daughter, was placed in an embarrassing position by a friend of the family, Mr McGee. He brought his friend, Mr Peat, to visit the family home, and introduced him as a very sincere friend. Euphemia and Peat fell in love, much to the chagrin of McGee, who evidently had hopes of winning Euphemia's love. McGee then told the family that he had been mistaken in his friend, and that he was not the wonderful man he had thought him to be. However, Peat and Euphemia married, without her mother's approval at the time. When their first son was born and brought to the family home, Euphemia's mother was so captivated by her new grandson that she relented and everyone was happy again, except Mr McGee, who did not ever marry but remained a friend of the family. Youngest of the six Bishop daughters, Henrietta, married Thomas Coulter, who was the schoolmaster at Titirangi School in 1878. Thomas Coulter is also listed as postmaster at Titirangi Post Office from 1877 to 1878. As a schoolmaster Thomas Coulter moved around New Zealand, but the family returned to Auckland in 1887. Of their five children three returned to live in Titirangi, as did Henrietta after her second marriage.

The two boys, William and John Joseph, were the youngest in the Bishop family. On 26 December 1893, William Thomas the elder son married Miss Alexandrina Sara Johanna Tinling, the School Mistress (1890–92) at a ceremony held in the school. They built a new house about a quarter of a mile from the old home on Huia Road. John Joseph, the younger son, married Emily Surman on 20 July 1892. John Joseph had bought two properties from Dr Mahon: Lot 26, 96½ acres and half of Lot 29, 44 acres. It was his intention to build a house on Lot 29, and he had cleared a site and planted some shelter trees. However, his mother wished him and her new daughter-in-law to make their home with her in the family home, Dunvegan. The house and eight acres of land were transferred to the newly married couple.

Elizabeth Bishop died on 18 September 1898. Her obituary in the *New Zealand Herald* on 20 September read:

> *Another old colonist passed away last week in the person of Mrs Bishop, widow of the late John Bishop of Titirangi. Mrs Bishop came to the Colony in 1840, and settled in the Bay of Islands, but had to leave during Hone Heke's war, in which her husband and brothers John and James McLeod, served as volunteers. After coming to Auckland the family settled at Titirangi, where Mrs Bishop's kind and hospitable nature endeared her to everyone that knew her. Mrs Bishop leaves a large family and numerous grandchildren.*

Gran Bishop, as she was affectionately known in the family, was loved and respected by all who knew her. A staunch observer of the sabbath, she brought her family up using strict lines, and it is very much to her credit that she not only reared her family single-handedly after her husband's early death, but also managed and maintained the property until her sons could take over. This was a remarkable achievement for her time. Her home was always a family home to her children and grandchildren and she entertained extensively, always welcoming travellers. She could speak Gaelic, so her home was a popular visiting place for those of Scottish descent. Lord Onslow, during his term as governor, was a frequent visitor, and a paddock was named 'Onslow Paddock' because the Vice-Regal party picnicked there on their visits to Titirangi. Another notable visitor was Lt Colonel Roche of the 18th Regiment, who was a keen photographer. He photographed the home and its occupants on Christmas Day 1868. The photograph remains in the Bishop family.

In July 1885, William Thomas Bishop sold to Henry Atkinson of Auckland, manager of the Auckland Gas Company, a parcel of land containing about 36-37 acres. This parcel of land included the ridge opposite Lopdell House and the site of the present Titirangi Primary School. Henry Atkinson was the brother-in-law of Mr J.S. Johnston, an old friend of the Bishop family. As a point of interest, Mr Johnston had married Miss Kitty Duane who was the first European child born in Titirangi, the daughter of Sergeant Duane, mentioned

The entrance to Dunvegan, c.1905.
Waitakere Library & Information Services, Print Collection (Titirangi — Bishop)

earlier as training the settlers in case of an attack. Henry Atkinson also bought Pugh's property when the latter left Titirangi. The Atkinson family were prominent in Titirangi for the next two generations. Their story is told in subsequent chapters of this volume.

The first Dunvegan and other Bishop family houses in Titirangi

The first Dunvegan was built on a site near to 25–35 Huia Road. The earliest photographs show a lean-to porch with a small room on either side, and the fireplace and cooking arrangements in a detached building. A later photograph shows the porch removed and two windows on the northern side. On the western side a lean-to comprising a kitchen and dairy had been added, and a double chimney built. The bricks for the chimney were made on a small hillside close by, which was then known as the Kiln Hill. Family tradition records 1000 bricks were used in the under-floor foundation of the chimney.

One fireplace was in the new kitchen and another in the large dining room. The house now had three bedrooms, a dining room, kitchen and dairy on the ground floor and two bedrooms and one large room used as a schoolroom upstairs. The space in one of the bedrooms under the stairs that served as a wardrobe was called 'the binker' ('binker' is possibly of Scottish origin, but no-one in the family seemed to know the exact meaning). Another strange name was the 'punky (or pokey) house'. This was a fairly large kauri tree and was hollow at the base with an entrance where a person could enter; it was a favourite trysting place for courting couples. Inside there was a seat nailed to the tree. The painting by Cameron Johnson of the punky tree (page ii, colour section) shows an old kauri, with a sparse crown, obviously not in very good health, so its later demise is not so surprising. The tree was weakened during the widening of Huia Road and was blown down in a gale some years later. The name has been the subject of many arguments as to its origin and meaning. One suggestion was that pumpkins grown nearby were once stored in the tree's hollow base. But there are other possibilities, perhaps of a more romantic nature.

(Above) Dunvegan, showing the original kauri shingle roof, later replaced by corrugated iron after the fire of 1894. New windows were in place by this time. W. Titchener Collection

(Right) 'In the punky house'. Mia Stein Collection

View in 1920 from Mt Atkinson down to Dunvegan and out to Little Muddy Creek (Laingholm). The entrance to the house is at the lower edge of the image. James D. Richardson, 18 February 1920. Auckland City Libraries Special Collections, 4-4082

The next alteration to the house was the removal of the two windows on the northern side and their replacement with one much larger window. No doubt on account of the fire that destroyed their home at Kororareka, Elizabeth Bishop was always afraid of fire. The children were never allowed a candle to light them to bed, and her grandson Gus (T.A. Bishop) recalled that during his childhood he had to go to bed in the dark. On one occasion, possibly in 1894, a spark from the chimney set fire to the shingle roof. Mrs Bishop refused to leave her home, but when her young grandson, a baby about a year old, was placed in her arms, she relented and left the house for safety. Her daughter-in-law carried buckets of water from the well to a helper and the fire was put out without much damage being done. No doubt the old bullock horn was blown as an alarm to bring her sons William and John home to deal with the fire. This old horn, which is still in the family, was blown to call the men home to lunch and as an alarm.

Some years later the shingles were taken off the roof of the old house and replaced with corrugated iron. The next and last alteration to the house was the construction of a verandah along the eastern and northern sides, finishing in a porch over the back door, and a small room on either side, one being a separator room and the other a bathroom. The door on this side now became the front entrance as the newly formed Huia Road passed in front of it.

Originally the water supply for the house was carried from the 'well', which was in fact a brick tank in the ground about 20 or 30 yards from the house. The water came from a spring, which was called the 'fountain', at the foot of a hillside some distance away, and was conveyed in field tiles laid in the ground. These tiles frequently became blocked with roots and had to be taken up and cleaned. About 1910, a windmill was purchased and erected by the spring and the water was pumped into a brick tank further up the hillside. From here it was carried in galvanised iron water-pipes to the house, and this allowed the luxury of a shower (cold) and no more carrying of water from the well. Over the years, the 'old house', as it was called, became hard to maintain in a habitable condition. Because it was lacking in modern conveniences, a new house was built close by. John Joseph Bishop and his family moved there in January 1927.

The new house retained the name 'Dunvegan' and the old house was demolished in

1935. Over 80 years the old house had served the family well and had also given service to the district.

Its schoolroom was the forerunner of the Titirangi School, it was the post office after Mr Pugh left the district, it was a store for rifles and ammunition, and was used as a training ground for the settlers in case of attack.

Huia Road, a new road, was formed from the entrance to the Bishop property at 'Bishop's Gate' through the Bishop and Brimner properties to connect with the existing road at Little Muddy Creek. This road eliminated the very steep hill down to Little Muddy Creek, and crossing the creek was no longer necessary. The land for the new road was given by the Bishop and Brimner families. The site of old Dunvegan is close to 25–35 Huia Road, and the new 1927 Dunvegan is at 25 Huia Road.

To mark the extent of their properties, early Titirangi settlers planted quick-growing trees at their corners to show where they turned an angle or ended. Bill Bishop recalled that

> 'his father Gus' two pines were in front of the house facing Exhibition Drive, one sporting his wireless aerial, that went down to his house below. Further along the Drive towards Aunty Christy (sometimes called 'Cricket') were two macrocarpa trees and two more pines. Further along still, was a gum tree at the corner of Bishop's property'.

(Right from top)

Garden party at Dunvegan, c.1919. Waitakere Library & Information Services, Bishop Collection

Children at the rifle range, a garden party activity. Waitakere Library & Information Services, Bishop Collection

Garden party at Dunvegan, c.1919. Mia Stein Collection

Manukau View, William Bishop's house at 18 Huia Road, was built in the 1890s for William and his new bride. The timber was cut on the property, rafted from Little Muddy Creek to the sawmill at Onehunga where it was sawn, and then carted back to Titirangi by bullock wagon. The house was still in a good state of preservation in the 1960s and is one of the oldest in the district, although it has been extensively altered from its original design. It was named 'Manukau View' for its good view of the harbour, eventually obscured by regenerating native trees. William Bishop's daughter, Mrs Dora Jones, occupied the house after her father's death in 1943.

The next generation of Bishops

John and Elizabeth Bishop's two sons both lived in Titirangi and raised their families there. William, the elder son, was a quieter personality who, while well respected, was not known for entertaining and did not have the public profile of his younger brother. Education was an area of interest to William and his wife, and he was for thirty years on the Titirangi School Committee. He was a foundation member of the Waitemata County Council and his wife was postmistress from 1909 to 1917. Of their five children, two died in childhood and their elder daughter Elizabeth Sarah (Bessie) married and moved away. Their son William Alexander (Alec 1898-1971) became a prominent Titirangi resident and represented the district on the Waitemata County Council, Power Board, Hospital Board, Titirangi School Committee, chairman of the Bus Committee and was active in many other local organisations.

John Joseph, the younger son born after his father's death in 1865, was known as 'Chappie'. The nickname had been given to him by the schoolmaster Ben Carrol when John was an infant and it stuck with him all his life.

Chappie and Emily married in 1892 and had three sons and three daughters. Their three sons were born during the 1890s, a fateful decade, as they were all old enough, just,

Bishop family members at the Punga House on the north side of the lily pond at Dunvegan. Chappie Bishop is standing.
Mia Stein Collection

Children of Chappie and Emily Bishop, c.1909. Mia Stein Collection

for the First World War. During that tragic conflict they lost two sons, John Joseph and William Norman. The remaining son, Thomas Augustus, (known as Gus returned) alive but had suffered injuries when a piece of shrapnel pierced his leg at the thigh and exited at the inner ankle. His son, Bill (named William Norman after the brother lost in the war), said that his father had been badly wounded and one ankle was 'as thick as a broomstick' all his life. Listed on the First World War memorial at Titirangi are several other names connected to the Bishop family: Pugh, Armstrong and Coulter, all probably grandsons or great-grandsons of John and Elizabeth Bishop. So many young men from the district did not return after the war, so there was much community support for the construction of the non-denominational Soldiers Memorial Church which was opened in 1924.

Gus Bishop was medically unfit for service in the Second World War but continued to live and work in Titirangi and raise his family. When he returned from the war he was confined to a wheelchair for some time, during which he attended lectures at Auckland University College, studying law. However, he never practised law, but continued to live by a combination of farm income and a war pension.

During the Depression life was hard for many families including the Bishops, and Bill Bishop recalled that when financially pressed his father occasionally sold timber from the Titirangi properties. Gus also served on the Harbour Board for a time. His concern for the welfare of returned soldiers saw him take an active interest in the RSA and he was the first

Chappie Bishop was a keen naturalist and became an authority on the plants in the Waitakere Ranges. Frequent visitors to Dunvegan were the botanist T.F. Cheeseman, who wrote the first *Flora of New Zealand* in 1925, prominent botanists T.L. Lancaster, D. Petrie and H. Carse, and probably the young Lucy Cranwell, who became the Auckland Museum botanist in the 1930s and an authority on pollen structure, and probably also her friend Lucy Moore, later a co-author of the revised *Flora of New Zealand* in the 1960s. Cheeseman brought many prominent overseas visitors to meet Chappie Bishop and be guided on plant-hunting expeditions in the Waitakeres. Emily Bishop was a vivacious and gregarious woman who was an excellent cook and enjoyed social occasions. Many memorable garden parties and other occasions were held at Dunvegan during these years. Chappie Bishop has a plant named after him, *Hebe bishopiana* (originally *Veronica bishopiana*) an endemic plant of the Waitakere Ranges, which is now quite rare in the wild (page iv, colour section).

Chappie Bishop on Huia Road on a supply trip, early 1900s. Waitakere Library & Information Services, Bishop Collection

The Bishops — an early settler family 35

Gus Bishop returned from the Great War, with wife Lilian, and Constance Lusty, c.1919. Waitakere Library & Information Services, Bishop Collection

The following text is an extract from a newspaper clipping of the time.

A largely attended and highly successful garden fete and sale of work was held at 'Dunvegan', the residence of Mr J.J. Bishop of Titirangi, in aid of the local Soldiers' Memorial church fund. Visitors were given the opportunity of making purchases from an interesting collection of native trees, ferns, and botanical curiosities... Music was supplied by an efficient orchestra... The fete was formally opened by Mrs C.J. Parr. The war, she said, had brought a great deal of sorrow to Titirangi homes. Of the 17 soldiers who went from the district no fewer than eight had laid down their lives.

(Above) Bishop garden fete, 1919. Waitakere Library & Information Services, Bishop Collection

(Left) Cars parked on Huia Road for one of the Bishop's patriotic days, in this instance a garden fete. Image taken from the veranda of Dunvegan, 1919. Waitakere Library & Information Services, Bishop Collection

Gus (Thomas Augustus) Bishop, late 1930s. Mia Stein Collection

Essie (Emily Elizabeth) Bishop, 1931. Mia Stein Collection

(Right) The home of Gus and Lilian Bishop at 75 Waima Road. Waitakere Library & Information Services, Bishop Collection

president of the Titirangi RSA, and later the secretary. Like his father, Gus was a non-drinker and regarded Sunday observance as important. His sons remembered that when they were quite young, on Sundays they would go to their grandparents, Chappie and Emily Bishop's house in their best clothes. Bill recalls, 'We weren't allowed to make a big noise or play cards. Sunday was an important day!'

Chappie and Emily's three daughters, born after 1900, also lived in Titirangi. However, they suffered from the shortage of young men in their generation as only one, Emily Elizabeth, known as Essie, married and had a family. Essie, (Mrs Hodge), and her sister, Ada were schoolteachers and Essie's evocatively written memoirs are reproduced in the second part of this book. Christiana (Cricket) became a nurse. Chappie Bishop died in 1933 and his widow Emily was cared for by her two daughters in her later years, living with them in a house on Exhibition Drive until her death.

The cousins, Alec and Gus, did not always see eye to eye, as Gus was known to be a teetotaller and opposed to the availability of liquor, while Alec was against prohibition and was involved in the setting up of the Titirangi Hotel which applied for, but failed to get, a liquor licence in the early 1930s.

The arguments for and against prohibition of the sale of liquor were prominent in local politics of the 1930s. According to the memories of his sister Dora Jones, Alec was only 21 years-old when he started the Titirangi Kiosk or tearooms, a tourist stop in the 1920s that was so successful that he was inspired to support the hotel. However, the failure to get a liquor licence and the oncoming Depression of the 1930s caused the failure of that venture.

In the early days, he also took the mail to Huia by horse. In 1919 Alec married May Louisa You and they had two daughters and a son. In 1927 he was the secretary of the Titirangi Ratepayers Association, when estimates for the concreting of Titirangi Road were received. He was prominent in local body affairs as the member for Titirangi Riding for

A busy day at Alec Bishop's tea kiosk, c.1926. Waitakere Library & Information Service, Print Collection (Titirangi)

(Left) Cars and buses parked at Titirangi's popular tea kiosk in the 1920s. W.T. Bishop's house, Manukau View, is at left. The pine tree obscures Alec Bishop's house, which is behind the kiosk. Waitakere Library & Information Services, Bishop Collection

some years. He was also the Waitemata Council chairman in 1939, when his influence was critical in the establishment of the new Titirangi School. His work for the school was honoured at the opening ceremony (*New Zealand Herald*, 18 February 1939), when he said that the new school building was the result of 10 years of fighting by the school committee.

Gus Bishop married Lilian Lusty and they spent their lives in Titirangi. They had three children: John (Jack), William Norman (Bill) and Mary Katherine (later Mrs Fraser and then Mrs Garbely). Bill Bishop spent most of his life in Waima, Titirangi, and retired to Mt Roskill. Mary Garbely built a house in Waima and lived in it for some years. Her brother

Early tour buses, charabancs, at the Bishop kiosk in its heyday, c.1925. Note the Laingholm Estate sign advertising sections for sale. W. Titchener Collection

38 *Titirangi*

Bishop family reunion, 1965. Mia Stein Collection

Bill recalls that as a child Mary had said that she wanted to live on 'Ruru Hill', Waima, and that was where she eventually built her house.

Other descendants of the Bishops who lived in Titirangi for many years were the Titchener family. The cousin marriage between Bertha, the daughter of Sarah Bishop and Thomas Robert Speer, and Frank Oscar, the son of Euphemia Bishop and Robert Betts Peat produced Frances Betts Peat, who married Arthur Lee Titchener, for many years the proprietor of the grocery at Titirangi. Arthur's father Walter Titchener had begun the business Titirangi Four Square Groceries in the building that now houses The Hardware Café. Walter was joined in the business by his two sons Arthur and Vernon. Vernon was disabled and had limited mobility but ran the post office and early telephone exchange situated in the grocery shop. Arthur ran the grocery and after their marriage, Arthur and Frances lived on the hill at the corner of Titirangi and Godley roads. The Titchener name is perpetuated in the street running off Golf Road. Their son Walter (Wallie) lived in Titirangi until 2009, and in 2010 still owned property and takes a great interest in Titirangi. The next generation of Bishops have scattered throughout New Zealand, but the family's contribution remains at the heart of the history of the area.

This account of the Bishop family was compiled from the following sources. T.A. Bishop, 1951–52 Family Reunion; T.A. Bishop, 1965 Family Reunion, Bishop family papers; W.N. Bishop, 2000–2009, oral histories, West Auckland Historical Society Inc.; Dora Jones, A memoir, oral history, West Auckland Historical Society Inc. Wallie Titchener, Remembrances of Titirangi, oral history West Auckland Historical Society Inc.

1   Bishop, T.A. Family reunion papers, 1965.

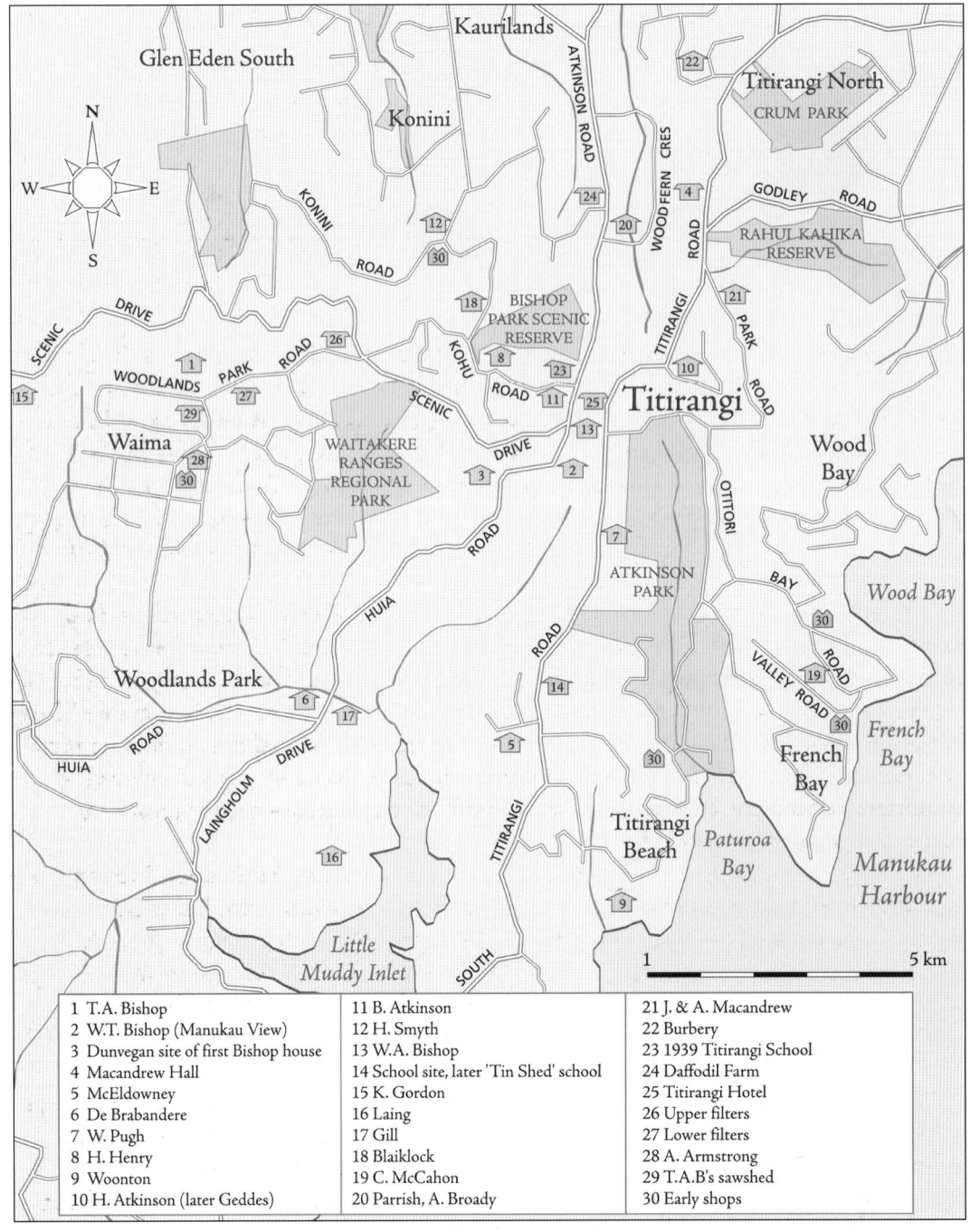

1 T.A. Bishop	11 B. Atkinson	21 J. & A. Macandrew
2 W.T. Bishop (Manukau View)	12 H. Smyth	22 Burbery
3 Dunvegan site of first Bishop house	13 W.A. Bishop	23 1939 Titirangi School
4 Macandrew Hall	14 School site, later 'Tin Shed' school	24 Daffodil Farm
5 McEldowney	15 K. Gordon	25 Titirangi Hotel
6 De Brabandere	16 Laing	26 Upper filters
7 W. Pugh	17 Gill	27 Lower filters
8 H. Henry	18 Blaiklock	28 A. Armstrong
9 Woonton	19 C. McCahon	29 T.A.B's sawshed
10 H. Atkinson (later Geddes)	20 Parrish, A. Broady	30 Early shops

Map of Titirangi district. Original by Marc Bonny. Drawn by Nick Keenleyside, Outline Graphics.

3

Early vigour

As well as the Bishop family, it is well to note some of the other families that lived in early Titirangi. The Brimner property adjoined that of the Bishops, and it was through these properties that the track, and later the road, passed to Little Muddy Creek.[1] Prior to this the road ran along South Titirangi Road and down the steep hill (at about the present location of Grendon Road) for this connection. In his memoirs, T.A. Bishop records:

> *The Brimners were engaged in farming and sheep rearing and later Mr Brimner had the first horse and cart in the district. He did all the carting for the settlers, his conveyance being left at the Bishops.*

John Porter, who owned 10 acres overlooking Little Muddy Creek near what is now McEldowney Road, was reported as being the first postmaster in Titirangi.[2] Unfortunately, he drowned a year later and the post office was closed. The fact that the first post office for the Titirangi area was called Little Muddy Post Office emphasises the importance of the Little Muddy area at that time. Until the 1860s the Little Muddy valley had been serviced by cutters and boats at the landing. It was an open muddy bay when first discovered by Europeans, but milling the forests and the run-off of nutrients hastened the growth of mangroves in the bay, as can be seen today.

The valley had been milled and was still providing kauri and firewood for Auckland in the last half of the nineteenth century. It was full of smallholdings, often leased from absentee land owners, as stated in a letter to *The New Zealander* on 7 January 1860.

> *The road continues through what was forest, but is still burnt shrubs and grass to the bottom of the hill affording the most delicious peeps of Little Muddy landing place where the Creek and the valley through which it runs, is dotted with small houses and pretty enclosures. The road leads to a creek easily crossed.*

Water was still the main means of access to Little Muddy and the general Titirangi area in 1860. This was reflected in the Electoral Roll of 1855 (p. 232): Titirangi had only 23 registered electors and Little and Big Muddy had 42 registered electors. An early public house existed at Little Muddy to service the local growing population. It was known that sailing vessels such as cutters and scows would come to the landing to enjoy this social amenity. Another attraction at Titirangi was a dancing floor without sides, walls or a roof, that had been constructed at the foot of Rigby's Hill (Rangiwai Hill); here the early settlers and pit-sawyers passed many a merry evening.[3] This amenity was probably connected with the sawing station in the Upper Atkinson Valley area, at least two kilometres from Little Muddy. Another public house, known as the Woodman's Inn, was built beside a wood

> *The Henry family must have been among the first families to leave the north and settle in the new town of Auckland. In Moodys Royal Almanac for 1841–42 they are listed as John Henry and Sons, sawyers, Durham Street. So if they originally came with William White their stay with him had been very short. William White (missionary and businessman) is known to have recruited sawyers from Sydney to Hokianga in 1838–39.*
>
> *On 7 August 1854 Hugh Henry paid £40 for a grant of land at what we now call Titirangi. It comprised 84 acres (Allot 28, Roll 15. Folio 400) and was in the shape of an irregular triangle with the apex where Lopdell House now stands, the Northern border along the line of what is now South Titirangi Road and the Southern irregular border between this road and the present Huia Road. Actually the apex of this triangle belonged originally to Hugh's brother John (18 acres, parts of Allots 184 and 48) but was sold to Hugh on 18 December 1855.*
>
> *Here Hugh made his home. There were three daughters: Eliza, Anna, who died in 1871, and Mary Jane, who died in 1854. Hugh cut and sawed the timber on his property and his father, who lived in West Queen Street (Swanson Street), attended to the sales, some going overseas. On 16 November 1862 Hugh was killed in an accident with his horse.*
>
> *Eliza married John Gittos whose father Benjamin took control of the farm in 1874, and the property was later sold to Thomas Matheson for 200 pounds in 1883.*
>
> Extract from Henry Family History supplied by the McCutcheon Family.

sawing station in Swanson Bay, past Big Muddy. This establishment was run from 1850 for some years by Cuthbert Leathart, but was burnt down in 1876.[4]

The first primary school in the area was opened in a shed on the property of William Pugh in South Titirangi Road. William was married to Hannah Bishop and was the first chairman of the Titirangi School Committee. He was also Postmaster of Titirangi when the post office opened in his residence in March 1873.[5]

Hugh Henry, whose land was between that of Hibernia Smyth and John Bishop, owned and farmed what was then known as Henry's Hill (also sometimes called Bishop's Hill in the old days), today known as Mt Atkinson. Henry was described as a sawyer in the electoral roll of 1855. He was locally respected and his home or station was listed as a polling place in both the 1856 and 1862 local elections. In the letting notice of his property in the *Daily Southern Cross*,[6] after his untimely death by accident in November 1862, his farm was described as 260 acres with a comfortable dwelling house, containing three rooms, a large commodious kitchen, dairy, stable, barn and cow shed — about 100 acres laid down with grass and substantially fenced.

The McEldowney farm was situated in South Titirangi and stretched almost to Little Muddy. James and his wife Lydia settled in Titirangi in the early 1880s, where later their son Arthur and wife Dot ran a dairy farm and raised pigs at their Grendon Road house. James and Lydia, who had emigrated from Ireland, grew apples and fruit for export. They took their produce to the Auckland market in a four-horse wagonette and were the only commercial growers at the time.[7]

Bordering Little Muddy Creek and in the area of the present Huia Road was the de Brabandere's farm, bought from the Brimners (the first settlers). The de Brabanderes had a herd of dairy cows, mostly Jersey, and some sheep. Originally from Belgium, they spoke Flemish and worked hard to get quality produce from their property.

Most settlers in the Waitakeres were described as sawyers when they first obtained their land, having first to cut and sell the timber, and then burning the scrub and sowing the grass seed for the farm. Later, as the farm became self sufficient and improved, they would describe themselves as farmers.

William Scarlett and his brother left England in the 1840s and came to New Zealand via the gold fields of Australia, a common route for settlers in the 1860s and 1870s. William stayed in Auckland, went gumdigging for a while, and then in 1877 married Henrietta Denyer from the family who were among the earliest settlers on the fringe of Titirangi, towards New Lynn. The original settler, George Henry Denyer, came to New Zealand in the early 1840s and farmed and cut timber on land between New Lynn and Mt Albert. By the 1860s there were five Denyer families living in New Lynn or on the northern Titirangi slopes near Golf Road.[8] William and Henrietta Scarlett lived at first in New Lynn, then on a small farm in Golf Road. Their son, William Henry, and his family continued to live in the area and his descendants have been prominent Titirangi people to the present day.

View to de Brabandere's property, c.1920. There is a boatshed in the valley.
Waitakere Library & Information Services, Bishop Collection

On 408 acres of land originally owned by the Denyers, a progressive social initiative in the 1890s saw the formation of the Hetana hamlet in the valley stretching below Old Titirangi Road. Its purpose was to provide land to working men, and returned soldiers from the Boer war. The initiative was named after the then Prime Minister Richard Seddon (Hetana is the Maori version of his name). The land was to be leased, but a preference for freehold resulted over time in the selling of individual sections, so the hamlet idea was lost, but a sign indicating the area, still exists at the entrance to 200 Old Titirangi Road. The West Lynn Garden now occupies a portion of this land.[9]

The boundaries of Titirangi, both present and past, have varied. In Maori times Titirangi was the whole range of hills that runs along the edge of the Manukau Harbour at right angles to the main Waitakere Range, but Europeans soon accepted Titirangi as a specific area/district of Western Auckland. It was described in 1855 as:

> *... a well timbered and hilly district between 10 and 12 miles from Auckland, west of the Great North Road, with a frontage to the Manukau Harbour. The land is very broken, good in the valleys. The scenery is remarkably fine and picnic parties frequently go from Auckland to a clump of kauri bush on the ridge, reached by road branching on the left side beyond the Whau Bridge. The district may be reached by boat (or cutter) from Onehunga (Manukau).*[10]

Earlier, Titirangi had been defined by the provincial government as the area where the village is today including a few kilometres south and west, but bounded by Avondale and New Lynn. Little Muddy and Big Muddy were looked upon as separate small districts in the 1855 Electoral Rolls.

From 1870 to 1886 Titirangi was a specific Highway District and extended from the Whau area to the Nihotupu Stream (Parau).[11] Today, Titirangi Village is the centre of the suburb of Titirangi in Waitakere, greater Auckland City, and is bounded by Laingholm and Parau on the west, Glen Eden to the north and New Lynn and Green Bay to the north-east and east. The Manukau Harbour frames the beautiful tree-covered slopes to the south.

In the 1860s and 1870s roads were becoming the lifeline of the growing communities, particularly for farming settlers and millers. In 1862 government legislation made local highway boards, elected by local ratepayers at annual meetings,[12] responsible for roading.

Board members in the 1870s and 1880s were:[13]

William Allcock	1873–74	Thomas Brimner	1873–74
John Dobson	1874–86	Augustus Gobbat	1871
James Hanson	1871–84 Chair	Reuben Haslip	1882–83
Caesar Hastings	1873–84	John Johns	1870–72
? Jones	1873–74	John Jones Sen.	1875–76
John King	1870–72	George Laing	1870–86 Chair
Walter Lee	1874–75	Gordon Lennox	1882–83 Chair
?Morrison	1882–83	?Nelson	1882–83
John Porter	1872–73	William Pugh	1870–76
Samuel Seymour	1870–73	Archibald Wilson	1872–73
John Wood	1874–75	Owen Yorke	1882–83

Local men improving the clay quagmire road with tea-tree fascines (layers of bundles of tea-tree) to improve traction, 1896. The group are near the corner of today's Park and Titirangi roads. From left: W.T. Bishop, J. Atkinson, P. Woonton, I. Matheson, J. McEldowney, ? Aitken, S. Woonton, A. Bulte, T.S. Armstrong, L. de Brabandere, Jim McCowan, J.O. Yorke, Joe McCowan, J.J. Bishop.

Photographer: J. Hibbs, Waitakere Library & Information Services, Atkinson Papers

The Woontons at Davies Bay

Davies Bay is to the west of Titirangi Beach. The land was originally bought by Greenwood (see lot numbers, p. 229, and map of 1870 Titirangi district, p. 40). In 1878 a piece of land bordering the harbour was bought by Edward Woonton and his wife, who came out from St Hellyers (St Heliers) in the Channel Islands. They brought with them the acorns that have now grown into the large oak trees that adorn the area. Edward Woonton bought more land from Laing (see appendix) in 1891. Today there is a walking track but no road access to Davies Bay.

The Woontons are remembered in the name of the nearby Woonton's Lane, but the name Davies Bay, although confirmed by historian Jack Diamond and now the official name, has an unknown origin. An article in about 1950 refers to the bay as Woonton's Bay.[14] Phillip John Woonton, Edward's son, also bought further pieces of land in 1900, but he was better known for his boat the *Pearl* that, after his death in 1944, apparently lay derelict in the sands of the bay. The *Pearl* had a romantic history and apparently was a very beautiful boat in her day. In his youth Phillip lived for a while on Manihiki, an island in the Northern Cooks group in the South Pacific. During that time a boat called the *Flying Venus* was wrecked on Manihiki and Phillip salvaged the main mast and used the wood to build the *Pearl*.

In an article written in the 1950s, Doris Burson recounts that:

> *Phillip swam out and saved the captain's life by bringing him to shore. Custom allowed a captain to sell a wreck to the highest bidder, and Phillip bought what was left of* Flying Venus. *At his bidding, part of the cedar wood mast was cut into planks and with this he built* Pearl, *an eighteen-foot vessel with a daisy sail. He later shipped his boat aboard* Richmond *and brought her to Auckland. A single cylinder Mianus engine was installed and* Pearl *became the second oil driven boat on the Manukau Harbour, Mr Grundy's pride and joy,* Mildura *being the first.*
>
> *In 1915 Phillip decided to lengthen* Pearl *to thirty feet. He sent to Manihiki for the remainder of the mainmast, and the Onehunga mills cut it into the required lengths. A border of diamond-shaped pieces of inlaid pearl wrought from the deep sea pearl shells of Manihiki ornamented the gunwhale, and the words 'Pearl Manihiki', also in pearl-inlay, stretched across the stern.*

Woonton family and friends outside the barn. Mrs Woonton is standing in the doorway with husband Phillip next to her (in hat). Harvey Waite Collection

Phillip Woonton (left) beside his launch, *Pearl*. Harvey Waite Collection

After his third marriage in 1914 to Annie, a local woman from Laingholm, who was also a sailing enthusiast, Phillip remained in New Zealand and sailing in the Manukau became the couple's greatest pleasure. A descendant, Harvey Waite, was interviewed by Marc Bonny in 2005 and recalled his family. His grandfather was Phillip Woonton, his mother, Phillip's daughter, went to school at Parau. Harvey Waite started school at the 'Tin Shed School' in 1937 and then to the new school at Titirangi in 1939.

Titirangi School

Education of the young in Titirangi began very early after the founding of the colony. In the early 1840s Miss Green, who lived on Mt Atkinson near Kohu Road, charged threepence per week to teach children (although T.A. Bishop's memoirs say one shilling). Miss Green was the first known teacher in Titirangi. As mentioned by T.A. Bishop in his 1951 memoir, John and Elizabeth Bishop, who had eight children, engaged a tutor, Mr Patterson, to teach the children. A large upstairs room, the attic, was converted into a schoolroom. Neighbouring children were allowed to attend for a small fee of threepence a week.

Mr Patterson died in the first few years of the Bishop children's education and Ben Carrol was engaged to take over as teacher. By the late 1860s the Bishop children had completed their primary schooling. Ben Carrol, who in 1884 worked in Titirangi's first hotel, then enlisted William Pugh to provide a shed on his farm in South Titirangi Road (46–48 South Titirangi Road). Later teachers were Mr Thomas Coulter, Mr Thomas Armstrong and Miss Alexandrina Tinling, who became Mrs W. Bishop.

After a year or two of teaching in the shed, in 1870 Mr Pugh encouraged locals to build a formal school in South Titirangi Road. Timber, mainly kauri, was pit-sawn and extracted from the Paturoa Beach area. Community volunteers built the building, which was designed as a comprehensive facility able to be used as a social hall, church and school. The address at the time was 181 South Titirangi Road, now renumbered 634 South Titirangi Road.

When Europeans first came to Titirangi, Maori residents seemed to be grouped in Paeroa Bay (Paturoa Bay-Titirangi Beach) and some later attended Titirangi School.[15] Concerts and dance fundraisers were held to repay Mr Pugh for the land and other associated expenses for the new school. From the attic classroom of her Dunvegan home, Mrs Elizabeth Bishop gave the school desks and forms and other items.[16] Titirangi School was finished in November 1873 and classes began in February 1874. It was handed over to the Education Board some time after 1874.

In a letter from around 1975, T.A. Bishop wrote:

> *I am not too happy about the newspaper reports of the school. Mr Pugh did not give the site, he sold it to the committee of which he was chairman. My grandmother offered a site on the other side of the road. Nor did he advance money for the building, the builder agreed to accept payment as the money came in from the functions held. Mr Pugh no doubt supplied the reports for the newspapers at the time and if any money was for him it was to pay for the land. The account given in the newspaper prepared by my wife for the Womens*

View to Pugh's farm and the Manukau Harbour from today's hall, pre-1920. In the distance on the right is the 1873 school.

Photographer: James D. Richardson. Auckland City Libraries Special Collections, 4-8260

'The Shanty', Atkinson's Bush, (1910), believed to be the house where the Pugh family lived.

Alexander Turnbull Library, Wellington, NZ, Price Collection, Ref. No. G-1584-1/2

Institute was verified by people who were alive when the building was built. It was built mainly as a dance hall with provision for the school and handed over to the Education Board when the committee would not agree on maintenance.

(Source: Waitakere City Library & Information Services)

Under the Education Act (1870) villages such as Henderson and Titirangi could take advantage of certain benefits. The roll at that time was 29 and the teacher, Ben Carrol, was given a salary of £100 a year. This was a half-time position. The Board also spent £30 on maintenance in the first year.

According to Titirangi District details filed in the Auckland Public Library in 1879, Titirangi residents applied to Auckland City for funds for a library but it seems that it was a number of years before this amenity became a reality. Proposed trustees were: Matheson, Rigby, Smith, Pugh, Carrol, Yorke, Martin, Woonton, Bishop, Porter, Capps, C. Otway, L. Otway. The interim committee were: Martin, Woonton, Porter, Pugh, Rigby, Smyth, Hill.[17] First name initials were not given.

From 1884 to 1890 the teacher for Titirangi School was T.S. Armstrong. He held classes at Titirangi and Laingholm schools. By 1890 the population had increased and Titirangi had its first full-time teacher, with a roll of 35 pupils. At the time, more than 35 pupils would have allowed for the Board to allocate another assistant.

The regular dances and soirees continued into the early 1900s and became part of the Titirangi scene. However, there were occasional complaints from residents living nearby.

Mrs Lily Witten taught from 1921 to 1934 and she gained much respect for her broad view of education. She introduced civic and cultural studies and she was applauded for the individual attention that she gave to each pupil.

Early vigour

The Soiree at Titirangi New School House on November 7th turned out as anticipated a complete success. A large assemblage of the surrounding settlers and visitors from town responded to the call of the committee, which resulted in a most enjoyable evening's amusement, and a substantial addition to the School Fund. The proceedings were opened by Mr. Carroll with a poetical address written for the occasion, and speeches, recitations, and songs, of no mean order, tended to pass the evening, which all seemed at parting to think much too short. They were all amateurs who kindly came forward on the occasion; it would be invidious to particularise, but we cannot help noticing the speeches of Messrs. Bollard and Hill, the former gentleman complimenting the committee and also Mr Forsythe the contractor, on the beautifully finished and substantial building, showing plainly that he (Mr. Forsythe) had, what England expects, nobly done his duty; and the latter gentleman's speech was given with great taste, and well suited to the occasion. Mr. Carroll's recitation of "Campbell's Last Man," and his burlesque medley of "Alonzo the Brave," were very well received, the latter bringing down the house with frequent bursts of applause. Mr. David Archibald's "Good Evening and Good Night, Darling," and last not least, was Mr. Brimer, with his venerable grey locks, who sang remarkably well. The Committee feel themselves very grateful to Mesdames Bishop, Dobson, Matheson, Pugh, Porter, and Wilson, who kindly provided trays for the occasion, and for the tasteful arrangements, and liberal supply of creature comforts, received many a hearty compliment from their guests during the evening. The Committee exerted themselves to the utmost to ensure the comfort of all, and as for Mr. Pugh the chairman, he was almost ubiquitous. Divine service was held in the School House on the following Sunday, when Mr. Hill officiated and gave an excellent discourse. We understand the Committee have prevailed upon the same gentleman to preach again next Sunday, and hope to be able to secure his services every Sunday, as the only place of worship is no nearer than the Whau, too long a distance for many to attempt.

A SECOND soiree in aid of the funds of the above school was held on Friday, the 22nd instant, in the spacious school-room recently erected, and like the first one was a great success. Whatever could add to the amusement and comfort of the large number of visitors assembled (over 150), was not omitted by the members of the School Committee, and Mr. Pugh, the chairman, through whose untiring zeal the district is indebted for the commodious school-house. The ladies of the district were not backward in coming forward to add to the evening's enjoyment. Trays were provided by Mesdames Pugh, Porter, Bishop, Wilson, Matheson, Spiers, and Dobson; and the appearance of the tables on entering the room had a very pleasing effect, decorated as they were and abundantly supplied with creature comforts, relieved by a stage front erected at the end of the room, which was tastefully decorated with ferns, nikau, pohutukawa blossoms, flowers and garlands, arranged by Mrs. Pugh, assisted by Messrs. Dobson and Hill.

A GREAT want is about to be supplied in this rising district by the completion of a school-house, the absence of which has been long felt by its population. Great credit is due to Mr. Pugh, the chairman, and the other members of the District School Committee, for their exertions in the matter, which has resulted in the construction of a spacious building adapted in every way for the purpose intended. We understand that a soiree is about to be held, for which several ladies in the neighbourhood have kindly promised to furnish trays. The entertainment, speeches, songs, recitations &c., will be given by well known amateurs, and the prices of admission being within the reach of all, we have no doubt the affair will be a great success.

TITIRANGI SCHOOL DISTRICT.

The first yearly examination of the pupils of the above district took place at the school-house on the 1st of January. The progress of the children reflected great credit upon the exertions of the school-mistress, Mrs. Colgan. After the examination, the prizes to the successful pupils were distributed by the chairman of the committee, Mr. Pugh. The children were afterwards entertained at a school feast by the committee and a few of the immediate settlers. The successful competitors were as follows:—1st Class: Miss Christiana Pugh, 1st prize; Miss Eliza Frances Knobbs, 2nd prize. 2nd Class: Miss Emma Mathieson, 1st prize; Miss Mary E. Pugh, 2nd prize. 3rd Class: Miss Agnes Smith, 1st prize; Master Evan T. Pugh, 2nd prize.

(Above) The first soiree, one of many such social occasions, held at the new school building.
Daily Southern Cross, 13 November 1873, p. 2

(Top right) The second soiree for the community.
Daily Southern Cross, 6 January 1874, p. 3

(Centre right) A school and community building were built in 1873 for the district. *Daily Southern Cross*, 3 November 1873, p. 3

(Bottom right) Prize-giving report for Titirangi School District, 1876. *Daily Southern Cross*, 6 January 1876, p. 2

A hand-coloured photograph of a picnic party on a horse-drawn jigger on the pipeline tramway, some time between 1911 and 1914. Chappie Bishop is carrying the basket. Huia Museum

View from present Titirangi Village to Little Muddy Creek and Manukau Harbour. This is a hand-coloured tinted lithograph by Frederick Rice Stack, 1850–60.
Alexander Turnbull Library, Wellington, NZ, C-060-023

(Above) *Untitled (Soldiers Memorial Church Titirangi)*. Cameron Johnson, oil on canvas, 305 x 460 mm. Mia Stein Collection

(Left) *The Punky Tree*. Cameron Johnson, oil on canvas, 700 x 350mm. Mia Stein Collection

(Top right) View from Titirangi to Little Muddy Creek, c.1910. The school, built in 1873, is at back left and the Bishop house is to the left of the tall tree. Alexander Turnbull Library, Wellington, NZ, G-292-1/2

(Right) 'Teddy McGee chasing the chooks'. A child's sketch of the Bishop home, 1878. Drawn by Robert Betts Peat. W. Titchener Collection

iii

(Above) **Whau Portage Sculpture on Great North Road, New Lynn.** The sculpture represents the route taken by Maori canoes from Waitemata to Manukau. Designed by Warren Viscoe and Bill McKay, Tai Whakarunga Tai Whakaroro, 2002, Portage Trust and West Auckland Sculpture Trust. Marc Bonny Collection

(Top left) **Bishop's hebe, *Hebe bishopiana*.** Bruce Harvey Collection

(Left) **Whau plant (*Entelea arborescens*) in flower.** Bruce Harvey Collection

(Top right) **Little Muddy Bridge.** Bruce Harvey Collection

(Right) **Mangroves in present day Little Muddy Creek.** Bruce Harvey Collection

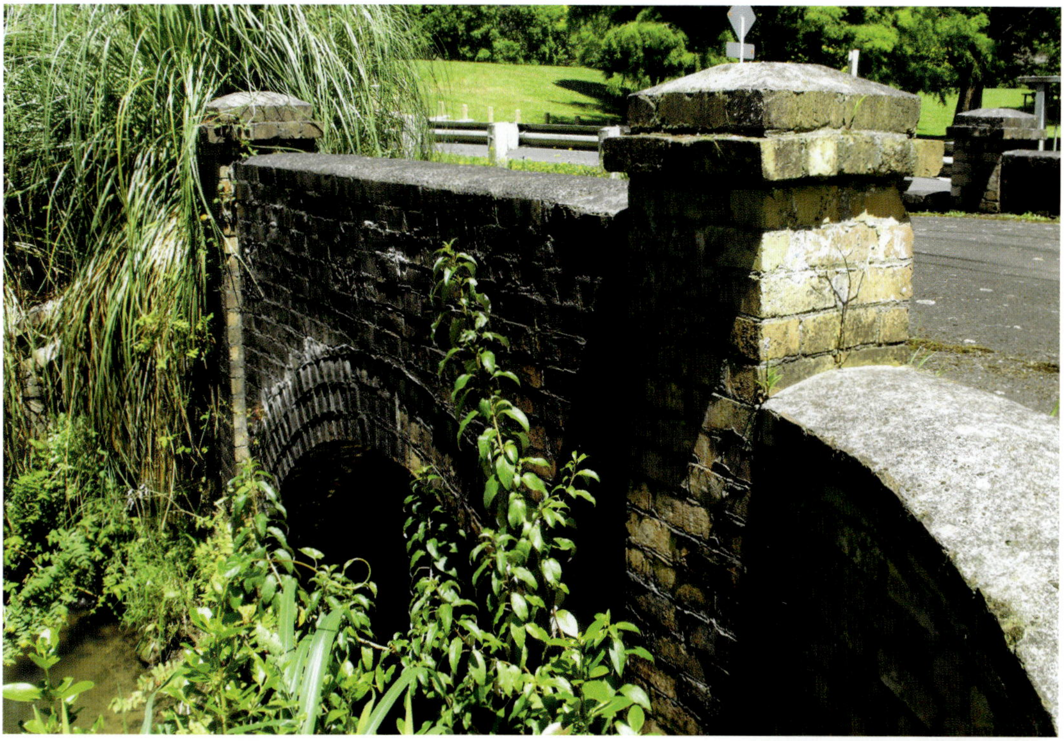

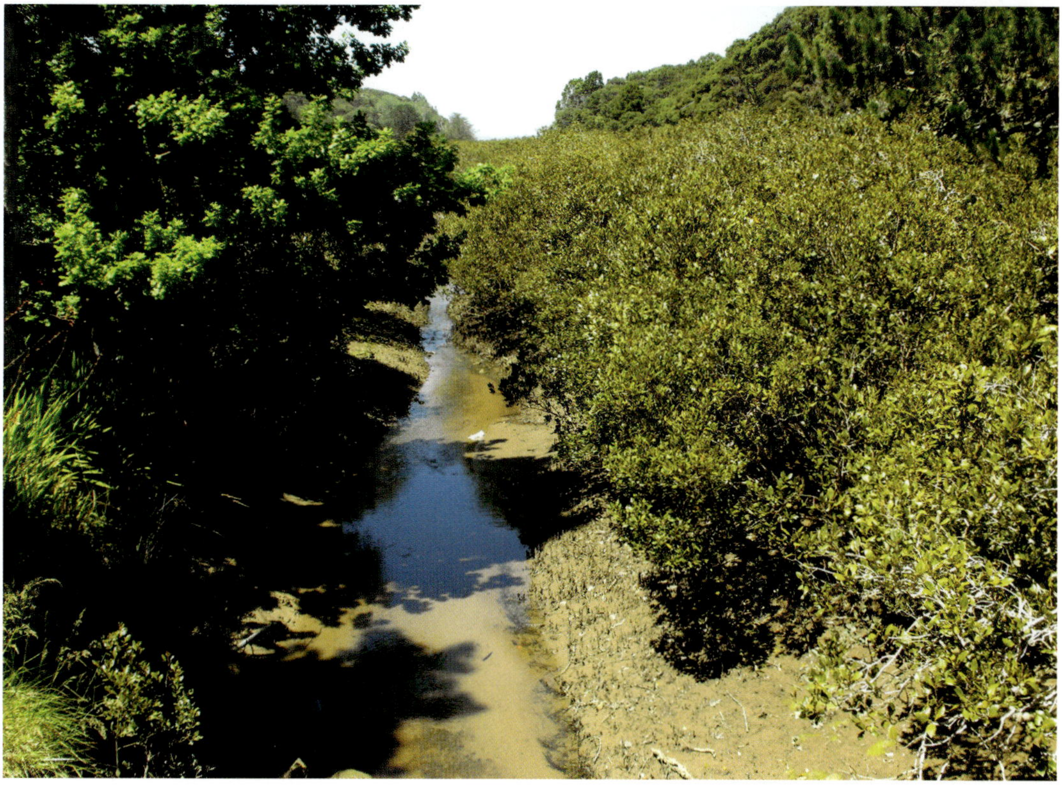

(Above) Lopdell House, November 2008. Marc Bonny Collection

(Left) Henry Atkinson's memorial statue, which now guards Lopdell House. Bruce Harvey Collection

(Below) This welcome sign is a locally crafted mosaic artwork, sited near Pleasant Road. It was erected by the Titirangi Ratepayers' Association and promoted by Ian and June Henderson. Marc Bonny Collection

(Above) *The Three Bush Markers* was sculpted by Lisa Higgins, assisted by Warren Viscoe. This image was taken in 2010. Bruce Harvey Collection

(Right) The war memorial obelisk at its second site, near the present War Memorial Hall.
Bruce Harvey Collection

(Below) A wooden sign for the district's Home Guard. Captain Arthur Parrish was the company commander.
Russell Parrish Collection

Peter Smeele's plan for Worley's Coffee Bar, December 1958. Peter Smeele

(Above) New Zealand Fire Service emblem. Ted Scott

(Left) The 25-year jubilee of the Titirangi Volunteer Fire Brigade, 1974. Trevor Pollard Collection

View southwest from Rangiwai Road showing Pugh's farm, left foreground, and 1873 school (white building on hill) behind. Photographer: James D. Richardson, 18 January 1920. Auckland City Libraries Special Collections, 4-4033

With the Depression of 1929 onwards, funds for school maintenance were limited. The school burnt down on 2 January 1930 and Mrs Witten lost all her personal possessions. It was a terrible blow for her as she was a widow and had seven children. With little funding and help from the Education Board, Alec Bishop, the parents and the school committee raised £180 to build a tin shed, 24 x 20 feet, which catered for 40 pupils. By 1935 another classroom was added by the committee. The roll was now between 70 and 80 pupils.

Because buildings that had been built during the Depression were very basic and the conditions for the pupils less than comfortable, by 1937 the situation at the school, with an increasing roll, had become acute. The Education Board at last began planning for the future and land was taken under the Public Works Act at the present site on the corner of Atkinson and Titirangi roads. This land was part of that which had been given to Auckland City for posterity (park land) by Henry Atkinson when he donated Mt Atkinson and the Zig Zag track area.

On 18 February 1939 the Minister of Justice, J.R. Mason, opened the present Titirangi Primary School. By 1940, with the Second World War under way, the roll had increased to 140. A bomb shelter was built in the school grounds and male teachers began disappearing to the war.

> *During the war there was quite a scare on around the country about the safety of children at school. So my father got cracking with some of the men on the gang at the weekends. We drove an air raid shelter right in under the hill at the top of Atkinson Valley Road, and put the big bomb blast shelters inside.*
>
> *After the war, the shelter was packed back again lest it become dangerous. It was a big job I tell you, wheeling clay in there, as it had 6ft 6in headroom. The shelter was wide enough for benches to be built along the side, with room for the teachers to walk up and down the centre. It was all timbered and all the timber was brought out.*[18]
>
> Bill Beveridge

With the war over, the roll increased to 210 pupils, and in 1948 Laingholm Primary School opened to relieve the pressure. By February 1953 the roll at Titirangi had doubled to over 400 and in October 1957 the roll climbed to a record 538, requiring the building of an extra block. Kaurilands Primary, which opened in 1955, and Glen Eden Intermediate School, that opened later, relieved the roll pressure.

The erection of the school at Laingholm arose partly out of a combination of transport and accommodation difficulties in the Titirangi area, moreover the Titirangi parents were not so convinced of the pedagogical advantages that were claimed for intermediate schooling that they wished to continue sending their children in overcrowded buses to Avondale Intermediate School. The Titirangi Committee, with a thoroughness of organisation seldom if ever equalled by a School Committee, conducted an investigation and presented its case to a large and enthusiastic meeting of householders on 19th May 1948. Facts and figures, lantern slides and the eloquence of J.M. Odlin, C.L. Carter, H. Atkinson and J. McKail Geddes persuaded Messrs Merrington, McCarroll and Smith who attended the meeting, that the people who chose to live in that hilly area and endure its bad roads and wayward bus services had genuine reasons for dissatisfaction. The outcome was the establishment of the school at Laingholm, the enlargement of the Titirangi Primary School and the return of standards 5 and 6.[19]

An early newspaper article from around 1893, possibly supplied by Mr Pugh, is very positive about Titirangi's progress.[20]

This district is keeping pace with others in the march of progress. One of our settlers, Mr McEldowney, has done so well with sheep this last year or two that he is moving his house to a better position near the school, where he will command a fine view of the Manukau Harbour. He is also adding more rooms to it. Another settler, Mr Aitken, contemplates building a new house in an improved position. The settlers here find sheep so suitable to the district that they are steadily increasing their flocks and felling the bush rapidly to increase their areas of grass. We have started the year with a new teacher (Miss Duncan), our late teacher having recently changed her name, and settled in the district. The school roll has increased and the new teacher is giving satisfaction to all. Some time since an attempt was made to obtain a bi-weekly mail service, instead of the present weekly one, but failed. We are hoping they are not too discouraged, and mean to try again. The residents of Brooklyn are moving for a school, as they are too far off to send their children to Titirangi School. The timber trade is dull owing to low prices, but firewood is brisk, and prices have advanced. As for fruit, plums have been a short crop, peaches are improving, and apples and pears very wormy. Our roads are now in a very fair condition. Lately a great improvement has been made to the main road to Huia, near the bridge that spans the Titirangi River. Several pipe culverts have been put in by Mr Parker, who has charge of the roads in the district, and the work has been finished in a very creditable manner. In fact ever since Mr O. Mays was appointed clerk of the Waitemata Council and Mr Wilson, engineer, our roads have been much improved, and the county generally has been benefitted greatly by the management of the funds and the engineering skill of those gentlemen respectively. Notwithstanding this fact there are a few dissatisfied persons who have axes to grind, and who would like us to return to Roads Boards and mismanagement and confusion. Mr H.E. Sharp, our able and just member, has made some enemies and they are now blustering about a division of the riding, or else joining Eden County. The latter means Roads Boards and waste of public money.

The Tin Shed School, 1937. Bill Bishop in dark shirt, top left.
Committee, Titirangi Primary School, 125th jubilee

Today, Titirangi Primary School is a decile ten school with a roll of approximately 500, and is equipped with a swimming pool and excellent room and staff facilities. One teacher, Margretha Banks, is known as the longest-serving teacher. She and other dedicated staff have taught many students, some becoming eminent in New Zealand and overseas.[21]

Much was to change towards the end of the 1800s. The children of the settlers were soon old enough to work, some stayed on the settler farms and others were caught up with the growth of the city and its variety of vocations. Brickmaking was in full swing in New Lynn and other surrounding West Auckland areas. From the 1840s ships were being built in Auckland and Onehunga. Timber was in full production and houses built with Waitakere kauri were filling the new suburbs of Auckland. With the land wars over, huge tracts of arable land were available in the Waikato and the pressure to produce on the farms in Titirangi had lessened. Young people were being enticed away from Titirangi farms to work in the city. By 1900 some land where bush had been burned and grass sown was reverting to scrub due to economic pressures and scarcity of labour. The regeneration of the original vegetation continued and small bush lots that had been unattended since the late 1800s became budding young forests.

The First World War dramatically withdrew labour from Titirangi. Wars denuded West Auckland's population of young men considerably and hastened the demise of farming in the first quarter of the twentieth century. The South African War (1899–1902) took a contribution of 6500 men from New Zealand. There is no direct record of local participation but no doubt there were a number

The War Memorial at its original site on the hill opposite the school, above the present roundabout, 1920s. West Auckland Historical Society, Kershaw Collection

Early vigour

The Ogier family's farm cottage. The family named their New Zealand home Guernsey Valley Farm. From left: Claud Ogier, Thomas Robin Ogier and unknown.

West Auckland Historical Society

of young volunteers. At the time there was an imperial spirit evoking visions of the rugged volunteer riding to war with his own horse and equipment. This view was captured again in 1914, with thousands of eager, young men volunteering for service. However, the statistics at the end of 1918 are very sobering. From a small settlement such as Titirangi, over one-sixth of the volunteers were killed in action and a larger number wounded, often incapacitated for life.

On the Titirangi War Memorial for 1914–18, the names listed as having served are the family names mentioned in this book. Familiar names, such as Armstrong, Bishop, Yorke, Coulter, Godley, Jones, Lawrence, McEldowney and McQuoid, are among the 68 names. The Bishop family had three sons in the war, of which two were killed, J.J. Bishop at Passchendaele on 12 October 1917 and W.N.C. Bishop in Northern France on 23 May 1918.[22]

> *My father came from a family of six children, three boys and three girls. Two of his brothers were killed in France and he was severely wounded when a piece of shrapnel from a shell pierced his leg at the outer thigh and exited at the inner ankle, leaving him crippled for the rest of his life.*
>
> *Before each Anzac Day, as children we picked the supple branches of young teatree and bent them into an oval to make the basis of a wreath. We then bound fine wire around and around and tied the ends together to make the circle. We plucked the leaves of a rhododendron tree, bound tooth picks on the leaf stalks and arranged them stuck into the wreaths to look like laurel leaves.*
>
> From W.N. (Bill) Bishop memoirs

In the first few years of the twentieth century, the sunny north-facing slopes of Titirangi were still productive lands. It was here that, in about 1910 the daffodil farm emerged.

In 1908 Thomas Robin Ogier bought about 80 acres of land in the Atkinson Valley area near present Daffodil Street. He named the property Guernsey Valley Farm. This would probably have been part of Hibernia Smyth's original land. Ogier began growing a variety of fruit trees and other cash crops such as vegetables, strawberries and flowers.

In a letter to his mother dated 22 December 1908, he wrote:

Ogier familiy members and dog on their property in the vicinity of today's Daffodil Street.
West Auckland Historical Society

It (the land) belonged to an Englishman who came out 20 years ago and who has lived there for a good many years. There is a nice 4-roomed house and several good sheds on the place — a beautiful valley nearly a mile long with a splendid stream running through. A lot of land is not much good but fit for strawberry growing which is a paying game here. Strawberries commenced about 5 weeks ago and they have not come down lower than 8 pence a pound. Should I discover kauri gum on the land it will be a fine thing for me — my fowls lay from 300 to 325 eggs a week and my cabbages will be ready to cut in a few days.

In 1910 Albert Peter Thomas (1885–1963) bought eight acres of Guernsey Valley Farm. Thomas was born in Ashburton, one of seven children, and came to live in New Lynn in 1898 where he began to learn farming, carpentry, brick-making and sailing. His father and mother had bought 88 acres in New Lynn but the family's main income was from a brickworks. The bricks were transported to Auckland and about the Waitemata Harbour by scow. It was on the scow that Albert learnt his sailing. Albert married Ethel Ladbrook in 1912. Albert and Ethel were the first couple to be married in Elim Hall, New Lynn. They had six children. Half of their eight-acre property was planted in daffodils and the balance was used for growing strawberries and other flowers. Daffodil Farm is presently remembered by the name of Daffodil Street.

The farm was owned and operated by the Thomas family, Albert and Ethel and their six children, during the period from 1912 to the 1940s. Initially consisting of only eight acres that had been planted in flowers and strawberries by Tom Ogier, the farm was added to in 1922 and consisted finally of 30 acres. The family all worked on the farm during the Depression, sometimes from before dawn and late into the night according to memories of Albert and Ethel's son Jim[23].

Ethel Thomas was a very devout woman who belonged to the Brethren Church and attended services every week. However, it seems the couple were often at odds with one another and their marriage broke down in 1934 and they separated. Ethel died in 1946, but Albert remarried. He died in 1963. In 1954 Albert still owned the land in Atkinson Road, however, the suburbs were creeping out to Titirangi and the land was being subdivided.

Alwynne Broady recalls working at Daffodil Farm in 1944 and photographs from 1948

View from Mt Atkinson to the Waitemata Harbour. The cleared land below the bush is Guernsey Valley Farm (later the Daffodil Farm area), with Kaurilands to the left. Titirangi Road runs along the flattened ridge in the background.
Photographer: James D. Richardson, 18 January 1920. Auckland City Libraries Special Collections, 4-4041

show girls picking daffodils. Alwynne thought the farm continued until about 1954,[24] operated by eldest son Cyril, who had worked with his father from the mid-1930s.[25]

1   District Highway Board Map, 1870. Auckland City Library.
2   *Auckland Provincial Gazette*, 19 August 1861. Auckland City Library.
3   T.A. Bishop memoirs. Bishop family papers, 1951. This may have been the milling of timber at Hugh Henry's establishment.
4   Harvey, Bruce and Trixie. 'That Noble Sheet of Water' in *West*. Finlay McDonald and Ruth Kerr (eds), Waitakere City Council, 2008, p. 91.
5   *Daily Southern Cross*, 22 January 1863. Auckland City Library.
6   *Brett's Auckland Almanac*. Auckland City Library, 1878, p. 106.
7   T.A. Bishop memoirs. Bishop family papers, 1951.
8   Diamond, J.T. 'Early Settlers of New Lynn'. *New Lynn News*, February 1952, Waitakere Library.
9   O'Grady, Alison, *West Lynn Garden: A Place of Beauty*. West Lynn Garden Society Inc., 2010.
10 *Auckland Provincial Gazette*, 1855. Auckland City Library.
11 Verran, David, in the *West Auckland Historical Society Newsletter*. No. 240, March 2002, p. 7.
12 Ibid.
13 Ibid.
14 Burson, Doris. Article about Woontons Bay, West Auckland Historical Society Archive, c.1950.
15 T.A. Bishop memoirs. Bishop family papers, 1951.
16 Sinkinson, Carol (ed.). *Titirangi Primary School 1873–1997*. Titirangi Primary School. Auckland, 1997, p. 3.
17 Titirangi District Library. Auckland Public Libraries, filed 12 August 1879.
18 Beveridge, Bill. Conversations with Marc Bonny. West Auckland Historical Soc. Inc., 1995–97.
19 Cumming, Professor Ian. *Glorious Enterprise, The History of the Auckland Education Board 1857–1957*. Whitcombe and Tombs Ltd, 1959.
20 Waitakere Public Library. This article was cut out from a newspaper at the time but the source was not recorded.
21 Sinkinson, Carol (ed). Op cit., p. 4.
22 Burton, O.E. *The Auckland Regiment NZEF 1914–18*. Bishop WNC 54813, Whitcombe and Tombs Ltd, Wellington, 1922, p. 307.
23 Memories of Jim Thomas. West Auckland Historical Soc. Inc., oral history, 1995.
24 Memories of Alwynne Broady. Oral History by Marc Bonny, West Auckland Historical Society, 2001.
25 Price, Trevor N. *William Thomas and Family of Devon and New Zealand*. T. Price, Auckland, 2001; Alwynne Broady, 'Memories of Early Titirangi' in *West Auckland Remembers*, James Northcote Bade (ed.), Vol. 2, 1990, p. 121.

4

The Atkinson story

The following narrative of the Atkinson family begins with the children of William Atkinson (1793–1862) and his wife, Ann (1805–1874). William was a maker of wooden ploughs, harrows and gates. William and Ann had 16 children, and although three of their sons were Titirangi residents at various times, it was their ninth child, Henry who had the most impact on Titirangi.

Born at Lindeth, Windermere in the Lakes District of England on 6 July 1838, Henry, became the most prominent and successful of the brothers. He was tall, well proportioned and wore a full beard in latter years. By the age of 25, Henry had been to Russia to work on water engineering and other briefs, and to Lisbon, Portugal, on a similar project. He was an intelligent and capable engineer.

Henry Atkinson.
Fane Kearney Collection

In 1863 he journeyed to New Zealand on the ship *Helvellyn* to supervise the erection of the Auckland Gas Works. He was manager of the company for 35 years. The first family residence stood on the high ground behind the gas works in Nelson Street, Central Auckland.

In about 1866, Henry married Jane Johnstone, aged about 15 years at the time. They had come out on the same ship in 1863, and no doubt a shipboard romance had developed. Jane, a small, extremely capable woman, was devoted to Henry, and immensely helpful to her husband. She had complete authority and control of the children and the household, and it seemed Henry took little part in managing the household except as a final adviser. They had three daughters: Ann Jane (Annie), Caroline and Adeline (Ida) and three sons: Henry William, Alfred Howard (known as Sid) and Hubert James (Bert).

Henry became interested in Titirangi from the 1870s. In the following three decades he acquired from settlers considerable areas of land on the bush edges, extending into the watershed portion of the Waitakere Ranges. His first purchase, about 1884, was the Pugh farm on School Road (now South Titirangi Road). Within two years he also bought a large block of scrub country known as Atkinson Valley, through which Atkinson Road now runs. He also acquired, from the Porter family, land running down to the beach from Park Road, now known as Atkinson Park. He bought a block known as the Maori Block, which ran from the school in School Road down to the beach, and also a block east of the Pugh farm, which included Hall's Hill (now Rangiwai Hill).

Almost from the time of his arrival in New Zealand in 1863, Henry Atkinson seems to

A steam traction engine transporting pipes for the Nihotupu Dam. The Nihotupu Main Trunk was laid between 1913 and 1920. Henry Atkinson gifted substantial tracts of land for the project.
Waitakere Library & Information Services, Print Collection (Titirangi) [from photocopies]

have taken a close interest in the water supply of the city. His earlier experiences in the United Kingdom, Russia and Portugal had given him knowledge about water reticulation that he put to good use in Auckland. In 1900, the Auckland City Council had decided on a scheme to obtain water from Canty's Creek (Oratia Stream) in the Oratia Valley, some six miles west of Western Springs. However, Henry Atkinson and civil engineer H. Munro Wilson suggested an alternative scheme: diverting the Nihotupu Stream. This scheme was accepted when Henry gifted substantial tracts of his own land in the catchment. The Oratia plans were abandoned but Auckland had to endure another trying summer before, in February 1902, the first Waitakere water reached Western Springs. In December 1900 Henry made another gift of two areas of land, one a water reservoir site in Atkinson Road (where the present Titirangi Primary School now stands) and the other area for the Nihotupu reservoir.

The permanent supply of water was the subject of reports over many years to the Auckland City Council, and cost was always a problem, but gradually the realisation grew that the growth of Auckland required the securing of a permanent supply and that the Waitakere Ranges were the best option. Henry Atkinson was a consistent advocate of water from the ranges. He sold a further block of land adjacent to the Nihotupu Stream to the council in 1906 for water reticulation, and his influence was undoubtedly critical in securing the scheme that gave Auckland City permanent supply for the next 60–70 years.

Henry was also very interested in the construction of the Whau canal, a proposal that would have connected the Waitemata and the Manukau harbours, along the line of the Whau portage, that ancient Maori route from north to south. A rival canal option was from Tamaki to the Manukau and for many years controversy and rivalry raged. In the end neither option was adopted, despite Henry's advocacy. Several of Henry's brothers also made their way to New Zealand and contributed to the early days of Titirangi. George, a witness to Henry's marriage, seems to have left New Zealand shortly afterwards, but William, who married the sister of Henry's wife Jane, was a gold prospector in Victoria and in Hokitika, but eventually took up 13 acres in Atkinson Road. His son, George Atkinson, recalled living with his parents, brothers and sisters in the Old School House on the former Pugh farm, one of the first purchases by Henry Atkinson in Titirangi. George also recalled working on surveying sections of 13–15 acres in Atkinson Valley for his uncle Henry. Another of Henry's brothers, James Atkinson, came from England in 1882 and established a watchmaking and jewellery business in Otahuhu. He moved from Otahuhu to Titirangi about 1907 and also lived in the School Road house (later sold to the Abbott family) while he built a house in Atkinson Valley on a large block bought from Henry. During his Titirangi time James was chairman of the local council and well respected in the area, and he was very interested in saving the volcanic cones of Auckland. He later returned to Otahuhu, where he died in 1932.

From 1900, Henry Atkinson was one of the most prominent citizens of Titirangi but he did not live in the area permanently, retaining his house in the city for most of the year and arriving in Titirangi for holidays. He built several houses in Titirangi including, in 1915, a 'holiday home' in Rangiwai Road. Jane Atkinson and her daughters, Annie and Adeline, lived there after Henry's death in 1921, until 1937. The imposing residence was leased to the Canadian trade commissioner for several years and then sold in 1941 to the Geddes family, who still occupy it.

The Atkinson Memorial on its original site, Mt Atkinson, c.1930s. West Auckland Historical Society

On the corner of Kohu Road (formerly View Road) and Scenic Drive is another large Atkinson house, which was occupied by Hubert (Bert) Atkinson, one of Henry's sons, until his death in 1941, and later by Hubert's daughter. The house that was the Community House for many years, on the slopes of Rangiwai Hill, was another Atkinson house, occupied by members of the family in earlier days.

Henry Atkinson died in 1921. The family-commissioned statue of Henry currently positioned outside Lopdell House was originally erected on Mt Atkinson, but was moved because of vandalism. It is well that Titirangi is reminded of Henry because most of his family has now left the district.

A great-granddaughter, Fane Kearney, still lives in Titirangi, as does one of Henry's great great-granddaughters, Michal Denny. His children all lived in Titirangi in their youth; son Alfred Howard (Sid), a gas engineer, did not outlive his father by many years, dying in 1927 and leaving a teenage family who were looked after by his unmarried sisters, Annie and Ida, in the Rangiwai Road house. One of these children, Henry Junior (Harry), was an optometrist and married Edna, the daughter of the schoolteacher of the Titirangi Primary School, Lily Witten. Harry built the house that later became the Community House in Rangiwai Road. The late Tibor Donner, a very well-known architect, designed it, and today it has a heritage listing.

While living in Titirangi, Harry and Edna contributed to social events such as the Music Society, local council, and community events, especially those held at the school during the 1940s and 1950s. Edna Witten's mother had been a skilled and respected teacher, and was principal at the school. She taught at the original Tin Shed School in School Road (now South Titirangi Road). Edna was a former pupil at the school.

Edna (Witten) Atkinson was always interested in landscape gardening and organised the Titirangi School Arbour Day plantings in the 1950s. She also was responsible for much of the native planting around the school, and even today the kowhai at the front gate provide a lovely sight in the spring. With the help of Ethelwyn Geddes, she started to create an

The Atkinson story

outdoor theatre on the lower grounds at the school, but unfortunately it was never completed due to her early death, although for some time the school did use it for concerts and other events. Edna died suddenly at a relatively young age, leaving a family of three boys and two girls. A plaque at Titirangi School was erected in her memory and for many years an annual competition was run in her memory. Children had to grow native trees and write about them, eventually planting the trees at the school.

Harry Atkinson was the chairman of the Titirangi School Committee for several years. Harry and Edna's daughter, Mrs Fane Kearney, continued the family teaching tradition and was a teacher aide at Titirangi Primary in the 1970s.

Henry and Jane Atkinson's eldest son, Henry William, was his father's main support in the family and became manager of the Thames and Whangarei Gas companies. Henry jun. married Lilian Young and the family lived in Auckland City and Mt Eden. Youngest son of Henry and Jane, Bert Jnr married Florence Leake and lived in the Kohu Road house until his death in 1941. One of his daughters, Annie Florence, known as Nance, married John Vernon Lane, who died in an accident. Nance continued to live in Titirangi and later at Karekare. Of Henry's daughters only Caroline married. She married late in life, in Australia and had no children. Annie, the eldest, and Ida, the youngest, were part of Titirangi society in the 1930s.

Auckland is richer for Henry Atkinson's energy and foresight due to his ideas about water supply and various other engineering works such as Grafton Bridge. Titirangi has benefited greatly from Atkinson's bequests of land, which now form several lovely parks immediately surrounding the village including: Atkinson Park with its Zig Zag Track from Park Road down to Titirangi Beach, Mt Atkinson, encircled by Scenic Drive and Kohu Road, and providing a wonderful view to the south and west over the Manukau, and to the north over the city.

The Henry Atkinson drinking fountain, which stood at the top of the Zig Zag Track on Park Road. The fountain disappeared many years ago. Photographer: James D Richardson, 1 September 1920. Auckland City Libraries Special Collections, 4-4077

At the top of Memorial Hill. Note the cannon in the display case and rustic fencing with seating. Bert Atkinson's house is behind. View Road, now Kohu Road, is to the right below the windmill. W. Titchener Collection

This narrative has been compiled from Atkinson family records and the memories of Mrs Fane Kearney.

5

Exhibition Drive

Exhibition Drive is now a walkway and provides vehicle access for the maintenance of the water pipeline to the filter station in Huia Road. However, its original purpose was grander; it was to provide access to the scenic beauty of the Waitakere Ranges. The history of Exhibition Drive was researched and written by Arnold Turner CMG and Fiona Drummond in 2004 and published in *Waitakere Ranges*.[1] It is reprinted here with some additions by the original authors and with their permission.

Exhibition Drive

In 1900, the Auckland City Council decided to augment the city's water supply by installing a 'run of the stream' intake high on the Nihotupu Stream and piping the water to the city through a light 12-inch steel pipe. In his booklet *Rails Across the Ranges*[2] David Lowe says, 'From the intake of the stream at the present main dam, until a public road was reached at Titirangi township, between five and six miles, a tramway was formed, mostly on a steep sidling that followed the many spurs with a uniform downgrade'. Lowe goes on to record that by 1910 it had been decided to build a storage dam at Nihotupu, and because the original light pipe had deteriorated badly, it was also decided to replace it with a larger cast iron pipe. Driving 23 tunnels through the spurs shortened the tramway route, and a narrow gauge tramway was built. The improved route carried both the pipe and the tramway.

A car on a section of Exhibition Drive, near Titirangi Village, which later became the beginning of Scenic Drive, c.1915. Alexander Turnbull Library, Wellington, NZ, Price Collection, Ref. No. G-1581-1/2

In 1911, Mr C.J. Parr was elected mayor of Auckland. (He had already been a councillor for about 10 years.) He was a very energetic mayor, particularly interested in the provision of parks for the city. He would have been well aware of the work going on in relation to the water supply from the Nihotupu Stream and no doubt he had visited the work from time to time. He would also have been aware of the nearly 3500 acres on the western side of the Nihotupu Valley, which the government had vested in the City Council

Horse-drawn transportation of pipes for the Nihotupu Dam.
Waitakere Library & Information Services, Print Collection (Titirangi) [from photocopies]

Pipes for laying to the Upper Nihotupu Dam (completed in 1923) lying on the ground where today's Woodlands Park Road crosses to the left. Exhibition Drive runs at the base of the hill. Mia Stein Collection

The official opening of Exhibition Drive on 24 January 1914. Members of the City Council, Waitemata County Council, Automobile Association and others were present at the terminus of the road.
Photographer: William Beattie. Auckland City Libraries, 7-A16459, Auckland Weekly News, 29 January 1914, p. 42

in 1895 as a reserve 'for purposes of recreation and for the conservation of Native flora and fauna'; and also of the 1927 acre Cornwallis Block (adjoining those 3500 acres), which the McLachlan family had given to the city in 1910 for reserve purposes.

Who conceived the idea of turning part of the tramway into a scenic motor road is now lost in the mists of time. But in February 1913, it was Mayor C.J. Parr who outlined to the Auckland Automobile Association (AA) a scheme for forming a road to give access to the 'Titirangi Reserve' by utilising part of the tramway. About the same time, Mayor Parr had persuaded Mr Henry Atkinson to give to the Council what is now known as Mt Atkinson and the reserve that runs down to Titirangi Beach (originally called 'Titirangi Reserve'). It may be that Parr's proposal for a road to give access to 'Titirangi Reserve' referred to the Atkinson gifted land. But no matter — his proposal would open up access to the southern part of the Waitakere Ranges.

It was seen that the scheme would benefit motorists. Therefore, the Association decided to do what it could to assist the scheme by 'raising subscriptions'. In March, the City Council recorded that it was willing to allocate £750 for the road if the Association would contribute £250 within six months. Apparently, the Association then agreed to that condition. In October, the president of the AA reported that he had inspected the road, some work had been done, and although 'motors could not yet use the road'. But the City Council was calling for payment of the AA's contribution. However, the Association wanted assurances that the Council had indeed expended £1000 on the road and that it would always remain open for motor traffic. By January 1914 those points had been cleared up and the Association had forwarded its contribution.

In its original form, Exhibition Drive linked Titirangi Village and Carter Road. Between Titirangi Village and what is now known as Jacobsen's Depot, it utilised the existing tramway route. About that time, that section of the tramway ceased to be needed, because by then supplies for the construction of the Nihotupu Dam were being hauled up from the head of Big Muddy Creek. But presumably that section required widening in places and the creation of a roadway around the spurs, which had been tunnelled for the tramway and pipeline. It seems that the link between Jacobsen's Depot and the top of Carter Road may have been the only section of completely new construction. A formal opening of the new Drive was held on 24 January 1914. The AA was fully represented.

The newspaper report[3] recorded the event.

> *The start from the Town Hall was made about 2.30 pm by an imposing procession of about 60 motor cars, and an hour later the present end of the drive at Cochrane's Saddle was reached, the cars drawing up on a commanding elevation of about 500 ft above sea level, near which a splendid panorama of the Manukau and a portion of the Waitemata is obtainable ... Mr Parr pointed out the advantage to the citizens of Auckland and visitors of having such a magnificent piece of bush scenery within such easy reach of the city, and urged the desirableness of pushing the drive still further ahead into the finest part of the bush ... right through to Nihotupu, thus ensuring a superb round drive by connecting with the Waikomiti-West Coast Road, near Waiatarua.*

Cochrane's Saddle is the saddle on Scenic Drive from which a road now leads down to Jacobsen's Depot. The new drive was named Exhibition Drive in view of the fact that a

A team of workers on the Scenic Drive construction project. Waitakere Library & Information Services, Print Collection (Titirangi)

large Mining & Industrial Exhibition had opened in the Auckland Domain on 1 December 1913, attracting large crowds.

In 1914, Wilson & Horton published a small booklet entitled *Titirangi Park and Exhibition Drive*,[4] written by F. Carr Rollett, with photos by Cyril F. Bell. This describes itself as the 'Official Handbook'. (The 'Titirangi Park' of the title is the reserve that runs down to Titirangi Beach.) There is little in the text about Exhibition Drive itself. However it does say, '… what a wealth of wonder and beauty is open to those who travel the first few miles on this Drive …' and continues that '… later the Exhibition Drive will be extended until it connects with the main West Coast Road near Waiatarua, and later of course the whole of the range system of roads will be connected and the thousands of acres of public reserves made accessible. But it is only the beginning. In a little while connection will be made with the Puponga Park'.

The map included in this publication is inaccurate insofar as it shows Exhibition Drive connecting with Parker Road. 'Puponga Park' is a reference to the Cornwallis Peninsula.

Another 25 years were to pass before Mayor Parr's vision of a road connecting Titirangi with Waiatarua was fulfilled. But, except for the first kilometre (from Titirangi to its junction with Woodlands Park Road), Exhibition Drive does not form part of Scenic Drive.

Throughout the 1920s and 1930s, thousands took advantage of the Drive's scenery and bush solitude. It was a one-way road, with travel times allocated on signs at either end of the road. The Drive was prominent in motor touring trips from Auckland for years, and hire cars charged 5/6d (53 cents) for the round sightseeing trip from the city. There were a couple of incidents in which motor vehicles went off the road, and the insurance companies would not pay out.

Following the opening of Scenic Drive in 1939, Exhibition Drive took on lesser importance as Scenic Drive became the main road. Exhibition Drive was closed to traffic in the early 1950s.

Exhibition Drive, as walkers and joggers know it today, lies between the Nihotupu Filter Station (on the east) and Mackie's Rest, overlooking the Nihotupu Valley (on the west). 'Mackie's Rest' relates to the original wooden seat inscribed by local farmer

Marshall Laing in 1913 (relocated from Huia Road to its present position overlooking the lower Nihotupu Valley) in memory of Mackie, who was a city saddler that made periodic trips into the bush to sell his wares, and who owned a house at Parau. This was also the site of a trampers' hut that stood for 40 years until destroyed by vandals.

Most of Exhibition Drive is not a public road, except for the link road between Huia Road and Mackie's Rest at the end. It is a private road maintained by Watercare Services Ltd for access to its pipeline. It is open to the public for other than motor traffic. Today it is a haven for those wanting an all-weather peaceful bush walk. It is dog and pushchair friendly, and an easy jog of 3.2 km on a near flat gradient. It is probably the most popular track in the Waitakere Ranges. Watercare recently provided an excellent parking area adjacent to the Nihotupu Filter Station. The southern part of Shaw Road links with Exhibition Drive about midway on the drive; there are several carparks available.

Group on hillside looking north over Waima area.
Waitakere Library & Information Services, Bishop Collection

There are a few properties with access from the Shaw Road end of Exhibition Drive. One of these is a notable garden, developed by the Bishop sisters over 40 years; the sisters were granddaughters of the original Bishop pioneers of Titirangi. Across the drive from this property, where only steps remain today, was a cottage, originally owned by Hermann Hoffman, who owned a considerable amount of property in the area. City Council Waterworks later bought this cottage and Joe Beveridge, who was employed by Waterworks, resided there. Joe was first employed by Waterworks as a tunneller. He later became foreman and helped maintain the tunnels and pipes on Exhibition Drive. He, along with his workmen, also did an excellent job of keeping the Drive open. Joe's son Bill followed in his footsteps, working for Waterworks and later as an Auckland Regional Council Senior Park Ranger.

In the paddock to the left at the end of Shaw Road was a storage depot, where much of the equipment and materials used in the construction of the Upper Nihotupu pipeline and tunnels were located. To the right of Shaw Road was a bunkhouse, which was accommodation for the conduit workers, an open fire cooking area and the cooks' quarters. Adjoining this building was a blacksmith's shop, and behind it were stables. This bunkhouse building was again in use in the 1930s to board the Scenic Drive survey and engineering staff. Late in the 1930s this building was demolished.

Long may Exhibition Drive continue to give enjoyment to the community. Perhaps one day the section between Mackie's Rest and Scenic Drive (at Cochrane's Saddle) will be re-opened as a track for walking and jogging.

Note from the editors: since the writing of the above history of Exhibition Drive, meaningful discussions have been held between Watercare, which owns the land surrounding the pipeline, and the ARC, which owns and manages the adjacent Regional Park, with regard to extending Exhibition Drive walkway to the Arataki Visitors Centre on Scenic Drive. The ARC has allocated money for preliminary work on this connection, so the hope for the connection previously expressed looks like it will become reality. It will become another walking and tramping asset for the Waitakere Ranges, and create another track with its starting point at Titirangi. It is envisaged that a bus service could run from either end of the track. Watercare will continue to use the track to service the pipeline, as it has done in the past.

And so Mt Atkinson and Atkinson Park (Titirangi Beach Reserve) came into public ownership. Paths had already been cut in Titirangi Park. The track to the summit of Mt Atkinson was opened in 1919.

The biography of Parr contained in the *Dictionary of New Zealand Biography* records that his interests were catholic, spanning parks, roads, public health, planning and organisation. He was the foundation President of the Auckland Town-planning League and the Federated Town-planning Associations of New Zealand.

Parr's vision of 'large reserves' became reality over succeeding decades. The 'Waitakere Hills' reserve has grown to become the Waitakere Ranges Regional Parkland, spanning over 17,000 hectares bordering Titirangi. In 1914, Parr had been elected MP for Eden, and he continued as an MP for 12 years. In 1920 he became a cabinet minister. In 1926 he was appointed New Zealand's High Commissioner in London. He died in 1941 aged nearly 72.[5]

Christopher James Parr

Sir Christopher James Parr was Mayor of Auckland from 1911–15. In the opinion of G.W.A. Bush[6], Parr was 'one of the most remarkable of Auckland's mayors'.

In February 1913, Mayor Parr outlined to the Auckland Automobile Association (AA) a scheme for turning the tramway between Titirangi and the Upper Nihotupu Dam into a road suitable for the new and popular motorcars. The AA agreed that the scheme would benefit motorists. It invited subscriptions and was able to make a financial contribution towards the cost of the proposal. The scheme was implemented, and Exhibition Drive came into being.

At about the same time as Exhibition Drive was being constructed, Mayor Parr persuaded Henry Atkinson to give to the Council, as public reserves, key areas of land at Titirangi. In his centennial history, Bush describes the gift occurring when:

> *Stopping for refreshments during an inspection of possible Scenic Drive routes, the Council was invited to view the summit of a small peak on the ridge behind Titirangi. Parr was so eloquent about the magnificent vista, that the owner ... was induced to offer to the Council both this area and a stretch of land running back from Titirangi beach (some 40 acres of bush). Parr accepted on the spot.*

1. Harvey, Bruce and Trixie (eds). *Waitakere Ranges*. Waitakere Ranges Protection Society Inc., Auckland, 2006.
2. Lowe, David, *Rails Across the Ranges*. The Lodestar Press, Auckland, no date.
3. Opening of Exhibition Drive. Newspaper report (newspaper unknown).
4. Rollett, F. Carr, *Titirangi Park and Exhibition Drive*. Wilson & Horton, Auckland, 1914. Auckland Central City Library refrerence: 995.722 T5:R7 (not for loan).
5. Bush G.W.A. 'Christopher James Parr', biography in *Dictionary of New Zealand Biography, Vol. 3*. Department of Internal Affairs, Auckland University Press, 1996.
6. Bush, G.W.A. *Decently and in Order The Centennial History of Auckland*. The Auckland City Council, 1971.

6

Improved communications

The following extract is by Peter Buffett[1] from his article, 'From Clay to Concrete Highway'. It gives a description of how Titirangi Road was originated.

The first weekend in August 1931 was a stormy one. Thunderstorms rolled over Auckland, fierce winds pounded the city, boats were washed ashore and streets became temporary streams. Despite the weather hundreds of people were pleased to assemble on Saturday afternoon at the corner of Titirangi and Great North roads. Those who had travelled three kilometres down from Titirangi were more than happy to venture out in the wind and rain to see Mrs. E. Mason, wife of the local Member of Parliament, open a gleaming white concrete highway leading back up the hill to Titirangi. Going up from New Lynn would never again be a mud-splattered nightmare in winter and a dust-filled, teeth rattling trip in summer. Titirangi people had long campaigned for a road into the Waitakeres from New Lynn that would make travelling more comfortable, especially for the increased numbers of weekend sightseers. The trip to the train in New Lynn for city workers who lived in Titirangi would also be less onerous on an all weather road.

Bert Atkinson and Alec Bishop led a deputation of Titirangi people to the Waitemata County Council in the late 1920s to press for a new road. Their requests received little sympathy. Local Riding member Marshall Laing thought it a huge joke that Titirangi should have a sealed road to itself. He had not counted on the tenacity of Titirangi ratepayers.

The next Waitemata County Council elections saw Alec Bishop stand against Laing for the position of Titirangi Riding member on the Council. Laing lost. However, the newly elected Bishop found that he and his Titirangi Road committee had a number of problems to overcome before their sealed road could be built. The road from New Lynn to Titirangi, known as Porters Bush Road for many years, passed through two local body areas. One kilometre was in New Lynn, and the remaining two kilometres passed through Waitemata County jurisdiction. Both local body councils needed to be convinced that

Titirangi Road leading to Rangiwai Hill. The photographer is standing just above Godley Road.
Photographer: James D. Richardson, 12 October 1919.
Auckland City Libraries Special Collections, 4-4076

continued

traffic volume warranted spending money on a sealed road. Mr Grierson, a Road Committee member, learned that the council was intending to do a lot of carting from its metal dump at the triangle in New Lynn up Titirangi Road. He suggested that a traffic count be taken, and the Council took up his suggestion. The traffic tally coincided neatly with the Council's own vehicles making dozens of trips carting gravel, thus proving the need for a road. Tenders were called after Titirangi ratepayers voted to raise a loan of $26,000 for their portion of highway. The National Main Highways Board chipped in with a 3:1 subsidy. Grinter Brothers successfully tendered for the job at $36,000 for the whole road from New Lynn to Titirangi, and a start was made in February 1931.

Built like the recently completed Great North Road in concrete mixed by batching gangs at the site, Titirangi Road was meant to have a top surface of bitumen, as was the case with similar roads in the United States. Local road builders found by varying the mix and deepening the layer of concrete, the expensive imported oil-based bitumen could be left off. The seven-metre wide road was completed in July 1931, extending from Great North Road in New Lynn to the recently opened Hotel Titirangi (Lopdell House). Cost overruns pushed the final cost to $50,000, one-third paid for by New Lynn Borough, the remaining two-thirds by Waitemata County. The surface of the road proved stable and finally it was covered, as originally intended, with its present surface of bitumen. (Note: sums of money have been converted to 1986 dollar values)

(Above) Car on lower Titirangi Road, c.1920, near the intersection of today's Croydon Road and Parker Avenue. Waitakere Library & Information Services, Bishop Collection

(Below) Titirangi Road near Golf Road. This section of concrete road from New Lynn to the village was completed in July 1931.
Photographer: James D. Richardson, 22 September 1935. Auckland City Libraries Special Collections, 4-7689

Hand-in-hand with the development of the new Titirangi Hotel and the concrete road, the little village continued to mature. Titirangi had long been a beaten track for tourists from Auckland City and visitors to the region. Alec Bishop and his family established his successful Titirangi Tearooms and the later hotel and petrol station for the growing number of cars. The concrete road's completion connected with that of Great North Road running through New Lynn and on to Henderson. An improved passenger system for cars, trucks and buses had evolved, which now also connected with the original rail link that had first run through New Lynn in 1880.[2] Many students, workers and shoppers from Titirangi and environs used this linkage to Titirangi's advantage.

Exhibition Drive, which originally began in Titirangi Village, became the beginning of Scenic Drive, which opened up more tourism for Titirangi. Scenic Drive opened in 1939 and began at Titirangi Village and ran along the crest of the Waitakere Ranges to Swanson, with links to Piha and Te Henga. At that time it was a huge project that had many benefits for working men in the later stages of the Depression. It opened up the ranges for tourists, who were given a new dimension to Auckland's beauty. Titirangi and environs began to expand in population and various individuals and firms began serious bus and transport operations. One of these was Gilbert Shaw's father.

> *It was my father who drove the truck before the 1930s, before the Depression. First of all they used a truck for carrying goods, then converted it into passenger use for use at weekends and later must have increased it into a regular service. I don't think Eddie McQuoid and my father were running at the same time. He came a bit after my father. I would say my father had the first regular bus service to Titirangi. He used to talk about his trucks and he talked about the Republics and a Bessemer; there is one at Western Springs Motat and he also talked about a truck called a United, which he hired or borrowed.*[3]

However, according to an article in *The New Zealand Bus and Coach Magazine* (October 1985), the first bus service in Titirangi was Eddie McQuoid's in the 1920s.

> *Probably one of the least known private operators in the Auckland area was the small western service pioneered by Eddie McQuoid. The McQuoid family owned a small dairy farm in Huia Road, Laingholm and in 1919 Eddie McQuoid started a bus service from Laingholm Beach to Titirangi, using a Model T Ford. He also ran a service to Cornwallis to connect with the boat for Onehunga. It is believed that Mr Hinge earlier ran a service to Huia.*

Around 1930 Eddie extended his service to Auckland City, but only on Sundays, mainly to cater for those who wished to view the building sections at Laingholm Beach. During the Depression years sections at Laingholm

Mr Gilbert Shaw Sr standing beside the Shaw bus. According to Mrs Doreen Shaw, wife of Gilbert Shaw Jr, the Shaw brothers owned a Bessemer truck, believed to be the only one in New Zealand. D. & G. Shaw Collection

Members of the McQuoid family. From left: Graham, Eddie, Lily, Evelynn and Elsie, c.1950. McQuoid Collection

Fred and Gilbert Shaw vehicle on a delivery run in the early 1920s. D. & G. Shaw Collection

were cheap: a deposit of only £2 and ten shillings was required. The bus would stay at the beach all day and Eddie would usually spend the time asleep on the back seat. There was no set time for departure; Eddie would take off back to town when everyone had returned to the bus. At this time the vehicle was a Republic, but was followed by a Dodge; both were painted in a red and green livery.

> Later, after more people had moved into the area, Eddie began a daily service but even this was not regular. For a time while men were working on the water pipeline from Huia to Mackies Rest there was a 2300 service from the city on Saturday evenings. With an increase in patronage, a Diamond T was purchased in 1933, followed by a second in 1937.
> In 1939 there was a dispute with the Auckland Bus Company, which also commenced running a service to Titirangi. The resultant court case found in favour of the larger Auckland Bus Co., and so Eddie ceased operations. Eddie was a quiet and kindly man who gave free rides to those short of fare.
> Commercial Buses started in 1953, until Titirangi was taken over by subsidised ARA Auckland Regional Authority (ARA) bus services.
> *Extract from* The New Zealand Bus and Coach Magazine, *October 1985.*

The Auckland Bus Company (ABC) was run by Bob McCrae and operated out of Titirangi well before the Second World War. The company seemed to run on a shoestring and according to Bill Shears, Bob McCrae was a real character who constantly battled the

According to an article in the *Western Leader*, A. Ainsworth and F. & G. Shaw owned Republic buses at similar times. Later, the Shaw brothers established Shaw's Titirangi Motor Bus Services, which ran on a daily basis.

F. & G. Shaw's bus parked up in a paddock for a picnic, early 1920s.
D. & G. Shaw Collection

authorities on regulations but kept the buses in good condition. He treated his older staff very well, particularly if they had to drive some of the older buses called the Stewarts. By 1956 ABC had their own new Bedford buses and the younger drivers excelled at driving these, but had to forgo a small bonus that the older drivers were entitled to for driving the old Stewart buses. The ABC ceased its service in 1958 after dissatisfaction between ABC and the ratepayers.[4] Some locals noted the Titirangi bus with wry amusement, as the following anonymous contribution from sometime in the 1950s illustrates.

The Titirangi Bus

The Titirangi bus
Future generations will envy us
The privilege of riding in the Titirangi bus
It doesn't run to schedule, its seats are seldom clean
Tearing down the concrete, its brakes emit a scream
The windows never open, but we feel with proper pride
In spite of overcrowding, it has its social side.

There's Mrs Mac of IYA on the right as you get in
Off to play a neat gavotte. We'll hear the merry din
Miss Austin with a satchel and then there's Mrs Ross
When it comes to conversation they're never at a loss
And valiant Mrs Odlin, with child on either arm
Is contemplating traffic without the least alarm
There's Mrs Luckens, cluttered up with books you may depend
Rushing to the city, a meeting to attend.
There are many other ladies I could mention, but I must
Conclude this panegyric to the Titirangi bus.

Other minor irritations, I could cite them by the score
Behaviour of the children is a thing we all deplore
At five o'clock you're hurrying to town to meet a Yank
The driver stops the engine to fill the petrol tank.
Those chops you bought are oozing through their paper on the rack
And the dust that's milling round you is like a gas attack
But the gossip you have gathered must more than compensate
For the fact the bus is running over twenty minutes late
Yes, future generations will surely envy us
The torture that is travel on the Titirangi bus!

Shaw's summer bus timetable.
D. & G. Shaw Collection

The effect of the Second World War on Titirangi was devastating, although less servicemen and servicewomen were lost in the Second World War than in the First. The war was two years longer and the menace of the Japanese was real and almost at New Zealand's doorstep. Again, many of the founder settler names appeared on the War Memorial and of the names listed, nine lost their lives. In some of the memoirs in part 2 mention is made of the blackouts, where no street lights and lights of any sort from businesses or homes were allowed and the adventures of people walking home from work in darkened streets. Even in daylight some steep and twisting roads might have been difficult, even more so during the blackouts.

ABC buses and their drivers in uniform in a line-up beside the concrete road in New Lynn. There are five Stewart buses on the right. In the background is the imposing Delta Theatre building, c.1934. West Auckland Historical Society

In the immediate postwar years the population in Titirangi increased dramatically. Many people wishing to establish a lifestyle connected with the natural environment or to work on artistic pursuits were attracted to the area. There was a proliferation of local clubs and societies and the new suburb gained a sense of cohesion. In the original settler society (the first 50 years) the school and church gave cohesion to the community but the wars and the Depression had isolated and depressed people. Following the Second World War a new and positive wave took over, art and drama flourished and clubs such as the Country Women's Institute, the RSA, Fire Brigade, fishing clubs and the French Bay Yacht Club were invigorated with new members, whose impact on Titirangi is still felt today.

Aerial photo (c.1948) showing Golf Road running right to left and the concrete Titirangi Road in the background at right. The original bullock track from Green Bay to Titirangi, to the left of Titirangi Tennis Club, is now Ava Avenue. This track would have been used by early settler John Bishop on his journeys to and from Auckland. William Henry Scarlett's home is first on the left, with outbuildings of a dairy, wash house, toilet (obscured under trees) and, further down, a cow shed, fowl house and vegetable garden. The Scarletts originally had a five-acre block.
West Auckland Historical Society, Scarlett Collection

1   Buffett, Peter. 'From Clay to Concrete Highway'. *Western Leader*, 15 November 1986.
2   Raw, June. *Rail Tracks and Chimney Stacks*. West Auckland Historical Soc Inc., Auckland, 1998, p. 62.
3   Marc Bonny interview with Gilbert Shaw, West Auckland Historical Society Inc., 2 April 2008.
4   Marc Bonny interview with Bill Shears about the Auckland Bus Company, February 2007.

7

Prominent buildings in Titirangi

The Hotel Titirangi and Lopdell House

'Built in the 1930s to be a California-deco-style overview hotel … a lovably clumsy pile'.

Don Binney[1]

The history of Titirangi's first and second hotels, and the building's reincarnation as an education centre and then an arts centre and Titirangi's most prominent building, was researched and written by Peter Buffett in 1987. His history is reprinted here and has been brought up-to-date by Kate Wells, present Curator of Lopdell House Gallery.

Titirangi's first hotel, John Rigby's 'Waikomiti Hotel', was built in 1884 near the top of School Road (South Titirangi Road), just south of where the shops are today. The two-storeyed building had 13 rooms; liquor and meals were served but paying guests were not taken.

Situated among puriri trees, the hotel was barely two years old when in June 1886 barman Ben Carrol, left in charge while John Rigby was away, let his Saturday lunch catch fire. Within 30 minutes the hotel was a tangle of charred timber and a haze of blue smoke.

William Parkes and Peter O'Brien, witnesses to the blaze, found Ben Carrol crying in the hotel yard. All three might have wept a little louder had they known that the people of Titirangi would wait 44 years for their next hotel and another 56 years before they could buy liquor with their meals in its restaurants.

Titirangi has been on the tourist trail for more than 80 years. Visitors at the Central Hotel in Auckland in 1902 were offered day trips to view the large kauri at Titirangi by wagonette and pair, with driver, for £1 10s a couple. The journey was described as long but interesting. No mention was made of the never smooth, muddy or dusty and rutted clay road.

By 1920, improved road conditions and increased numbers of motor cars and buses had brought enough passing traffic through Titirangi for the Bishop family to establish a successful tea kiosk. Tea, soft drinks and snacks were sold to day trippers, who would also top up their cars and buses from the 'Big Tree' petrol station, hand-pumped of course.

Enough tourists were attracted to Titirangi by 1927 for Frank Oscar Peat (grandson of John Bishop) to build a museum in classic style. Called the 'Treasure House', the building, behind present Lopdell House, housed an outstanding collection of kauri gum,

> **TELEGRAMS.**
>
> [UNITED PRESS ASSOCIATION]
>
> AUCKLAND, 23rd July.
>
> At the inquest to inquire into the circumstances surrounding the destruction by fire of Rigby's Hotel at Titirangi, on the 19th ult., a verdict was returned to the effect that the fire was purely accidental, but that gross carelessness was shown by the barman in leaving a pan with fat on the fire unattended for a quarter of an hour. The house was insured for £650 in the Norwich Union.

Fire destroys Rigby's hotel.
Daily Southern Cross, 24 July 1886

Alec Bishop's first house (where Lopdell House stands today) just prior to being opened up as a tea kiosk. On the left is the path up to the First World War memorial site. Photographer: James D. Richardson, 12 October 1919. Auckland City Libraries Special Collections, 4-8273

Frank Oscar Peat, owner of the Treasure House.
W. Titchener Collection

(top right) Early photo of the Treasure House before the souvenir shop building. Mr Peat's house, built c.1927 (later known as Quamby) is in the background, with the Alec Bishop house at left.
W. Titchener Collection

(right) Mr Peat's Treasure House and Souvenir Shop. Mr Peat's house (Quamby) is in the background at right, with Alec Bishop's house at left. W. Titchener Collection

(below) Interior view of the Treasure House. The Treasure House's own brochure said that the collection within was 'worth travelling miles to see. Every visitor should seize the opportunity to visit this altogether fascinating and unparalleled collection of treasures'. Buses would leave the General Post Office in Auckland twice daily.
Photographer: James D. Richardson, 14 April 1928. Auckland City Libraries Special Collections, 4-4075

Hotel Titirangi before the Concrete Road and the additions on top, 1935. Note the petrol bowser, and that the alignment of South Titirangi Road is different to that of today. Auckland War Memorial Museum, Una Garlick Collection, C6598

mounted specimens of native birds, seashells and historic artifacts at that time and was used as a hall afterwards.

With his tea kiosk doing well from visitors to the Treasure House and Titirangi's natural attractions, Alec Bishop decided the time was opportune to build a hotel in keeping with Titirangi's scenic grandeur.

In September 1928 the Hotel Titirangi Ltd filed their prospectus with the Registrar of Companies at Auckland. Under its Board of Directors, Alec Bishop, James Kemo from Ponsonby, John Ellis of Avondale and Gideon Lund, a Devonport hotel manager, the company tried to raise £50,000 in £1 shares from the public. The shares were to be fully paid up in 20-cent installments within two months of issue.

The directors hoped that a soon-to-be built concrete road from New Lynn and the expected grant of a liquor licence would convince investors that the hotel could attract sufficient trade to be profitable. Unfortunately for the directors, Aucklanders seeking a return on their investment capital did not share the board's confidence that the plans for a 'castle on the fringe of heaven' would prove popular with the tourists or gain a liquor licence in a 'dry area'. Despite local support, the share issue, usually in small parcels of £10 worth of shares, was undersubscribed. An Englishman, Mr L.J. Shrubsall, who arrived in New Zealand with his family of seven daughters and two sons in 1928, guaranteed the outstanding funds so that the project could be started.

Built in reinforced concrete with a tiled roof for £20,000 by contractor P.W. Peate, the Hotel Titirangi occupied an enviable site on the main road with panoramic views to the Manukau and the Waitakeres. Designed by Shortland Street architects Bloomfield and Partners, the hotel was originally envisaged as having four main levels, courtyards, and colonnades in the front and arched windows.

The building, completed in November 1930, was less magnificent and a lot starker than the original concept. It did, however, as it does today, dominate the village of Titirangi.

Lopdell House and its designer is a special interest of architect D. Oldham, who has identified the designing architect as William Swanson Read Bloomfield. Bloomfield was the first architect of Maori descent and the grandson of pioneer William Swanson. Bloomfield designed the Yorkshire Building and the Station Hotel in Auckland City.

Prime Minister Gordon Coates opened the Hotel Titirangi on 20 November 1930 at a ceremony attended by local politicians and 300 guests. The same evening, at 8 o'clock, the hotel staged its most glittering occasion, an invitation-only opening ball, using for the first time the hotel's sprung dance floor. Catering for 63 guests in fully carpeted rooms with attached bathrooms, Hotel Titirangi had drive-in garaging for guest cars, a piped

The construction of Hotel Titirangi, which opened in November 1930.
W. Titchener Collection

Shares for the Hotel Titirangi were £1 each. This certificate shows that Mr Leslie Williams of Parau had 10 shares.
West Auckland Historical Society

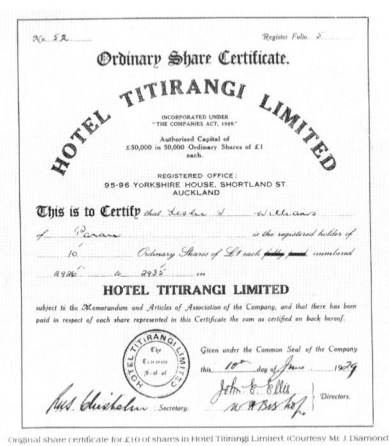

Original share certificate for £10 of shares in Hotel Titirangi Limited. (Courtesy Mr J. Diamond)

radio/music system to all rooms, an observation roof, and furnishings by the same firm that had appointed the Auckland Railway Station, which opened the same week.

Included within the hotel were a small shop, a tearoom and a restaurant. The hotel had a direct telephone line to Auckland, a facility not lost on local people who often used the line to save on toll bills. The post office used the same line to take telegrams for passing on to Titirangi residents.

Vacancies outnumbered paying guests in the first year of operation, and the hotel was handed to Reg Nicholas and Percy Levy to manage. As the depression deepened, they fared little better in turning Hotel Titirangi into a profitable business, and by 1934 the hotel had closed its register to the travelling public.

The Shrubsall family, in an effort to realise something from their investment, took on the venture two years later, moving in as a family in June 1937. Still without a liquor licence, and trade constricted by the continuing depression, the accommodation side of the business continued to run at a loss, although the Shrubsalls managed to make the dining and tearooms pay the hotel's keep.

Weekend business began to pick up in the late 1930s with up to seven tour buses arriving for tea in the afternoons. Tour bus drivers would phone in before they left town with the number expected for tea on their sightseeing trip along the recently opened Scenic Drive.

Doris Shrubsall-Jenkins remembers arriving home in the evening from her city office job and being expected to help sister Phyllis and the staff with a sudden influx of guests. Fortunately local people, including the Shaw sisters, could be relied upon to carry out duties in the hotel. Several of the Shrubsall children attended city schools, travelling in by bus each day. The driver of the morning bus, who began his run from Titirangi, would often wake the children before having breakfast at the hotel.

Doris recalled that, with theatre associations from overseas, her parents played host to many of the famous companies and singers of the era, including Gladys Moncrieff, who stayed with the family while sightseeing in the North Island.

The hotel also had regular guests for dinner, including the local doctor and the manager of a city theatre chain, who had his own suite in the building.

A nightclub opened in the hotel at the end of the 1930s run by 1ZB personality Nedo (Mr Silver). The club featured singing, music and dancing and a grill supper but still no liquor. Lack of a liquor licence cramped the hotel's style for most of its existence. This resulted in prosecution of the management for supplying liquor without a licence to a private club set up in the basement billiard room by workers on a nearby dam project. The dam workers, finding the city pubs shut by the time they arrived after journeying in from the Waitakeres, arranged for the hotel to buy their beer, which they then sold amongst themselves. This raised the ire of a local citizen who reported the management to the police.

The quiet and reserved L. J. Shrubsall and his wife had seen their business through a difficult time, always making the final decisions in the complex running of the hotel themselves. They sold the Hotel Titirangi to Mr Hunter in 1939. The new owner allowed the nightclub to continue, but with the start of the Second World War, apart from a few honeymooners and armed service guests, the hotel days were nearly over.

Hotel Titirangi from Memorial Hill in 1936. Beside the memorial is a small canon enclosed in a display case. On top of the hotel building are several additional display areas, including a fernery, which Gus Bishop had instigated.
Auckland War Memorial Museum, E. Cowan photograph, C23629

The School for the Deaf

In 1942 the building was passed to the Department of Education to use as a school for the deaf, beginning a 40-year association with education for Titirangi. Moving into the former Hotel Titirangi during term three in 1942, the School for the Deaf admitted all deaf children between five and sixteen years old who lived north of New Plymouth and Gisborne. The first temporary headmaster was Cyril Allen, who was answerable to the former principal of the Sumner School for the Deaf, Mr Pickering, in Wellington. The main hotel building was used by the children as sleeping and eating quarters. Boys and girls occupied separate floors. A rubella epidemic in 1941 resulted in increased numbers of children born deaf or hearing impaired, so there was a greatly increased roll for a few years from 1946. John de Vere, former principal of the Glen Eden School, taught at the School for the Deaf for many years during this period of growth. To occupy the children there were walks to Titirangi Beach, gymnastic classes in the ballroom, and a huge fancy dress party every Christmas. The school had many visitors over the years, including in 1948 the most famous, Helen Keller, the world-renowned deaf and blind teacher. Because of limited space, poor acoustics and traffic noise, the School for the Deaf was transferred to Kelston in 1960.

> *In 1940 H. Pickering from England was appointed Principal of the School for the Deaf in Sumner. In February 1942, he came to Auckland at the Board's request, to investigate the facilities for teaching deaf children. When the Army took over the Sumner School some of the children were temporarily housed in Christchurch and others were transferred in September to an extremely depressing 'hotel' at Titirangi with C.L. Allen as temporary Headmaster. The Titirangi experiment was looked upon as a part of the Sumner School, it was of course under the control of the Department. The Board closed the (Sumner) School for Deaf on 5 March 1943.*[2]

The Education In-Service Training Centre

In 1960 the Titirangi Hotel was renamed Frank Lopdell House after a former principal of the Auckland Teachers College, superintendent of education and New Zealand's first director of in-service training. The building became a residential centre for teachers from all over New Zealand who were participating in week-long courses. Thousands of teachers attended Lopdell House courses in the 22 years it was operating. In 1982 in-service training was transferred to the former North Shore Teachers Training College and once again the original building awaited its next occupants.

Lopdell House Gallery

At this stage the Titirangi Community Arts Council petitioned Waitemata City Council to acquire the building for an arts centre. Public support was sought and gained, and in 1983 Waitemata City purchased Lopdell House with the intention of using it for community purposes. A steering committee was established in 1983 to turn the old building into a lively arts centre. The committee included the Titirangi Arts Council, Titirangi Ratepayers Association, the Drama Society and the Businessmen's Association, plus Council representatives. Heather Carter was elected Chair of the committee. An open day in November 1983 enabled 1000 members of the public to see the inside the building. The first exhibition, of Japanese folk crafts, was held in June 1984, despite the less than ideal interior. Leases were arranged and the Drama Club put on its first performance in April 1985.

Governor-General Sir Paul Reeves officially opened the Waitemata City Arts and Cultural Centre on 19 November 1986. The first director was Margaret Burton, who resigned later that year.

Gallery spaces were on the ground and first floors, as was a seminar room. The top floor was re-roofed, covering the old observation deck, and the space was let as a restaurant. The Drama Group created an intimate theatre in the basement (formerly the garage) and studio space was created in the sub-basement. The second floor was originally meant to house a residential school but, after the opening, financial difficulties persuaded the committee to let these spaces as offices. An artist in residence, Hal Martin (a fabric artist), occupied the studio but the position was not continued after he left due to the financial difficulties. A weavers group then occupied the space he had used. Cost overruns from the refitting of the building caused some anxieties during the first few years, but the community generated funds and held many social and exhibition functions in the building and eventually these difficulties were overcome. From its grassroots volunteer base the gallery has grown over the years into a flourishing regional arts centre, exhibiting the work of many local, national and international artists. In 2006 the Lopdell House Gallery presented a milestone exhibition: 'Colin McCahon — the Titirangi Years 1953–59', in which 40 of the artist's works filled the gallery. Since 2001 the Gallery has held the exhibition of all entrants in what is New Zealand's most prestigious award for ceramic work, the Portage Ceramic Award. With the support of Mayor Bob Harvey and the Waitakere City Council, the maintenance of the building was assured since the 1990s, and Lopdell House has become 'the jewel of the west'.

The future

A Lopdell House Redevelopment Trust was formed (2002) to explore options for the use of the building to optimise its artistic and economic future. The proposal is to have an extensive seismic upgrading, and to add a new gallery using museum standards for showing art works. A new basement theatre is planned, an upgrade of the interior and extension of the car parking space. Lopdell House looks to have an exciting future if this work comes to fruition, although, in 2010, difficulties due to the reorganising of local government in Auckland and economic recession have cast a shadow over the plans.

Macandrew Hall and the musical Macandrews

In the bush on Titirangi Road, opposite the entrance to Godley Road, is an old Titirangi building that has been an important venue for the artistic endeavours of generations of people. It is Macandrew Hall, recently (2009) sold to a private buyer.

This Titirangi icon is embarking on a new era, but it is as well to remember its past.

The musical Macandrews, Arthur and Jennie, who lived at 4 Park Road from the start of the First World War to the end of the Second World War, bequeathed the building to Titirangi.[3]

Jennie Macandrew (nee West), born in Dunedin in 1866, was an outstanding musician who had studied piano in London and on her return to New Zealand had taught music and accompanied singers and instrumentalists on their tours of the country. She conducted choirs and performed as a soloist in Dunedin and Christchurch.[4] Arthur Macandrew was the son of the Hon. James Macandrew, MP for Dunedin and various Otago electorates, and a member of the Cabinet in the Stout and Vogel ministries between 1856 and 1884.

Arthur was a telegraph engineer who worked for the post office, and was a keen amateur musician. Arthur and Jennie married in 1900 and shortly afterwards moved to Auckland. After a few years they moved to Titirangi. The Macandrews had no children but put their energies into promoting music in their home area. As was the custom in those days, Jennie did not teach music after she was married, except in an informal sense. She became involved with the Country Women's Institute and in 1935 purchased the land on which the hall stands. Arthur provided the funds for construction and the hall was built and bequeathed to the Country Womens' Institute for community events such as meetings, plays, musical evenings and social events. For many years it was the venue for the Drama Group productions, the Light Opera Society, community working-bees during the war, Red Cross lessons and many other events. In 1946 the hall was the scene of Jennie Macandrew's eightieth birthday party and

Macandrew Hall on Titirangi Road. This image was taken from the concrete road in 1935. The valley behind is where Atkinson Road runs today, previously known as Atkinson Valley Road.
Photographer: James D. Richardson, 22 September 1935.
Auckland City Libraries Special Collections, 4-7697

Arthur and Jennie Macandrew.
West Auckland Historical Society

from then on was always known as Macandrew Hall. Jennie died on Christmas Eve 1949 and Arthur a few weeks later. Both are buried at Waikumete Cemetery.

Another prominent building in Titirangi is the War Memorial Hall, also housing the Library and Plunket, and formerly also home for the RSA. The history of its beginning is recounted by architect Geoff Hole, a long-time Titirangi resident, who was central to the building's construction. He remembers how the War Memorial Hall almost got 'the chop'.[5]

The War Memorial Hall, 1979. Waitakere Library & Information Services, Print Collection (Titirangi)

> *My contact with Lopdell House and the Titirangi War Memorial Hall began when my wife and I, looking for land on which to build, came across a section with a frontage of about 100 ft widening to about 300 ft at the bottom, situated on a slow bend on a road then called School Road (South Titirangi Road) because there had been a school there earlier.*
>
> *The section was very steep. But from a small flat area at the top covered in tall gorse, the magnificent view convinced us that, despite the distance to the city, it would be worth the travel. Thus began our sojourn in Titirangi.*
>
> *This section and others from Lopdell House to near Grendon Road, was owned by Mr Shrubsall, who acquired them in settlement of debts as a result of his support of the Titirangi Hotel. As I understand it, this land had been formerly owned by the Bishop family who, after it had been cut over for timber, used it for farming and grazing cattle. However, it was contaminated with the seed of the foxglove, a plant poisonous to animals. Thus the farming venture failed. As the Bishops had financial interests in the hotel that eventually failed to pay, Mr Shrubsall acquired the land in settlement of his contributions.*
>
> *When we arrived in Titirangi in about 1947, Lopdell House was partly occupied by the School for the Deaf. The property on the other side of South Titirangi Road consisted of an area part-grass and part-bush. The grassed part was a large mound and as there was no suitable area on the other side for the deaf boys to exercise, they were encouraged to play on this mound.*
>
> *The area had been subdivided into sections for sale. When Cyril Allen, the headmaster, learned this he contacted someone he knew in government asking him to take the property under the Public Works Act. At the same time the Post & Telegraph requested a part on the corner of South Titirangi Road for a telephone exchange. Thus the land was acquired and became for a time a public park, and some work was carried out under the auspices of the Titirangi Beautification Society to form paths, a pool with surrounding plantation and some aquatic species.*
>
> *Mr Harry Atkinson welcomed to his house other residents, and in the course of a visit there he spoke to me about the pound-for-pound subsidy the previous government had been offering for war memorials. The newly elected National Government intended to cancel this subsidy after a certain date, which was only two weeks away!*
>
> *It seemed incredible to me that such an opportunity should be missed. I had served four years in the New Zealand Forces and was lucky enough to return home in one piece. I also felt strongly that a building of use to the public was a better reminder of the sacrifice of the*

Prominent buildings in Titirangi

fallen. Therefore, for the next fortnight I dropped everything and we succeeded in putting in the application on time.

Harry Atkinson rounded up Alec Bishop, chairman of the Council, and got his signature on the papers which were forwarded with my sketch plans for the hall and the various other rooms required by the conditions and functions. These included a room where returned soldiers could meet (now occupied by the Plunket Society,) a plaque and flagstaff.

I was greatly assisted by a lady from the Ministry of Works who gave me sizes, heights etc. for different functions, especially indoor sports. The plan placed the subsidiary unit in a line connected by a covered porch enabling additions to the units laterally without disruption to other areas. This has subsequently happened, in particular, the library has been twice extended. It so happened that the authorities forwarded the plans to an architect in the Ministry of Works who happened to be a Titirangi resident. Although it was a general rule that Registered Architects did not do buildings of a charitable nature free of charge, permission could be given in specific instances by the chairman of the local institute body. The chairman at this time was Professor Knight, who approved.

Before these events the RSA had built a hall in Rangiwai Road with volunteer labour and gifts of materials. Also with volunteer labour and some material, a small lending library had been constructed in the basement.

As the proposed memorial hall and the RSA building were duplicating functions, it was decided to sell the RSA building in Rangiwai Road and put the funds together with those for the hall to obtain the pound-for-pound subsidy. As the Catholic Church was looking for a property we managed to sell it to them.

At some time later the RSA obtained funds to build separate rooms below the Memorial Hall. That was when Plunket obtained the use of the space originally intended for the RSA, and the library expanded into the vacant space previously occupied by Plunket.

As I was very busy with my own practice, the final plans for the hall itself were undertaken by a committee with Graham Fox as chairman, representing architects, and Morgan Lewis representing the RSA. A young architect, Fred Whitehead, now in Australia, offered to do the working drawings at a reduced fee, the remainder being counted as a donation towards the subsidy.

When these drawings were complete, the plans were sent to me as a courtesy for my suggestions. As it so happened I had quite a lot of experience with this type of building having done a public hall for a thesis in connection with my degree, which involved a close study of acoustics and also the electrical work needed for such buildings to function.

On reporting this to the committee, they employed an acoustic engineer to deal with the problem which included a special reflective surface on the ceiling (this was later taken down without serious consequences) and absorbent and reflective surfaces where required. I also wrote to the committee with regard to the electrical requirements from my experience in this field; including a much greater power intake that would be required, and the positioning of the mains switchboard and meters, and power points on the stage floor and in the wings for use for dimmers and sound effects. These provisions have not had much use up to now but would have been very expensive to install at a later date. In particular the Drama Group decided not to use the hall in the meantime since its capacity was too large to run at least the three nights they required. They therefore furnished an alternative space in Lopdell House.

1. Binney, Don. *Drawing the Waitakere Coast*. Godwit (Random House), Auckland, 2010, p. 10.
2. Cuming, Ian. *Glorious Enterprise: History of the Auckland Education Board*. Whitcombe and Tombs, Auckland, 1959.
3. Butler, Mike. 'The Musical Macandrews of Titirangi'. *West Auckland Historical Society Journal*, Auckland, 1997.
4. *The Dictionary of New Zealand Biography 1870–1900*. Department of Internal Affairs, Wellington, Vol. 2, p. 288.
5. Hole, Geoff. 'Close Call for the Hall', *Titirangi Tatler*. Auckland, March, 2004; oral history, Marc Bonny, Auckland, March 2004.

Aerial image of Titirangi Village. Ted Scott

Aerial shot over Titirangi School. Ted Scott

Titirangi's longest serving eatery is Tobys restaurant (formerly Reekies).
Bruce Harvey Collection

(Top right) Cyril Whiteoak's 1983 watercolour, *Titirangi Village*. The picture shows the dairy that was originally owned by the Shaw family.
Cyril Whiteoak

(Right) Local artist Edith Diggle's painting, *The Hardware Cafe*, 2000. Edith Diggle

The COLONIAL WINE SHOPPE
Tip Top
Titirangi Dairy
WINES
OPEN
Cyril Whitcombe 1985

ASB BANK
THE HARDWARE CAFE

A display of works by local potters at Titirangi School, c.1957.
Photographer: George Bonny, Marc Bonny Collection

Cyril Whiteoak carrying his easel to his space on the school verandah at the art display, c.1957. Photographer: George Bonny, Marc Bonny Collection

The Titirangi Village Festival was an annual event. Ted Scott

Titirangi painters exhibit their art at an annual show held in the War Memorial Hall. Ted Scott

Bruce Henderson's set design sketch for *A View from the Bridge*, 1962. West Auckland Historical Society, J. Geddes Collection

Geoff Hole and Ethelwyn Geddes at Rangiwai with Geoff's set model for *Physicists*, 1965.
Scott Hole Collection

Looking down Park Road. Photographer: Ted Scott

John Geddes with his band LLBs, at one of the garden parties held at Rangiwai c.1986.
Janet and Andrew Geddes Collection

The Titirangi Light Opera Company's second production in 1958 was HMS Pinafore *by Gilbert and Sullivan. Rev. J.T. Gunn was the producer, with leading roles taken by Graeme Cass, Fred Watson and Davon Unsworth.*

(Above) Geoff Hole's set design sketch for *Time Remembered*, which was produced in 1961.
West Auckland Historical Society, J. Geddes Collection

(Top right) The cover of the programme produced for *HMS Pinafore*. West Auckland Historical Society, Gunn Family Collection

(Below) A scene from the production of *HMS Pinafore*, 1958. West Auckland Historical Society, Gunn Family Collection

'H.M.S. Pinafore' raises £65 for school pavilion

8

Community gatherings

The Park Drive Kiosk

The building on the corner of Park and South Titirangi roads has a long history as a gathering place for Titirangi people, and often was the scene of social occasions from the 1920s onwards. It has been variously known as Park Drive Kiosk, Reekies, The Toby Jug, and more recently, Tobys.

According to previous owner Logan Gregg, in an interview with Marc Bonny in 2007, before the alignment of the present Titirangi Road people approached Titirangi through Park Road and stopped at the corner for a rest before going back up the road (South Titirangi Road). This suggests that in the 1920s and 1930s, Park Drive Kiosk (its original name) rivalled Alec Bishop's tearooms further up at the (present) village. The date of the original construction is not known, but newspapers found behind the wall or over scrim suggested the original building was built in 1924–25. On Henry Atkinson's authority, gas from Auckland was laid to his own home (Rangiwai), to Park Drive Kiosk and probably also to Titirangi Hotel. This would have been some time in the 1920s.

Council correspondence shows that R. Reckie took over Park Drive Kiosk in the early 1930s, and early photographs show that the name 'Reekies' was written on the side of the

Reekies Park Kiosk and Store, the Bishop's Tea Kiosk opposition.
Photographer: James D. Richardson, 2 December 1934. Auckland City Libraries Special Collections, 4-7688

(Right) The Park Kiosk before becoming Park Kiosk & Store (Reekies).
Waitakere Library & Information Services, J.T. Diamond Collection, Research Papers, Box 55 No. 788 (Envelope: booklet: Auckland City of Flowers published by the NZ Tourist League)

The delights of a Cup of Tea at the Park Kiosk

It is from the Waitakeres and their forest loveliness that any true appraisement of Auckland may be made

and

Titirangi is Queen of the Ranges and the Park Kiosk is conveniently situated on the bus and car route so that from its calm atmosphere the glories of cliff and valley cloaked in unspoiled native bush can be seen at their best

Morning Teas, Hot Luncheons, Afternoon Teas
Parties catered for

Proprietress: M. I. JONES

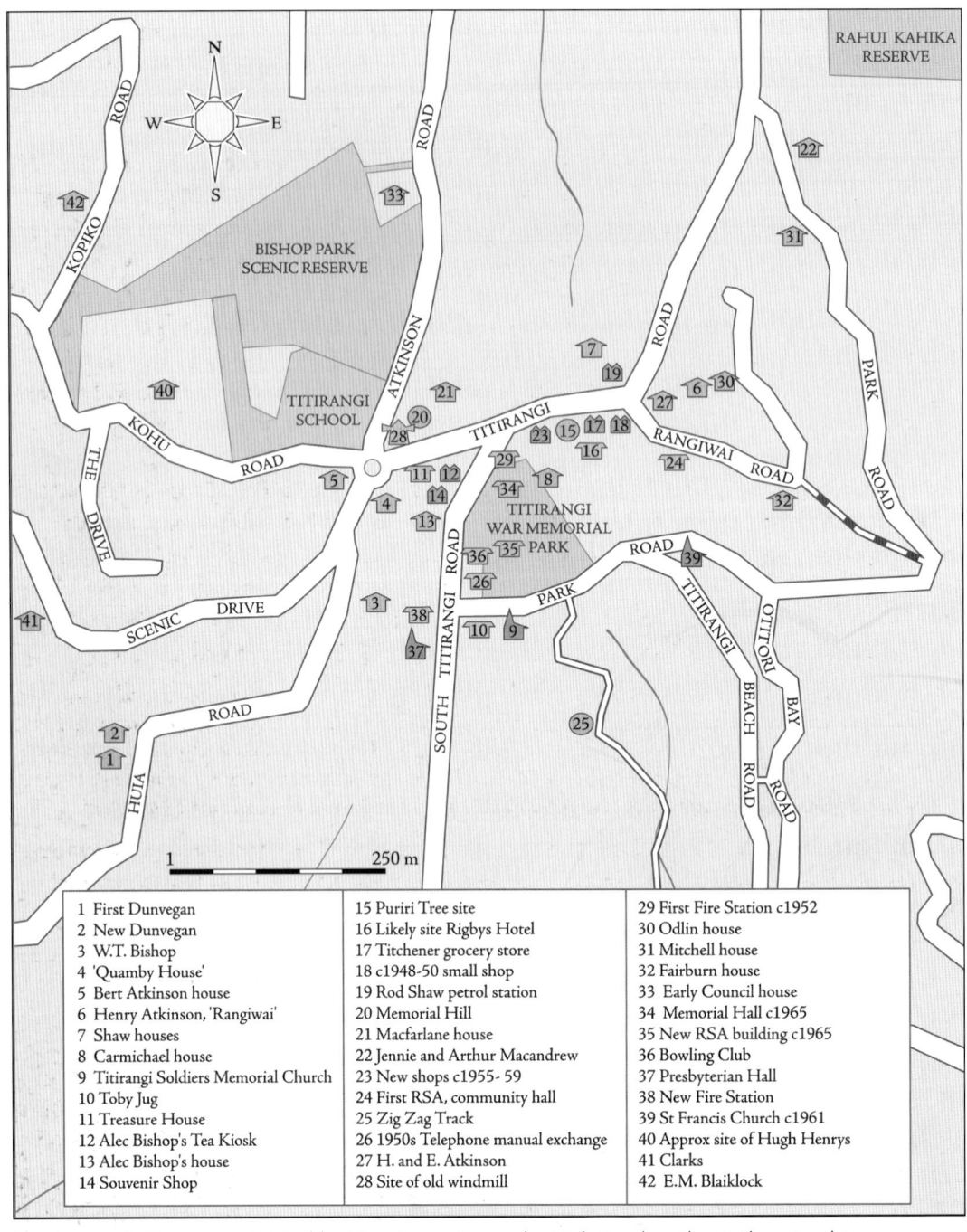

1 First Dunvegan	15 Puriri Tree site	29 First Fire Station c1952
2 New Dunvegan	16 Likely site Rigbys Hotel	30 Odlin house
3 W.T. Bishop	17 Titchener grocery store	31 Mitchell house
4 'Quamby House'	18 c1948-50 small shop	32 Fairburn house
5 Bert Atkinson house	19 Rod Shaw petrol station	33 Early Council house
6 Henry Atkinson, 'Rangiwai'	20 Memorial Hill	34 Memorial Hall c1965
7 Shaw houses	21 Macfarlane house	35 New RSA building c1965
8 Carmichael house	22 Jennie and Arthur Macandrew	36 Bowling Club
9 Titirangi Soldiers Memorial Church	23 New shops c1955-59	37 Presbyterian Hall
10 Toby Jug	24 First RSA, community hall	38 New Fire Station
11 Treasure House	25 Zig Zag Track	39 St Francis Church c1961
12 Alec Bishop's Tea Kiosk	26 1950s Telephone manual exchange	40 Approx site of Hugh Henrys
13 Alec Bishop's house	27 H. and E. Atkinson	41 Clarks
14 Souvenir Shop	28 Site of old windmill	42 E.M. Blaiklock

Local map of village area. Original by Marc Bonny. Drawn by Nick Keenleyside, Outline Graphics.

building. In a 1934 letter, R. Reckie wrote to the Council requesting permission to erect a large sign advertising his kiosk, but this was opposed by Alec Bishop, his competitor and influential councillor.

At this time, an addition was made to the original building. Mick Dromgool, who renovated the building in the 1970s, described steel rods on plates forming the bracing in the roof, with flying Dutch gables and crossmembers being viewed internally, as an early mode of construction. New, mostly cosmetic beams were put in then over areas that were structural. These beams, some six inches thick, came from the old trambarn in Manukau Road. The property area is roughly 2000 square metres. In an interview with Dora Bishop Jones in 1997, she recalled that the early owner, Mr Reckie, sold the building to a woman named Mabel Downes.

Other former owners were Bob Massey (Massey Quarries), Rod Campbell and Logan Gregg. In order to get a liquor licence, more parking was needed, so Gregg needed to acquire the piece of land next door (adjoining the property) to create the L-shape. The property adjoins the Soldiers Memorial Church. The long part of the L-shape is virtually on the boundary of South Titirangi Road, but the car parks are on Tobys' property, the footpath belonging to the Council. In various articles and memoirs from the 1930s and 1940s, the building was referred to as Reekies but the name of the owner was R. Reckie and Company.[1] All Titirangi residents remember Reekies or Tobys' from the 1930s onwards. Bernard Holibar remembers Reekies in the 1940s[2], when he was a child.

> *On School Road, now called South Titirangi Road, Reekies had the kiosk, now called Tobys, and there we bought ice cream and confectionery, it was more like a milk bar. They also had a grocery shop in a different part. It was L-shaped with a large room bordering School Road with a confectionery counter in one corner and the remainder as a tea room. In the part bordering Park Road was the grocery shop and I presume behind were the living quarters.*

During the Second World War and afterwards, before the RSA had their own premises, Reekies was the venue for meetings and social occasions. Harry Morgan Lewis[3] recalled:

> *We were the First 2nd NZEF members to join Titirangi RSA and we were given the first year free membership.*
>
> *There were about 30 First World War men in the Titirangi Branch of the Western*

View from Mt Atkinson over Titirangi to the Manukau Harbour with Mangere mountain on the left horizon. Reekies, the building with writing on the roof, is between the church and a house.
Photographer: James D. Richardson. Auckland City Libraries Special Collections, 4-7692

Community gatherings

Suburbs RSA (as it was called). The men would meet at what was then Reekies Kiosk, on the corner of South Titirangi and Park roads, once a month with indoor bowls each Monday night. The farewell 'send off' by residents to those departing for overseas and for those returning a 'welcome home' was also held at Reekies.

Angela McKnight, the present owner of Tobys and long-time Titirangi resident, remembers her father talking about his family coming from Richmond Road in the 1900s, in horse and cart to their bach, via Woontons Lane to Davies Bay.

The previous owner of Tobys was John Walsh from whom Angela bought the building and business a number of years ago. She is conscious of the history of the place, where many businesspeople 'had a go' at the restaurant and retail trade. For many years there was a tin cat attached to the roof of the building, and Angela has reintroduced this symbol. Although for most of its more recent life it has been known as Tobys or Toby Jug, at one period it was running under the name of Arlingtons. About 15 years ago the building was put up for auction; later, part of the old building was removed to make way for offices and car parks at the rear. Angela would like the building to be placed under a historic places category.

Pinesong

Although now a thriving retirement village occupies the land on the edge of Green Bay and Titirangi known as Pinesong, the area has an interesting history and was the site of the original house whose owners gave their name to Godley Road.

According to the Land Information Office, Pinesong was originally Lot 293 of 41 acres bought for £40 in 1881 by Paul Joseph Murphy. Various other owners used and sold the land until a sale to Lena Godley in 1907.

The Godleys built a substantial cottage and established an orchard sheltered by previously planted macrocarpa. Pine trees and magnolias, which had been planted 30 years previously, adorned the property. At that time the property was a well-kept oasis in the

A gathering of children at the Godley house, c.1911.

Clark Family History, p. 43. Permission of Dave Harre (Gardner family)

midst of scrubland covered in manuka. E.M. Blaiklock[4] wrote:

> *The old house, occupied in summer only, stood with moss grown orchard, behind, jonquils a twinkling galaxy when in flower down the grassy drive, and the great dark pines all round, pines spilling in their second, self-sown generation down the brown slopes to the shore — and there it was, a manuka wilderness running south to the Manukau, and southwest to the Titirangi oberland. The wide, grey oval of the valley was broken only by a copse of pines on the cliff over the harbour, where an old house and equally ancient orchard stood. It is a restaurant now. Dotting the wild acres were isolated pines, where seed had blown and somehow rooted in the heavy soil.*

Pinesong before major additions. Dalys Newman Collection

Pinesong prior to the 1990 fire. Dalys Newman Collection

In 1911 Charles Fisher Gardner (of New Lynn brickworks) bought the Godley property and the family owned it until 1941. The Gardner family came to New Lynn about 1901 and used to take the family to 'Godleys'. Mary Taylor (nee Gardner) says many members of their wider family, including the Clarks, walked over to the property. Blackberry picking seemed to be a great attraction at the time. The original Godley house became derelict as the years passed, with some of the roof and floorboards missing. In the local children's minds it became a haunted house.

During the Second World War, when visiting friends Frank and Kathleen Gratton in Green Bay, Thora Conlon saw how beautiful and captivating the old Godley orchard and land where the old house once existed was and wrote about it to her husband, an army captain serving in Egypt. In due course, with the war over, the Conlons purchased the property. Captain Sydney Conlon left the army in the early 1950s, cleared the bush by hand and, because the wind in the pine trees caught his attention frequently, named the property Pinesong.

The Conlons began growing strawberries, commercial poultry keeping, beekeeping and sheep farming. However, friends suggested a restaurant, so Pinesong became a restaurant and function centre. From small beginnings, using the dining room of their newly built home, the

The popular restaurant at Pinesong. Dalys Newman Collection

Community gatherings

function centre blossomed to become a catering business with a large permanent staff and a dine and dance venue with a resident musical quartet, one of the first postwar Auckland innovations.

In 1980 Martin Conlon, son of Sydney and Thora Conlon, developed a successful private nine-hole golf course at the property, where weekly twilight tournaments were held. From 1970 to 1982 the restaurant was leased to Logan Gregg and his wife, and then to several other people until tragedy occurred when the main Pinesong building was burnt down on Guy Fawkes evening, 1990.

Conlon family at Pinesong, c.1961. Sidney and Thora holding the goat, Martin feeding the lamb and Dalys on her pony. Dalys Newman Collection

In 1992 it was rebuilt, but Thora Conlon died shortly after. After a few years of ownership by Mr Tsenge, Metlifecare bought the land and buildings to form the present retirement village.

The cafés

Titirangi is now famous for its cafés, but it is often not appreciated that the village led the way in the 1950s in catering for a more sophisticated clientele who were demanding more European-style social gathering places.

Peter Smeele was a designer who came to live in Titirangi in the early 1950s. He was part of the large number of Europeans who emigrated from Europe in the aftermath of the war, bringing their ideas and relative sophistication to a New Zealand that was conservative and still colonial in many ways. Coffee bars were the latest level of sophistication to hit New Zealand and Titirangi was at the forefront. A coffee bar was set up in 1959 by the Worleys, in the building that is a café currently known as La Vincci. Peter Smeele did the original interior design.

The original Titirangi Coffee Bar had only a limited view out the end of the building . Peter at once realised the benefits of lowering the windowsills to the present level to make the most of the magnificent view of the Manukau. Adjoining shops successfully followed this alteration.

Marc Bonny — a recollection

Peter's design for Titirangi Coffee Bar was for the most part carried out according to the sketch he lent me. So for me, as a 12 year-old in a non-TV household in 1959, a coffee stop at Worleys Coffee Bar Titirangi, with an art exhibition presently on display, following a library visit on Friday evening, was eagerly awaited. One of the most fascinating exhibitions was a display of insects made out of brass and copper and hung on the walls by Titirangi artist David Kennedy. My parents bought a couple of these objects and I still have one at home. The funny thing is the coffee bar is still a great place to be, 43 years later, and a great place to take a friend. Peter explained to me how in the 1960s the first exhibition of his furniture for sale was organised by Peter Webb, auctioneer of art and antiques, and displayed at John Cordy's in Customs Street, Auckland. To get recognition and understanding in those days was difficult and the exhibition was not a financial success, but looking back now it is apparent that a new style was being set. The souvenir edition of *Home and Building* says 'the reality for the innovative artists and designers in the fifties, it must be concluded, was that they were not accepted by most of the general public, who viewed the arts with intense unease'.

The Hardware Café

Titirangi now has several cafés; the one known as The Hardware Café occupies one of the older commercial buildings in Titirangi Road (see page xi).

In the Bishop family the children of the sisters Euphemia Peat and Sarah Speer married, and this couple's son, Frank Oscar Peat, built the Treasure House in the 1920s. Peat's daughter Frances married Arthur Titchener, whose father had opened a stand-alone grocery shop in Titirangi in the building that now houses The Hardware Café. The shop was built about 1934. Before it was built some groceries were supplied from the hotel or from the tea kiosks. The shop remained a grocery until the 1960s, although Arthur Titchener sold it to Mr Chermside about 1949. In the early 1960s the supermarket was built on its present site and Mr Chermside became the first manager. During the late 1960s and 1970s the premises were sold to Jock Reith who used it as a hardware shop; Bill Strid remembers being involved with the saw-sharpening side of the business.[6] The name was retained for

---

Designer given full Scope for Ideas in New Coffee House[5]

Strong bold colours, blending furniture and light fittings, a charming balustrade, plant box, recessed wall panel and highlight of all, a full-length window that frames a magnificent panoramic Manukau Harbour view. These are the features, which give the new Titirangi Coffee House its charm and appeal — features which interior designer Peter Smeele has been able to blend together. In planning many designs the designer, at best, must compromise — incorporating his ideas as best he can in a building already completed. But in this case, Mr Smeele, with the full encouragement and support of Coffee House owner Mr Worley, was given a wonderful start, enabling him to advise and suggest certain features before the building was completed. In addition to designing and choosing interior fittings, Mr Smeele made many of the fittings himself. The mahogany counter, mahogany-edged Formica topped tables, comfortably shaped tops to the bar seats, for which he also designed the novel metal sprung supports, were all made in his own workshop. Both bar stools and lounge-type woven rattan seats were chosen and designed with an eye to added comfort — being in each case slightly lower than normal; the light fittings were judiciously picked to contrast with the bold wall colours, which give an appearance of extra depth to the room and lead the eye automatically to the panoramic view through the rear window. The whole room reflects the individuality and imagination of Mr Smeele's ideas — and the interest and helpfulness of all the contractors engaged, which greatly assisted in putting these ideas into such pleasing effect.

the café when it opened in 1999. The old building has been extensively renovated and is now a very popular meeting place. The site of The Hardware Café coincides with the entrance to the original Bishop property, then known (rather jocularly) as 'Bishops Gate'.

The Titirangi RSA

The Titirangi RSA was begun and promoted by returned soldiers from First and Second World wars, but its present form is largely the result of enthusiasm generated by Harry Morgan Lewis on his return to civilian life after the Second World War.

Harry Morgan Lewis moved to Titirangi in 1931 and lived in the area for 48 years. He was interested in sport, and was given life membership to the French Bay Boating Club, mainly for tutoring young people in the art of sailing. Morgan was instrumental in obtaining and negotiating with the New Lynn Borough Council for the use of Ken Maunder Park for cricket, and he helped to lay the first pitch there. He was a foundation member and prime mover in the formation of the Titirangi RSA Men's Bowling Club and a wily and clever bowler, well known in the Western districts, having won 17 club championships. He also skippered for the Western Services RSA indoor bowling team at the national championships on five occasions. He was elected Vice President of the Western Suburbs RSA in the late 1960s but was unable to take on the presidency due to business commitments. He was made a Life Member in 1967 and received the NZRSA Merit Award and Certificate in 1970, then the NZRSA Gold Star in 1979. After retirement from the executive he became a trustee of Homes for the Elderly Trust and continued to be interested in welfare. For nine years he was a trustee, then vice patron from 1989. During the 1990s he continued to oversee the outside maintenance of the Homes for the Elderly. In an interview with Marc Bonny[7] he gave this account of the beginnings and growth of the RSA in Titirangi.

RSA sign, April 2010. Bruce Harvey Collection

RSA gun, April 2010. Bruce Harvey Collection

> *I arrived back in New Zealand in August 1943 with the first furlough draft after spending three years in the Middle East during the Second World War along with Sid Bingham and Bill Carr-Rollett, the three of us having left from Titirangi to go overseas. We were the first of the 2nd NZEF members to join Titirangi RSA and we were given the first year free membership. There were about 30 First World War men in the Titirangi branch of the Western Suburbs*

RSA at that time. They used to meet at Reckies Kiosk. I was elected Secretary in 1945 and again in 1946; elected President in 1947 and 1948. I served continuously on the executive for 35 years, and as president again in 1961–64. I was 20 years on the Titirangi War Memorial Hall and Recreation Committee. This committee consisted of Alec Bishop, member of the Waitemata County Council and Chairman of the Titirangi Riding, Rex Congalton, Secretary Treasurer from the RSA, and myself as Deputy Chairman. The Committee was made up of three from the Ratepayers Association, three from the RSA, one each from the library, Plunket Society, playcentre and School Committee. It was set up in 1946 or 1947. The committee's objective was to obtain the land known as the Philcox estate bounded by South Titirangi Road and Park Road, then in use as a playground for the School for the Deaf who were housed in what is now Lopdell House. The committee had been given the undertaking by the then MP for the district, the Hon. H.G.R. Mason, that the land would be handed to the Waitemata County Council as the site of the Titirangi War Memorial when the School for the Deaf vacated and moved to Kelston.

All sorts of fundraising efforts were entered into, including a hair-raising one-off motorcycle race meeting around Mt Atkinson, along Kohu Road and the Scenic Drive. Fortunately no serious mishaps occurred during this effort! Through the efforts of Alec Bishop and the Hon. Mr Mason, Ardmore Aerodrome was obtained for the race meeting, but unfortunately a higher bid from the motor racing fraternity obtained the rights to run the race at Ardmore and that was the end of the committee venture. The committee bought a section in Rangiwai Road in 1947 and built a temporary hall with voluntary labour. This was opened in 1948 and served the district for all kinds of activities, the RSA using the hall each Tuesday night for indoor bowls and highly successful monthly dances. The hall was sold to the Catholic Church in 1955 to obtain enough to qualify for the pound-for-pound government subsidy for war memorials, thus raising £4000. The next 'home' for the RSA was a prefab vacated by the School for the Deaf, directly below Lopdell House, opposite the entrance to the War Memorial Reserve. We carried on there until 1962 when the original RSA clubroom was built to the covered-in stage. Then the RSA, with its own resources, finished it off with voluntary labour. The RSA building has been altered or added to on at least six occasions and now is a superb functioning building. Although the Titirangi War Memorial and Recreational Committee had completed its task, it carried on for a couple of years until the Waitemata County Council terminated it because the committee wouldn't bow to pressure to replace Alec Bishop as chairman. He had done a fine job in that position for 20 years but had unfortunately lost his seat on the Council. The Council has been responsible for the War Memorial Hall ever since. Western Suburbs RSA consisted of delegates from the various branches in the area from New Lynn to Waimauku. I was Titirangi's delegate for many years and we originally used to meet at the Glen Eden Library once a month. It was quite a ride home with George Soutar in his Model A as he never changed gears and it was often a struggle getting up the hill to Titirangi. Later when Henderson was built, provision was made to use a room under the stage. Western Suburbs' only income was from levies on the branches and the welfare account needed finance so I moved 'the interest received from the branch poppy day funds be used for that purpose'. Also I was responsible for the First World War men receiving free membership of the RSA in 1965 on the occasion of the 50th Anniversary of the landings on Gallipoli. Other RSA groups throughout New Zealand followed our lead. During the late sixties and early seventies it was impossible to obtain suitable accommodation for single First World War men in need; so Titirangi recommended to the Western Suburbs RSA a suitable home be set up in the West, hence the birth of the West Auckland Combined RSA Homes Trust for the Elderly.

The Anzac Day services were held on the hill at the corner of Atkinson Road and Scenic Drive prior to 1965. We used to truck seating from the Titirangi Women's Institute, cart them up the steep path and return them after the service, borrow the Anglican Church electronic *organ, and lay 50 metres of power cable from the house nearby with Mrs Soutar providing the music. The memorial contains the names of those who left the district during the First and Second World Wars and Vietnam with those killed inscribed. This memorial stands adjacent to the car park in the War Memorial Reserve on South Titirangi Road. When the hall was opened in 1965 the Anzac service was transferred there. I have attended the Anzac Service at Titirangi since 1944 and from the humble days of that period ever increasing interest, particularly among the young people, is apparent by the larger gatherings at recent ceremonies.*

In November 2009 Dave Lawrence, Titirangi RSA and immediate past secretary-manager, was interviewed by Marc Bonny[8] so the story of the Titirangi RSA could be brought up-to-date.

Before 1984, Titirangi area members of the RSA were a sub-branch of the Western Districts RSA. However, after this date Titirangi members became a branch in their own right and became Titirangi RSA Incorporated. At that time the membership was about 500. When the Wellington Headquarters of NZRSA changed the rules of membership, allowing not only servicemen who had not served overseas but also Compulsory Military Training (CMT) men in as members, there was a huge boost to membership. The law under the Flags and Emblems Act required that at least 50 percent of members had to be either ex-servicemen or returned servicemen but Titirangi found no problem with this, unlike some of the other clubs in the surrounding areas. In 2007 the law was changed and now there is no proportion required. This is a decided advantage for the future as servicemen age. At the moment we have returned servicemen, other military men and women who have served but not necessarily overseas in action, and associate members.

In 1984–85 the building was renovated and enlarged, with a poolroom being built at the back using voluntary labour, almost doubling the size of the building. Before, in the long narrow room, every time it was required for a dance or other event, the pool table had to be shifted by six people, usually the committee members. Later, another large addition was built, including new toilet facilities and a dining room. In 1985 we had our 50th Anniversary, which was extremely successful, with many members of Second World War and some older men from the First World War, including Gus Bishop, present. Old members were given a book and life members were given an anniversary pewter mug plus other items, such as anniversary badges and spoons.

The bowls started in the late 1960s and began with a black 'green' made from synthetic rubber, which was used for coaching schools on Saturdays throughout the winter because all the local grass greens were closed being too wet. Then about 20 years ago the 'green' was changed to Astroturf and bowls have gone from strength to strength.

Other clubs make trips to Titirangi RSA as we have very good caterers, for example Devonport RSA members come here for Christmas lunch or Onehunga or Papakura RSAs come by bus for a visit. Over the years we have had socials, indoor bowls, dancing, pool and snooker.

After much negotiation, land belonging to Telecom, facing South Titirangi Road, was purchased, allowing for a car park and the building of the new dining room. The latest extension was the room for the library and computer facilities for Senior Net training. In addition, in the last six years a gymnasium, believed to be the first in Auckland RSAs, was created for members only.

In the 1980s a friend of mine, Terry Keenian, who was in the Navy, and myself began collecting memorabilia, for which we started advertising. Soon it snowballed and Army men joined in with a great number of items, now displayed on our walls. Titirangi has a Women's Section, with Angela Logan who was Vice President, as a strong promoter. This group has an affiliation with Titirangi and do much work in raising money for charities and so on. The

RSA gives a lot to the community in supporting schools, Scouts and Guides and they support us in their own way, particularly with increasing attendances at Anzac Day ceremonies. With regard to this, although I have retired from my formal work with Titirangi RSA, I have been asked to continue to look after the Anzac Day services, which I will do with pleasure.

The churches of Titirangi

The first church built in Titirangi was the Soldiers Memorial Church in Park Road. The loss and trauma of the First World War was the driving force for its construction, and for Emily Bishop it was a memorial to her two sons killed in the war. An early painting of this church shortly after it was built is that by a friend of the Bishops, Cameron Johnson on page ii, colour section). Emily's grandson Bill[9], recalled:

In 1922 the local residents, under the leadership of my grandmother, Emily Bishop, organised the construction of the beautiful Titirangi Soldiers Memorial Church in Park Road, in memory of those brave men from the Titirangi area who gave their lives for their country. My father was trustee of the church until just before he died aged 93.

About 1936 a bell tower was added at the front section of the church grounds' entrance; great were the protests from people who said it would spoil the look of the church. One of the loudest protesters was the proprietor of the tea kiosk next door, now Toby's, who claimed the morning 9 o'clock tolling of the bell would wake him from his Sunday slumbers. However, his lolly counter was always open as we went into Sunday school. Dare I confess for the first time

Opening day of the Titirangi Soldiers Memorial Church in 1924.

Photographer: James D. Richardson, 18 August 1924. Auckland City Libraries Special Collections, 4-8241

(Below) The boy in the doorway of the newly completed church is Cliff Kershaw who, as a seven year old, helped his father and uncle at their home in New Lynn pre-cast the concrete blocks for the building.

West Auckland Historical Society, Kershaw Collection

(above) The church with lych gate, 1960.

Photographer: John T. Diamond. Waitakere Library & Information Services, J.T. Diamond Collection, 1102 (10A)

that there were Sundays when my parents' hard saved penny was used to purchase a half-penny liquorice strap and the other half-penny was dropped loudly in church plate so as to make the same noise as a penny?

The church was interdenominational, the church services were taken by the Anglican vicar one Sunday and the Presbyterian minister the next. We were told that we children were being given a good grounding in Christianity and that we would be allowed to make our own choice about religion when we were old enough to make a balanced decision.

From a generation earlier, Essie Hodge[10], daughter of Chappie and Emily Bishop, wrote:

John Bishop was a friend of George Augustus Selwyn, who styled himself as 'the first white Minister of New Zealand'. He invested in John Bishop the authority to carry out the offices of the Anglican Church. The Bible guided the lives of these pioneers who faced so many dangers in the early years of settlement. Elizabeth (Bishop) never called her children by name until they were baptised. The baptism took place soon after birth, as there was a belief that an unbaptised child would not go to heaven should it die. We have a lovely bowl that was used in the baptism of most of the infants in these parts.

As the district grew there was need for a place to worship as there was no church. The old school on School Road, now South Titirangi Road, was built as a community centre and was the natural venue. From then on, the Anglicans and the Presbyterians held services on alternate Sundays. What a squeeze to fit into those old school desks. The school owned a harmonium on which instrument the hymns were played. What a business it was to keep the bellows full of air! The Anglican services were very much simplified. The hymns only were sung. Chants and psalms were spoken. What dedicated men those vicars and ministers were! There were no cars and they had to get from a service in Avondale to Titirangi, either on horseback or bicycle. I have never forgotten a Presbyterian minister, Rev. Marsh, who arrived exhausted. He, no doubt, left Avondale late and had to cycle to Titirangi, uphill most of the way, before the road was concreted. I thought he might collapse during the service. So much devotion for a pecuniary pittance.

After the building of the Soldiers Memorial Church, which catered for Anglicans and Presbyterians, other religions have built churches in Titirangi: the Roman Catholic Church bought a large hall in Rangiwai Road, overhauled it and altered it to serve as their church. The Baptists have built a fine modern church at the beginning of Victory Road, Laingholm, and the Presbyterians have a fine church complex in upper Atkinson Road.

Now came the big step that I think the Anglicans were looking for. We became a Parish on our own, separated from New Lynn. In August 1971, Rev. Vernon Robertson became the first vicar. During Rev. Robertson's term as our vicar the Church celebrated its 50th anniversary.

The Anglicans built St Francis' Hall on the corner of Park Road and Park Beach Road. The Memorial Church is too small to accommodate large Anglican gatherings.

1 Waitakere City Council Archives, 2 May 1933.
2 Holibar, Bernard. Oral history by Marc Bonny, West Auckland Historical Soc. Inc., January 2004.
3 Lewis, Harry Morgan. Oral History by Marc Bonny. West Auckland Historical Soc. Inc., November 2001.
4 Blaiklock, E.M. *Between the Valley and the Sea*. Dunmore Press, Palmerston North, 1979.
5 *New Lynn News*, 26 February 1959 (abridged).
6 Strid, Bill. Memories, oral history by Marc Bonny. West Auckland Historical Society Inc., 2006.
7 Lewis, Harry Morgan. Oral History by Marc Bonny, West Auckland Historical Society Inc., November 2001.
8 Lawrence, Dave. Oral history by Marc Bonny. West Auckland Historical Society Inc., November 2009.
9 Bishop, W.N. Oral History by Marc Bonny. West Auckland Historical Society Inc., 2009.
10 Hodge, Essie. 'Memories of Titirangi,' Bishop family papers.

9

Sports and services in growing Titirangi

The French Bay Yacht Club, the Coastguard and the Fire Brigade

According to *Place Names of New Zealand*[1] French Bay was previously known as Opou Bay. The bay took its present name in the 1920s, but the origin of the name is not known. The French Bay Sporting Association was inaugurated in 1938 and formed the tennis club, clearing the bush on Opou Point Reserve. They held beach carnivals to raise money, and it was natural that boating, fishing and yachting interests took hold,[2] eventually giving rise to the formation of the yacht club.

Martin Northcott, the present (2010) commodore of the French Bay Yacht Club, wrote the following account for this volume, of the early days of the club, particularly in the 1960s when his architect father, Brian Northcott, was commodore, and the building on the waterfront at French Bay was constructed.

> *The origins of the club began in 1956 when it operated from an old building located where the present pumphouse is. This building was moved on rollers and manually pushed by volunteers to a new site near the present coastguard building shortly after this. The club operated from this building until the 1960s when the new clubhouse was built. In 1961 the reclamation was constructed where the first ramp is. It was all done by volunteer labour. The patrol boat* Otitori *was built in a garage by dedicated members and launched in 1962. In 1964 a subcommittee of four people was formed to prepare plans for the new clubhouse, which proudly serves the club today. Final designs were completed and an estimate of £7500 ($15,000) was approved. A fundraising project on a monumental scale was launched. The*

The Young People Seaside Mission on a church youth rally at French Bay in 1938. Waitakere Library & Information Services, Print Collection (Titirangi)

Opening day of the tennis club at the end of Opou Road, 1938. Waitakere Library & Information Services, Print Collection (Titirangi—Lewis)

By 1939 French Bay had become the favourite local swimming beach; the seawall was completed a few years previously and furnished with seats (long gone today) and pohutukawa trees, now providing shade. Waitakere Library & Information Services, Print Collection (Titirangi)

The rock wall under construction at French Bay, 1937. Keith Hewitt Collection

Swimmers and boats compete for water space at French Bay in 1958. The yacht club building (at left) was new in 1956. Keith Hewitt Collection

Aerial photo of French Bay, 1955. Alexander Turnbull Library Wellington, NZ, Whites Aviation Collection, Ref. No. 3890

The new clubrooms at French Bay opened in 1968. The Lewis' house is in the bush on left. Waitakere Library & Information Services, Print Collection

club was incredibly frantic with fundraising projects including carnivals, sausage sizzles, garden parties, stalls, even building a P-class yacht and raffling it. Most of the funds came from bottle drives, which were superbly organised by dedicated club members. We can recall the hilarious antics and occurrences on these expeditions, convoys of cars with trailers and trucks, any form of transport and an entourage of youngsters scurrying off to find all the local caches of bottles.

On 31 May 1965, £1000 ($2000) was allocated to start the project and the Harbour Board was approached for a loan for the remainder. Later that year a modified plan with a smaller budget £5500 ($11,000) was approved. As one can appreciate, to some members the cost was all important. However, the members of the day must take the credit for pursuing the dream of a building that would stand proud over the sea.

The new plans were prepared for a building with a design that allowed for further expansion. The expectation was that the foundations would be in before Christmas, but the steering committee had the foresight not to nominate which Christmas! The project stalled for a while and more engineering was required. Bob Foster, a structural engineer and a club member, was again called on. Bob was responsible for all the engineering on the new clubhouse and new reclamation on the seaward side. This was no mean feat and countless hours were put in by him and other hardworking volunteer club members. In June 1966 the permitted plans were estimated at £5300 ($10,600) and the club passed a motion calling for club members to do the actual work. A timeframe of 10 weekends was set; the backbreaking work of forming the concrete foundations anchored into the sea floor, and the retaining walls, was done by volunteer members reducing the deficit by thousands of dollars, and allowing the club to proceed with the building. In February 1967 a full contract was let to finish the clubrooms, which were opened in 1968.

Memories of the beginnings of the French Bay Yacht Club were also part of an interview with Morgan Lewis by Marc Bonny, in 2001.

Mrs Whyles had a corrugated iron kiosk at French Bay and shifted it to the beach for the first French Bay Yacht Club building.

The yacht club started in the early fifties, I got involved in the sixties particularly. They made a nice job of the new yacht club building. Wally Silva was the foreman for Downer Construction Company and he supervised it most carefully. He had the foundations bored right through the sand to the papa rock and filled it with concrete. Eddie Bougher had a trimaran and also there were the Newbys. They used to have winter programmes building the moth class yachts, which could be built cheaply, and my boys had several of them. Before marine plywood came in it was usual to use solid wood very thin that could be built to shape. I remember Jack Newby built one out of pukatea, a greenish soft wood but solid wood hulls were heavy which was a disadvantage. Gordon Addis was Commodore and the yacht races were usually held on Sunday.

Bob Foster recalled that he and Ted Franklin both had sons who sailed small yachts, when they as structural engineers were roped into helping with the building of the yacht club. Brian Northcott was the architect and Wally Silva was the foreman and both did great work. The work of building was done almost entirely by club members. Later it was decided to build a new launching ramp and a retaining wall was also built by members, supervised by the two engineers. From the late 1960s the club went from strength to strength and the building is now used extensively by club members and other community groups.

The French Bay Yacht Club still runs a full programme of sailing each year, as it has done for the past five decades. The accent is on family sailing with junior racing programmes, dinghy sailing and schools for young people to learn to sail. The club is West Auckland's premier yacht club and caters for all ages.

The Manukau Volunteer Coast Guard also operates from French Bay, from a separate building that is adjacent to the yacht club. The following account of its founding and activities was given by Peter van Rooyen for this volume.

The Manukau Volunteer Coastguard is one of three coastguard units on the Manukau Harbour and is the only unit on the northern shoreline. The coastguard base is situated at French Bay in Titirangi and was formed 40 years ago. Its founding members were local boaties who, either through an incident on the harbour or tragedy on the water, formed the unit using their own vessels as rescue vessels. Manukau Volunteer Coastguard is a purely volunteer organisation, relying on charities and foundations for its ongoing and ever-increasing running costs. There have been various sized vessels used over the years and at present the coastguard has a 12.5 metre Rayglass Protector with twin 300 hp Suzuki outboard motors. The vessel can carry just under 1000 litres of fuel, giving it a substantial range of operation. The Manukau Volunteer Coastguard is also the first response coastguard unit to an airport incident and any incident on the notorious Manukau Bar.

The operating patrol area is from South Kaipara Head in the north to Raglan in the south and 12 nautical miles off the coast. Although the majority of the work is carried out within the Manukau Harbour, when the game fishing season arrives, the rescues tend to extend a little further afield. The types of incidents that the Coastguard commonly attends are engine failure or fuel problems, but there are more serious and tragic incidents that are the reason all coastguard units train to the highest standards expected of a rescue organisation.

At present (2010) the Manukau Volunteer Coastguard has 23 active volunteers coming from all walks of life and professional backgrounds, but sharing a common goal: saving lives at sea. The volunteers in the unit each bring skills and attributes that when combined allows the unit to function in a professional and efficient manner. The unit is very much a community-based group of individuals and has a very close association with the local residents. The volunteers participate in local community activities and educational programmes involving the Sea Scouts and local school children. The aim of the educational programmes is not only to teach the pupils safe boating practices, but also to educate them on the dangers to look out for and to enlighten them to the role coastguard has in keeping the harbour safe. When an education program is being run emphasis is always made on checking the weather and telling someone where you are going and when you will be back.

A bottle drive collection point for French Bay fundraiser. Behind is the early Manukau Coastguard building.
Trevor Pollard Collection

The Titirangi Volunteer Fire Brigade

Not long after the war there were many ex-servicemen, well disciplined and motivated, moving to the outer suburbs of Auckland, to Titirangi, Glen Eden and Henderson. There were also growing concerns being expressed by insurance companies, councils and the Auckland Fire Board regarding fire risk, boundaries, delays and costs. For example, the following abridged extract taken from the Waitakere City Archives of 3 December 1948 shows the concern of the local council.

Linden Coleman, Titirangi's first fire superintendent.
Trevor Pollard Collection

Town Clerk: Fire Protection, Titirangi

Arthur Mead made recommendations referring to minutes of Council dated 11-11-1948 about fire protection in the Titirangi area. Arthur Mead's recommendations established that although the cost to upgrade to a fire service in Titirangi would be substantial, the value of the property in the area would justify it. It would mean replacing small, galvanised pipe and upgrading to 4-inch main or larger, the fitting of fireplugs to these and the existing 4-inch mains pipe. Also, there would be a need for additions to reservoir storage and the inclusion of the area in the Metropolitan Fire District, which would mean the building and equipping of a suitably placed station. It would take time to set up a special rating area in the portion of the County concerned. The preliminary cost figure came to £30,000, and included salvaging the small galvanised pipe for extending other rural areas. Work was to be spread over two or three years, commencing with the most valuable areas. Financing the work could be done in one of two ways; either by putting an extra water meter charge to the individual customer or by a special rate levied by the County to reimburse the City Council for the annual extra cost. Alternatively, the County could take over the reticulation and bring it up to standard and buy water in bulk for resale to its own consumers. Mr Mead went on to explain the importance of the area's large water supply mains, the Upper and Lower Nihotupu and Huia supplies converging. An independent organisation to handle reticulation would increase the ultimate cost to the consumer. The Superintendent of the Fire Brigade advised the local representative present to organise a volunteer fire brigade for the district to operate pending the establishment of the major scheme.

Titirangi 1949: formation of the Titirangi Volunteer Fire Brigade[3]

Dr Guy Chapman, a local dentist, recommended that Linden Coleman from Tanekaha Road should take on the responsibility of forming such a brigade. The early volunteers were George Wilding, Harry Lawrence, Tom Johnston, Lloyd Gerrard, Alf Veart, Ian Clarke, Fred Lavers, Norm Hewitt and John Aitken.

The first fire appliance, named the *Grey Ghost*, was a 1942 International crash tender that had been in the Pacific Islands during the war. A pump and 400 gallon tank was fitted. Early temporary housing of the brigade was in the basement of the School for the Deaf (Lopdell House).

The Waitemata County Council allowed the brigade to build the first fire station on the corner of South Titirangi Road opposite Lopdell House (currently parking area). It had a gravel floor with a large bench at the rear and a big vice for hose-coupling replacement and a hose-patching machine. It also had a room for meetings, a small kitchen at the rear and a

Grey Ghost at the rear of Lopdell House. This was the brigade's first engine, which arrived in February 1949.
Trevor Pollard Collection

longdrop toilet out back, all voluntarily built by the firemen. The Waitemata County Council provided the materials. Communication was a problem as not every fireman had a telephone. Wires dangled from the trees through the bush from Harry Lawrence's house in Opou Road down to Norm Hewitt's home in French Bay. The manual telephone exchange, operated by Peggy Holmes-Libbis and her husband and Vernon Clarke, would receive the 333 Fire Brigade emergency number. In those days the exchange would then have a list of numbers to ring, starting with the superintendent. The first to receive the call would then frantically wind the phone handle for 30 seconds to activate the phone circuit, connected to all firemen's homes, and say twice where the fire was located; this operation was done by the wife or family.

The first person to get to the station would set off the siren and write the address of the call on the blackboard for those who came after the appliance had left and who had to make their way in their own car. In the 1950s, when the siren by Lopdell House would go off the residents of Titirangi would count the seconds and minutes wondering how long it would be before the mobile siren sounded, signifying the engine was on its way. Sometimes it was too late save the house but in time to prevent fire spreading.

To bring the story of the Titirangi Fire Brigade up-to-date, in 2010 Trevor Moreland and Randolph Covich presented the following summary for this volume.

> *To residents on South Titirangi Road who regularly pass the Titirangi Fire Station, the only changes they may have noticed since the early 1990s are the occasional upgrading of a fire appliance, or maybe the tinting of the engine-bay door windows, along with a coat of paint now and again. To those in the wider Titirangi/Green Bay community, some may have wondered why they never hear the 'air raid' siren alerting volunteers to a fire call anymore. Those closer to the action will know that technological advances to the volunteer paging system made the siren redundant in 2006. They will also know that the windows were tinted to afford better ultraviolet protection for the newer turnout gear hanging ready inside the engine bay doors.*
>
> *District Fire Chief Trevor Moreland, and his Deputy Chief Randolph Covich, both Gold Star veterans of over 25 years' service, took up their current roles in 1994, and along with their 28 volunteers have been part of the ongoing changes from the 1990s to the present,*

which has seen the evolution of the New Zealand Fire Service to what we know today as the New Zealand Fire and Rescue Service.

Traditionally volunteers generally had a trade background, which fitted in well with the practical nature of a firefighting role, however, due to the changing demographics of Titirangi, volunteers now tend to have a more academic background, and they require more formal recognition of training and achievements. Thankfully this seemed to be a common theme among many urban volunteer brigades, and the Fire Service recognised this in the early 1990s, adjusting training accordingly. It now runs comprehensive structured training and qualification programmes, making it one of the largest government training establishments in the country.

A card giving details of the fire emergency number used during the 1950s. Trevor Pollard Collection

Equipment added to Titirangi appliances since the early 1990s now includes such things as a thermal imaging camera, hydraulic cutting equipment, and more advanced medical equipment, meaning that increased training is required to achieve regular recertification in the required skill base.

Along with this, the introduction of computers in all stations has meant that Titirangi firefighters can now tap into a wealth of fire/rescue-related training and information from a central networked resource, which means knowledge can be easily shared with all.

Fire turnout gear now includes a 'flash hood' worn under the helmet, which along with superior fire-fighting uniforms and the 'Safe Person Concept', health and safety philosophy, decreases the chance of fire related injury markedly. Along with a good-sized gym building constructed in 2004, the current complement of firefighters, both paid and volunteer, are arguably the fittest and most health conscious to pass through the Titirangi ranks.

Risk is still part of the nature of fire-fighting, and as part of their 300 plus calls per year, Titirangi volunteers and their daytime paid counterparts are called upon to attend many varying types of incidents, ranging from a child with their finger stuck in a shower plughole to greater alarms on the other side of Auckland, or perhaps a motor vehicle accident just up the street.

Titirangi also carries out the role of helicopter support unit, and provides manpower and equipment for helicopter operations at large fires over a significant part of the Auckland rural region, which places a heavy brigade commitment at these lengthy jobs.

A large workload is taken off the volunteers by the dedicated commitment of Titirangi paid staff, which covers the district with a crew during weekdays when volunteers are unavailable at their daytime jobs. Fire safety matters and the constant upgrade of risk plans and the like, along with the regular in-district fire calls and backup requirements for other neighbouring fire districts, place a heavy responsibility on the four paid yellow watch staff.

The 1990s also saw the placement of the Police Community Constable at Titirangi station, which continues to this day. As can be expected, with all these changes and increased administration requirements of managing a busy brigade such as this, a business case has been put forward for much overdue building extension work, which when done will help carry this community asset ahead into the future.

1   Reed, A.W. and Dowling, Peter. *Place Names of New Zealand*. Raupo, Auckland, 2010.
2   Council Correspondence, Waitakere City Archive, 1938.
3   Pollard, Trevor, Ingold, Bruce, Scott, Ted and Rotondo, Margaret (eds.). *Titirangi Fire Brigade 50th Jubilee 1949–1999*. Ted Scott Fotofile International Limited, Waitakere City, 2000.

10

Early days in Titirangi arts: a recollection by Lois McIvor

From the early days, Titirangi has had a reputation for being a place that had a highly scenic quality about it, and from the time that Scenic Drive was constructed during the Depression by relief workers, it has been taken for granted that this was a very special area, renowned for its beautiful views from the Waitakere Ranges of Auckland, the Waitemata Harbour, Rangitoto and other islands in the gulf.

The Manukau Harbour is a shallow enclosed harbour with an entrance through the Manukau Heads. In earlier days it had a reputation for being a dangerous place for the boats that had to use it to go up the harbour to the Onehunga wharf with their cargo.

In the early fifties, with my husband James, and my son Mark, I moved into Wood Bay Road extension on the Manukau Harbour, and although it was beautiful with the waters rippling into the bay and the bush surrounding it all, it was very primitive.

That part of Wood Bay had only recently been opened up and the baches were made from car cases or fibrolite and the water had just been laid on. There was a vast amount of mud and the road had a rough metal surface, which the council grader used to smooth out once a week! We bought a small cottage that had no conveniences and no power for six months—it was very rudimentary indeed.

I don't think I was aware of much in the way of artistic happenings at the time but I joined the Women's Institute, the only group that one could join to meet up with other women. By chance I became involved with the Drama Club that was a part of the Women's Institute and which met at the Macandrew Hall in Titirangi Road. The club was one of the most alive and interesting groups in Auckland, run by Ethelwyn Geddes, who was the producer. She was a knowledgeable and powerful woman who was greatly respected by the local community.

Geoff Hole was a local architect who was painting some scenery for the next play. We offered to help. That was my first contact with Mrs Geddes, although I never got to know her very well as my interest was in painting, not the theatre, but I saw a number of very good productions over the years. Their star was a man named Bruce Henderson, who was one of the finest actors I ever saw but who died young. Chris Cathcart later worked with the Drama Club too; he was a very talented producer, and also a friend of the McCahons.

Colin McCahon, who worked in the Auckland City Art Gallery, was my teacher and mentor. I met him through going to Summer Schools at the Auckland City Art Gallery, and he lived in French Bay Road with his family from 1953–60. Later the family sold their house and shifted into Newton to live. At that stage of his career he was not well known but later

Wood Bay in 1955, about the time the McIvors arrived.
Alexander Turnbull Library, Wellington, NZ, Whites Aviation Collection, Ref. No. WA-368905

on he became quite famous, and the little house in French Bay has become a museum and an artist-in–residence apartment with a studio that was built next to it by the Council.

After the war, Titirangi was full of people who had emigrated from Europe and who had bought their skills with them, and they made pottery or sculptures or almost any kind of craft you could think of. There used to be annual exhibitions of arts and crafts in the Titirangi War Memorial Hall, and also people would open their homes and workshops to visitors and sell their work in that way. The community was very cosmopolitan and the beauty of the environment seemed to attract people from all around the world. Some joined a craft collective at Browns Mill (originally an old flour mill) in the city, behind His Majesty's Theatre.

The New Vision Gallery in His Majesty's Arcade in Queen Street was run by Kees and Tine Hos, who had arrived in New Zealand in 1956 from the Netherlands. They sold a lot of pottery from Titirangi in their craft shop. They put on large exhibitions that were very popular, by potters such as Barry Brickell, Len Castle, Patricia Perrin, Graeme Storm and Doreen Blumhardt, in their upstairs gallery. The gallery also exhibited paintings and other art works and I showed paintings there. I had 14 exhibitions over the years.

The Hos were a great influence on the development of the craft movement in New Zealand. Artists such as Len Castle had a wide audience, and people collect his work to this day, as evidenced during his exhibition called *Mountain to the Sea* (2009), and his book, *Making the Molecules Dance*.

There were a large number of potters in Titirangi and out west, and possibly one of the reasons for this was that the area was one where you could have 'cottage industries'. This meant that craftsmen could work at home and have a kiln in their own backyard, where they could have a firing. Because of the possibility of fires in the bush, great care was taken over the years, and some potters had electric kilns that were regarded as being less hazardous. There was a young Chinese potter named Wailin Hing who lived in Wood Bay, and she had the first electric kiln that I ever saw. Later she married a woodcarver named Tom Elliot and they now run Barry Brickell's railway at Coromandel.

Also, there were many weavers in Titirangi and you might be invited to someone's home, perhaps for a house concert, and there would be a large shining wooden loom dominating the living room with a pattern on it that was being woven by the proud owner.

House concerts were held in private homes for some years and they had an enthusiastic audience. Neil Duff, who lived in Waiatarua, had a fine high quality piano that he had brought with him to New Zealand and it was a great treat to attend concerts in his house, with its wooden flooring and wooden ceilings and great acoustics. We also went to other houses in the district, and often the architecture and furniture showed a strong European influence that reflected the life the owners had left behind.

Zena Abbot, who was a weaver trained by Ilse von Randow, had a workshop in Blockhouse Bay, and she employed several women to weave her handmade products, which were beautifully done. I can also remember going into the main room of the Titirangi Community House, full of women talking and laughing while working away on their spinning wheels, creating large balls of wool, which would then be woven on a loom into fabrics that people could wear or hang on the walls, a lovely sight!

There were a number of jewellers who produced original and traditional work and who made a living from it and there was a large audience who appreciated all this. Andrew Ventor from South Africa worked in pewter and later on started the craft school at Hungry Creek, Puhoi, which continues to this day.

Dutch furniture-makers used their skills and created traditional rocking chairs and all sorts of furniture. I have a rocking chair made by Peter Smeele, a Dutch interior designer. Another one of my favourites was Levi Bergstrom, a Swedish carver who made beautiful handcarved spoons from native puriri wood.

John Crichton was an English designer, with a shop in Kitchener Street, and he designed the Java Chair, which had Asian influences, and was very popular.

There were painters like Ted Smythe, who had exhibited at the New Vision Gallery, and who was highly regarded and became one of our country's leading landscape gardeners. Odo Strewe was a landscape and garden designer who lived up on Scenic Drive. He brought in subtropical plantings that have greatly altered the appearance of Auckland gardens.

The Titirangi Coffee House was a well-known meeting place, with a beautiful view out over the bush and the Manukau Harbour, and many local painters and sculptors used to show their work there. One of the artists that I particularly remember was David Kennedy, who was a painter who designed murals and also used bronze in his work. I think he left Titirangi and went to live in Greece.

Cyril Whiteoak was also a popular artist and there were other painters who belonged to clubs and exhibited as an enthusiastic group.

Maurice Shadbolt was a highly regarded New Zealand writer, and he and photographer Brian Brake co-authored a book called *New Zealand, Gift of the Sea*, published in 1963. It was very successful! The photographer, Brian Brake, was a lovely man. He had an international reputation but preferred to use Titirangi as his base. He lived on Scenic Drive in a beautiful Japanese-style house designed by Ron Sang, and planted camellias in the bush, which was very unusual at the time.

John Caselberg was a poet who lived in Wood Bay with his wife Anna Woolaston; he collaborated with McCahon on his written paintings and provided the texts he used. Dick Scott lived up the hill for many years and was also a prolific writer.

Then there were talented people like Graeme Tidman, who had originally worked for BBC Bristol, and who on several occasions took photographs of my paintings for me.

Arne Loot is a Dutch photographer who I met at Bill Moller's farm, which was a social centre where the Folk Club had festivals. He took photos at the Art Gallery opening functions. Mrs van Zon taught modern dance and today her daughter is well known for continuing her work in the arts.

The creativity and the aesthetic feeling in Titirangi was quite remarkable and very unusual at that time. When I look back on it I wonder at such a concentration of talent.

I exhibited at the New Vision Gallery, and in the 1970s I was awarded an Arts Council Travel award and went to England, Holland and France to look at paintings. When I came back I joined in what was beginning to happen in Titirangi, hoping to make some kind of recompense for my trip overseas, which had been a wonderful experience for me.

The role of the Arts Council was to help develop the arts in New Zealand, and one of the ways that they did this was by giving grants to encourage local artists who might never have seen great art to travel and visit the major galleries.

The QEII Arts Council of New Zealand was supported by the Regional Arts Councils. Below this were the Community Arts Councils, spread out around New Zealand. In 1977, when I returned from Europe, I joined the recently formed Titirangi Community Arts Council (CAC), which was linked to the Auckland Regional Arts Council and had its office for a while in His Majesty's Arcade in Queen Street.

Our local CAC was given the use of the old council office in Rangiwai Road, where we used to pay our rates. It was an attractive architect-designed house that had once belonged to the Atkinsons, but was no longer being used by the Council.

Community houses were just coming into fashion and they seemed to fill a need for a place where locals could meet and discuss what was important to them. It was something new and we asked the Council to let us have the use of the Rangiwai Road house as a community house. This was welcomed and it became very popular as a public centre, which had been lacking before in Titirangi. All sorts of events took place there including yoga classes, art classes and meetings, discussions and exhibitions. Downstairs was turned into a pottery workshop, with a kiln out the back on the lawn.

When Brian Brake gave a talk at the War Memorial Hall, he let us arrange an exhibition in the Community House of his huge Egyptian photographs that he had taken for *Time-Life* magazine. What an honour that was! He gave some illustrated talks at the library, including his famous 'Monsoon essay on India,' 1961.

Lopdell House, which belonged to the Education Department, had been The School for the Deaf until a new one was built at Kelston. The house stood partially empty for some time. There were various options available but there was a strong feeling that the building should remain in the community, so we sent a delegation to the Mayor, Mr Covic, and asked that Lopdell House should become an art centre for the west of Auckland as there were few alternatives available. Finally, permission was granted, and representatives of groups such as the Ratepayers Associations formed the Lopdell House Committee so that the City Council had a formal body to deal with.

A theatre was built downstairs in the former garage, and on the top floor a restaurant, which had a magnificent view; we even held a weekend conference for the local Auckland Community Arts Councils there. It was all rather fun although not without controversy.

Bill Haresnape, who was chairman of the ratepayers association, suggested to me in my capacity as chairman of the CAC that we organise an exhibition at Lopdell House to show the House to the local people, but it wasn't an 'official' opening of the building. That came later. I invited several artists and craftsmen to take part and it was called 'Titirangi Fiesta' and it was very successful. Those involved included Len Castle with his superb pots; Zena Abbott, weaving; Brian Brake, photographs; Richard Cadness, pottery; Graham Barton and myself, painting; and Ruth Castle, woven baskets.

Titirangi Beach Hall was the meeting place for the Titirangi Folk Club, of which I was a member for about 30 years and I believe it is still going strong. We sang our hearts out and I made many good friends within it such as Leo Cappel, a Dutch musical instrument maker who made a variety of instruments including flutes and drums and stringed instruments.

Frank Carpay has come into prominence recently and he brought his skills as a trained ceramics designer to Crown Lynn Potteries and designed wonderful hand-painted plates under the name of Handwerk. The New Zealand public did not appreciate them so they were withdrawn. I think this happened to many of the artists and craftsmen and craftswomen who were ahead of their time!

Each year we had a very popular beach day for the locals on Titirangi Beach and many residents took part, including the Folk Club, who sang and played guitars. One year we asked Tim Shadbolt to get up on a soapbox for us and he willingly obliged. In the midst of a large circle of local residents he started to rail against everybody who was there and abuse them. Initially I was horrified, but afterwards it seemed very funny and I never forgot it! He was a hard case and no one escaped it, but later on he became mayor and more respectable!

In 1997 an exhibition called 'Western Lights: Art and Design in West Auckland 1945–80' was shown at Lopdell House. It was an overall survey of what had happened over the years and very good. It created the impression that the centre of the arts was out west and perhaps this was true. It has become obvious that the craftsmen and craftswomen asserted an influence over our architecture and the design of the times.

Lopdell House was well worth the troubles we had with it as it has been an excellent centre for many years and I think its climax came in August 2006, when The McCahon House Trust and Lopdell House Gallery put on an exhibition that was a tribute to Colin McCahon's early years in Titirangi, 50 years previously. The exhibition was very beautiful and appropriate, attracting a large audience, and the paintings, which had been painted 50 years ago in French Bay, were well preserved and very poignant.

Now the Lopdell House Society Committee is working with the Redevelopment Trust and there are plans to extend the building, as it has to be strengthened against earthquakes, and more room is needed for exhibitions and storage, and so things change and grow. Lopdell House has been a wonderful place as a focus for the art that has flourished and developed in Titirangi over the years. There is still much to come.

At home among the trees

Comment on the history of architecture in Titirangi — Megan Edwards and Jacqueline Bell

Over almost 100 years, the gradual opening up of land for subdivision in Titirangi has produced houses in a large range of architectural styles. The eclectic housing stock is also reflective of Titirangi's past as a holiday destination and its popularity with artistic people, who were open to developments in modern architecture and looking for freedom from conformity in a like-minded community. Before the 1920s European settlement in Titirangi consisted of villas and cottages on small farmlets in clusters around the Manukau. By the 1920s and 1930s small baches and grander holiday homes, some in the Art Deco style, dotted the hills and bays. As roads improved and more people bought cars, many baches became permanent homes with additions made as needs changed, more often than not without the input of an architect. In the post-war period, professionals who had set up businesses in New Lynn commissioned architect-designed homes in the hills on many of the best flat sites with views. The sixties boom in housing was assisted by further subdivision down to a quarter-acre. An increasingly design-aware clientele and the unique bush environment provided the opportunity for architectural innovation throughout the 1950s and 1960s with many outstanding houses built. In the 1970s, pole house technology allowed sites previously deemed too steep or unstable to be developed. In the four decades since, architect-designed houses have continued to be built on the few sites still remaining.

From a town planning perspective, Titirangi village is blessed with a main road on a splendid ridge, standing high above the city and providing an important point of access into the Waitakere Ranges. This busy ridge road is complemented by the winding crescent of Park Road, off which roads trail down the valleys, giving access to the beaches on the Manukau. Lopdell House, built in 1929–30 as a hotel in Mediterranean style, is most potent as a landmark, defining and holding the principal corner of Titirangi and South Titirangi roads. The building is a critical element of Titirangi's identity, now housing professional and community art galleries and a theatre.[1] Its form marks the edge of the city, representing both earlier glamour and somehow still, the prospect of leisure. The rest of the commercial buildings on the main road are undistinguished, but the sunny ridge bustling with traffic, together with the market space to the south (framed by the Memorial Hall, library and community house) forms a successful village scheme.

Titirangi's architectural excitement lies in the experimental and modernist houses built from the late 1940s through to the 1970s. There had been few opportunities for architectural projects throughout the Depression years and the Second World War, however an influx of European architects well versed in the tenets of European Modernist architecture as well as New Zealanders returning after the war, contributed to debate in architectural circles about how one should and could live in houses. New Zealand journals *Home and Building* and *Landfall*, as well as overseas journals such as *The Architectural Review*, were highly influential. Against the backdrop of social conformity and the prevalent English cottage style domestic architecture, a small group of artistically minded people were excited by the prospect of modern living. They were attracted to the idea of houses designed to facilitate the lives of their inhabitants, in which all the arts would be integrated, creating a life of vitality and originality. Houses that explored the idea of continuous horizontal space offered the opportunity for buildings to relate to their particular sites in new and exciting ways. Titirangi, being at a remove from the conventional suburban plots of the city and offering affordable sites within a distinctive natural environment, provided the ideal location for this project. The area attracted potters, artists, weavers, painters, designers and architects — people in general less concerned with status, open to the mix of housing quality and passionate about the opportunity at hand.

Alongside interest in modern living was the exciting prospect of creating architecture that was somehow particular to New Zealand. Centennial celebrations in 1940 and New Zealand's involvement in the Second World War had prompted consideration of national identity. There was interest in the idea of generating a distinctly New Zealand voice in all the arts, suitable to a new chapter of social history. As poet Allen Curnow declared with requisite monocultural bias in 1945, New Zealand 'doesn't exist yet … It remains to be created — should I say *invented* — by writers, musicians, artists, architects, publishers'.[2] As New Zealand was considered a modern country, many architects believed it should also have a modern architecture, reflecting the particularities of this place.[3] Alongside attempts to find historic New Zealand prototypes for an emerging vernacular, architects borrowed from abroad. Rather than pursuing European models of international modernism, New Zealand architects increasingly looked to other regions with local traditions of building in timber — to California, Japan and Scandinavia. This was part of growing interest internationally in the idea of regional modernism. California and Japan were also part of the 'Pacific Rim' and as such considered better sources for the development of architecture appropriate for this place.

In Titirangi, architects' own homes were the ground for experimentation. In 1947 Tibor Donner, acclaimed architect[4] and chief architect of the Auckland City Council during the years 1946–67, built his own house on a steep site overlooking the city (page xix, colour section).[5] The beautifully refined plan and careful detailing of the house are clearly influenced by European modernism. The lower floor is essentially one open living-room contained on one side by a stone-clad retaining wall, and open on the other to lawn and views by way of a gently concave glazed wall. This distinctive, white painted timber-clad house incorporates a perforated sun shade to the north, a curved deck on a single steel post, which doubles nimbly as entry canopy and an exterior spiral steel stair to an upper floor roof deck — all architectural elements familiar from the work of European modernists. The interior incorporates subtle gestures such as the built-in plywood furniture and a curved balustrade leading to the upper floor at the far end of the living room.

The Atkinson house, 1945–46. Built for Donner's friends, Harry and Edna Atkinson, at the beginning of Rangiwai Road and later used as the Titirangi Community House. The elegant 120º L-shaped plan has a mono-pitch roof and includes two covered outdoor areas modelled within the form of the house. Architect: Tibor Donner. The Architectural School Archive, University of Auckland

Donner designed several houses in the Titirangi area, all different, apt for their sites and with an assured modern aesthetic.

At architect Bill Haresnape's[6] own large family house, built between 1955–58 at the top of Otitori Bay Road, the influence of international modernists is also much evident, in this case Californian residential architecture and in particular the houses of émigré architect Richard Neutra.[7] The house has a cruciform plan anchored on a spur of rock beyond which the land drops away steeply to the Manukau Harbour (page xxii, colour section). While the dramatic siting of the house may be worthy of Frank Lloyd Wright, the planning and detailing is clearly indebted to Neutra. The cool rectilinear geometries of the house appear to materialise from the site, as stone walls (hand-hewn by the architect) extend from within the building to without. The house explores the notion of fluid space with intersecting spatial volumes that open with extensive glazing and large sliding doors on all four sides of the home. The rich materiality of the interior (stone chimney, built-in timber furniture, timber finishes and expressed timber beams) combine with the generous interconnected spaces to produce a wonderfully comforting ambiance. The Haresnape house has an epic quality — in the New Zealand context the scale and ambition of the house were unprecedented. At the time the house was dismissed by some as 'too American, too Australian'[8], but was recently awarded a New Zealand Institute of Architects Award for Enduring Architecture.[9]

Another nearby house designed by an architect for his family was the Henderson house, situated on a flatter, more open site at the top of Titirangi Beach Road. Indeed, the old farm road that trailed along the contour of the hill from Reekies Tearoom (now Tobys) past the Henderson house, along the drive to the Haresnape house at the top of Otitori Bay Road, down past the Swinburn house (also designed by Haresnape) before dropping into

The Henderson house, 1949–55. Stage 1 was completed in 1950. This image shows the floor to ceiling glass. Architect: Bruce Henderson. Sparrow Industrial Pictures Ltd, Sylvia Henderson

Avonleigh Road, afforded quite an architectural tour. Bruce Henderson's[10] house preceded his friend and neighbour Bill Haresnape's family house. Both men not only designed but also built their houses over several years on lean post-war budgets with determined ingenuity. The two collaborated in importing large panels of glass from England that would allow them to realise their vision. The families of these charismatic men were often involved with the various building projects. The stone walls on the Haresnape's property were an ongoing project over endless weekends, involving trips to the Bombay and Bethells quarries. When Bruce Henderson began building in 1949, his Remuera-based family were reputedly rather shocked that Bruce was determined to take his bride out to the Titirangi hills, but it was here he found the freedom and opportunity to explore his architectural ideas. Built in stages, the Henderson house was largely complete by 1955, with a pool and gazebo added in the early 1960s. Stage one of the house was uncompromisingly modern: rectilinear, flat roofed, rigorously based on a three-foot module frame and with large areas of floor to ceiling glass. An arresting feature of the house was the 'sgraffito' (painting technique using scraping) mural featuring dragons by artist David Kennedy, which was purpose-made for the house. Apart from creating necessary additional space, stage two of the building involved the extension of the modern grid of the house into the garden. A large rectangular flat roof was projected out from the house, providing outdoor covered areas and walkways and doubling as a deck for the upper floor. An opening in the flat roof allowed light into the house, illuminating a beautiful garden planted with an ornamental Japanese maple adjacent to the entry. Careful design of screens, planting and paving enhanced the Japanese-inspired exterior spaces. The result was a sophisticated house and garden, where traditional boundaries between inside and outside were broken down (see image on p. 109).

Several houses in Titirangi were designed by architects with an affiliation to the company known as Group Architects.[11] The 'Group' was active in the design and building of houses

In 1955 stage 2 of the Henderson house was completed. This image shows the covered exterior areas. Sylvia Henderson

The Henderson house. Exterior screens extend the 3-foot module. Sylvia Henderson

Exterior spaces of the Henderson house. The Japanese influence is evident. Sylvia Henderson

from the late 1940s and adhered to many modernist notions: a free plan based on peoples' activities rather than separate rooms, continuous horizontal space, rational planning, economy of structure and the use of modular building systems. They were also keen to develop a vernacular style, which they sought to do by drawing on utilitarian rural sheds and simple settler dwellings, adopting visible timber-framed construction, pitched roofs and expressed sloping ceilings. As harbingers of a modest New Zealand style, members of Group Architects saw themselves as pioneers facilitating a modern distinctly New Zealand way of life. Local houses designed by Group Architects include the Worley house in West Lynn Road (1948) by Bruce Rotherham, the Hunter house in Rangiwai Road, the Tibbles house in Golf Road (1952) by James Hackshaw, and the Heine house (unbuilt) in Tinopai Road (1952) by Alan Wild. There is also a house in Scenic Drive designed by Group founder Bill Wilson in 1955 for landscape designer Odo Strewe and his wife Jocelyn and family.

In 1959–60 James Hackshaw, who had been a key figure in the Group, designed a house for the well-known artists, potter Len Castle and weaver Ruth Castle.[12] The long gabled living space that is at the heart of this design is lit with high level glazing at either end, creating a chapel-like ambiance in the interior.[13] The open plan of the living room is designed to facilitate both work (the loom and display of pottery) and home life. The house can be seen as a modern take on settler dwellings with its barn-like form and vernacular materials — corrugated asbestos (originally) and creosoted weatherboards. The architect

The Castle house, 1959–60. The central gable form with lean-tos clad with creosoted rough-sawn weatherboards and corrugated asbestos roofing — 'humble' New Zealand materials. Architect: James Hackshaw.
Barry Mackay, reproduced from *Home and Building* magazine (September 1960)

The Castle house interior, which facilitated the work and life of its artist occupants.
Barry Mackay, reproduced from *Home and Building* magazine

submitted the house for publication to *Home and Building* magazine with an article entitled 'Toward an Indigenous Architecture',[14] in which Hackshaw emphasised that the design of the house was based around the lives of two New Zealanders and the 'possibilities of the site'. Despite this emphasis on local origins, the house accomodates the Castles' interest in the art and design of Japan. A Japanese sensibility is evident in the vertical panelling of the glazed gables, the zoning of the living space and in various landscape features.

In 1962 Hungarian émigré architect Imi Porsolt, teacher, critic and practitioner, designed the Pollard house for fellow central European immigrants in Wood Bay. The house, suspended above (now amongst) the bush canopy on steel poles, has an experimental radial plan that fans around the brow of a hill (page xx, colour section). The planning is not unlike some of the Group's houses, with open-plan interconnected living areas at the heart of the house, and a play space for children off their bedrooms instead of a corridor. The distinctive butterfly roof is expressed internally with exposed rafters radiating from the entry over the kitchen and living spaces and then up into the bush. The house is notable for the beautiful interior quality of its living spaces, with several opening into one another, subtly defined by level changes, the placement of the chimney and cabinetry, and changes in interior linings.

The Orr-Walker House of 1965, by the partnership of Alan Fairhead and Peter Mark Brown, was based on the aesthetic of linked pavilions, another Japanese concept that was being explored internationally by modernist architects. In this instance the design-aware clients[15] had stipulated that the bush-clad site remain as undisturbed as possible. The pavilion concept allowed minimal disruption, as the pavilions and linking walkways could be disposed along the natural contours of the land in such a way that larger trees could be retained (p. 112 and xxiii, colour section). The flat-roofed structures have large areas of floor to ceiling glazing, allowing views through from one space to another and to the garden. The main pavilion opens on the downward side to a deck overlooking the native bush and on the upward slope to a courtyard (designed by pioneer Modernist garden designer Ted Smythe) cut into the hill. The proximity to bush allows a high level of glazing without the risk of overheating. The living room in particular, largely glazed and with no eave, creates a most intimate relationship between interior and exterior. The house was noted at the time for its successful integration of interior design, architecture and landscape, and won a Bronze award in 1965 from the New Zealand Institute of Architects.

From the 1970s most of the houses built on steeper sites utilised pole house technology imported from California. Poles were in some instances helicoptered into steep sites with difficult access. The system minimised the number of foundation holes required, leaving the bush largely intact, and allowing houses to be built in close proximity to the bush. Pole houses of this period were characterised by steep roofs and stepped plans with dramatic split levels. Natural timbers were used extensively on both interiors and exteriors. Floor plans were often based on a 2.3 metre square pole grid, which optimised bearer spans, with poles taken up higher than the building platform and expressed as part of the design. The system was cost-effective. The expression of roof planes internally, often with high clerestory windows to let in light, was also an important feature in these sometimes dark, steep sites shrouded by bush. The technology was embraced and championed by architectural designer Peter Norton, who designed several of the earliest pole houses in Titirangi, including his own (p. xxiv, colour section).

In 1976 architect Ron Sang designed a pavilion house par-excellence on Scenic Drive for internationally renowned photographer Brian Brake, whilst working in the partnership of Mark Brown, from Fairhead, Sang and Carnachan. The design can be seen as a development of the earlier Orr-Walker pavilion house for a client who was both interested in and informed about Asian architecture. Situated on a steeply sloping north-facing site with views back to Auckland city, the house is comprised of a sleeping and a living pavilion lined up along the contour of the site and linked by a glazed walkway. Two additional square forms project and hover above the bush — the 'tatami' room (based on Japanese tradition) and an open deck, each supported on a single concrete pier. The rectangular forms of the house are detailed in a restrained fashion — generally flat roofs with no eaves and a neat copper flashing at the top of walls that are clad in horizontal shiplap cedar boards (p. xx, colour section).

The quiet detailing and rational plan provides a wonderful foil for the dramatic and ceremonial moments the house delivers. Visitors to the house are required to traverse a long raised walkway to reach the oversized solid entry door. A contained entry space contrasts with the relaxed unfolding of the open plan living areas beyond, and the striking immediacy of the garden and views afforded by the glazed northern walls. Dramatic advantage is derived from the steepness of the site. The glazed walkway offers views to a stream below, which is developed as a beautiful landscaped pool. A raking roof to the stairwell soars in the opposite direction to the descending stair, creating an unexpectedly sheer window. The tatami room and the deck place the occupant carefully into the space and light of the garden. The house is an example of the exquisite engagement of architecture with a specific place, and has been honoured with a New Zealand Institute of Architects 25 Year Award.[16]

During the decades following the Second World War, a distinctive artistic community developed in Titirangi, enamoured and influenced by the unique physical environment. The artists and architects who made their homes in Titirangi were engaged in various ways with the project of making New Zealand 'home' through the creation of an artistic culture. Local artists and architects and their families spent their time together and shared ideas. The Henderson children recall assuming everyone lived in architecturally designed homes. Many of the architects had working connections as well as friendships.[17] On talking to people who remember these times, there is the prevailing sense of a community of clients and architects, experimenting together. One imagines that the kinds of debates going on at parties at the McCahon house were being enjoyed throughout the suburb.

The Orr-Walker house, 1965. Separate living room and main pavilions from the north. Architects: Peter Mark-Brown and Fred Whitehead of Mark-Brown, Fairhead and Associates. Studio 57, reproduced from *Home and Building* magazine (March 1965, pp. 52–55)

The well-known 'Case Study' house programme in Los Angeles, sponsored by the *Arts and Architecture* magazine during the years 1944–65, produced a series of seminal and highly influential designs for modern living. It's tempting to see Titirangi as the site of our own mini 'Case Study'. In Los Angeles many people thought young clients and architects were mad building up a dirt track in the hills; there were certainly those in the conservative post-war years in Auckland who regarded the Titirangi experiment with equal scepticism. But the availability of cheap land in an area outside the suburban norm, at the very time that there was the taste for artistic and architectural experimentation, did produce a concentration of most interesting houses. The houses mentioned in this article are fine examples and Titirangi contains many more hidden gems, obscured by ever-increasing bush cover, that are deserving of record, presentation and discussion. Whilst the intellectual fervour of the modernist and nationalist project has dimmed, the physical particularities of Titirangi and its history as a site of key social and architectural developments in New Zealand provide ample ground upon which contemporary architects may draw and build.

1   Plans by Mitchell and Stout Architects for the redevelopment of Lopdell House as a regional gallery capable of hosting important touring exhibitions are, at time of print, lodged with Waitakere City for granting of Resource Consent.
2   Allen Curnow, in Curnow and Ngaio Marsh, 'A Dialogue by Way of Introduction', *First Yearbook of the Arts in New Zealand*, H.H. Tombs, Wellington, 1945, p. 2; quoted in Francis Pound, *The Invention of New Zealand: Art and National Identity 1930–1970*, preface, p. xviii.
3   Paraphrasing Clark, Justine and Walker, Paul. *Looking for the Local: Architecture and the New Zealand Modern*. Victoria University Press, Wellington, 2000, p. 7.
4   Architect of the Parnell and Point Erin baths, the Savage Memorial and the City Administration Building among other significant buildings. Tibor Donner was born in Hungary in 1907,

(Above) The Brake house, 1976. The tatami room projects out and hovers above the bush. Architect: Ron Sang. Simon Devitt

(Below) Looking outwards from the tatami room in the Brake house. Simon Devitt

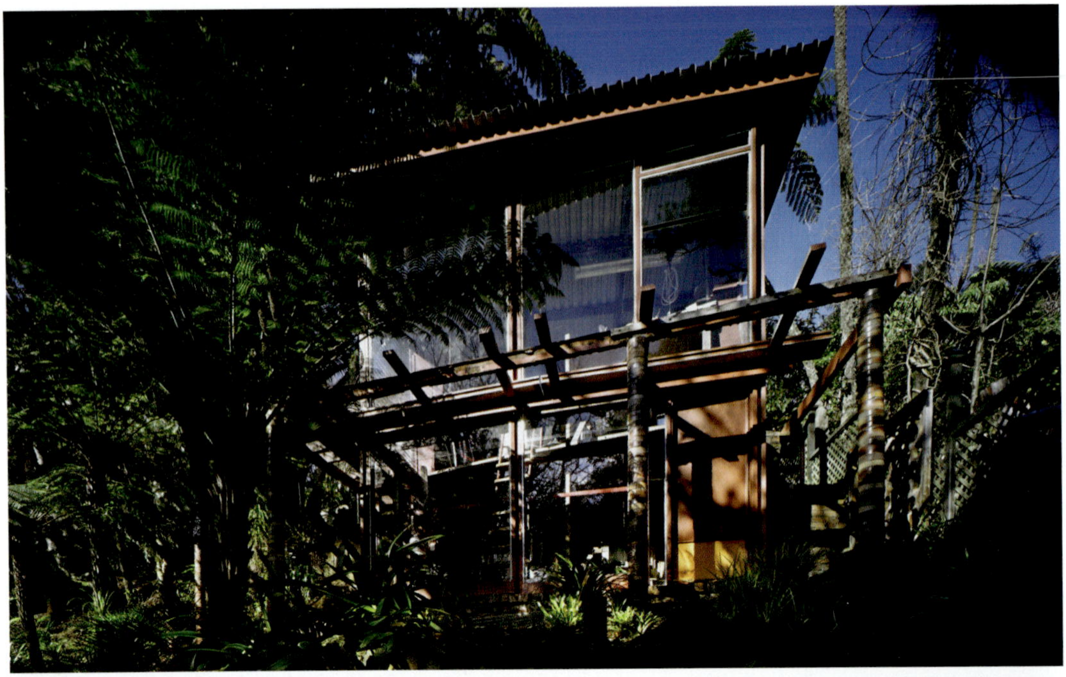

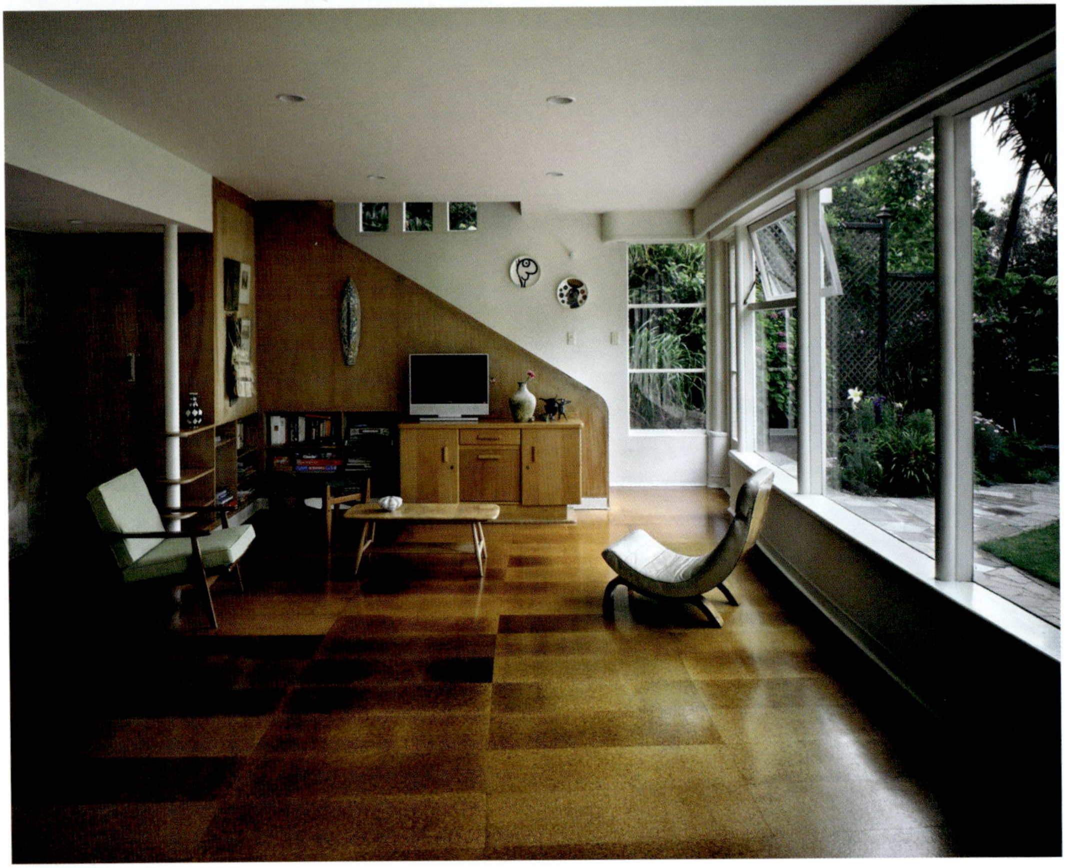

(Above) The Donner house from the entry, 1947.
Simon Devitt

(Right) The Donner house from the northwest.
Simon Devitt

(Top left) One of two studios on the Donner property, 1960s. The concrete-filled ceramic rings of the pergola posts mimic the banding of the nikau trunks. Architect: Tibor Donner.
Simon Devitt

(Left) The living room in the Donner house.
Simon Devitt

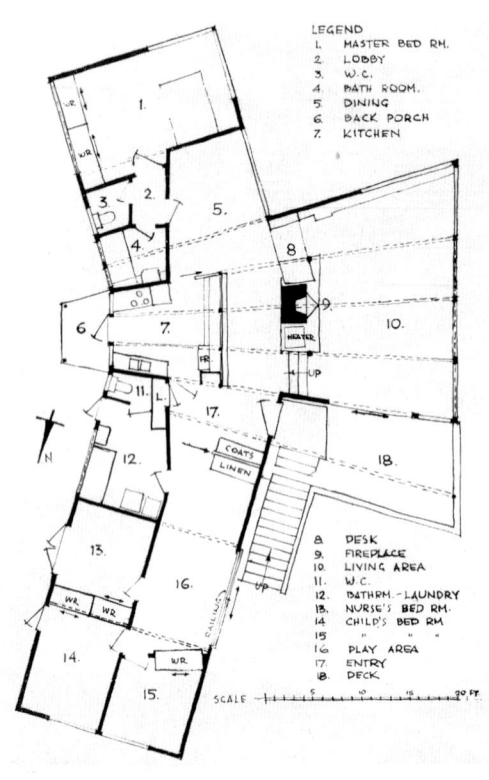

The Pollard house, 1962. The floor plan fans around the brow of a headland above Wood Bay. The dotted lines indicate exposed rafters above. Architect: Imi Porsolt. Reproduced from *Home and Building* magazine (August 1963, pp. 36–39)

Pollard House on the brow of the hill

Photograph by Rod Harvey, reproduced from *Home and Building* magazine (Aug 1963, p 36-39)

The wood-lined interior of the Pollard house. The entry space with the living room to the right and the kitchen behind a partition to the left. Simon Devitt

(Above) The Haresnape house, 1955–58. The house is now the Fringe of Heaven Bed and Breakfast. This is the northern wing of the cruciform plan. The cladding is industrial aluminium sheeting. The stone wall continues into the interior. Architect: Bill Haresnape. Simon Devitt

(Left) View from the Haresnape house, looking north from the deck that is located above the natural rock spur on which the house is sited. Simon Devitt

(Right) The rich and accomplished interior of the living room in the Orr-Walker House. There is a ceramic pipe screen in background. Rees Osborne

(Below) The Orr-Walker house: floorplan showing the concept of linked pavilions.
Reproduced from *Home and Building* magazine

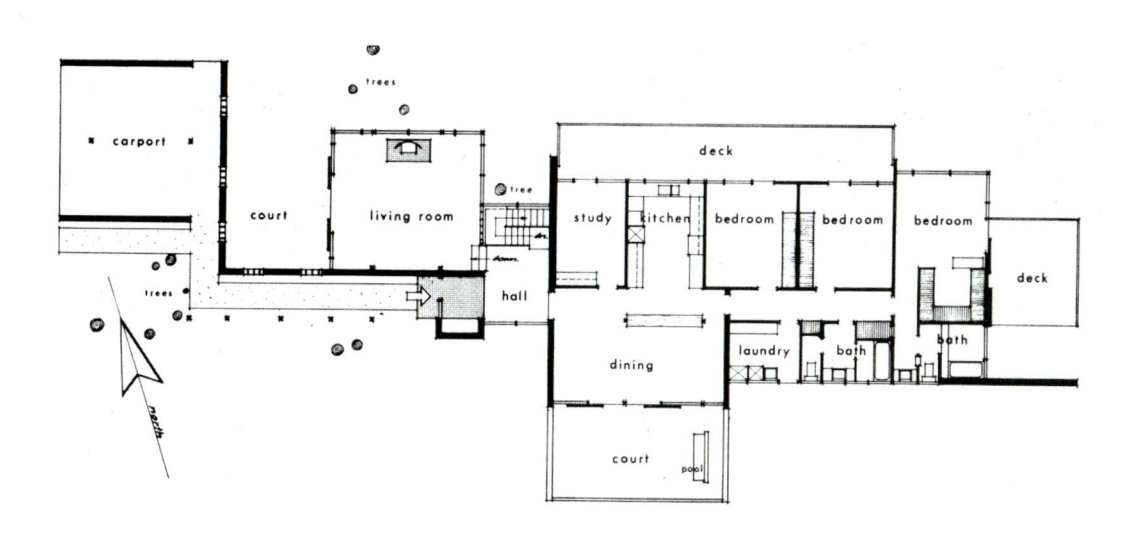

Peter Norton photographed outside his house, designed and built in 1973. Norton placed the poles on the outside of the building to allow clear expression of the pole and bearer structure, which was stained green to contrast with the warm stain of the kahikatea shiplap wall cladding. Courtesy Peter Norton

5   emigrated with his parents to New Zealand as a young man and obtained his architectural degree from Auckland University College. He was appointed the first City Architect in 1946, and was awarded a NZIA Silver medal in 1956 and a Gold medal in 1957, died 1993.
5   The Donner house has recently been given a Category 1 listing in the Heritage appendix of the Waitakere City Council District Plan. One of the two studios on the property designed by Donner was given a Category 2 listing.
6   Bill Haresnape, 1921–91, local councillor, teacher, campaigner for the protection of the native bush, architect, according to some the unofficial mayor of Titirangi. (As noted by Jane Blair in the *Western Leader*, 13 June 1991, p.1, 'Bill Haresnape — he was Titirangi', quoted in McKay, Bill, 'A Possum in the Kiwi Bush'.
7   Richard Neutra, a Viennese architect who initially worked in the office of Frank Lloyd Wright, and later with Schindler before setting up his own practice around 1927.
8   Interview with Val Haresnape, 9 June 1998, quoted in McKay, Bill, 'A Possum in the Kiwi Bush'.
9   October 2009, an award 'for buildings which have stood the test of time', NZIA website. The citation read, 'this jewel lost in the Titirangi bush … inspired by Californian designers of the era — a style rarely seen in contemporary domestic architecture'.
10 Ian Bruce Henderson, 1925–73. His own partnership with John Wheeler focused on commercial and public buildings. Bruce previously worked for the Education and Hospital boards. He designed the two-storeyed extension to the Titirangi Primary School incorporating the staffroom in the early 1950s. His other buildings include the Waitakere Obstetrics Hospital in Henderson, Auckland Blood Transfusion Centre (opposite Auckland Hospital), and the IDAPS Building, corner Khyber Pass and Grafton Road (now renamed the Southern Cross Building).
11 Begun by a group of graduating architects led by Bill Wilson, the Architectural Group's philosophy was first articulated in their 1946 manifesto, *On the Necessity for Architecture*. In 1949 Group Construction Company was established, which designed and built three seminal houses on Auckland's North Shore. In 1951 Group Construction Company coalesced into Group Architects.
12 The Castles built another home in Paturoa Road in 1971, designed by architects Gillespie, Newman, West and Pearce.
13 As noted by Douglas Lloyd Jenkins in *At Home: A Century of New Zealand Design*. Random House, Auckland, Auckland, 2004, p. 180.
14 *Home and Building* 51, September 1960, pp. 50–53.
15 John Orr-Walker, who still owns the house, attended architecture school with Peter Mark Brown and others, before training as a dentist.
16 Although Ron Sang recalls no discussion of the connection between the two projects in the office.
17 Awarded September 2000.
18 For example, Fairhead had worked for Tibor Donner and Ron Sang worked with Fairhead.

Bibliography

Clark, Justine and Walker, Paul, *Looking for the local: Architecture and the New Zealand Modern*. Victoria University Press, Wellington, 2000.

Gatley, Julia (ed), *Long Live the Modern, New Zealand's New Architecture 1904–1984*. Auckland University Press, 2008.

Lloyd Jenkins, Douglas, *At Home: A Century of New Zealand Design*. Random House, Auckland 2004.

McKay, Bill, 'Modern Houses in the West' in *Block: The Broadsheet of the Auckland Branch of the New Zealand Institute of Architects*. Itinerary n. 13, 2008-4.

McKay, Bill, 'A Possum in the Kiwi Bush' in R. Blythe and R. Spense (eds.), *Thresholds*. SAHANZ, 1999, pp. 209–212.

Norton, Peter, *The New Zealand Pole House*. Hickson's Timber Impregnation Co. (NZ) Ltd., Auckland, 1976.

Pound, Francis, *The invention of New Zealand: Art & National Identity, 1930–1970*. Auckland University Press, 2010.

Shaw, Peter, *A History of New Zealand Architecture*. Hodder Moa Beckett, Auckland, 1997.

Shaw, Peter, 'Modernism in New Zealand Architecture' in Daley, Debra (ed), *New Zealand Home and Building: The Newstalk 1ZB 1950s Show*. Robin Beckett, Auckland, 1992, pp. 22–31.

12

Performing and literary arts in Titirangi: 1950s to the present

Titirangi has always been a place where the arts have been taken seriously; this has included the performing arts as well as the visual arts. The 1950s was a time of clubs and societies that provided entertainment, often of very high quality, at a local level. During this time Titirangi had a Light Opera Company and a theatre that produced many outstanding entertainments. Sandy Matheson was a member of both of these clubs and remembers the fun and achievements of those times[1].

> **Theatre memories by Frank Broad**
>
> As long as there are a few theatre groups such as the Titirangi Light Opera Company, lovers of flesh and blood theatre should never be frightened of television competing to the detriment of live shows. The Titirangi Company is to be commended for its courageous efforts in staging the Gilbert and Sullivan operas.
>
> Extract from a newspaper article published during the season of *The Yeoman of the Guard,* 1960

The Rev. Jim Gunn formed the Titirangi Light Opera Company (TLOC) in 1957. For the first few years Gilbert and Sullivan operas were produced and performed by local talented singers. The Pirates of Penzance *was first, performed at Macandrew Hall, followed by* HMS Pinafore, The Mikado *and* Iolanthe. *The performance venues included Laingholm Hall then Kelston Boys' High School, which became the favoured venue. Jim Gunn produced the first two then became Musical Director while his wife Margaret was for many years a most capable accompanist. As a chorus member for the first productions I recall the pleasure and fun that we all had during both rehearsals and performance. Fred Watson, Davon Unsworth, Graeme Cass and Doris Owen were outstanding soloists with Jim and Margaret Gunn holding it all together. The company continued into the mid-sixties with a departure from Gilbert and Sullivan and the addition of a fine orchestra. The personnel in the company changed over the years too, but we had a variety of fine singers with productions of* Tom Jones, Amahl and the Night Visitors *and* Katinka.

Jim Gunn[2] recalled:

In addition to the venues noted by Sandy we also did shows at Pukekohe and at the big Technical College hall in Wellesley Street. I think it was Amahl *we did there and I remember a spotlight crashing to the stage floor while we were setting up, fortunately missing anyone on the stage. We did* The Mikado *in the Macandrew Hall and with its low ceiling we had to fight our way through cherry blossoms. I did that part at Kelston Boys' and had wonderful makeup done by (I think) Gil Cornwall. We did* Amahl *on the Manse croquet lawn, Margaret playing more mosquitoes than notes and Gil Cornwall getting temporarily lost in the bush! Roland Everard, who had a beautiful baritone voice, went on to entertain on*

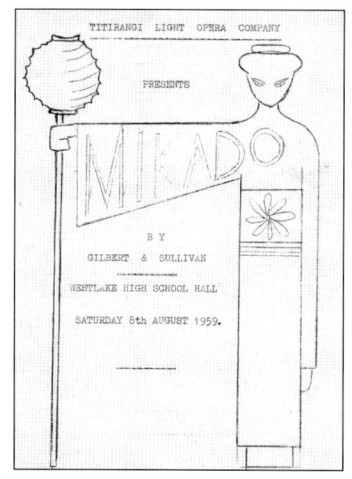

(Above left) Programme cover of The Mikado. West Auckland Historical Society, Gunn Family Collection

(Left) Programme cover of The Pirates of Penzance, the Titirangi Light Opera Company's first production and the first of a run of Gilbert and Sullivan works. West Auckland Historical Society, Gunn Family Collection

(Above right) Margaret Gunn at the piano rehearsing 'The Chorus of Fairies' for the 1959 production of Iolanthe. Rehearsals and productions were held at Kelston Boys' High School. West Auckland Historical Society, Gunn Family Collection

(Right) Graeme Cass as the Lord Chancellor in Iolanthe. West Auckland Historical Society, Gunn Family Collection

cruise ships, Mark Pedrotti, who sang the part in Amahl *in that opera had a marvellous reedy treble, ideal for the part. He, of course, became quite a famous opera singer overseas later. Davon Unsworth was an excellent soprano, true and strong and now lives in Napier. The late Jack Hunter reckoned that his days with the TLOC were the happiest in his life. Margaret accompanied all the rehearsals most efficiently and once did the whole of* Tom Jones *when the orchestra walked out at the final dress rehearsal in the Titirangi War Memorial Hall. Others who come to mind are Ray and Audrey Saunderson, Wally and Beth Round and Don and Gilda Aitkin, Mrs Machellan and Bette Lott. I think some of our music is in the Playhouse Theatre Library. When the TLOC packed up, the costumes were given to St Simeons in New Lynn, who had a drama group. We were a very happy group. I can't remember any dissention in the ranks. I doubt whether we ever paid royalties and certainly never had a constitution or such like. We just did shows and enjoyed ourselves.*

Titirangi Theatre is still a strong society producing quality shows. Its origin was with the Country Women's Institute. Sandy Matheson recalls its history:[3]

In the early years of the war, small groups of New Zealand women in country areas would meet for friendship and support in troubled times. This was the beginning of the Country Women's Institute (CWI). At Titirangi a group was established in the newly built Macandrew Hall about 1940; besides companionship, knitting and other handcrafts were encouraged. Ethelwyn Geddes, who had recently arrived from Melbourne and had an interest in drama, soon had a play-reading group under way. This became 'The Drama Circle' and one-act plays were put on for and by the members.

It was not long before other groups in the Auckland area showed their interest and soon competitions were held for the Drama Cup of the CWI Federation. By the late 1940s this interest had spread throughout the country and many drama groups keenly competed for the British Drama League Cup. Titirangi had some success with Orphelia *in 1951, together with the* The Snow Queen. *Ethelwyn Geddes[4] commented:*

Last year we spent the best part of six months rehearsing and playing Orphelia *and the experience was invaluable. But we do not mean to make a habit of entering BDL competitions, as we would rather do a three-act play in the winter months. So we do not intend competing unless we have something very good indeed.*

Up to this time the cast consisted solely of women, but as productions became more ambitious, men were drawn into the group. It was also a practice that the principals in the current play would assist in another capacity, such as backstage, in the next production. With their production of Sordid Story *in 1956 they won the North Island Section of the BDL Competition in Wellington and received high commendation.*

Following on from this success, many three-act plays were produced in the next few years, including Still Life, The Cherry Orchard *and* The Diary of Anne Frank. *It was not unusual for the 'House Full' sign to be displayed at Macandrew Hall. As a consequence of this, a decision was made to enlarge the stage and improve the seating.*

By the early 1960s further plays were produced, including View from the Bridge, The Heiress, Uncle Vanya *and* Photo Finish. *It was at this time that the name was changed to Titirangi Drama. An era of excellent amateur theatre ended with Ethelwyn's death in 1967, but its very fine reputation has been maintained by others, right up to the present day.*

In 1982 the club moved to the Titirangi Beach Hall, sharing the space with the Folk Music Club. This, however, was not ideal, as many prospective audiences did not enjoy the thought of driving down the long, very windy, bush-lined road to the hall, especially on a wet winter's night. When the Waitemata City Council decided to buy Lopdell House from the Education Board for use as an Arts and Cultural Centre, President Heather Mogridge

The 1956 cast of *Sordid Story*. Standing (from left): Ethelwyn Geddes, Margaret Donner, Jean Cheal, Beryl Scott, Bruce Henderson, Helen Turvey, John Osborne. Sitting (from left): Pera Jackson, Rosemary Edgar. Janet Geddes Collection

The 1959 production *The Diary of Anne Frank* was fully booked due to its popularity. Lavender Sansom and Mac Geddes at the noticeboard by the Four Square store (now The Hardware Café).
Janet Geddes Collection

Geoff Hole's stunning set design for the 1962 production of Arthur Miller's *A View from the Bridge*. Glen Lester helped paint the set. Scott Hole Collection

Fred Watson as Bread in *The Blue Bird*. Janet Geddes Collection

David Booth and Ingrid Strewe in the production of *A Touch of the Sun*, December 1963. Janet Geddes Collection

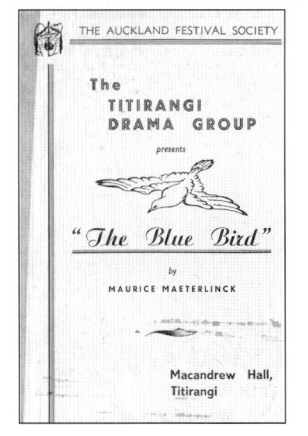

Programme of *The Blue Bird*, a 1964 drama group production.
Janet Geddes Collection

saw the opportunity to provide a permanent home for the theatre. After a good deal of fundraising and much back-breaking work, a basement garage was converted into a working space, and Heather's vision became a reality.

Since then the theatre has changed its name once more, this time to Titirangi Theatre. Many presidents and committees have contributed to an ongoing process of refurbishment, which has resulted in the intimate and attractive place that patrons enjoy today. Seating 90 people, the theatre is often a delightful surprise for those accustomed to paying town prices for their entertainment. The theatre's programme each year caters for all tastes, from Shakespeare to contemporary and locally written plays, and great pride is taken in maintaining a consistently high standard of production.

Ethelwyn's son Andrew[5] and daughter-in-law Janet recalled the 1950s and 1960s with enthusiasm. Indeed, earlier in the 1940s his mother carried Andrew on stage as a baby when she was directing productions.

Apparently Ethelwyn involved the wives of men who had been caught in the Malay Peninsula during the first part of the war. These women had been evacuated to New Zealand and were understandably anxious and lonely. Ethelwyn persuaded them to participate in the early plays and because of her magnetic appeal, obtained critics from the *New Zealand Herald* and the *Auckland Star* to give publicity to the productions. As well as providing friendship and interest for these women, the productions were welcomed by the entertainment-starved public of Titirangi. Other memories from later in the 1950s and 1960s were the drama club balls and the garden parties, where all were dressed up to raise funds for the group or additions to Macandrew Hall. *Titters for Tatters* was a very popular comedy review commenting on local body politics. Andrew and Janet remember the period when the Drama Club moved from Macandrew Hall to Titirangi Beach Hall as a very

Vi and Ron Gibbs (centre couple) in a scene from *Simply Spymen*, 1964. The Gibbs' were strong contributors to the group.
Janet Geddes Collection

British Drama League Cup certificate.

creative period, when the restrictions of the venue resulted in some avant-garde theatrical arrangements, and then the shift to Lopdell House with the formation of the basement theatre, which is still in use today.

Titirangi people involved in art and design in the 1950s and 1960s

In 1953, when Frank Carpay emigrated from Holland, Crown Lynn was run by Amalgamated Brick and Pipe, and was experiencing unprecedented growth. The company employed Frank in experimental design work, looking to develop new styles after the rather conventional and safe designs of the past.

Carpay was to teach design in conjunction with his work at Crown Lynn and in 1961 set out on his own as a printer of textiles. His designs had a strong Picasso influence, which were distinctive. It was difficult to make a living in original design in those days, as the New Zealand consumer was rather old-fashioned and conservative. However, it is generally agreed that in this field Frank Carpay was a pioneer, and his work is better appreciated decades later. An exhibition of his designs was held in 2002–2003 at the Hawke's Bay Museum, and a book was produced by the school of design at Unitec. During his most productive period, Carpay was a Titirangi resident; he built his own home by adding to a previous structure with the help of friend and fellow designer Peter Smeele, and architect Graham Smith.

Rosemarie Muller and her husband Harm were also part of the post-war emigration from Holland to New Zealand in the 1950s. They brought with them the house that they had designed and prefabricated in Holland. This house at 180 Atkinson Road is still occupied by Rosemarie, now retired from business. She had studied dress design in Europe and wasted no time in starting her own business, with a cutter, finisher and team of seamstresses making her designs, in the basement of her house. She sold to boutiques all over New Zealand and eventually had her own shop in Parnell. She specialized in knitwear

Frank Carpay and David Jenkin display their Handwerk ware. Hawke's Bay Museums Trust, Hawke's Bay Museum & Art Gallery

and employed several knitters to execute her unusual and attractive designs. She also gathered gem stones that were made into necklaces to complement her garments and two of these are in a permanent display of New Zealand haute couture at the Auckland War Memorial Museum.

The visual arts tradition continues in Titirangi. Past-president of Titirangi Painters, Edith Diggle[6], describes the club's early days in the 1980s and its continuation into the twenty-first century.

> In 1980 a small group of Titirangi residents who had a keen interest in art got together with the idea of creating a club. They advertised in local papers for members and with approximately 20 artists, Titirangi Painters was formed. Monthly meetings took place in various members' homes, where they shared ideas and encouraged each other. Tony Goodison became the first President, Stuart North was Treasurer and Lin Fleming was Secretary. Life membership has been given to those original members, including the above-named, Glen Anderson, Frances Baker, Isobel Cahill, Geoff Hole, Bruce Loretz and Dorothy White.
>
> Within the new club there was a group interested in creating their own gallery. At a Rotary luncheon in April 1983, Tony Goodison voiced her concern over the lack of local exhibiting facilities. Two days later she was offered the second floor of the barn in the forecourt of New Lynn Timbers by Mr Murray Williams, a partner in the firm.
>
> They set to work with each person contributing $100, and after almost two months of hard work transformed the unlined, cobwebbed loft into an art gallery. It was officially opened with an exhibition on 8 August 1983. In this venue members and invited artists could sell, hire, display and demonstrate art. Exhibitions were changed every two weeks and one part of the gallery was set aside to display young adult art. It was a non-commercial venture with profit going back into the gallery. Unfortunately The Loft closed after 12 months, when the building was sold.
>
> Meanwhile, Titirangi Painters continued developing enthusiasm by holding exhibitions all over the Auckland region, including at Lopdell House in Titirangi. The increasing membership led the club to hiring Macandrew Hall in Titirangi Road for meetings and eventually a move was made to the Green Bay Community House.
>
> When Avondale College was severely damaged by fire in 1990, Titirangi Painters put on a special exhibition and contributed $772.50 towards the new gymnasium.
>
> In 1992 Bruce Loretz, then President, suggested Titirangi Memorial Hall as the venue for an annual winter exhibition. With encouragement from Bob Harvey, the Mayor of Waitakere City, the winter exhibition has become an important event in the local calendar.
>
> In 2010 the club has 50 members and still holds to the original concept of sharing experiences in painting as being the essence of the organisation. As a result of this support, several artists have achieved recognition. Monthly meetings continue to be held at the Green Bay Community Centre, where artists bring their paintings for criticism and advice. Demonstrations and talks are also given. The club holds several exhibitions each year, in the Rose Gardens in November, St Heliers and Mission Bay during the summer and then the highlight, the winter show at Titirangi War Memorial Hall, featuring between 400–600 paintings. The exceptionally high standard of these exhibitions attracts buyers and viewers from a wide area.

Present head of the Elam School of Art and Kaitiaki Maori Hon. Curator of Maori Art, Jonathan Mane-Wheoki, of Nga Puhi and English descent, was educated at Titirangi Primary School. A graduate of the School of Fine Arts Canterbury and Trinity College of Music, London, Jonathan was previously Dean of Music and Fine Arts at the University of

Canterbury and Director of Art and Visual Culture at Te Papa. Perhaps some of the artistic enthusiasm of Titirangi influenced him as a child to pursue this distinguished career in arts. Auckland and Titirangi welcome him back.

Music and literature have never been forgotten in Titirangi. In the 1950s and 1960s Harry Atkinson, Thayer Fairburn and others formed an informal classical music club, which met to listen to recordings. In more recent times, musical interests have been catered for by several different groups. A number of Titirangi classically trained musicians are members of the Waitakere City Orchestra led by Titirangi resident Brigid Bisley, which delivers high quality concerts to wider Waitakere City audiences. The Waitakere City Orchestra gave its first free concert in the Titirangi War Memorial Hall in March 2003 to an appreciative audience. Conductor and indefatigable worker/manager Brigid Ursula Bisley[7] recalled that Titirangi had several prominent classical musicians in previous generations, especially after the war with the influx of European migrants such as Otto Hubscher, a fine musician of the 1950s who taught in schools around West Auckland. Even famed conductor Georg Tintner lived in the west for a time in the 1950s. Singers from western areas are drawn into Show West, a group that contains several Titirangi musicians, including the musical director Judy King.

The Folk Music Club has been active for many years and still meets regularly in the Titirangi Beach Hall. Interest in modern music is also high and the Titirangi Music Festival held each year attracts listeners and participants from all over the Auckland area. The Music Festival was instituted in 2005 and brings a wide variety of folk, jazz and band music to Titirangi village venues.

Novelist and playwright Maurice Shadbolt is a major New Zealand writer who lived in Titirangi for 42 years of his productive working life. His works of fiction often used New Zealand history as a setting and basis for his plots and his stories; *Among the Cinders* (1965), *A Touch of Clay* (1974), *Season of the Jew* (1986), *Monday's Warriors* (1990), *One of Ben's* (1993), and *Dove on the Waters* (1996) are widely read and appreciated for their distinctively New Zealand flavour. Maurice Shadbolt lived in Arapito Road overlooking the Manukau, and after his death his house was bought by the Waitakere City Council with the aim of turning it into a writers' residence.

The Going West Books and Writers Festival, a literary festival held in Titirangi annually since 1995, is supported by the Waitakere City Council and organised by Oratia residents Murray Gray and Naomi McCleary. It is an event that attracts literary people to the War Memorial Hall from far and wide to analyse and discuss books. Thus, Titirangi maintains its reputation as a centre for quality arts, crafts, music and literature begun in the 1950s and still attracts many people to this small community on the fringe of Auckland.

1   Matheson, Sandy. Oral History by Marc Bonny, West Auckland Historical Soc. Inc., 2009.
2   Gunn, Jim. Oral History by Marc Bonny, West Auckland Historical Soc. Inc., March 2006.
3   Matheson, Sandy. Oral History by Marc Bonny, West Auckland Historical Soc. Inc., 2009.
4   Geddes, Ethelwyn in archives of Country Women's Institute
5   Geddes, Andrew and Janet. Interview by Marc Bonny and the editors, 2010.
6   Diggle, Edith. Interview by Marc Bonny and the editors, 2010.
7   Bisley, Brigid. Interview with the editors, 2010.

13

Rangiwai and the Geddes family

The story of Titirangi would not be complete without writing about the Geddes family who, in 1940, bought the Rangiwai property from the Atkinson family. One of Henry Atkinson's three houses in Titirangi, Rangiwai, built in 1915, stands on the top of the hill adjoining Titirangi Village.

In the early days Rangiwai looked out at all of Auckland, including over both harbours and the Waitakere Ranges: a 360-degree panorama. Today, Rangiwai is surrounded by beautiful trees, some from the Northern Hemisphere and some New Zealand natives. The view is still there, but screened more than it was in the early twentieth century.

Herman McKail Geddes was a third generation New Zealander, one-eighth Maori of Ngapuhi (Hokianga) ancestry with traceable whakapapa. His great-grandfather, Colin Gillies, had settled in the north in 1828. Gillies' daughter married William Webster, a sawmiller from Scotland, at Wairere near Mangungu in the Hokianga. Their daughter, Mary Annabella Webster married John Geddes, who had come to New Zealand from Scotland in 1840 at the age of 19. John eventually set up his own business, Brown Barrett and Co., in Auckland. The firm made sauces, including tomato-sauce products, which were very popular.

Ethelwyn Geddes, who married H. McKail Geddes (he never used his first Christian name and was generally known as Mac), was of Australian ancestry. Ethelwyn's mother was from the Melbourne family of Robert Reid, merchants. Her father was Edward Bates, an architect in Melbourne who had designed the Melbourne Library. Ethelwyn was an intelligent, well-educated woman, having gained a Master of Arts with honours in History and a Diploma of Education in 1923. Ethelwyn met H. McKail on the ship *Niagara* in 1927 and then she came to New Zealand from Melbourne.

In 2010, John Geddes, his wife Claire and their son are residents at Rangiwai. John's brother Andrew and his wife Janet live in an adjacent house on part of the original property.

H. McKail Geddes had an abiding interest in the environment and was involved in many local affairs. Ethelwyn Geddes was a dynamic woman and a leader in many community endeavours in Titirangi during the thirties, forties and fifties. They had three sons, John, Edward and Andrew. As Edward died at an early age, John and Andrew inherited Rangiwai.

Death of former Councilor H. McKail Geddes[1]

His worship the Mayor I.G. McHardy Esq. paid a tribute to the services of the late H. McKail Geddes who had been a member of the Waitemata County Council from 1962 to

Rangiwai.
John Geddes Collection

1968 as a Riding Member for Titirangi. While a councillor he was a member of the Finance, Parks and Pension and Housing Committees. He represented the Council on the Auckland Suburban, Local Bodies Association and the Auckland War Memorial Museum Council. He was also chairman of the Titirangi Fire Services Committee. Prior to this he was a member of the Titirangi County Town Committee.

One of his prime concerns was the protection of the natural environment. He played an extremely active part during the development and bringing into operation of the County's first District Scheme, in which the retention of bush areas of Titirangi was encouraged by providing minimum sized sections. He also immersed himself in many of the local activities, including senior citizens, scout and war memorial functions and he was a former president of the Auckland Tree Society.

John and Claire Geddes completed a significant renovation to Rangiwai in 1978, just after they occupied the residence. The late Vernon Brown was the architect, and Waitakere City has now listed the home as one of historical and architectural significance.

John McKail Geddes was educated at Auckland University and admitted as a barrister and solicitor in 1954. He has emulated his father's interest in environmental matters; during his career as a partner of Rudd, Garland and Horrocks, he was one of a group with D.A.R. Williams who formed the Environmental Defence Society. His interest in the environment also led him to the organisation for the Protection of Trees in Urban Areas, which prepares submissions to parliament on Property Law, the Fencing Act and Removal of Trees. He is also a member of the Tree Council for Auckland, a protagonist for the preservation of historic buildings, and is one-time president of the Auckland Society of Arts. Music is an abiding interest in the Geddes family and John plays in a Law Society Dixieland Band, which entertains with great fervour and some comedy.

Rangiwai has been the venue for a number of functions and garden parties over the years and Claire and John have been very much amiable hosts at this historic residence.

1   Minutes of Waitemata City Council, 26 October 1978.

14

Nature and nurture

In pre-European times, dense subtropical rainforest clothed the hills around Titirangi. On the ridges kauri (*Agathis australis*) reigned supreme, trees up to 1000 years old with huge, spreading crowns full of epiphytic asteliads, orchids and ferns. On the ground grew kauri grass (*Astelia trinerva*) and various small shrubs. A remnant of this forest can today be seen in the area on Scenic Drive opposite the Arataki Centre, where a small area of the original forest has been retained. In pre-European times this type of forest was probably found on many ridges around Titirangi. The only rival to kauri was rimu (*Dacrydium cupressinum*), found extensively throughout the Waitakere Ranges and in some places more dominant than kauri. Both these great trees, along with kahikatea, miro, and matai, belong to the same southern gymnosperm family. Kahikatea (*Dacrycarpus dacrydioides*) and miro (*Podocarpus ferrugineus*) are also found in the Waitakeres; the former is common in wetter, lower areas and stands of kahikatea can be seen at Titirangi Beach and in other gully areas. Miro is less common but formed part of the ranges flora in pre-European times. Another

The village in the 1920s. The famous puriri tree at left (cut down in the early 1950s) and the tea kiosk and Bert Atkinson's house in the background. The fence is in front of the three Shaw family houses.
Mia Stein Collection

large tree still common in regenerating bush is rewarewa (*Knightia excelsa*), and on coastal slopes puriri (*Vitex lucens*). Some large puriri are still standing; one was a landmark in Titirangi Village in the early years of the twentieth century.

Around the village today, what we see is regenerating forest. During the mid- to late-nineteenth and early twentieth centuries, all the forest except for tiny remnants was milled, then the smaller shrubs were burnt and the ground was sown with grass to provide pastures for the farm animals of settler families. It was not until the 1930s and 1940s that large areas were left to regenerate. Fortunately, seeds in the ground responded quickly to the opportunity and it was not many years before the scrub and tree fern cover reappeared; in the shelter those plants provided the seedlings of the larger trees started to flourish. Protection of the regenerating forest was achieved, firstly due to the demand for water catchment areas, then with the formation of the Auckland Centennial Memorial Park in 1940–41. The expansion of the park during subsequent decades brought into protection areas near Titirangi Village, including Exhibition Drive, Clark's Bush between Huia and Woodlands Park Roads, and Atkinson Park, with its track to Titirangi Beach. The City Council reserves also were largely left to regenerate, so Rahui Kahika (on the slope between Park Road and Green Bay) and numerous smaller reserves acquired their bush cover, adding to the green woodland image of Titirangi.

Today the trees are synonymous with Titirangi and most private landowners value their woodland image, although the bush has been invaded by numerous exotic weeds that flourish in the well-watered soil. Various drives to stem invasion by the most troublesome weeds such as kahili ginger and flannel or tobacco weed have been initiated by citizens, but

View from Rangiwai Hill to Mt Atkinson. Photographer: James D. Richardson, 16 December 1921. Auckland City Libraries Special Collections, 4-4089

inroads into some bush areas have been made. Some garden plants, such as jasmine and asparagus fern (not really a fern), have been planted and have subsequently proved to be aggressive weeds in the Titirangi environment. Education of private landowners is an ongoing task in an effort to keep the park areas from weed invasion. On the other hand, the planting of some garden plants, for example camellias and rhododendrons, particularly suited to the environment have added welcome spots of colour to the native green. The introduction of foreign animals, notably possums, pigs, stoats, cats and dogs, has also modified the native bush, and has impacted negatively on native birds. During the early twenty-first century, control of possum numbers by the Auckland Regional Council has helped particularly in the regeneration of certain plants such as the native kohekohe and fuchsia, but private citizens have been urged to help by trapping possums in their gardens (thereby saving their vegetable gardens as well). It is questionable as to whether the area will ever be rid of possums entirely, but efforts to keep numbers down are essential for the well-being of the woodlands. Proximity to the large regional park where the Auckland Regional Council and conservation organisations, such as the Forest and Bird Society that have made huge efforts to re-introduce rare native birds, means that Titirangi residents are urged to keep domestic animals such as cats and dogs under control and not allow them to become feral. This responsibility is usually eagerly undertaken by people who wish to live in the area.

Aerial image showing Titirangi and Waitakere Ranges, 1947. Alexander Turnbull Library, Wellington, NZ, Whites Aviation Collection, Ref. No. WA-07556

Park Drive (now Park Road) in 1919, with Rangiwai on top of the hill. The tall teatree growth indicates the first stage of bush regeneration after the logging of the 1850s. In this picture the dirt road is in good shape, but for most of the year it would have been a muddy trench, like many other roads in the area.

Photographer: James D. Richardson, 12 October 1919. Auckland City Libraries Special Collections, 4-4085

Among Titirangi's eminent residents was former Professor of Classics at Auckland University, biblical scholar and ardent conservationist, Edward Musgrave Blaiklock. His pupil, John Staniland said of him,

> His appreciation of nature was aesthetic and scenic rather than biological. He had an intimate knowledge of landscape and his favourite trees but did not pretend to be familiar with all the species.[1]

He so loved Titirangi and the Waitakeres that even with a full career as an academic and writer of about 80 books and numerous articles, he managed to write four especially personal books about his life,[2] in which Titirangi features largely.

His childhood before and during the First World War was spent on a farm of 30 acres, the dream of his English emigrant father, in the area that is now occupied by the Green Bay Schools, in Godley Road. He includes lyrical references to the coast from Green Bay around to Titirangi Beach, and also to the old Maori track that traversed the farm in the region of Godley Road. His philosophical and poetic essays in the newspapers the *New Zealand Herald* and *The Weekly News*, under the pen name of 'Grammaticus', were read and appreciated by thousands throughout the country. He spent a large part of his adult life in Titirangi, and one of his sons, David attended the Titirangi School. His sons and their families are still well known in the village.

Kauri is regenerating profusely around Titirangi. Most are young trees less than 100 years old, but they hold the promise of becoming forest giants in another few hundred years if they can be kept in good health. A present worry is the occurrence of a soil water-borne pathogen called PTA (*Phytophthora taxon Agathis*), which targets kauri in areas of the Waitakeres, and particularly in the semi-urban areas around Titirangi.

Present research is being performed in an attempt to discover more about this disease, its cause and possible prevention or cure for infection, but at this time (2010) there is no cure and infection rates seem to be increasing. There are a few mature kauri that escaped the axe in the nineteenth century; these give visitors an idea of the grandeur of the original forest. Two in Clark's Bush near the Village can be seen on the track between Tainui and Manuka roads, Waima.

There have been a number of organisations created in the area for residents and ratepayers, but two organisations stand out because of their age and durability.[3]

The Titirangi Beautifying and Bush Preservation Society, formed in 1920s by 50 ratepayers, was instrumental in keeping a strong watch on the ecological shape of Titirangi and was, in a sense, giving voice to the desire not to sacrifice any more forest or individual trees. Many voices in Greater Auckland in the early to mid-1900s expressed a desire to enhance the Waitakere Parkland.[4] This society vigorously protested some council decisions and made some constructive suggestions, as is recorded in the press and in early council archives. Early correspondence shows a very vital Beautifying Society, in a letter dated 27 January 1926, referring to an arrangement for six County Council workmen to plant trees under the direction of the Society. The Society lapsed for a short period but was revived at a meeting held in 1933 that was initiated by Messrs N.G. Hawkins and A.W. Campbell. In

Professor Blaiklock at the gate to Exhibition Drive. West Auckland Historical Society, Blaiklock Collection

1936 the Society became incorporated. Mr Holt became Secretary and later President of the society. One of its first acts was to plant the Pleasant Road corner reserve opened by the Governor-General Lord Bledisloe.[5]

Often led in mid-twentieth century years by Professor E.M. Blaiklock, the Society seemed to have had the respect of the Council. Its aim was to preserve the natural beauty of the Waitakere Ranges, to prevent destruction, and to maintain vigilance to prevent unnecessary destruction by Post and Telegraph and roading contractors. Professor Blaiklock deplored the practice at that time of giving felled timber for firewood to the gangs of men who worked on roading contracts.[6]

In August and September of 1941, the Waitemata Council threatened to cut down the famous Titirangi Village puriri tree, which had stood as an arboreal post office, goods delivery location and meeting place for decades. Later the Council denied that this was their intention, and controversy lapsed during the dark days of the Second World War. At the time the tree was calculated to be upwards of 150 years old.[7] The tree was reprieved for the time being, until in 1952 when commercial interests decided its fate.

Nature and nurture

In 1935 Waitemata Council offered an innovative idea: that the Beautifying Society would be subsidised £50 per year by the Council for beautifying work and making bus shelters. This demonstrates that the Society was well supported by the community. In 1926 the Titirangi Bush Preservation Society (consisting of 50 ratepayers), in a letter to Council, made certain demands for bylaws such as keeping speed on roads down to 12 miles per hour and that section size be kept to half an acre or more and that bush be preserved where possible.

In 1952 correspondence shows the Titirangi Beautifying and Bush Preservation Society was still writing to protest against Council allowing another large puriri tree to be cut down in Titirangi Beach Road. However, in June 1952 Titirangi's puriri tree, saved some 11 years before, was finally cut down by Council contractors to make way for a commercial development; so ended the puriri tree saga. The Waitakere Ranges Protection Society, the Royal Forest and Bird Society and other smaller conservation groups in the ranges have now taken up the bush-saving ethos of the Titirangi Beautifying Society with a wider focus.

Specifically concerning itself with Titirangi, the village and immediate environs, is the Titirangi Ratepayers' and Residents' Association Inc. (TRRA). This group has had an equally long history, with slightly different concerns. Correspondence in Council archives shows the Titirangi Ratepayers' (not incorporated) in action in 1926 with regard to roads. This topic is again evident in correspondence during the last war and under the presidency of John Grierson, also in 1947 and again in 1949 concerning bus routes and roading. Although residents had long sought improvements in roading, it was not until 1955 that the existing metal roads began to be improved by tarsealing. The Ratepayers' associations seemed to be very local during these times, indicative of the isolation of groups of houses on the fringe of the urban area. In 1952 the Titirangi Filters Ratepayers' and Residents' Association suggested to the Council that a playing area be set aside for development in connection with a Titirangi Town Planning Scheme, and that this be on de Brabandere's property, Huia Road. This area is now part of Tangiwai Reserve.

It would seem that the TRRA fell into a period of recess in the early 1970s for several years, but the catalyst that restarted the association was roading and child safety when getting to and from Titirangi Primary School. The intersection modifications at the junction of South Titirangi and Titirangi roads were highly contentious, as was the meeting of five roads outside Titirangi Primary School. TRRA were highly critical, as it seems were most of the local residents, of the Waitemata Council Works Committee in the late 1970s, and made vigorous deputations to drive the 'Murray North' proposal for the roundabout, widening and safety of the Atkinson Road, Scenic Drive, and Huia and Kohu roads intersection. Sewer reticulation was also controversial and TRRA became a strong voice for Titirangi residents.

Pim van der Voort, who has served several terms over 12 years on the Committee and is a past president, said the catalyst for the redevelopment of Titirangi Village in 1993 was TRRA. This occupied the Association for over four years. In 1982, 1600 residents joined the organisation because of restrictive building regulations that became evident when Waitemata City Council presented the District Plan.

Through the years TRRA have kept Titirangi's well-being in mind, with strong committees and an emphasis on a beautiful and tidy Titirangi. In recent years, the Association has produced folders with information for new residents about living in the bush, pest and weed removal and other helpful ideas. A titoki tree was planted outside the supermarket by Titirangi schoolchildren, an event fostered by TRRA in the late 1990s. Of late, TRRA has been concerned with the development of the Village, including the enlargement of Lopdell Art Centre and new commercial developments. As the road rises towards Titirangi Village, TRRA has erected a mosaic sign indicating the suburb at the junction of Titirangi and Pleasant roads. The Association also keeps a good watch on ecological matters, often joining in support of like-minded organisations in the Waitakere Ranges.

The unveiling of the Waima Stone

The Waima Community Group was formed several years ago to promote community spirit, understanding of nature and a sense of history. It was decided to give the area identity and a sense of belonging by erecting a stone with the name Waima on it at the entrance to the area. The stone was set in Woodlands Park Road near the junction of Scenic Drive to commemorate the history of Maori and early settlers. It also defines the location of the film set for Rudall Haywood's film *Rewi's Last Stand*.

Horticulture and an interest in plants have always been popular in Titirangi, so in addition to the natural woodland there are some gardens specially planted for enjoyment that are open to the public. Foremost among these is the volunteer maintained West Lynn Gardens, situated on the cusp between Titirangi and New Lynn. Its history and description is contributed by Alison O'Grady.[8]

> *West Lynn Gardens is a beautiful place. Its environment contains a variety of birds, native and exotic trees, landscaped lawns, rose-covered arbours, secret pathways among colourful shrubs, gazebos, seats and tables, a petanque court and a butterfly house.*
>
> *The stated vision of West Lynn Garden Society is to encourage people to learn more about the interactions between horticulture and ecology so they will have greater appreciation of the need to protect our country's unique heritage through responsible gardening practice.*
>
> *The garden is situated at 73 Parker Avenue, New Lynn, and has its origin in 1981 when Eden Garden Society decided to purchase the Lyndale Nursery property in Parker Avenue and transform it into a community garden. At the time of purchase the 2.5 hectares carried two titles, one held by the New Lynn Borough Council, the other by the Waitemata County Council (now the Waitakere City Council).*
>
> *After two years of intensive development by an enthusiastic band of volunteers under the direction of horticulturist Jack Clark, the garden was ready to welcome its first visitors. The official opening took place on 11 November 1983. The Mayor of New Lynn Borough Council, Bruce McNaughton, and the Mayor of Waitemata County Council, Tim Shadbolt, were both present, along with other dignitaries and members of the public, and a cedar tree was planted by Tim Shadbolt to mark the occasion.*
>
> *A further milestone took place in February 1992 when the West Lynn Garden Society was formed with Bruce McNaughton, former Mayor of New Lynn, as patron, and a number of West Auckland enthusiasts elected to serve on the committee. Although the Committee enjoyed the freedom to make decisions about the daily running of the garden,*

the land was still owned by Eden Garden and the Society felt vulnerable. They did not wish to see their garden sold at some future date by Eden Garden so they set their sights on gaining ownership.

In 2005, with generous donations from the Waitakere City Council, Portage Licensing Trust and the Auckland Savings Bank Community Trust, the land was purchased from Eden Garden Society. As the major donor, Waitakere City Council secured their interest in the property by way of a Conservation Covenant under section 77 Reserve Act 1977.

The West Lynn Garden Society is now proud owner of this wonderful asset in Waitakere City, responsible for the maintenance and development of the garden but working in partnership with the Council. Following a thorough survey, Council provides a two-year management plan to the Society outlining the work that needs to be done in the various areas of the garden. At the end of the two-year period, a further inspection of the garden is undertaken by Council and goals set for the ensuing two-year period.

Many community events have taken place at West Lynn Garden over the years. Notable among these are tree plantings by five Governor-Generals, (Sir Paul Reeves, Dame Cath Tizard, Sir Bryan Hardie-Boys, Dame Sylvia Cartwright and Sir Anand Satyanand), by Prime Minister David Lange and by New Zealand hero Sir Edmund Hillary.

West Lynn Garden is a popular place for weddings and wedding photos and an endowment scheme provides opportunity for people to endow a particular tree or seat in memory of a family member or friend.

The idea of incorporating a butterfly conservation programme was first raised in 1989 by entomologist Dr Peter Maddison. Today the monarch butterfly house education programme provides schools with a unique educational opportunity. Each butterfly season thousands of junior school students (years 1 and 2) experience the joy of being among butterflies and learning about the monarch butterfly's life cycle.

West Lynn Garden has no paid staff. It owes its existence entirely to the hard work and continuing commitment of a group of dedicated volunteers who manage and maintain it, keeping it open daily from 10 a.m. till 4 p.m. for the enjoyment of everyone.

Titirangi today could be proclaimed as the most beautiful suburb of Auckland, the bush regeneration from the degradation during the settler period is spectacular and the village is the focal point of West Auckland for art and tourism. Tourists from everywhere flock to the coffee houses and restaurants and tour groups into the Waitakeres often make Titirangi their first stop for refreshments. Everywhere one looks there is a sense of beauty and neatness, and gone are the days of rough tracks and clay roads; the Waitakere City of the past several decades has ensured that services including roads have been well maintained.

In 1993 Titirangi Village went through a major upgrade with a pleasant rock wall providing a secure and interesting area outside the shops for pedestrians to walk and communicate. Extra pavements and crossing shelters were erected, native trees were planted in the main precinct, lighting fixtures were improved and there was a major project to place electricity cables underground.

The *Titirangi Tatler* newspaper/magazine was first published in December 2002; its focus on Titirangi helps to give residents an increased sense of identity, as well as keeping residents up to date with local events and people in the news. Groups such as the Titirangi Ratepayers' and Residents' Association Inc. and various clubs and organisations, including the RSA and the churches, maintain the values of the past.

Because of good communications, residents work in all areas of Auckland. Young and old enjoy the bush feel of Titirangi and included in all this there is a wonderful community spirit that is not necessarily engendered in a more traditional urban situation.

One can sit in the village and see tui and kereru, especially since the bird populations have been enhanced by pest control. Weed control is still needed in the village and immediate environs, but the planting and saving of trees is a typical Titirangi activity. The local library has recently been modernised and the War Memorial Hall is used extensively for functions including the annual Going West Books and Writers Festival, monthly art and craft markets, and the Titirangi Painters' exhibitions. The old Atkinson house in Rangiwai Road, for many years the Community House, has given way to a modern Community House complex in the grounds of the War Memorial Hall. Lopdell House, a Titirangi landmark, is shortly to be upgraded with expanded room for art displays and an enlarged theatre. The three fungal-like sculptures on the roundabout, which locals now regard fondly as another landmark, continue to stand and are repainted every few years. Titirangi Primary School has a swimming pool, extra rooms and grounds and a thriving roll. There are now many schools in the area catering for all ages. The Titirangi Rudolph Steiner School offers an alternative view of education that attracts many from the area and also from outside Titirangi. The Steiner School is also the organiser of the monthly markets at the War Memorial Hall attracting buyers and sellers from all over Auckland and as far as Coromandel who sell arts and crafts of high quality. At the bottom of the hill leading to Laingholm, Landing Road marks the historic site of water access to Titirangi, and the old bridge spanning Little Muddy sits alongside the new sealed highway that leads to Laingholm, Parau, Huia and Whatipu.

History still permeates the area but increasingly the landscape is covered more with the beautiful rainforest that is Titirangi and the Waitakeres.

As noted amateur historian Jack Diamond said just before he died, 'I don't like coming so much now out West as you now can't see where the history was'. How interesting! But the history is still there if you look closely.

1. Staniland, John. 2006 'Professor Blaiklock' in Harvey, Bruce and Trixie, *Waitakere Ranges*. Waitakere Ranges Protection Society Incorporated, Auckland.
2. Blaiklock, E.M. *Ten Pounds an Acre*. A.H. and A.W. Reed, Auckland, 1965.
3. Waitakere City Council, Waitemata County Archives.
4. Turner, Arnold. 2006 'History of the Waitakere Parkland in Waitakere Ranges' in Harvey, Bruce and Trixie, *Waitakere Ranges*. Waitakere Ranges Protection Society Incorporated, Auckland, 2006, p. 343.
5. Automobile Association Official Bulletin, May 7 1949.
6. Ibid.
7. Waitakere City Council Archives and *New Zealand Herald*, 30 August 1941 and 1 September 1941.
8. O'Grady, Alison. *West Lynn Garden: A Place of Beauty*. West Lynn Garden Society Inc., Auckland, 2010.

The following memoirs have been extracted from oral and written articles. The oral histories have been collected by Marc Bonny and other members of the West Auckland Historical Society over a long period of time. A few have been previously published, such as the memoir by Essie Hodge about her early schooldays, which was previously published in the magazine celebrating the 125th anniversary of the Titirangi School. Some extracts have been previously published in the *Titirangi Tatler* and West Auckland Historical Society newsletters. The editors have tried to choose a variety of points of view from different periods and different areas, but have not attempted to be comprehensive in any respect. The works have been lightly edited to preserve continuity and delete digressions, but effort has been made to retain the style of the original.

W.N. Bishop at Clark's kauri in 2007. Marc Bonny and Mr Bishop were visiting the three major remaining kauri trees in the area: Bishop's kauri, Clark's kauri and Alley's kauri. Marc Bonny Collection

Part 2
The Memoirs

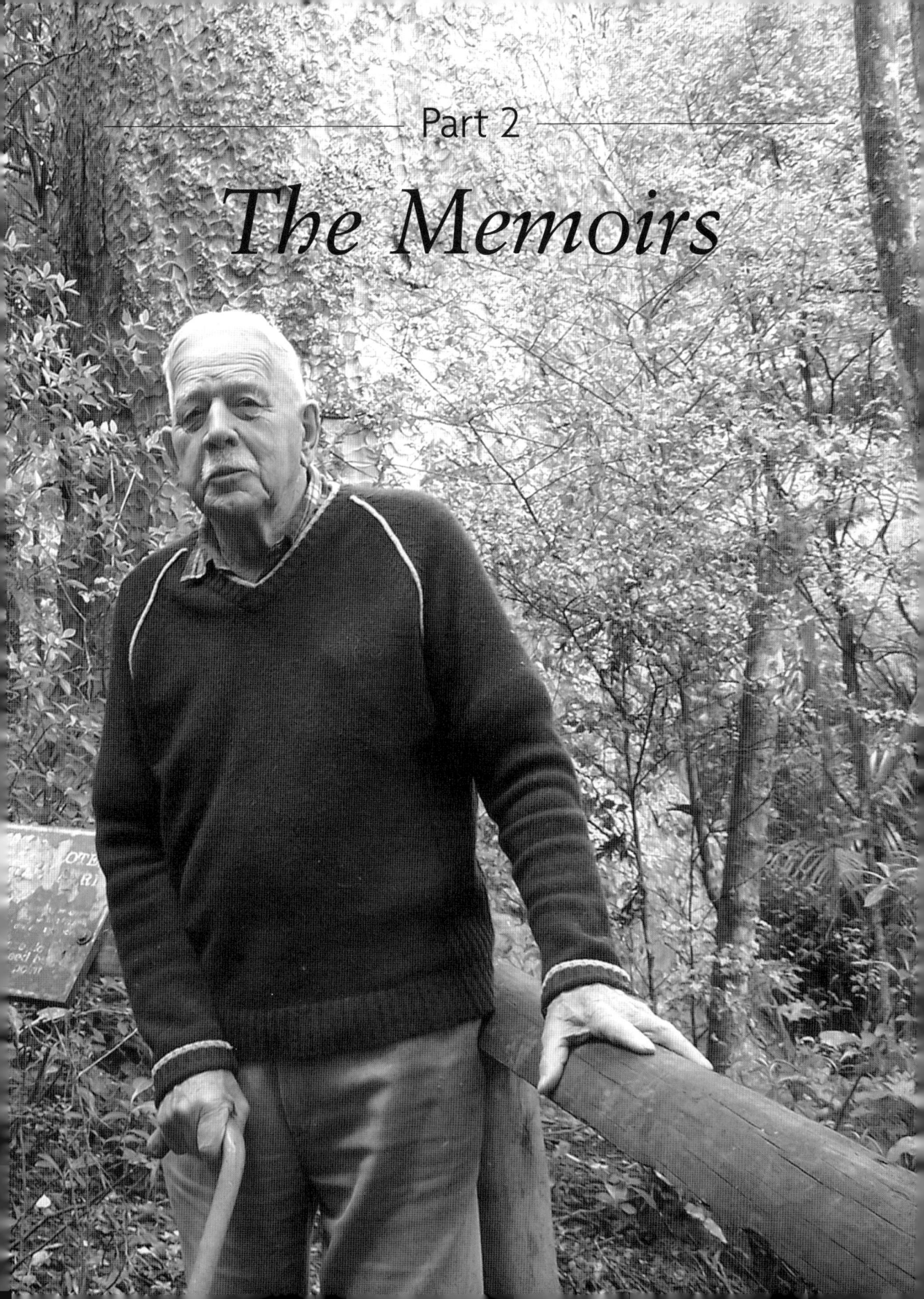

Essie Hodge

Essie Hodge was a granddaughter of pioneers John and Elizabeth Bishop and daughter of John Joseph (Chappie) Bishop. This essay was written in the early 1980s; Essie recalls the Titirangi of her childhood, which spans the early years of the twentieth century. This memoir was first published in the West Auckland Historical Society Newsletter 109 in March 1989.

Early Titirangi

Many people have the idea that Titirangi was always covered with dense native bush. This may have been true at one time when Titirangi was part of the great Kauri Forest but it was not so in the days of my childhood. So much of the kauri timber had been cut out by the early pit-sawyers. Then came the early settlers. Mr and Mrs John Bishop, my grandparents, were the first among these. The timber for their buildings were pit-sawn on the place and sent, by boat, to Onehunga to be dressed.

My grandparents had an interest in a sawmill in Freeman's Bay (later known as the Kauri Timber Co.) and owned an extensive property which has been described in early Year Books as a well-established and well-run farm. My father was their son, John Joseph Bishop (called Chappie). The entrance to my grandfather's property was a large wooden kauri gate called, of course, 'Bishops gate'. When I was a small child it seemed as if we owned all of Titirangi. What is now called Mt Atkinson, was known by the humbler name of Bishop's Hill. Everywhere one looked was under cultivation. The main road to Huia was via South Titirangi Road and in those days was called School Road because the old school stood on an elevated spot there.

Just past the school was a large fruit farm that extended from the road almost down to Little Muddy Creek. This farm was established by Mr McEldowney and his family. He and his wife with two sons had just come out from Ireland. Other children were born later. How I admired these people: homesick they may have been but

Bishop family member sitting on log, Clark's kauri. Waitakere Library & Information Services, Print Collection (Titirangi—Bishop)

prepared to start again from scratch. Our pioneers were truly the backbone of the country. By sheer hard work from dawn to dusk the McEldowneys established an orchard producing fruit for export. Very early in the morning, before 5 a.m. at least twice a week, the long wagonette drawn by four horses, laden with cases of fruit securely anchored, went into market. Although most farms had their own orchards to provide them with fresh fruit for eating, the surplus for preserving, McEldowneys was the only commercial orchard. I often wish that I could taste again some of the old varieties, especially Irish Peach apples, so delicious for eating. My sister and I often took our books and a cushion and sat under the tree and indulged ourselves. The Pairmain apple, regarded as good for making cider, was another favourite. Almost all of Titirangi was under cultivation. Most of the farms were mixed farms.

Adjoining us, down the valley, bordering Little Muddy Creek, was de Brabandere's farm. These folk came from Belgium and spoke Flemish. Once again by sheer hard work they established a good sheep and dairy herd, mostly Jersey cattle. When Robert de Brabandere sold off most of his animals he bought a pedigree bull for breeding purposes.

Anne Lydia Dagley (b. 1885) and her husband, Arthur Dagley. Anne was the only daughter of James and Lydia McEldowney. Joyce Clark (nee McEldowney) Collection

Farms stretched all the way through Brooklyn (now called Parau) to Huia. Here I will digress to tell you that my grandson, a ranger at Huia, recently came upon the remains of a pit-sawing site. It even had some of the structure that held the logs in place still standing.

Now to get back to the farms. There was one in Brooklyn that I must mention, owned by Mr Duff Laing. It was a very well-run farm, but what impressed me, when I was a girl, was the large expanse of concrete in the dairy area. With the aid of a hard broom and plenty of water it was kept spotlessly clean. The farm is now submerged beneath the Parau Dam. Duff Laing's son Leslie drove the cream wagon. On his return journey he drove his horses at breakneck speed down the winding road (mostly downhill) but never had an accident in spite of all the predictions of the local folk. He was an excellent horseman.

I learned from my father and his eldest sister, Aunty Winder (Christiana Bishop) of the early days on the Bishop farm—the paddocks of buckwheat, oats, barley, maize and other crops grown to make the farm self-sufficient. In those days before my lifetime, there were working bullocks. Outside on the grass at the entrance to our place was one of the old bullock wagons on which my sister and I used to play. But during my young days Mr Hibernia Smyth's bullocks were still a common sight. If anything very heavy was to be hauled they were in demand.

Essie Hodge

Grandfather died of pneumonia at the early age of 52 and Gran Bishop was left to carry on. On this large farm there were shepherds who controlled certain areas. These shepherds, of course, stayed on and helped to run the farm after Grandfather's death. When they died they were not replaced, although in my time the paddocks bore their names: Smith's paddock, Nixon's, Jack Nelson's, Jack Parr's. This last name was famous for the interest it aroused. It was believed that Jack Parr buried his money, and so when he died the hunt was on. When my boy cousins came to stay with us digging for treasure was one of the highlights of the visit. We never found it, but my parents were convinced that they knew who got it.

McEldowney's homestead, once surrounded by orchard and farm paddocks, now hemmed in at 18 Grendon Road. At the time of this image, 2007, the owners were having new decks built. Marc Bonny Collection

For the early part of my girlhood Uncle Will and my father ran the farm, but on a reduced scale. Later, as often happens when brothers marry, the partnership was broken off. We still had paddocks of oats and maize and some paddocks closed off for hay. The maize was so high that we used to hide in it. When the hay was cut and dried we loved riding on the haycart to the barn where it was stored. Haymaking was a special time. The grass was cut with scythes and the men seemed to develop a rhythmic pattern. Of course this hard work had to be rewarded and we children loved to carry over from our kitchen the food provided and partake of it. A specially made cold drink was a feature. It was made from oatmeal, lemon juice and cold spring water. Sometimes when there was no more sleeping room in the house, we brought blankets and slept in the hay. It was lovely if you didn't mind an inquisitive little mouse!

There was no modern machinery; we had horse-drawn ploughs, harrows, spades for all types of work, and scythes and pitchforks for haymaking and many, many more implements and tools. During the haymaking, should my father see a skylark fly up, he would hunt for the dear wee nest with its tiny eggs, and having found it, leave that small patch of grass uncut. Have you seen a skylark soaring into the sky, up and up, singing until it becomes a mere speck? They are rarely seen in Titirangi now, but I believe that they are plentiful further towards Huia. Another bird that we have lost is the weka; a friendly, mischievous ground-dwelling bird.

There was no water laid on to the homes in my early years; most depended on tanks, but we depended largely on underground springs from which we got beautifully clear, cool water. Later my father installed a windmill over one of these springs and this windmill pumped water up into a large brick tank, enabling us to have cold water laid to the house. Before this happened, we had a covered well with a bucket attached, a short distance from our back door. Here we drew up the water we needed. Not far from the well we had a stand into which a basin was sunk and there were containers for soap. These we had to keep closed to prevent the wekas from stealing our soap! There we performed our morning ablutions.

The reservoir at Titirangi put us on the map. Auckland was dependent upon it for their water supply. I remember pulling apart the sliding doors of the reservoir and feeling awed and terrified by the sound of the machinery and the roar of water. No doubt we would have been 'for it' if anyone knew we went in, but our neighbour was the grandson of the caretaker and this boy was a real daredevil. I was almost sick with fright when he crawled around inside. During World War I this same lad, Clarrie Tarlin, was taken prisoner of war by the Germans and shot for insubordination. Today the modern buildings that make up the upper filter tanks stand on the reservoir site. During World War II these buildings were well camouflaged because should anything happen to the water supply it could have had serious consequences for Auckland. I suppose that you might think that we were isolated. In fact, townspeople would say, 'Oh, you live up in the bou-hoy!' But we were a close-knit community and did not lack sociability. In our home I know that we often had musical evenings; people performing on the piano, violin, cello and also lovely vocal items by both men and women.

Most contact would be made through the mail. Should any businessman come up hoping to speak to my father, my mother would go up to Kiln Hill and blow the horn. This was a big horn from one of our working bullocks of earlier years. There was an art in blowing the horn, which could be heard for miles around. They would say, 'There is Mrs Chappie calling her menfolk home'.

At this time there were no telephones in the homes. I remember when the first were installed. Instead of dialling a number we would ring 3 shorts for 'S' I think. Our code was short-long-short.

What I think caused the disappearance of the farms was lack of labour. The pioneers

Bob de Brabandere's house on Huia Road, close to the brick bridge, c.1948. Gill Collection

Painting of Chappie Bishop's three boys. From left: Jack, Will and Gus. Beneath the painting are some artefacts from the family's earliest days; a bullock horn (left), a mashing tool (centre) and a metal cow bell. The bullock horn was used by Mrs Bishop to call the men back for meals or any other event, such as visitors calling. Marc Bonny Collection

The Bishops attended the opening of the Upper Nihotupu Dam, 14 April 1923. Waitakere Library & Information Services, Bishop Collection

The Bishop family supplied botanical decorations for the Auckland Town Hall when Lord Jellicoe visited in October 1920. Waitakere Library & Information Services, Bishop Collection

were sturdy independent folk who gave their children the best education that they could afford. So instead of making a living off the land, these boys were scattered throughout the North Island in professional jobs: teaching, accountancy, the law, banking and so on. Then when World War I broke out there were no young lads left in Titirangi as they all joined up, so the bush was taking over again.

After our father sold off most of our stock, our income came from the bush. He gathered sacks of rich brown leaf-mould and various kinds of moss, sphagnum being the most sought after, for the making of wreaths and other floral works of art. Shapes were made of wire and stuffed with moss, which when dampened kept the flowers fresh. Gilbert J. Mackay, a florist in Queen Street, took all we could gather.

I remember when I was at school being taken to see over the HMS *Renown*, which brought the Prince of Wales to our shores. He was a very popular prince, the eldest son of King George V and Queen Mary. My father supplied a great part of the native bush decorations for a reception in the Town Hall for the prince. Several whole nikau palms, festoons of lycopodium and other attractive offerings from the bush. Coloured lights made the Town Hall look like fairyland! Conservationists where were you then?

In the bush, not far from our home, there was an old abandoned Maori canoe in which we children often played. It was amazing to see how beautifully shaped it was, especially as the tools used would have been so primitive, probably stone axes. It was always called 'Aid-ee's Canoe'. I've spelt it as sounded but don't know the origin. As we grew up and left home we didn't often go there. The last time I saw it the moss and ferns were growing in it. My old aunt, who was in her nineties and spent the winter months with us, told how she had seen the Maoris launching their canoes. Amid heaving and chanting they made their way through the bush to Little Muddy Creek. Running beside them were the Maori women, who were feeding them hot food from flax baskets.

Another interesting thing that happened in Titirangi was the opening of Exhibition Drive on 24 January 1914, by the then Mayor of Auckland, C.J. Parr. The name came from the big exhibition which was staged in Auckland. I remember that vividly. It was so exciting!

I remember Mr Ned Taylor, a caretaker of the City Council Waterworks in Titirangi, who arrived in 1902 and was our next door neighbour. Two of his workmen whose names will be remembered were the Jacobsen brothers, Matt and Ambrose (Brosy). They gave their names to the longest tunnel: Jacobsen's Tunnel. Glow-worms were to be seen in all the tunnels. To transport equipment from the reservoir to Nihotupu were horse-drawn railway wagons which ran along railway lines. In Jacobsen's long tunnel there were alcoves cut into the walls so that if a pedestrian was caught in the tunnel with horses coming through, he could step off into one of these. If too far from one of these, the pedestrian would have to press himself against the tunnel and, of course, he would get wet through.

Before Exhibition Drive was opened there was a lot of work to be done. The influx of workers made an impact on Titirangi, because board had to be found for the workmen, and as there was no boarding house local people had to help out. Near the reservoir was a Smithy where the big draught horses belonging to the Council were shod. I remember one horse in particular: Victor. One horse was remembered in the name 'Bill's Paddock'.

There is something fascinating about watching a blacksmith at work. Jim Rankin was head blacksmith. He was later killed at Gallipoli.

Exhibition Drive, stretching from the reservoir to Mackie's Rest, was really beautiful: flowering native trees, hanging ferns and native trees in many parts meeting overhead. The road was just wide enough for two cars to pass. Along this drive, my sisters owned a property, a feature of which was their beautiful garden. Many visitors from garden societies came to see their garden, set in such beautiful bush surroundings. Almost opposite their home was a City Council cottage (later demolished) where Mr Joe Beveridge lived. Joe Beveridge was a great raconteur and a true lover of the bush. He did a wonderful job with his workmen in keeping Exhibition Drive open. It was not long after his retirement that the Drive was closed to all traffic and is still closed. (It is now a pedestrian only track, Ed.) While work was being done on the Drive, it was decided in 1910 to build the Huia Dam. This was concluded in 1928. All the smaller waterpipes carrying water to Auckland were later replaced by huge cast iron ones.

The home where I now (1989) live is over 60 years old and part of the original farm on the old homestead site. The original home was pulled down during the Depression. There were so many needy families, my parents gave the timber free and there was sufficient to make two lovely homes. A direct member of the family has lived here these last 133 years. First my grandfather John Bishop, then after his death Gran carried on. Later my dad, their youngest son, married. They were to have built on another part of the farm but Gran asked my mother to stay on. After my dad's death, my husband Bob and I bought the property (25 Huia Road). When our younger son, Leicester, and his wife Julie and our two grandsons came from overseas they needed a home. By this time the children of our family were all married and had homes of their own. The place was getting too much for us and so Leicester and Julie bought the place and built on a 'granny' flat for us. This place has been crammed full of happy memories for many generations. There are still remains of huts built in the trees, a place to dream, a place of contentment.

School days

Written by Essie Hodge, this piece was originally published in the 125th Anniversary booklet of the Titirangi Primary School.

The early colonists of Titirangi were people of high ideals; they knew that the education of their children was of prime importance. My grandparents, Mr and Mrs J. Bishop, settled here in 1855 and had tutors for their children. Any of the local children, for a small sum, could attend these classes in the Bishop home. I'll mention the first tutor, Mr Patterson, who gave my father a pet-name that stuck to him. My father at that time was an infant and Mr Patterson referred to him as his 'little chappie'. Throughout his life my father was known as Chap. Even my mother called him Chap. Officially he was John Joseph Bishop. After the death of Mr Patterson, Ben Carrol came as tutor.

Now, it wasn't long before the people of Titirangi wanted a hall. Mr Pugh (husband of Hannah Bishop) suggested a site on School Road and offered to finance the building if he was reimbursed. So, the timber was pit-sawn on the site and sent to Onehunga, a busy port in those days, to be dressed. The hall was built with voluntary labour and dancing and other money-making affairs soon had it paid off.

For a short time before the hall opened, school was held in one of Pugh's sheds. Gran Bishop gave all the school furniture from her home to the school in the hall: desks, blackboards, easels, books, maps which could be rolled up when not in use, seats etc, to say nothing of a very large globe.

Emily Bishop, wife of Chappie Bishop, 1916.
Mia Stein Collection

View from Titirangi, 1920. Atkinson Road in the foreground, Mt Albert and Mt Eden in the background.
Photographer: James D. Richardson, 18 January 1920. Auckland City Libraries Special Collections, 4-4042

One of these was held back and my sister Ada and I, when we were very small girls, delighted in seeing how fast we could make the world go around. Ben Carrol was the first teacher.

Later in 1872 our school in the hall, one of the oldest in Auckland, was handed over to the Education authorities. There it stood in an elevated spot, overlooking the Manukau Harbour, until it was destroyed by fire on 2 January 1932. Three generations of children went there. I was a second-generation pupil.

Do you know how we learnt to read? A very large chart with coloured pictures was hung on the blackboard. When we were word perfect, then that page was turned over, but not before. Now comes the spelling. In sing-song voices we chanted 'a-t at, b-a-t bat, c-a-t cat', etc. Then we went back to our seats and wrote (no script print in those times). Our first writing lessons were making shapes called hook and hangers. We sat two in a desk. The wooden desks had two slits along the top into which we put our slates. The pencils, pens etc lay in a groove the length of the top of the desk. There were holes into which the water and ink-wells fitted. Writing in ink began in Standard 1. Each Monday morning monitors filled the ink wells. In the

The first Education Board school building, 1873. The building was burnt down in 1932. Mia Stein Collection

Essie Hodge

Titirangi School pupils, 1911. From left, back row: Herbert Bishop, Frank Smith, Eugene de Brabendere, Harry Rush, Norman McQuoid, Melville Henry, George Burbery, Fred McQuoid, Henry Hart, Hazel Tarlin, Bessie Bishop. Middle row: Jack Russell, John Smith, Ernie Smith, George Smith, Boyce Rutland, Graham Russell, Keith Rutland. Front row: Olive Burbery, Dorrie Armstrong, Dora Bishop, Christie Bishop, Essie Bishop, Ada Bishop, Winnie Rutland. Mia Stein Collection

primmers we cleaned our slates using the water in the well and dried them on rags brought from home. The boys often found that the sleeves of their shirts were handy for this job.

Of course Titirangi was a 'one-teacher school' and if the teacher was busy taking oral lessons with the upper classes, the lower grades would be doing written work. I remember an incident when the teacher was taking a lesson on wool. She asked, 'From what parts of New Zealand it came?' A little boy with a loud drawly voice interjected, 'Yer do not, yer get it off Bishop's fence!'

We had a wonderful view through the back door of our school. It overlooked the Manukau Harbour. There we saw steamers, barges, scows and other vessels plying between Onehunga and the Huia, Cornwallis, Parau, and Little Muddy Creek. There were all types of cargo: firewood sent to Bakers in Onehunga, cattle and timber. On sparkling days we might see the *Rarawa* looking lovely sailing out to cross over the Manukau Bar on the way to New Plymouth. On stormy boisterous days she had to wait inside the bay until the bar was manageable and how the bar could roar! Whether it was a dull moaning or an angry roar, all old Titirangi residents knew the roaring of the bar! Nobody had to explain Tennyson's poem, *Crossing of the Bar*. It could have been written for us, 'May there be no moaning of the bar when I put out to sea'.

The reasons that the bar is not heard now is threefold I think, traffic noises in the sky, and on the roads, and also the bush growing up again to dampen the sound.

I remember with love all my school teachers, but the one I must mention is Patience Windust. I am sure that all the pupils at the Titirangi School when she was a teacher would join with me and say, 'Thank God for Mrs Windust!' We were thoroughly taught in all subjects. In those days 'English' embraced so many aspects of the subject. We had to be able to parse every word in a sentence, divide a sentence into subject, predicate and object, analyse it into principal and subordinate clauses, correct and comprehend, as well as writing essays.

At the end of our Standard 6 year (equivalent to Year 8 now) we sat for our Proficiency Examination. The three sitting from Titirangi were Frank Smith (a boy fostered by Tom Armstrong and his family; for many years they fostered state children), my sister Ada, who was only ten-and-a-half years old, and me. On the morning of the Great Day we had to get down to New Lynn Station, just over 3 miles, to get to the Henderson School where the examination was to be held by 9 a.m. So that we should not be too tired my dad drove us all to the station. My mother and Aunt Countess, who came for company, took us to Henderson.

Ada and Cricket (Christiana) Bishop.
Mia Stein Collection

We were all examined in all subjects even reading, recitation, writing and drawing. Because we came from afar and my sister was very young, one of the examiners came rushing out and gave Mother progress reports. We three scored very high marks thanks to Mrs Windust. We learned a lot of poetry and prose at school. Later I thought of these as treasures of the mind, and in my old age I felt enriched by them.

Team sports, due to small numbers, were not known. Girls and boys were not allowed to play together. There was the girls' shelter-shed where we ate our lunch or sheltered from the weather and there was a separate boys' shelter-shed. While the girls for the most part played genteel singing games like Poor Jenny is A-weeping, Green Gravels, Drop the Handkerchief or Hide and Seek or tag, the boys were rough and rumbustious. Among the games they played were Prisoner's Base, King-a Seen-e and 'Cock' Fighting. In this game, a small boy rode piggyback on a senior boy's back. He challenged another small boy thus mounted. The winner was the one who could unseat his opponent. At the same time the older boys leapt about to give help to their mounts. I can never remember a serious

Titirangi School, Standard 4 pupils in 1945. Essie Hodge's daughter, Mia, is in the second row, fourth from left. Mia Stein Collection

accident. My sister Ada and I had no trouble competing with the academic side when we went on to the Girls' Grammar but we were disadvantaged by not having taken part in organised sport or physical drill.

On account of the small area of playground space Mrs Windust let us go into the bush to play. This was a real treat. We had supplejack swings and our imaginations ran riot at the number of games we invented. To call us back for the beginning of afternoon school, two bells were rung at ten minute intervals. We knew that if we were late for the second bell we would be forbidden the bush. Mrs Windust was strict without being harsh.

At the beginning of 1915 Ada and I went off to Girls' Grammar School. From our home to New Lynn station was just over three miles. The roads at that time were roughly metalled and full of potholes. We wore old shoes and carried our good school shoes into which we changed at the New Lynn railway station. These old shoes were left under the seats that went all around the waiting room. We left the train at Mt Eden Station and walked across the Newton Gully to AGGS at Howe Street. Coming home after school we had to go at a trot across the Gully to catch the 4 p.m. train to New Lynn where once again we changed our shoes and walked off home. I don't remember missing a day. After a year of this we boarded in town during the next winter, not because we were afraid of a bit of rain, but because we couldn't afford two sets of clothes. When we came to New Lynn station after being away for a week our shoes were just where we left them. Life was grand!

The Burberys and the Thursbys

Extracted from The Memoir of Ethel Black formerly Ethel Burbery nee Thursby, *an oral history recorded by Mike Butler (photos in Henderson Library), 1997*

The Burberys came from Adelaide and 'Old man Burbery', — George, used to work in the mines. He had a certificate for having taken part in the Broken Hill miners' strike about 1900. The family moved to Hamilton first and from there to Titirangi in 1904. George was a contractor working in Avondale when they purchased the farm (Allotment No. 129, 37 acres).

Mr Mealing purchased Allotment No. 130 in 1906; about 40 acres on the other side of Titirangi Road from the Burberys, in the valley where Crum Park is today. He was a great painter and used to have the most fantastic paintings in his house covering the walls. He lived in a cottage next to Godley Road in the 1930s.

The Burbery's dairy farm ran almost directly opposite Golf Road on Titirangi Road, as far along as Macandrew Hall, which was their boundary, and swept all the way down, almost to Atkinson Road. Their homestead is still there: No. 3 Highland Ave. Of course, Highland Avenue was just a driveway to their house and not a road in those days. Theirs

View from Atkinson's paddock showing Titirangi Road winding down towards the Burbery farm (today's Highland Road area). Godley Road cuts across on the right. Photographer: James D. Richardson, 17 October 1920. Auckland City Libraries Special Collections, 4-4848

was the only house apart from a small chicken barn and it was set amongst macrocarpa trees, one of which remains on the corner (opposite Crum Park).

I married Arthur Burbery, the youngest son (Jane Burbery was his mother and an old lady by then) in 1937. George, the father, had died around 1934. Arthur was born in the Highland Ave. home, just before the outbreak of World War I and, as the youngest, was called 'Mate,' which stuck throughout his life.

My father was Fred Thursby and we bought a 12–14 acre farm in Atkinson Road in 1933 from a Mr Rau who was a European, possibly German. The Thursby house is still there at 136 Atkinson Road. Our farm backed onto the Burbery's larger farm, that was how I met Arthur.

The Burberys and ourselves had a milk and cream round that started with a horse and cart, then a motorbike and side-chair, and finally a Model T Ford. With deliveries, Arthur had to go through the gate and around to the backdoors; he wasn't allowed to climb fences, which would have been much quicker but it would not have been proper. With some of the old dears, heaven help you if you dropped any milk on their step! We carried the milk in cans, with a dipper to pour the milk out. All of the milk and cream was our own, the Burbery's and Thursby's. I had to wake up at 5 a.m. in the morning on our farm in Atkinson Road to separate the milk in a wooden butter churn and milk the cows. With my dad we used to sell butter, milk and cream in the city markets, at Radleys on the waterfront. We had our own label: 'F.W. Thursby' for the butter.

I was told Atkinson Road got its name because it was logged and farmed by 'poor' man Atkinson, as distinct from the rich Atkinsons later on. His old cottage was on our property. Behind a cleared bit of Atkinson Road was Smyths bullock track (refers to Hibernia Smyth). In those days, Atkinson Road was a rough metal road and I have heard it called Happy Valley. There was a beautiful rimu tree growing right in the middle of the road, long gone now.

I worked on Alby Thomas' daffodil farm in Atkinson Road. There was a big packing shed and their cottage alongside a bamboo hedge (it was about where No. 161 Atkinson Road is now). It was called 'Eureka'. Mr Thomas also built a little cottage a bit further up the road to spend the nights in because he and Mrs Thomas didn't get on so well at times. The Thomas' also grew daphne, violets and strawberries in the summer. We also grew daffodils on our farm. With Alby Thomas' kids (who ran the daffodil farm), I have vivid memories of getting hold of a big wind-up siren and walking back and forth from one end of Atkinson Road to the other at midnight on New Year's Eve with this wailing siren, waking everyone up. We couldn't see the harm in it then as kids, but it must have created an awful racket.

Martin Thomas rode Jess the horse that used to graze on the farmland around the packing shed. He used to chase us around on it but we made for the daffodils because he wouldn't dare ride through them.

We used to follow the route of the 'pipeline' to Pleasant Road to catch the bus or to New Lynn for groceries and I remember clearly that a loaf of bread cost two and half pennies. There was a pig farm at the back of the substation in Atkinson Road run by a one-armed Scandinavian man. We used to marvel that he could manage a pick or a hoe with one arm. The shops on the corner of Kaurilands Road weren't there then and it was all just farms.

There were other Titirangi families I can remember. Wally Hay lived down School Road; he was a bachelor. George and Katie Murch lived in Atkinson Road; he was a 'salt of the earth' type of interesting character. The Boyes lived down West Lynn Road. The older son, Neville, was called Captain Boyes for some reason, probably because he looked like a pirate. He lost the sight of one eye when he got a gorse prickle in it when he was young. There were also a few girls in that family. The Griersons lived up on View Road (Kohu Road). They were a big family and later some of them became solicitors in the firm Simpson Grierson. They used to buy cream from us. Mr Godley lived on Titirangi Road, a little bit above Macandrew Hall opposite Godley Road. We used to call it 'Ungodly Road' because it was so roughly metalled and muddy. Mr Peat had the kauri museum below Lopdell House and they had a house in Huia Road called Quamby.

The Atkinson girls, Jean and Nancy, lived in the white villa you can see from the Titirangi roundabout. Their dad was Bert Atkinson. Nancy went to live opposite Macandrew Hall on top of the hill where the wall is. The Witten Hannahs lived down School Road. The MacFarlanes lived in the house atop the hill next to the old soldiers' memorial (opposite Lopdells) before they moved out and eventually sold their farm to a young couple, who farmed it for a while.

My father Fred later sold the Thursby farm and shifted further up Atkinson Road and built a house on a 2–3 acre property. Arthur and I married in 1937 and returned to Atkinson Road in 1941 and built a house, still there: No. 184 Atkinson Road. Arthur died in 1947 when a horse float fell on top of the car he was in on the Whau Bridge.

Thayer Fairburn

> *This memoir was recorded in 1981 by Jay Hoby. Thayer Fairburn was a member of the distinguished Fairburn family that lived in the Titirangi/Green Bay area for decades. His brother Geoff was a poet, and Thayer was the author of the definitive book* The Orpheus Disaster, *published in 1987.*

I was born in Parnell in 1909. My father, wishing to play golf, decided to move out to New Lynn and had already bought about an acre of land next to the golf links, just next door to Charlie Gardner's place. We shifted out there over the Christmas/New Year period 1919–20.

Coming from the rather overpopulated area of Parnell, at New Lynn I felt like a young puppy let loose in the field to run around. At the age of 10 I was, no doubt, very impressionable, and I remember the great joy of walking across the golf-links rather than walking on the rough Portage Road to Green Bay, and being charmed by the immensity of the harbour.

Our family had a coal range, so we were always on the lookout for kauri gum in the golf-links. There was no one there very much as it had only recently been established, but the clubhouse was there and a resident secretary. There used to be two Irish brothers by the name of Timmins, who had presumably come out to New Zealand just before or after World War I, and we always used to remark that they looked as though they had been in a gunpowder explosion, having short coal-black hair and a sallow complexion. They were in charge of the horse teams, there being no bulldozers in those days. They were employed in clearing out the gullies, and smoothing out the contours around and about and forming the golf links, but they left us boys mostly alone.

The kauri gum that we found was great for lighting our coal range. As I remember, the gum burnt very readily with a lurid yellow flame and great quantities of black smoke that you could smell throughout the house. We were really burning money because we could have sold the kauri gum. The pits dug by the kauri gum gatherers were still to be seen in various parts of the district, although the gumdiggers had left much earlier. There was an old gumdigger's hut we boys found in a section not far from our house, in a very thickly wooded teatree area. Exploring it with two other boys one time, we discovered it had a sod chimney and a solitary window, and the whole thing was barely 10-foot square. The teatree was growing up so closely that it was pressing in on the walls. We were told that it had been the property of a solitary gumdigger who had gone to the Great War and hadn't returned. It was built in a period before 1914 and was obscured from the road. For us it was a great adventure, as we explored and found our way into it. Later it was demolished for housing. This place was quite close to the house owned by Mr Marshall Laing, a well-known figure in those days.

I used to love searching for golf balls; the ditches were of a fairly uniform size, about two-feet wide and about three-feet deep and nearly always covered with a growth of ferns on the walls. There were a lot of these ditches and it was quite impossible for the golfers to avoid 'duffing' some of their driving shots and the ball would go whizzing down to the rough area into these partly formed ditches, and it was very difficult to find. Rummaging around in the mud was no difficulty for a small boy without any shoes and I used to go burrowing along under all the ferns looking for the tell-tale round hole, where a golf ball had fallen. With a stick you could poke into the hole and sure enough you'd feel something hard. A bit of digging and out you'd come with a 'Silver King' green dot floater, which the ladies used to use. They were ideal for a small boy to play with, and I used to have a little driver club. We used to know all the weights and colours on the balls, such as the beautiful 'Colonel' or 'Zodiac'; the Zodiac was marked all over the circle. Great finds!

My brother Geoff and I at one time had a pillowcase filled with golf balls that we sold back to the golfers. When we had 120 we were golf ball billionaires! To repaint the balls we used to drive three nails into a flat bit of wood, a bit smaller than the golf ball, then got some special golf ball enamel, poured a little into the palm of your hand, and between the palms of your hand you would roll it around so the ball took on a nice coat of gleaming white paint. Gingerly you would lower the ball on to the three protruding nails, which made practically no mark on the ball, to dry. When it was dry we had the effrontery to go up to the clubhouse and use the golf-ball marking machine. It had a dial on it and if you wanted to impress your name on the ball you put it in the proper holder, select a letter, and push the handle down and the letter would be indented. With a bit of care you could impress your name. However, we soon discovered that balls with our own name wouldn't sell, so we would try to caddy for somebody and sell some of the surplus golf balls to the golfers.

I also used to be interested in the motorcars that came to the links. There was a car called an 'Axiom 8', a huge eight-cylinder unusual American car. There were 'Stucksa's Oakland' cars and Buicks, as this was the early 1920s, when American cars were very much 'the style'. English cars were not so often seen as they didn't suit the roads. I used to go around peering rather shyly through the slits in the bonnet to see what the engine was like, and inside to see what the driving compartment was like with its instruments.

Most of the golfers were affable nice people, kind to small boys who just wanted to caddy for them.

There was a man called Tommy Rogers, who used to carry a bag around filled with many different types of club. There were 'Cliquer' medium irons, driving irons, 'baffee' driver, 'brassy'— all these old names remain with me. Tommy Rogers was a very tall man with iron-grey hair and rather aristocratic features, who wore a bright red coat and hunting cap so was easily found on the golf course. If my father had been playing a round with him, sometimes he came in and had lunch with us. I remember him coaching my brother Geoff in maths, because he was also a very good mathematician. However there was a sorry ending: because his wife wouldn't come out from England and join him, in the end he put a revolver to his head and committed suicide.

There were lady players too. Fay was a very nice youngish lady and she always asked if I would like to carry her clubs for a small sum of money. I have fond memories of all these people. On the walls of the clubhouse were quite a number of enlargements of well-known sailing vessels photographed by Mr Caneer, a well-known dentist and photographer. They were quite unusual, showing a lot of sailing vessels that sailed around the coast. The photos contrasted with the rather austere furnishings of the clubhouse, no carpets or anything of that sort.

I remember the secretary was Maurice Ward, a single man, and rather lonely I used to think. He and my father, at the beginning of the century, had gone on a long walking tour having taken the train to Taumaranui, and walked from there across the country, past Ruapehu and Tongariro mountain huts, past Lake Rotoira, and over the top of a mountain and then round the shores of Lake Taupo, to Rotorua. In later years I wondered how they could have done it because there was no walking track at the time.

I had to attend the New Lynn School, which had been rebuilt in 1914 (demolished in 1980). The previous school had been closer to Glen Eden, and had been established in the late 1880s. The New Lynn School in Hutchinson Avenue at that time was a rather grim looking place, the usual design of those days, with the curious motto incised in the concrete over the main entrance: 'Fear God, Honour the King'. Mr Ellis was the headmaster there, and I remember being taken by my mother to be enrolled and thinking Mr Ellis was a very mild looking man who invited us in. Later I knew how wrong I was as he turned out to be a positive devil who could lose his temper very readily. We were told that he had prohibition notices issued against him when he was in charge of Dargaville School. He used to terrify the lot of us, including the lady teachers, and we often wondered if he should have been locked up! He managed to teach me precisely nothing in the four years I was there. Mr Hodson, his second-in-command, was another very grim gentleman. I always thought of Mr Hodson as being much older than even Mr Ellis, all of 55 or 60 years old, but looking back in later years I realised he must have been all of 25 years old or so at the time!

When I went to Mt Albert Grammar in 1924 it was into an entirely different atmosphere. I had young men to teach me and two masters, whom I liked very much: Mr Grey, Latin teacher in Titirangi, and Harry Calder, history and geography. Mr Perry, who later became chief inspector of schools, taught French, and the headmaster was Mr Gamble, both of whom died just before 1981. I spent only two years there, and in the second year I made a proper mess of things. 1925 was a very bad year for young people because schools were closed for the first three months of the year owing to a polio epidemic.

Today it's a thriving community compared to what it was when we came to New Lynn in 1920. I guess the population then was about 800–1000 people. It consisted mainly of the pottery place, Gardner Bros, and Parkers Brickworks, with houses of brickworkers scattered about the landscape. None of the brickworkers were very well paid and New Lynn certainly didn't look affluent at all. It was always a source of grief to our family that the footpaths and roads were so terribly rough. To walk down to the railway station a mile away at night was quite an undertaking. There were no footpaths at all. I have in mind looking across Blockhouse Bay and Mt Roskill, photographs showing very few houses there too in those days. Others considered that it was a foolhardy thing for my father to want to leave St Stephen's Avenue and come out to New Lynn, the back of beyond. There was the railway of course, but a mile walk to the station wasn't very pleasant when it was raining hard.

If you travelled at night you had to take rather unusual precautions to make sure you got home. For instance, we spent the first year (1920) living in a house belonging to Mr Arthur Jenkin, which was actually at the Green Bay end of Portage Road, and in those days was a mere little lane shrouded with bush on either side. Godley Road was much the same. During that period, if we decided to go to town maybe for a concert, we had to leave the kerosene lights of the old car my father used at Gardner's house opposite the railway station, and when we came home, arriving at the station late, we had to pick up the lamps to guide us home. In autumn and winter there was frequent fog. This was very common over the golf course, being low-lying. We could find our way without much difficulty as far as the clubhouse, the fog was not too thick up to that point, but after that we lit the lamps and headed in the general direction of Green Bay. There was very little in the way of markers on the golf-links although there was a track (now Golf Road) dividing the two parts of the links. There were gates in the barbed wire fence and we would try to steer a course in the fog that took us the 3/8 of a mile to the first gate, which we would find if we were very lucky. If not, we were just confronted with the barbed wire fence, and one wouldn't know whether to move left or right. Often we had to walk the full length of the fence and come to the corner post and then have to retrace our steps in the other direction. Having crossed the road, one had to then do the same thing with the second paddock. We had to come out at a certain spot where there was a bridge that crossed a stream. You wouldn't believe how confusing it was at night, not knowing where you were.

Such was our life in the early 1920s. My father bought an old car, a 'Crit' car 1914 model, which my father said used as much oil as petrol, a really strange looking contraption. Getting in from Green Bay to New Lynn railway station in winter he had to use the car. Before moving to Links Road it was quite a business in winter, ploughing through heavy mud all the length of Portage Road, to the tannery and right along Clark Street to the station was quite an adventure.

On one occasion my parents had been in town, having left the car at the station. Father cranked up the car, drove off as far as the tannery, then along Portage Road in teeming rain. At the culvert near the intersection of Portage and Golf roads they found the dip in the road had several feet of water in it. My father plunged down into the water ahead, illuminated by the acetylene lights of this ancient car, which chuffed through none the worse except for everyone getting wet. Returning next morning when the water had subsided he could see the wheel tracks of his car. Half the culvert had been washed away and by some fluke he had chosen that part with just enough height to take the car. Right beside it was a seven or eight foot drop.

For us children it was a marvellous place to explore, and we would follow the coastline right around to Wood Bay, or Titirangi Bay, and follow up a very primitive road.

I remember the Titirangi School site being just a flattened area with a windmill. At Green Bay there was no dressing shed for swimmers and only about two houses a good hundred yards from the beach. It was popular with school children for swimming. There were two or three boats including a nice launch out there, and we used to climb on it and dive off. It's a wonder we didn't drown. There had been an old house but only the untidy gardens were left and no one could remember the house. That part of the land between Godley Road and the Manukau Harbour had been in pasture probably in the 1900s, and then it was covered in low 'heath' of teatree and blackberry.

Driving along Godley Road was just the same as along Portage Road, the car having to

Wood Bay c.1920. Waitakere Library & Information Services, Bishop Collection

Thayer Fairburn

shoulder the bushes to one side in order to get through it, much to the detriment of the car's paintwork. Godley Road used to be joined by Avonleigh Road although it was entirely a 'paper' road in those days. It was years before Avonleigh Road was actually formed. The road came up from the shopping centre at Green Bay close to the cliffs. It was a very beautiful drive continuing under the tall pine trees, some of which can still be seen and with Godley's garden lasiandra trees in flower and a lot of fruit trees. The owners were the Gardner family. They didn't mind us going along the clifftop from Green Bay to get fruit. Actually this track from Green Bay to Godleys was the original Maori track, from the Blockhouse to Huia. You can still see the remains of an old road coming out at the Toby Jug and going down South Titirangi Road to Grendon Road, then descending steeply to Little Muddy Creek.

Golf Road joined Titirangi Road where the tennis courts are now, and continued over and down the valley to Atkinson Road, where just a track turned left up the valley. In 1922 the top of Atkinson Road was merely a walking track. The top of present Titirangi Road going uphill from Godley Road didn't exist, nor downhill on its present route to the Toby Jug. The road from the shopping area down to Little Muddy Creek was also non-existent then and even wheeled vehicles would have to use the rough road that ran down from the end of Grendon Road to Little Muddy Creek.

A photo I have shows my parents' house in Links Road taken about 1920–22 when the house was just finished. Above it is Charlie Gardner's house built about the year before. There are only two houses there, as well as the clubhouse, then an ordinary looking domestic house. Our house has no trees around it at all, an entirely bare section then, which seems so strange as for many years now it has been thickly surrounded with oak and pine trees.

My father's house was a very unusual design, and I believe it is still on the list of unusual houses held by the architectural faculty at Auckland University. It was called a Californian bungalow. It has double cavity brick walls, none the worse for wear after 60 years. I look at it with nostalgia, having lived in it until nearly 1938. The architect was Kenny Aimer of the firm of Grierson, Aimer and Draffin, who built the War Memorial and a lot of houses here. The house itself was largely to my

Thayer Fairburn. Fairburn family

parents' design, and they had their own ideas that might have seemed a bit unusual to Mr Aimer. However, it proved to be a comfortable house, and a great many people showed interest in it.

My father wrote musical reviews for the newspaper for many years, and our house was visited by many visiting musical celebrities. My father would invite them because if they did not know Auckland at all they would have to spend a dull weekend in their hotel. Some of them played our piano. I remember some of the more unusual characters. One was Edmund Kurtz, a well-known cellist, brother of Charles Kurtz who conducted the Philadelphia Orchestra. Kurtz was here with the Spivokoski Brothers, who brought their wives along. The Spivokoskis were very frosty in manner; I think my parents must have had a job entertaining them. Having an old Ford car I was round the back of the house tinkering with it when I looked up and there was Edmund Kurtz. 'What are you doing?' he said. I replied that I was just tinkering. He replied that he lived in Melbourne and had a Buick car that he told me all about. I asked him if he had ever ridden in a Model A Ford. He replied no, but he would like to. So Edmund Kurtz the famous cellist drove my old jalopy round the back streets of Titirangi, New Lynn and Glen Eden and thoroughly enjoyed himself, saying, 'I don't want to stay inside with those people I see every day'. As there weren't many people in New Lynn you were thrown on your own resources, you had to find people with which you had something in common. There were no dances except miles away on the other side of Auckland.

New Lynn was a very healthy place, and we were told at one stage that New Lynn School's loss of attendance due to illness was the lowest in the whole of New Zealand! I was immensely interested when I first saw the sundews and little fly-catching plants. A child could run loose and explore to his heart's content, and of course the chance of finding the odd golf ball in the scrub was an amusement.

Many years later I went down to the golf links, after an absence of about 35 years, and asked the secretary if they would mind if I walked across the links. I walked all over the links trying to locate which hole was which. They had changed the layout of the course several times in the intervening years. I found memories coming back to me, it was quite an experience to go and explore once again a still lovely place.

Walking from Green Bay to New Lynn School in winter, I remember a sheet of white frost that you don't see these days because of enclosure by houses. We built mud dams in the stream and created wonderful 'hydrostatics', whereby the stream could be released with a tremendous wall of water that went plunging down to the creek to the Whau River. I've known the Whau all my life.

At the age of 16 I gained a job as office boy with the architectural firm of Gummer and Ford, which in 1926 was the largest firm of its type in New Zealand and was irreverently known as 'Fummer and Gord' by its employees. On one occasion Mr Ford directed me to clean out an untidy cupboard that no one else wanted to do. He said if I made a good job he would suitably 'reward' me. If I'd known what the 'reward' was to be I don't think I would have done it so well, even though it would have incurred his wrath, as he was a peppery little man. I must have done it correctly for I was invited to the 'Ford Summer Camp', which was on the Atkinson tennis court just below Butcher's Alley, Ti Ray Road as we call it. It hadn't been used as a tennis court for some time, and although there are houses all down there now, it was almost completely free of houses and trees then. Mr Ford, having been an officer in the Navy, actually had had an interesting career; as a young man he went with Captain Scott on one of the expeditions to the Pole.

He had tourniquets set up at one of his tents and his seaman-like qualities required that all the ropes be tightened to exactly the right amount; there was to be nothing untidy about the property at all. Fortunately he didn't have a lawnmower or I would have spent all my time mowing lawns. Scraps of paper or any litter wasn't to be tolerated. Anyway, we went swimming at Titirangi Beach and had quite a good time, but he was quite a disciplinarian. Once, we were having lunch and a little boy of about seven came up to us looking a bit bashful and smirking at us, wanting a little bit of notice taken of him. Mr Ford turned around to him and said, 'Well young man, what's your name?' 'Billy Haresnape,' said the little boy. 'Oh,' said Mr Ford, 'then where do you live?' 'We live just down here,' he said, pointing to the foot of Butcher's Alley. Apparently the Haresnape family had a summer cottage where Mrs Isobel Haresnape lived later. We were amused at the time, but Bill Haresnape became a very well known resident of Titirangi, and town councillor. I also remember Mr Ford's brother coming up to visit, and he invited Donald, his son, and me to the pictures in town. We came home by bus to New Lynn and had to walk up to Titirangi. Going through Park Road I remember it alive with glow-worms on the sides. The picture was *The Black Pirate*, with Douglas Fairbanks in unusual Technicolor in 1926.

As a young man in my early twenties, I was collecting information about the loss of the *Orpheus* at the Manukau Heads. At that time very little was known, but I was told to see Mr Bethell who lived in Avondale between the Whau Bridge and the convent, and was often to be seen sitting on a chair outside his front gate. I remember him as a short man, rather fierce looking, with high complexion, a little pointed white beard and an old slouch hat. He had a piercing gaze from a pair of very blue eyes. I actually wanted a bit of wood from the *Orpheus* to include in a model I was making of the ship. Mr Bethell used to spend some of his time at Bethells Beach. I went to his Avondale residence one evening and was admitted into his bedroom. There he was in a huge bed, a sea of white, snow white hair, which suited the white sheets, and his very high-coloured cheeks showing up strongly. 'Well boy, what do you want?' I said rather timidly that I wanted a bit of wood from the *Orpheus*.

Thayer Fairburn and Mona Freeman in *The Heiress*, 1960.
West Auckland Historical Society

Alwynne Broady

Alwynne Broady was an enthusiastic and long-time member of the West Auckland Historical Society. She lived all her life in Titirangi. Alwynne's memoir was recorded by Marc Bonny in 2001.

My earliest trips out west were to our family friends, the Boots. They moved to Parau in 1921. My mother died in 1944, and I came out from Mt Albert to live in Titirangi. My uncle and aunt had 22 acres at Titirangi, 12 acres of grass and 10 acres of bush. When my uncle subdivided it, the City Council required him to donate some property as reserve land, in our case about three and a half acres. Part of the bush and farm is now Woodfern Crescent. The farm went up towards Titirangi Road. There was the creek on the lower part and my cousins and I used to go and fish for eels.

Atkinson Road was called Atkinson Valley Road in those days, and only went as far as the old macrocarpa tree to be seen on the left-hand side going down just past the Titirangi School gates. There was a track after that, leading up to Titirangi Road. Atkinson Road had no footpaths and you wouldn't want to try walking it in high-heeled shoes!

Around 1944 there was a tearoom where the chemist shop is now, in a double storey house standing on its own; downstairs there was a little lending library. The tearoom was called 'Zella Rouell's Home Cookery Tearoom'. I worked there for a few hours per week in between working on the farm. Mrs Luckens had another little library at the Macandrew Hall. Mr Titchener was the grocer, and there was a garage across the road.

We didn't have mail delivery so the back corner of the grocery was the post office

Mrs Luckens' cottage, 2003. Marc Bonny Collection

The Village, c.1919. Kohu Road is in the foreground; the charabanc is where the roundabout is today.
Waitakere Library & Information Services, Bishop Collection

Alwynne Broady with Christine Seymour sitting on 'Sue', c.1948. In the background are houses in Koromiko Road (now Kopiko Road).

West Auckland Historical Society

corner. Rural delivery came later and you could get money orders and stamps by just putting in a note and the money.

We had electricity but it was quite a long time before the power went out beyond Titirangi. About 1945 there was a drought and there was no grass whatsoever and we used to put the cows out on to the 'long acre' (the roadside). I would go out on my bike and see how far up or down they had gone and turn them around. Gradually they returned, eating as they went.

Some of the ladies up at the Macandrew Hall had arranged for us to 'do our bit' for the war so about 10 or 11 Titirangi girls would do spinning sometimes. I learned to spin there. Mrs Luckens had the little cottage that is down in the bush behind the hall. Mrs Macandrew lived in Park Road. From Atkinson Road we used to go up through our place and there was a track to just below the Macandrew Hall, about 10 to 15 minutes walk.

We attended the Titirangi Memorial Church in 1944. Reverend Boyd from Blockhouse Bay or Reverend Martin from New Lynn used to come out once a month to take services. Then Jim Gunn came around 1950. I was asked to take Sunday School and felt a bit nervous about it at first, but the children were mostly well-behaved. This was at a hall now demolished, just below the present fire station. Then Mr Sage came, and some parents would come to the Sunday School with their children. Mr Sage was very good at drawing stick figures on the blackboard.

I didn't have a bike when I came out to Titirangi but I wanted one. So, I went over to Newmarket and bought one for £16 and rode it back to Titirangi.

Mr Thomas had the daffodil farm where Daffodil Street is now. It went from Kilgours down the road to where the Lachberrys lived. Mr Thomas imported bulbs from Holland. I used to go over in between milking and pick daffodils. He had a special way of tying them up with raffia and they went into the city market in boxes. He had several varieties of daffodils planted in rows. At first Mr Thomas lived in a little cottage right in the middle of a pear orchard. Another neighbour was Mr Lunn, who had an orchard.

We had a milking herd but there was no vet handy and one of our cows used to get milk fever every year as soon as she calved. We had a special attachment to a bicycle pump

Daffodil Farm where Alwynne Broady used to pick the daffodils. From left: Mia Hodge, Ann Hodge, ? Shaw, Lynn MacLean, Irene Sharp, c.1947. Mia Stein Collection

to pump up her udder, and as soon as she calved we put her into the barn to prevent her from lying down. We made hay also and had about 150 hens and used to sell eggs.

We had a good horse called Lassie. She was easy to catch and I used to go around the paddocks with the konaki, or sledge, and get cow manure. Then my uncle bought another horse. We didn't have a fence down by the creek, and every morning this horse would be in the hay paddock and at first we couldn't understand why. It was jumping the wide creek. I had to put in a fence, quite hard work. Also, we had an orchard of about 100 Eureka lemon trees. The cows were quite partial to a feed of lemons; they would eat straight off the tree, the juice pouring out of their mouths.

Washing was in a copper and with a wooden scrubbing board. We had a long washing line between the cottage and the house. My uncle used to wear long johns and one day I looked out the window to see the calves sucking at the legs of his underwear!

Using the horse for traction with the sledge or konaki, a combination of runners and wheels, we could ride up and down Atkinson Road no trouble at all.

I can remember the Titirangi School site being just a flat section when we visited Titirangi in 1939. Two little rooms were built at first and the rest came later. After my uncle subdivided the farm I got a job in Albert Street in the city, and used to get the 7 o'clock bus in the morning. I remember first the Transport Bus Service, and then McCrae's ABC.

We used to have electrical blackouts occasionally, so my uncle put in a wood range. Maybe it was during the war and the electricity was rationed. My aunt did all the groceries and Gillian and Bell used to supply us from New Lynn. I remember the railway bridge on Titirangi Road being built, and I often used to bike down to French Bay, but coming back was an effort as my bike had only handbrakes and no gears.

I can remember quite well going along the railway line to my 'relations', the Boots, at Parau. Mrs Boot and my mother were at school together, and we always called them 'Aunty Violet' and 'Uncle Alf'. Aunty Violet (nee Pugh) had to cook on a wood range. Parau was considered 'out in the sticks' at that time as it was all bush and farm. Where the pumping station is now there was a little shed with a little train engine in it and they used to take the material up to the Upper Nihotupu Dam. We went out there when my brother and I were quite young. They had an orchard, and a barn with hay and there were macrocarpa trees that I believe are still there. The site is now part of the watershed area of the Lower Nihotupu Dam. The cowsheds and pigsties are covered with water now. Along Exhibition Drive or towards Arataki you can see the trees where the homestead used to be, up on the hill.

On the old railway line, my brother used to push an old wagon up a little hill and sit on it and come roaring down. If we went by car we left the car down the bottom and then walked up to the house.

The Presbyterian congregation in the early days was not very big. Dr Blaiklock used to have bible studies in his home at Kopiko Road and my aunt and I used to go there about once a week. He had a big library underneath the house. Titirangi had always been a combined congregation and it made for a good community atmosphere, although of course the Anglicans have a church of their own now on the far corner of Titirangi Beach Road off Park Road.

Reekies used to have wedding breakfasts and other functions as well as being a restaurant. There was a little grocery shop there as well that was part of the main building. We had grape juice at our church communion, and although Presbyterians used to be very strict, I don't think it matters so much these days. The church in Titirangi had this great community spirit of helping people out. We had a ladies group (Presbyterian Women's Union) meetings up at 'Mrs Macs'. For Sunday School picnics we used to go to Tui Glen or Redwood Park. My aunt, my father's sister, was most hospitable, she was a stalwart Presbyterian and a very lovely person.

I got to know one of the attendants at the School for the Deaf and then she became a teacher and it was her job to look after a group of children. She used to bring her group down often on a Saturday to the farm. The children ran around and my aunt gave them biscuits. One little boy called Billy used to come in and out of the house and I got to know some of the sign language. Billy would come in and turn on our radio to the point of just about blasting our heads off, and he would put his head to it and say, 'I can hear it! Can you?' He was very good at drawing and I wish I'd kept some of his work. German measles were considered to be the cause of much deafness in children in those days.

The Bright family

Ellen Bright built a bach at Titirangi Beach. Harry, George and Margaret, her grandchildren, all remember Ellen and the happy holidays they spent with her at Titirangi. This oral history was recorded by Laurel North for the West Auckland Historical Society in the 1980s

Titirangi Beach in the 1920s

George Bright

I suppose my most vivid memories of Grandma Bright were those associated with Titirangi Beach and the bach, built in 1922. The timber was floated into the beach from a scow. The road down to the beach was pure clay and impossible to travel on in wet weather.

Every year during the Christmas holidays the family would come together at Titirangi Beach. The small bedrooms had bunks, two lower and two upper. The heating and cooking were on a wood stove and the lighting was oil lamp and candles. The water came from a tank.

We used to have great times swimming, rowing, fishing, looking for crabs, exploring the bush and walkways, sand activities and on wet days there was plenty to do with indoor

'Bowness Bay', which is today's Titirangi Beach, no doubt named by the Atkinsons who had come from the Windermere area in the Lake District of England. Alexander Turnbull Library, Wellington, NZ, Price Collection, Ref. No. G-491-1/2

games and so on. We would catch fish and spear flounder or gather pipis, cockles, mussels and scallops, and Grandma Bright would fry the fish and cook the shellfish. They were so fresh; the taste was out of this world.

To summon her flock to meals she used a cowbell, which when rung could be heard right across the bay. Sometimes in dry weather the tank would run dry and water would have to be carried in kerosene tins from a tap near the beach.

Harry Bright

It was the August term holidays in 1921 when they started building the house on the beach level. It amounted to picking down a clay wall about 12 feet high and we spent a whole morning doing that. Then somebody yelled down, 'there's a better site up here,' so we all stopped picking clay and they had a look at the site and decided that was where the house would be. The materials were water freighted from Onehunga and floated to the beach and carried up by hand.

I went back to school but by the time of the Christmas school holidays the bach was ready and Grandma started her long sentence looking after the boys during the school holidays.

Margaret Bright

There are two things I remember most about Titirangi. One was the nights when we all used to go out as a family to the Zig-Zag Track where all the delightful glow worms were in the bush. We used to all go with our torches and lanterns and walk up the roads then go on to the Zig-Zag and I always remember the magic as we approached the little wooden bridge over the stream. The water would cascade down a mossy bank, and all round there you'd see these dozens of little lights. It was beautiful.

The other thing I remember were the dances that used to be held on a Saturday night at the Kiosk. It was when Uncle Ernie and Auntie Win ran the Kiosk at Titirangi and every Saturday night everybody at the beach would go to the dance. We used to love it. All ages would be there and there was a lovely friendly atmosphere with everybody singing and dancing.

Wonderful meals were prepared on the old coal range by 'Great-gran', as we used to call her. I always remember the tremendous preparation, there were so many of us and Gran was in charge. We would be there peeling masses of peaches, apples, potatoes, and shelling peas and preparing all sorts of foods for the evening meal, while the boys went fishing — it somehow didn't seem to be a fair balance!

When we used to play on the beach, each family had a bell that would let their youngsters know when it was time for meals. Each one had a different bell, so we always knew our bell because we could tell by the sound of it. We'd tear up the track and be just in time to sit down round the table. It was a big table, and in the evening there used to be a kerosene lamp lit in the middle of the table and we would all sit round it playing cards — sort of old-fashioned card games like Snap, or Old Maid or Donkey.

The Gordon family

The Gordon family have lived on Scenic Drive since the 1930s. Ken and Esme Gordon were interviewed by Alwynne Broady in 1985; Graham Gordon was interviewed by Marc Bonny in 2008.

Ken Gordon

I bought my 28½ acres from John Shaw of Titirangi. I was not able to sign the Deed as I was just 20, and in those days you had to be 21. To get there you had to go via Exhibition Drive, as Scenic Drive had not then been made. A huge 24-inch water pipe followed down the edge, and I had to get over the pipe to get on to my place, so I asked Joe Beveridge if he could lower it. He said yes, but I would need to go to the Auckland City Council first. When I went to the Council they said it would cost me £3, which would have been a month's ordinary wages.

I paid the money and Joe and his gang took a week to lower the pipe. As soon as the pipe was lowered I built a drive up into my place and it is still there. When the Labour Party won the election in 1935 they started to look around to make work, and one scheme was to make Scenic Drive. I went up there on a Tuesday afternoon and there was this track cut right along the ridge for 14 chains (a chain is 22 yards). The surveyors were camped in the old cookhouse on Shaw Road, so I went round to see them. The boss said, 'We've been told to keep to the top of the ridge'. I said, 'But you have taken 14 chains of my land'. When I went up later, they had brought it down to where it is today.

Years later I asked what they were paying me for the 14 chains of road, one chain wide, but I was told 'betterment', so I gave the Government 14 chains of my place. I had to wait until 1948 for electric power to come, 1960 or so for the telephone, and 1970 for city water. In the meantime I did four years' war service as a soldier, raised four children, and cut up the frontage, which I sold as sections. Since then the Council took 15 feet of land on one side of the Scenic Drive in case they wanted to widen the road, and a further piece of land for a footpath in front of the sections on the remaining side. The road wasn't widened, and the footpath was never provided!

Esme Gordon

In 1945 my husband Ken was discharged from the army, and we came to live in the little cottage he had built as a young man when he bought his land in Titirangi. It had two bedrooms and a long passage. The largest room had a little Dover stove, a sink and an open fireplace. The other room was furnished as a bedroom, and the long passage had my piano at one end, storage shelves on the walls, and behind a curtain was the bath. Outside was a lean-to with a copper and two tubs, and this was also used to store firewood. We had to walk a mile to the nearest bus service, and there were no near neighbours.

Early picnic party at Titirangi Beach, barbecue facilities in place. Shag Point is at the base of the headland.
West Auckland Historical Society, Kershaw Collection

However, the two Bishop sisters, Ada and Cricket, lived on Exhibition Drive, as did Joe Beveridge, and I could walk to their homes.

I really felt I was living as Ken's pioneer family had done in Pokeno. Ken's grandmother, Isabell McPherson, had arrived in New Zealand as a child with her parents on the *Helenslea*, which sailed from Scotland in 1864. They lived in a little cottage at Pokeno that is still in use today, as the property is now owned by two of Isabell's great grandsons. Isabell left the family farm when she married Sam Gordon. When Isabell was 90, Ken's father and I organised a birthday party for her at his home.

Our little cottage had no electricity. We used kerosene lamps until Ken bought a white spirit lamp. When our second child Glenis was due, Ken added another room to our little home as a children's bedroom. Our eldest son Graham was a schoolboy when our house was burnt down. We had only tank water, and there was no fire engine at Titirangi until after our fire, so the cottage was completely destroyed. We had to go back to Mt Eden where we lived in two rooms of my parents' home. They lived in Hamilton, but had kept part of the house for their use when visiting Auckland, and let the rest.

We moved from there when other members of the family wanted the rooms. We moved to Ken's large shed that he had built prior to going overseas in the war. Fortunately, in 1948 he had managed to get power to the shed. With the help of my father, brother, and a neighbour, Ken and I were able to move into our present home when our third child was born. We have added on to the original plan, and have always kept an open home, sharing it with family and friends. At present our grandson and his wife, Richard and Melanie Gordon, are living in our basement. Over the years I had Guide friends from England, Ireland, Switzerland and Australia to stay.

Graham Gordon

(Interviewed by Marc Bonny, 10 September 2007.)

My father, Ken Gordon, worked at the box company in New Lynn originally, then got a job with the Huia Filter Station. My father came here in 1932, although his lawyers advised him not to buy the property, 20 acres originally. Esme, my mother, was involved with the Guides for a long time. She travelled all over the world to England, Ireland and Scotland to groups over there.

We kids went to Titirangi School, and then we went to Kelston High School as there was no intermediate school in those days. When I was at Kelston High School, it was boys and girls together in the present girls' school. While I was there they separated the boys into another school lower down Archibald Road, and the girls remained up at the corner of Great North Road.

Odo Strewe bought a half-acre section from my father and in the early days we used to play with the Strewe and Mason children. In the fifties I used to be friendly with Geoffrey Clark, Tom Clark's son, and the Bishops. I used to go around to see Joe Beveridge, the ranger, and the Bishop sisters, Ada and Cricket. The Chant boys lived right on the corner. Then there was David Cotton, whose father used to be in charge of the filter station. Mrs Roxburgh, now long gone, was our neighbour, and used to make us apple pudding when we were kids. It was a fairly hard life; there was no money in the family, although we had no concept of the hardship suffered by our parents in the Depression.

Originally we grew potatoes on our small farm. We specialised in 'Cliff's Kidney' potatoes, that were especially for Christmas dinner. My father grew them and then I grew them later. They were barely economical to grow because they had to be dug with a fork instead of a tractor because it was so muddy. The income was hardly worth it after all the trouble of getting the seed and the fertiliser. We still sell firewood and native trees and that's about the only income we get off the land now. My father used to cut the teatree, which he sold as firewood. He used to pack it so well in the bags that you could hardly lift them. By the time he had cut the teatree right around the section it was back again, so it was like a continuous thing. When we got tractors with slashers we cut it down and planted a citrus and macadamia orchard, and some pine trees. All around the house originally was bracken so high I had to stand on the seat of the bulldozer to see over the top. All the area between Kaurilands and Titirangi Road used to be gorse years ago, with no houses at all.

We also grew tamarillos; we had 3000 trees in the 1960s. With gate sales and selling jam and native trees we were quite busy. Then, later when Saturday and Sunday shopping came in, that was the end of that business; it just died overnight. I had intended to do orcharding, but found I had to go back to doing cars. Having an orchard is full of problems. The neighbour's washing ends up yellow from lime sulphur spraying or copper sulphate when the wind starts blowing. Also, you have an endless fight with rosella birds, rat problems, possum problems, and wind problems when all the fruit ends up on the ground.

Ian Gordon, my younger brother, went to work at the DSIR and there he found out about macadamia nuts, and so from then on we grew macadamias. We had all sorts of macadamia nuts from all over the world. Dick Endt (owner of Landsendt, Parker Road

Oratia) was also selling macadamias. We are not harvesting anything off the macadamia trees now. We use them instead for propagating. We get the best varieties from everywhere and choose the best for the oil content and production, and then propagate. Our trees are sold all over the country. We have never concreted our property. The roads are quite good now, until we get a storm. Every time it rains all the water comes off the road.

When I was at school I had a 1931 Austin 7, which I pulled to bits and fixed and made into a little two-seater. I went to work for Seabrook and Fowlds, Austin agents, in Symonds Sreet, and worked there for 20 years. While I worked there I also tried to make an orchard. Originally I was in spare parts, but when working for myself I had to do everything because just one thing wasn't enough. Because I had the knowledge of the cars, people kept coming to me with cars they didn't want or cars they wanted fixed, and it grew from there. I only did classic cars, 1950 to 1980, Austin and Morris, MG and Wolseley. I did not do vintage cars. I only did one brand, and got very specialised in that brand. We overhauled the gearboxes, especially Austin Maxis around 1972 era. They were five speed gearboxes and awkward to fix. My wife had a Morris Minor and that's how I met her, when she came around to get it fixed. We had a workshop there and basically did every aspect of car repairs. We used to make leigh shafts and sell them all over New Zealand. Every gearbox in an Austin had a leigh shaft and they often failed and we used to make them in the workshop.

One of our sheds burnt down, caused by a guy who was smoking in the shed. We lost a lot of parts and there were so many gearboxes lost that the melted aluminium ran down the road. We rebuilt that shed but couldn't recoup the loss because I had so many tractor parts in there, a huge collection that was irreplaceable. I used to do earthworks too, all around this city, 30 years ago. I did site work, driveways and all that for many houses around here. I used to have diggers and also a traxcavator and two trucks. I think they should still make concrete roads because they are the cheapest by far.

W.N. (Bill) Bishop

In this memoir, W.N.(Bill) Bishop recalls his childhood at Waima during the 1930s. Recorded by Marc Bonny in 2007.

Catching the cow

During the winter there wasn't enough grass in the paddocks to feed the cow so she was allowed to roam in the bush. The cow had a bell round its neck so we could tell where it was in the bush. Often I was told to bring the cow home, but she soon learned to be very cunning and would sit down alongside a log on which the bell would rest so that when she chewed the cud the bell wouldn't ring. As darkness fell we used to get so exasperated when we couldn't find her. Every so often we would hear one ring and you had to try to find it in the dark. Once found we had to hang on to the cow's tail for grim death in case you got lost yourself. Finally the cow and you would emerge to the paddock.

In 1936 my father sold some of the big native trees on our side of Waima Road to a timber company because he was so desperate for money. The contractors set up a hauler on the first knob underneath Waima Crescent, and hauled up to there. They used to hook on to the log and then a fellow would run or walk alongside it and when he came up to the block and tackle, he'd knock the pin out of it so there would be a straight line for the log to be pulled all the way up.

When they had got a big collection part of the way to the top side of Waima Crescent, they would send the hauler up to the foot of Dad's drive and do another haul. Because it was a straight haul they didn't need any block and tackle at this point. Just before they came to Waima Road, the log would drop down and gouge a big hole, which became a swimming pool or pond for quite some time afterwards. Trucks would then come down Waima Road and go in and load these logs and take them to the mill.

At the Nihotupu incline, which used to go down to what we called 'Island Creek', there were the biggest blackberries you've ever seen. We weren't allowed to swim in the stream until we had filled a seven-pound golden syrup tin with blackberries. We used to have a day for collecting blackberries and we each had to fill a tin.

I was born in 1925 and left school in 1941, so I can remember the two gates next to my father's drive and the gate on Waima Road. I remember the telephone party line and how you could tell who it was by the Morse code. In 1930 I was five, so I would have been nine when I went to Titirangi's old Tin Shed School. In 1934 I used to come home, through Dora and Will Bishop's place from School Road to Huia Road, down the Huia Road to my grandmother's place to eat scones, and then my mother would ring up to see if I'd left to go home. My mother felt I was more inclined to stay with my grandmother, especially if there was a job at home she wanted me to do! So the phone would ring and my grandmother would say, 'Get up the "golden stairs" so I can honestly say that you've left to go home; I won't say how long ago, but you have left'. So I would belt out the front door and start up the stairs.

Jack Nelson (Essie recalls that the supposed hoarder was Jack Parr) who farmed on land leased from Elizabeth Bishop in the late 1890s and early 1900s, was reputed to have his savings in a tin that he hid, supposedly under a large rata tree or in a hollow log. When he was taken ill and taken to the Auckland Hospital and was dying, he sent for Chappie Bishop, presumably to tell him of his secret cache. However, he died before Chappie's arrival, so the secret was never revealed. A frantic search by the neighbours, which culminated in the demolition of his house, proved fruitless. Generations of Bishops and others kept searching but nothing was ever found.

My brother Jack was working for the *New Zealand Herald* after he left Grammar and they kept his job open all the time he was at the war. He was a sergeant at Mt Albert Grammar cadets and I was a private. He went to Papakura camp but after a week was sent to the Cheltenham Officer Training Unit on the North Shore. When he finished there he was given the rank of Second Lieutenant. As there were enough men in the army at that time he was sent to Wigram, in the South Island, to become a Second Lieutenant in the Air Force. There he had to learn to fly. After he got his wings, Jack was sent to the United Kingdom via Freemantle and Durban. Here he found that the Air Force and the Army had too many officers, so he was sent to the Navy and joined the Fleet Air Arm. He was one of the few officers to be in all three services in the war. On VE Day 1945, Jack was in the sky over the Irish sea with an aircraft carrier below him heaving in the rough swell, and a number of pilots had previously crash-landed or overshot into the water. Fortunately, before his turn came to land on the carrier, a message came through to return to base. The war in Europe was over. Jack's wife Josette, nee Heymans, said she knew when Jack was flying the plane above her as he would cut a motor and the noise the plane made would let her know he was there.

Our roaming and play area was along the Exhibition Drive to Mackie's Rest and Jacobsen's Tunnel. We did not go in the 'old' tunnel as we were told it was unsafe. It is concreted up now at the entrance. We admired the glow worms in Jacobsen's Tunnel and were frightened by the telephone wire that went through the third tunnel as it twanged when we unknowingly hit it. We thought a train was coming! We climbed above Exhibition Drive in front of the house by 'Breakneck Track' to what is now known as the Scenic Drive, and then sledged down the Auckland side of the hill at Pascoes. All of the places covered in teatree now are where the farmland used to be. Pegler's house was below my Uncle Will's, before Dunvegan. After the Peglers the Peaces lived in it. That house was built before my time and belonged to the Council or Waterworks.

The front paddock was between Exhibition Drive and a line across the front of the house roughly just on the far side of the kauri tree. It had slip-rails on the right-hand side. The back paddock was below the concrete water pipeline down the drive and near the road. It was an oblong but irregular shape, with Waima Road as part of its edge. My father, Gus, made hay in it one year by hand-scything and then towing the hay on his tarpaulin and stacking it in the hayshed. He also did the same in the front paddock. There were slip-rails where the top corner of Waima Crescent is now. On the downhill corner was the saw shed, garage and hay barn, in that order, all in one building.

Just below was the lake. It was a hole in the ground that I think used to be a saw-pit and I saw many eels there. At the back paddock was an old high stump, used for years as a support for the Guy Fawkes fire we held each year. It was down Lake Road that Nobby the horse died, when I was very young, and because disposing of it could be difficult, a funeral pyre was made right across Waima Road at the end of the bottom leg of Waima Crescent.

Looking up you would see Rawlings' house, made of chipped bricks and timber, leftover war surplus material from the American camp. Beneath it was the old bullock track that ran down the ridge, passing where the store is now, and more or less following the road downhill. This piece of land belonged to Emily Bishop, my grandmother, and it was known as The Bo'Tom'. I think it was sold to Alley when he bought the lower end of Tainui Road, about 1945.

This land was in grass, just starting to revert back when I was a boy, and later on I used to shoots rabbits there. Hoffman had a red house along Exhibition Drive. My aunties, Cricket and Ada Bishop, bought a house in Exhibition Drive, that had belonged to Mr Hoffman. They lived in it for a while, sometimes with Gran Bishop, their mother, my grandmother (widow of Chappie Bishop). Then Ada and Cricket built a new house on the old site and kept a big garden, including fowls and wild rabbits. They had a dog and an old van, and my father used to supply them with firewood. I cut a set of steps up to Exhibition Drive in front of our house for Gran Bishop. Bruce Fraser made a track for his motorbike from our place to Exhibition Drive later. The bush on the right-hand side of Gus' drive was called Hybie's. In this bush, just above the concrete pipe, is an old saw-pit, full of rubbish but still reasonably intact in 1999. On the right of the drive was a narrow strip known as Jack's garden. The main item was a kaikawaka tree, which had a stringy bark.

When I was a child we would go to Morepork Hill, and Mary always said she wanted to have her house here, and she did. Later she called it 'Ruru Hill'. We used to go to the highest place and loosen big boulders that rolled down to the concrete. This spot was called McKenzie Road and came down from Exhibition Drive. The workmen brought material for the concrete down this road before my time.

'Gus' lot'. Gus and Lilian Bishop with children Jack, Bill (front) and Mary, and relatives, on the steps of 75 Waima Road, c.1936. Mia Stein Collection

One day in 1936 we were coming home from school and we found a film crew working. It was Rudall Haywood, and he was making a start on *Rewi's Last Stand*. I said to him, 'You don't want to play around in this type of second growth; come down the road a bit to my father's place and you'll get some proper scenery!' I must have been persuasive because sure enough they came down and talked to my father. Most of *Rewi's Last Stand* was made on the Bishop property. Most of our 78 acres had undisturbed forest on it. The fight between Robert and the Maori in the film was held in the front paddock. The Bishop boys held the screens up to reflect the light on the scenes being filmed. In another scene, where the leading lady was being followed by Robert, she jumps on a log and talks about 'utu' being expected; this was filmed on the right side of the bottom leg of Waima Crescent, and the dying scene was filmed close by. The scene where Robert has his head bandaged sitting on a log took place across the road. There was a lot of criticism of this scene as it showed that the log had chips cut from it. The scene where the rangers meet the Maori war party was shot on Boylan Road. Both Jack and I were in the line of bush rangers and I had the musket with the dummy round. The first time I fired it I shot the microphone box out and the chap who did the recording swore. The second time I fired elsewhere and all was well.

Bernard Holibar

Bernard Holibar lived in the Tanekaha Road area during the 1930s and 1940s. He was interviewed by Marc Bonny in 2005.

In 1939, Titirangi was fairly isolated. Arthur Titchener's grocery shop is now The Hardware Café. Arthur ran the grocery part of it and every week he'd come round and deliver our grocery order. One of us had to take the order to the shop a day or two before, as there were few phones around at that time. Arthur Titchener's brother Vernon was very crippled. He ran the post office in the back of Titchener's shop. Later there was a taxi stand on the opposite side of the road, then later again, a fish and chip shop. In the thirties I'm sure there wasn't anything else except the hotel on the corner of School Road, now South Titirangi Road. Reekies had the kiosk (now Toby's), and there we bought ice cream and confectionery; it was more like a milkbar. They also had groceries in the part bordering on Park Road. It was L-shaped, with a large room bordering School Road with a confectionery counter in one corner and the remainder as a tearoom. Here they held New Year dances.

In School Road there was Alec Bishop's house, and another house with a different pitch to its tiled roof. Tiled roofs were not common at that time. It was behind Alec Bishop's house but you approached it from Huia Road. It has certainly been there for a long while.

In those days we all relied on buses. Often the bus only went to the hotel or sometimes down to Reekies and we had to walk the rest of the way. We'd go along Park Road, a short way down Titirangi Beach Road and cross over on that short track linking it with Otitori Bay Road, which we'd go down until we reached Tanekaha Road. Nearly at the end of that we branched off to Ridge Road (now Miha Road) and our house was the first (apart from a bach) on the left. After some years they remodelled the turn-off to Tanekaha Road. It used to go parallel but at a higher level to Otitori Bay Road, for perhaps 60 yards, and then turn the corner. Later they made the turn-off directly into the corner so the short stretch of upper road was derelict. It was done after the war, quite a long while after we came. The upper section was very narrow and there was no way of widening it.

Dr Chapman used to live on that corner of Tanekaha Road, where the new section came in, on the right. He used to have a regular morning session on the radio, 1ZB I think, and was a dietician, and frankly, as kids, we literally had a gutsful of his ideas. He was always suggesting weird recipes and my mother used to follow them religiously, testing them out on her poor unsuspecting offspring. One of these was to boil linseeds until a horrible gelatinous mess was obtained and you were supposed to eat this with milk. Absolutely revolting! Another of his fads was to cook up fowl wheat and put sugar and milk on it. That also was awful, terrible stuff, so his name was mud to us. Every week he'd come up with some new recipe. Of course in those days the radio was the only means of mass communication, apart from newspapers.

My father was mad on radios. To digress a little; when we lived in Oratia he invented a type of crystal set that operated in the earphone alone. This he connected to any fence that happened to be handy and listened in without any trouble. In 1936 we had a battery radio, with batteries somewhat bigger than torch batteries. Years later, when my mother's house was sold (1989), that old radio was part of the household goods which I had to dispose of. It could have been worth a bit even just for curiosity value!

We always had a piano and my younger sister learned. I was dying to learn, but I needed money to pay for lessons. I did some 'slave labour' and saved up enough money to learn, but when I started at 16 it was really too late as my hands were fully formed.

Further down Tanekaha Road on the left and down below the road were the Palliser-Smiths, in a house behind trees. For ages we thought, with a name like Palliser-Smith they must have been very high-class people. But then the lady told me her husband had 'information' on the stomach. In my mind's eye I saw the poor man with perhaps a large dictionary weighing down his stomach! I think I inherited my interest in malapropisms and mispronunciations from my mother because I can never remember a time when I wasn't aware of them.

Continuing down Tanekaha Road, Miss Allen lived a few sections below Dr Chapman on the right-hand side. She probably died in the late forties. There were bach-type houses on the right that weren't occupied very much in our early days. Later on some were permanently occupied.

Lower down Tanekaha Road and on the left was the Cottingham family. Lynn Cottingham, later wardrobe mistress for the Drama Group, is probably a relation. Morgan Lewis later built a house a bit further up on the right, a little below Miss Allen's and around the corner. Around the next corner, still on the right, was Mrs Henderson's house. Some years later she married Morgan Lewis' father, Harry. Her family consisted of two sons, Peter and Alan. Alan married Letitia Lott. The Lotts lived a short distance up Otitori Bay Road. Snow and Grace (Lott) had two children, Letitia (Leta) and Ken.

On the opposite side, on a relatively straight section of this twisty road, were the Mellars, with daughters Judith and Lyndell, in a two-storeyed wooden house. The Cottinghams lived next door. Around the next corner but on the right, a family called Mitchinson arrived some years later. Besides the parents there were three children: Billy, Lesley and Rae.

So now we come to what was Ridge Road, now Miha Road. At the intersection with Tanekaha Road there is the old stone bus stop. Ridge Road just went a couple of chains but on each side tracks led the left down to French Bay and to the right to what we called Wattle Bay, sometimes called Little Beach. I would think the stone bus stop was built in the early 50s when the buses started coming down Tanekaha Road.

Morgan Lewis' father's house was on the left, where Tanekaha and Okewa roads joined just above Wattle Bay. In the fifties this house was owned by Jack and Essie Jones; their son Boyd became a senior veterinary lecturer. Okewa Road was quite a new road, built about 1949–50. I don't think there was anyone very much on the right hand side of Tanekaha Road.

The Bentons were on the left-hand side, not far before the turn into Okewa Road. Pauline Groves lived with her family nearby, and Eunice Campbell lived next to the Groves family. Down Ridge Road, as it was then, we were on the left side with the Newbys a section away, and the Millets beyond them. In the Newby's family were Gary, Fay and another girl. I can recall only Jackie Millet from that particular family. On the right-hand side of Ridge Road I cannot recall anyone living there for quite a while after we moved in.

Later, Mrs Taplin and her infant daughter Lorraine arrived; then later still, the Quinns. Young Lorraine Taplin, when aged about 5, often visited our house. At 16 years old, having mastered the piano sufficiently, I sometimes played her Johann Strauss' *Voices of Spring*. She would arrive at our door asking to be entertained with *Horses and Springs*.

The French Bay Yacht Club started a long while after my childhood. Our house was the one that used to belong to Tattersfields, the bed and mattress people. It was more a bach to them but to us it was a big, two-storeyed house. We had it from 1939–64, but did not buy it until 1948 when it was offered to my parents for £600. My father vetoed the whole transaction; but as we knew our mother dearly wanted it, my two younger sisters and I made all the necessary arrangements. Because I was the only one over 21, I stood guarantor and so was the legal owner until, on my marriage, I signed it over to my parents.

As the years went by a few more people moved into Ridge Road. My mother had an unwritten rule that we didn't mix very much and we didn't bring anyone home, so we were rather socially inept. I think it was that we were such a big family, and having just gone through the Depression not knowing where the next meal was coming from, she thought that we couldn't afford anyone coming in for 'stray meals'. It was only later on that we could bring the occasional person home. However, towards the end of the war, in spite of rationing, things had changed to the extent that we regularly had visitors to 'high tea' on summer Sunday evenings. But among those visitors there were not many of our own age.

At French Bay beach, Captain Hewitt, Norman Hewitt's father, and his wife lived up the middle of Valley Road behind French Bay. Further up, on the left-hand side, were the Sextons, who usually had with them their friend Uncle Horrie, as we called him. Nearer the beach was a lady called Elva MacBeth and the Thuells lived in what was later Webber's house and shop. Norm Hewitt's sister, Kitty Laurence, lived up near the Opou Road Hall with Harry, her husband, and Dawn, her daughter. Others I can remember who lived in the area were the Caseys and the Cashmores.

The original track from Ridge Road down to French Bay was gravel and we used to 'skate' down it or we often walked around the beach when the tide was out. We often used the track from Park Road to Titirangi Beach, the Zig-Zag Track, and we'd even go up there at night when it was pitch black to see the glow worms. Because of the wartime 'blackout' we got used to darkness. Going through the Zig-Zag Track in one of my long walks through the bush I got bitten by something which must have been quite venomous because inflammation began midcalf and then slowly but steadily it climbed right up my leg. That night I became completely delirious. Luckily, in the room next door was Auntie Ada, who heard me yelling out about spiders all over the sky. My mother moved me up to her bed where she could keep a constant eye on me. My leg was so painful I couldn't put it to the ground. I was ill for three weeks, couldn't keep any food down and lost quite a lot of weight. In Titirangi in 1939 the nearest doctor was in Avondale; and we had no money for a doctor.

At French Bay beach the Webbers came either in 1949 or 1950. The Thuells formerly lived in that house, which was noteworthy because it had its own tennis court. The Webber's house, which was turned into a store on the front ground floor, was built by Hardley's, plumbers, of Newmarket. The Webber boys, Robert and John, were good yachties. Webber's shop was a sweets and ice-cream-type shop.

The war years

The Caseys, from Opou Road, made a significant impact on French Bay life. They lived in a brick house with lots of windows looking down on to French Bay beach. The eldest son, Jack, was a pilot in the war and was killed. His name is on the Roll of Honour outside the Titirangi Library. However, my most vivid memory is of his father just before the Battle of the Coral Sea. We had had nothing but bad news, getting worse. All the big battleships, the *Repulse* and others, had all been sunk. Impregnable Singapore had just fallen. It withstood the Japanese onslaught for only a few days and we were really quite desperate.

Later, we found out that Winston Churchill had just 'abandoned' us because our troops were needed in Egypt, which was much more important to him than far away New Zealand. However, we all idolised Winston Churchill at this stage and it was only years later that we realised our idol had feet of clay.

With affairs in such dire straits, we were all stressed out. At school we had had months of air raid training which, if there really had been a raid, would probably have proved completely useless. But at least they were trying to do something. We didn't know what might happen next.

After Jack had been killed Mr Casey became the air raid warden for the district. Two days before the Battle of the Coral Sea he came to my father and me when we were digging our own air raid trench. (Also probably useless in a real air raid.) He said to my father, 'The Japs will be here in two days'. We were terrified. 'For God's sake,' he continued, 'get hold of a gun of some sort and when they arrive, shoot all your women folk, shoot the boys and then shoot yourself'. I was about 15 years old at the time, very naive and impressionable. It was like a death sentence. The Battle of the Coral Sea hadn't been fought at that stage, but it was well after Pearl Harbour, which had brought the Americans into the war in 1941. The Japanese were just coming down inexorably towards New Zealand and Australia. The Germans had already ridden roughshod all over Europe. It looked hopeless. Even the Americans seemed helpless at stopping the Japanese, and we were really frightened. We had reports of submarines in Auckland Harbour and Japanese planes going over Auckland. We had been living in total blackout. Nobody had petrol except for the direst emergencies. You walked everywhere, no lights anywhere. Besides the curtains, we had blankets and things up over every window to keep everything as dark as possible. From about 1940–45 if you went in a car the lights had to be dimmed. Not just low beam but down to parking light level. I used to walk down Tanekaha Road from the hotel in the dark, right down to Ridge Road quite often, and somehow or other you developed 'night eyesight'.

Anyway, terrified as we were by the situation outlined by Mr Casey, it was not until a couple of days later that we heard the American Seventh Fleet had defeated the Japanese in the Battle of the Coral Sea, and we were saved. It may not mean much to young people today but those were days of absolute terror for us. We didn't need much in the way of propaganda to realise the Japanese treated their prisoners terribly. They would have been here had it not been for the Americans and we were eternally grateful. Once, an American plane loaded with personnel and bombs took off from Whenuapai and crashed. We in French Bay were asleep, with the blackout everywhere, when we heard this gigantic explosion. We were quite sure the Japanese had started bombing Auckland. Immediately, in the pitch black, the searchlights from North Head began combing the sky. Only in emergencies did we see these lights. But with this terrific explosion about 4 o'clock in the morning, everything went on high alert. We all got out of bed and wondered what was happening. (In those days we didn't say, 'What the hell?', but 'Oh dear, what must be happening?') Nothing about this incident appeared in newspapers or on radio. The military authorities knew its cause but the civilian population was left in complete ignorance for decades.

My eldest sister often worked late in the office of Bycrofts, making 'service bread' as fast as they could to help feed the troops overseas. After coming home on the 11 o'clock bus she had to walk down from the hotel in the dark by herself. One night there was a man some distance in front of her with a trilby hat pulled down over his eyes and collar pulled up giving the impression of a proper gangster. She followed him as quietly as she could, and lo and behold he turned into our own pathway and went down our steps and then around the house and continued on down to the beach. She came inside terrified and, having locked the door, came and woke me. My father was pretty old then. For several nights we would be inside and we would hear these footsteps going around the house late at night. Who that man was we never found out. There was an unsolved case about that time when a woman went missing and the police suspected that her husband had killed her. We often wondered if this was the man! Perhaps he had buried her in the bush!

We had electricity but frequent power failures. In the blackout if any lights were showing outside you could be prosecuted. From our house we had a beautiful view but much later the trees had grown up so much the view was restricted.

Among the young men who went to the war some returned. Some like Jack Casey did not. My eldest brother returned from service in the Air Force and Norm Hewitt returned from the Navy.

We would have been at French Bay about two years and I would have been about 13 years old and at school. We had to walk up to Reekies to get the bus, which left about 7.45a.m. The bus would drive up to the hotel where the Shrubsalls got on. Also, John and Edward Geddes, who were going to Kings School. There were some Seddon Memorial kids also. This was the Auckland Bus Company with their depot in New Lynn. Although we weren't encouraged (by parents or schools) to fraternise with other bus users we gradually got to know the names of some regulars. Further down Titirangi Road we would pick up other kids. Derek Simcock, with his sisters, used to get on at Golf Road. Some of us went to Catholic schools. The rule was that we were not allowed to talk to girls at all. You couldn't even talk to your sister till you got home. It was absolutely ridiculous. I was one of those that always obeyed rules, so I never talked to anybody unless it was 'okay'. We looked on the Seddon Tech people as a bit rough. Today their talk would be seen as mild but in those days they seemed beyond the pale. The trip took an hour and we had to stand up for adults because, of course, we paid only half-fare. The New Lynn railway bridge hadn't been built and was just a level crossing. When the bridge was built we thought it was wonderful.

People would drop off at New Lynn and Avondale, and by the time we got to town it was less full. I used to get off at Pitt Street, just opposite the big Methodist Church, walk along Karangahape Road and get the tram at Grafton Bridge going up Symonds Street to Khyber Pass to attend St Peters College. The brothers there had very rigid discipline.

About 1929 the Great Depression took hold, and I'm afraid to say that my father, who could have established himself in Oratia, left the family and went to Australia. My mother had to deal with five children: feed them, clothe them and keep a roof over their heads. I think my father was away for a year or so. Within a few short years of his return the family had increased to eight children. It was fortunate that my mother had her own father and with his help, and the charity of neighbours, especially the Dalmatians in the Oratia district, she managed to scrape through. My mother was the strength of the marriage.

At that time Glengarry Road just went up a short distance from West Coast Road. It didn't quite reach where the Salvation Army establishment is today. Mrs Silich with her daughters lived where the road ended. She was a Dalmatian lady who spoke very little English and consequently got me to do some of her shopping. Mattie Vulinovich lived in a corrugated iron-fruit-packing shed at right angles to Mrs Silich's house. Between his shed and our house there was a field with several old tree stumps, surrounded in summer with long, sticky paspallum grass. On our other side were the Levys, who were well-known in Glen Eden, with a road named after them. There were no other houses in the road. The right-hand side was all fields. Where the road ended was a clay track with a gate across it that continued for a while. We'd sometimes go there to collect wood for the fire, around 1935.

We rented in Glengarry Road until I was 11. At that stage the mortgagee foreclosed on the place so we had to move. My father eventually found a house available to rent at French Bay. To our large family it seemed just the thing. A big house with two huge verandahs, electricity and a flush toilet (the first time we'd had either of these last two amenities) suited us so well.

So we left Oratia behind. Within a week of our departure, our old house was burned to the ground. Our association with Oratia, where some of my elder siblings had attended school, was later continued by our children and then our grandchildren attending Oratia School. While at Oratia we had no car, so were quite used to walking long distances, for example up to Waiatarua, to Te Atatu, to Waikumete Cemetery or to the bottom of Hepburn Road. We'd visit the grave of the brother who had died, aged three, on the family's arrival in New Zealand. It was taken for granted that we should do this on a regular basis.

My father was a lot older than my mother and he had never been trained in any job. In 1935 the Harres were just down West Coast Road from us in the old homestead. Bill

Harre used to bring us milk. Mrs Harre was a cousin of the Bethell family at Te Henga. Nell Harre, whom everyone later called Micky, was the one I knew best. When the Bethell family told their Harre cousins that they were in need of another child to keep their tiny, beach-side school open, the Harres thought of our large family. In those days Bethells Beach was totally isolated, so they were allowed the services of a state-paid teacher provided they could keep up a minimum roll and supply a schoolroom and board and lodging for the teacher. The Bethells still had three children of primary school age but their two elder boys had gone to high school. This left the school two short of the required five pupils. To fill the vacancies their cousin, young Nell Harre, was called on. But they still needed a fifth one, so I was sent. I came home only once during that year. I remember being terribly homesick the night I arrived at Bethells. I'd been put on the train at Sunnyvale by my elder brother. The two elder Bethell girls, Trudy and Nancy, were already aboard and we all got off at the Waitakere Station, where Mr Bethell awaited us with his tourer.

Pa Bethell was the grandfather who lived in Avondale. Besides the Harres, the Gardners from New Lynn Brickworks were also the Bethells' cousins. I stayed at Bethells till late November. At first I felt lonely and strange out there. To accommodate the guests there were little chalet-type buildings, little cottages more like huts, around the place. Right beside the main homestead there was a place with a bedroom at one end with a verandah stretching to another bedroom at the other end. The building is still there but it has been altered. I was given one room while the teacher, Miss Drummond, was already installed in the other. Later on a family moved into a third room attached to the rear of the building but having its own entry.

As I had always had to share a room or even a bed with brothers or cousins, having my own room seemed quite a special thing. After I had got over my shock at being out there, and being attacked by one of their pet rams up against their picket fence (I was rather small and I thought I was going to be killed!), I settled in and loved it there. I turned eight in September. In August I went home for one day to Glengarry Road, but everything seemed so shabby and dull. I didn't want to stay there.

At Bethells, with a teacher among five pupils, it was like having a governess. We used to go down to the beach to Sunset Point and slide down the sand dunes, just the three of us, Nell Harre, Jocelyn and me. The schoolhouse was near the homestead and from there we had a good view of the sea. There was a generator, operated by the stream, which also fed the duck pond. It provided just enough power to light one room. Mrs Bethell was in charge of the boarding house and the kitchen but also they had a Maori woman helper, her name sounded like Rewi, however, because I couldn't get my childish tongue around it, I called her 'Weewee'. I think she took a shine to me. In spite of the isolation of Bethells she managed to get bananas, oranges and grapes and would every so often give me a feed. At home the fruit we had was just the usual orchard pears and apples from Oratia. I was certainly being spoilt. Mrs Bethell used to cook big apple pies and tapioca puddings, and we also had the usual things such as roasts and stews.

It was only me amongst all girls. Nancy and Trudy were older. They seemed very grown up to me but the other two, Jocelyn and Nell Harre, were nearer my age; Jossie, as we called her, was one month older and Nell about a year. We used to have a lot of fun together. They had a long verandah and at the end was a partitioned-off ironing room. Of course tablecloths and serviettes were starched in those days, so an ironing room was necessary. Every afternoon after school, at around quarter past three, we had afternoon tea in the ironing room, where we had our own enamelled cup and saucers, properly shaped miniature cups and saucers, which we used. My cup was a blue-green colour. The teacher would sit down to these afternoon teas with us and quietly teach us good manners. I revelled in it.

Then in November it was back to Glengarry Road and the harsh reality of the Henderson Convent. Henderson Holy Cross was an awful shock after this lovely Scottish teacher at Bethells who had treated us strictly but kindly and looked after us as if we were her own children. After about three years I was sent to St Brides Convent, Avondale, where the present day health clinic is and, for a while, my schooling was much happier. This was when we moved to French Bay.

My father was pro-Social Credit and pro-Labour, writing letters to the papers. He walked everywhere to my knowledge, 10 miles a day often. Much later on he got a little 'bubble car' in his nineties and was driving around in that. One person only could get in. It was like a small aircraft where you climb into the cockpit. That was after I left home.

It was building up to the great 1935 Labour election win and we were all excited about that. My father always claimed he had helped with the propaganda campaign to get Labour in. At that stage Labour was going to adopt Social Credit, and then they didn't so my father turned against them. However, H.G.R. Mason, the Attorney General and the MP for our district, used to come and visit my father at French Bay, arriving in a big black chauffeur-driven limousine. Forbes and Coates had been the main figures in the previous government. Their names were anathema in our area.

Next door to us was a bach that was owned by Mr and Mrs Surman, who had no children. We called Mr and Mrs Surman Uncle Bob and Auntie Belle. They were a dear old couple who lived in Mt Eden but came to the bach at French Bay. The bach had three rooms. Of course my family, having a superfluity of children, was only too pleased to 'farm' a few out and so this elderly couple sort of 'adopted' us. Uncle Bob taught me how to look after a boat, to caulk and paint it, and took me out fishing. I remember one special time when we went fishing in his boat, just off French Bay. We had only basic lines with sinker and hook, nothing fancy. Within three-quarters of an hour we had caught 44 snapper. Really good going! We must have landed right in the middle of a school of fish. After that any fishing experience was so tedious I nearly lost interest in it.

We discovered a seven-foot dinghy in the boathouse belonging to our house and got it all up to scratch. My elder brother was off overseas but I was around 14 years old. The little old ramp in Wattle Bay was built while we were there. We used to row all over the place. We'd go over to Wood Bay and also further on to where Pinesong is now. They used to call that Tommy Mason's Bay. We used to go out in this dinghy without lifejackets to the middle of the harbour to fish, and to the sandbanks for scallops. We did the most stupid things. The Manukau is a terribly dangerous harbour. I know the younger ones got friendly with one group of yachties who had an 18-foot boat. They were quite experienced yachtsmen. Yet they were all drowned in a sudden squall or storm. I used to stay with Uncle Bob (I think he must have been Gus Bishop's cousin) and Aunty Belle sometimes at their Mt Eden home and walk up there from secondary school. They loved us and, being childless, they were so good to us. Edna, my second eldest sister, also often stayed with them at Mt Eden. They sold the French Bay bach when they became too old. My youngest sister, Joy, who had just got married, bought it. There was a main kitchen/living room and two quite small bedrooms. We looked down on the right-hand corner of French Bay or had a more extensive view out towards Onehunga. There were two beautiful big kowhai trees, one on each corner, and a big puriri tree that we used to play on. Over a bit of a gully we used to swing on supplejacks, Tarzan style. We had a lot of fun there.

Estelle Bray

Estelle Canter Visscher (nee Bray) was interviewed by Marc Bonny during February and March of 2008.

A Titirangi childhood

My grandfather, Charles Bray (1864–1932), was the first of our family to be associated with this area. He was a civil engineer and during the first part of the twentieth century was the County Engineer for the Ohinemuri County with his office in Paeroa, where my father, Alan Bray, and his brothers and sisters had most of their schooling. My father then did his Mechanical Engineering apprenticeship with Price Engineering in Thames and later worked for a Waihi gold mining company.

In 1915, Langlands & Co. of Gisborne won the contract to build the Upper Nihotupu Dam for the Auckland City Council and they employed my grandfather to be the Engineer in Charge of Works. The family moved to a house in Sandringham and also used a house on the worksite in Parau, where my grandmother, Wilemina Mary, and her daughter Elsie ran a small post office; I think for the men working on the construction of the tram tracks, tunnels and pipeline. My father worked with my grandfather and he said that a number of the local young men, including Rod Shaw and other Shaw boys, worked with him. A jetty was built at Parau and the equipment and supplies for the construction site were shipped to there from Onehunga. The levels of the site of the dam were measured by my grandfather and Arthur Mead, who was

Charles Bray. Estelle Canter Visscher (nee Bray) Collection

then a young man and later became the Auckland City Engineer.

My father said that on Saturday nights the young men walked out to the old Titirangi School in School Road (now South Titirangi Road) for the Saturday night hops. After the dance the boys dossed down for the night on the verandah at John Bishop's house and would then walk out to Parau on the Sunday. One day Mr Langlands visited the site. He was talking with my grandfather in the contractor's office when the hooter sounded for a blasting. My grandfather went out to check and considered it safe for them to stay in the shed. However, when the shot was detonated a rock tumbled down, crashed through the roof of the shed and struck Mr Langlands on his head, fracturing his skull. They made a stretcher and carried him out to Greenwoods, which I presume was Greenwoods Corner, and there he died.

It was the time of the First World War. Many men, including my father, were called up for military service and with this loss of labour the work on the site was curtailed. My grandfather then became the County Engineer for the Mangonui County with his office in Kaitaia.

After Dad returned from the war, my mother, whom he had met in England, came out to New Zealand. They married and lived for a time in Cambridge in the Waikato. My sister Pam was born and then the twins, Nola and myself. My mother suffered ill health so they looked to moving to Auckland and Dad got a job as a mechanic at the Auckland Bus Company in New Lynn. He stayed in a boarding house in Rata Street until he found a house for us. That house was Punga Slopes, Titirangi. And so, during the May holidays 1938, when Nola and I were eight years old and Pam was 13, we came to live in Titirangi. We were not very happy to leave Cambridge where our life had been wonderful, but Dad encouraged us by telling us that we could not get lost because we

Alan Bray and co-worker during construction of the pipeline tunnel. Estelle Canter Visscher (nee Bray) Collection

Trench cut for foundations of new (Upper) Nihotupu Dam. In foreground is the auxillary dam temporary diversion pipe. Waitakere Library & Information Services, Bishop Collection

could follow a white concrete road all the way from Auckland City to the Titirangi Hotel and that budgies flew free in the bush. Indeed some did; a few years later when we had a budgie in a cage outside it attracted another budgie out of the wild.

When we moved from Cambridge, Dad brought our furniture up to Titirangi in a truck. Mum and my sisters and I stayed the night with friends and then came the following day by train from Hamilton to Auckland, each of us with our own little suitcase. We took an ABC bus destined for the 'TITIRANGI HOTEL' from the city, and followed the concrete road along the Great North Road through Avondale to New Lynn and then up to Titirangi. As we later learned almost always happened, chugging up the last hill into the village, the radiator blew its top and boiled over. I remember it was a lovely sunny day. The bus pulled over and stopped in the gravel in front of Mr Titchener's Four Square Store (now The Hardware Café) and there we got off.

Mrs Shaw had a very small tobacco kiosk to the left of Mr Titchener's Four Square store and on the other side of the store was a very nice house set down a driveway that ran parallel to the road. A big puriri tree stood a bit further along. It is said that people left messages on that tree but that was no longer so when we arrived in Titirangi.

There was the lovely view out to the Manukau Heads. Fortunately it is still there today, only then there were no public toilets to mar the scene. The Titirangi Hotel (minus Henry Atkinson who then stood undamaged on top of Mt Atkinson) stood as now, at the junction of the old School Road, which was narrow and very steep. I can't remember whether the red telephone box stood on the corner then or whether it came later; certainly it was there before the little wooden post office was built there, which no longer exists either. Near the end of the hotel a very rough Huia Road ran downhill, parallel with the main road.

There were no shops on the other side of the road opposite Mr Titchener's. Rod Shaw lived in a villa set back from the road behind a farm gate, and beyond that Gibby Shaw's family lived in a house well back from the road along a wide driveway (where the supermarket is today). They had a workshop there that later was a treasure trove for kids wanting trolley wheels. Punga Slopes was on Scenic Drive, just before the first big bend up from the filter station, and the house stood at the top of 118 steps; there was also a track which zigzagged up through the pungas. There were windows all along the front of the house and part way around the two sides and the view was spectacular: from the radio masts and the Whenuapai aerodrome in the northwest, across the city to Hillsborough and around to Little Muddy Creek and the Manukau Harbour in the south. We could hardly believe that we had come to live in such a magical place. At night the city was a fairyland of lights, with coloured neon lights flickering on and off. We could see the old scows sailing up the channel to Onehunga on the Manukau and when the sea was rough the 'white horses' scudding along. In wet weather Dad said that when the clouds lifted off Rangitoto and there was enough blue sky to make a pair of pyjamas then the rain would go away. Dad hung a piece of seaweed at the back door to tell us when rain was coming: it was dry and stiff in good weather and limp when it was going to rain. With our house perched high up on the hillside just beyond the gap in the range of hills, the wind would howl through the gap so that stormy weather was hurricane force around us and smoke from our cosy fire would blow down the chimney into the living room. There were all sorts of peculiar devices on the chimney to prevent this but they didn't work.

Our landlady was Miss Porter, who rode a motor-bike with side-car and lived with her cousin in Sunnyvale. She had built the little house herself and had dug the 118 steps. There was a small lawn at the back with a path around its edge to a tin-can dunny, just hidden in the bush. The first thing Dad did was to dig a very deep pit with a hand-held extended posthole digger (I have always thought it was 16 feet deep, perhaps it was), and so it became the sweetest dunny that ever was. The only hassle was that the wetas liked it too.

The house was really too small for us but we girls loved it. There was power to the house and water was laid on from rainwater tanks out the back. Water for the bathroom was heated by a chip heater. We inherited a semi-wild cat that Dad named Felix, who used to chase possums up the tall kanukas in the back garden. Possums sometimes sat on the windowsills at night and sometimes a morepork would sit on a punga frond just outside the window. There were grey warblers' nests hanging in the teatree scrub and often a hawk flew overhead, possibly in search of Tommy Belsh's Muscovy duck, Widdy, who lived in Waima Road (Woodlands Park Road) below 'The Filters'.

Huia Road winding down to Little Muddy, c.1920s.
West Auckland Historical Society, Kershaw Collection

We looked across the valley to see the Sowrey children playing in their garden on the corner of Westridge Road and hoped that we would soon be able to play there too. We did eventually. In those first days we entertained ourselves. We built a hut in the teatree scrub using puka leaves for roof tiles; very effective in the rain, and later we fished for craydaddies in a stream in the bush off the upper end of Konini Road. We walked for miles in all directions along the roads out to the Waitemata Harbour in one direction and down to the Manukau in the other. We never had time to be bored! We had been given a large sack filled with odd balls of wool and under Pam's guidance we knitted dozens of six-inch peggy squares, which Pam sewed together into a beautiful woollen patchwork blanket that she sent to Dr Barnardos. Later, during the war when wool became scarce, we could well have done with some of it for ourselves. Soon after we arrived at Punga Slopes one of Dad's cousins, with her big sons, came to visit us one evening and thereafter we looked forward to their coming most Wednesday evenings. The oldest boy, Arthur, made mandolins, and he loaned one to Pam who was then 13 years old. Pam went to the 1ZB radio station on Saturdays for mandolin lessons with the 1ZB "Musical Army", and then came home and taught me how to play by ear. I soon learnt to play a lot of the cowboy songs such *The Streets of Laredo, Tumbling Tumbleweeds* and *Home on the Range*, which were popular at the time. Later it was *A Sleepy Lagoon* and wartime songs such as *Coming in on a Wing and Prayer* and *Lili Marlene*.

In the evenings radio was the main form of entertainment. Dad had an American Bosche. We listened to *Fred and Maggie Everybody*, *The Lone Ranger* with his horse Silver, and spooky things like *Drums* and *Four Fingers and a Thumb*, which scared us stiff. We didn't have a car so we listened to a radio broadcast of the Dawn Service at the Museum on Anzac Day. I remember hearing the heavy tread of the boots of the many old soldiers as they marched through the Domain to the Cenotaph. It was so well commentated that afterwards we felt that we had been there. It was the same when the first Solent flying boat flew in to Mechanics Bay from Sydney; if I remember rightly, it was called *Aotearoa*.

We listened to Pam playing with the Musical Army at a concert in the Town Hall. I wonder if there is a recording of it in the radio archives? Then we heard King George VI announce the Declaration of War against Germany and thereafter Dad was glued to the radio. We (not understanding a word) heard Hitler ranting away and Lord Haw Haw spouting his propaganda and, after the start of the Pacific War with Japan, we heard Tokyo Rose. The Scenic Drive had been opened just the year before we arrived and it had become a favourite Sunday drive. From our house we could see the endless row of cars that wound up Titirangi Road and eventually passed the bottom of Punga Slopes. We didn't want to venture out on to the road on a Sunday afternoon in those days because we believed that we would not be able to cross through the continuous file of cars. With petrol rationing during the war, Sunday drives came to an end and never did return in the numbers of those first years.

When we arrived in 1938 the only shops in Titirangi other than Mr Titchener's Four Square Store and Mrs Shaw's tobacco kiosk, were Reekie's grocery and vegetable shop, which was an annex of the Tea Kiosk (Toby's Restaurant), and Mrs Jones' souvenir shop tucked in on the left at the top of the driveway, now down to the kindergarten. There was a little store opposite the old school in old School Road, but I have forgotten the name of the man who ran it. There was also a store at a house in French Bay and another just up Mahoe Road at Titirangi Beach that sold ice-creams and soft drinks in the summer time. Paturoa Road didn't exist in those days.

Reekie's Tea kiosk was sometimes used for public meetings, such as when a Chinese missionary gave a talk about his work in China. He spoke some Chinese, which we found very strange. Years later Pam's wedding reception was held there. It was a very nice, simple and cosy venue, furnished with the wooden chairs and tables typical of kiosks at that time, with a fire burning and a lovely view out to the Manukau Harbour.

Pam was married in the nearby Soldiers' Memorial Church, just as I was years later. At the gateway to the church there was a rustic archway of branches with a rambling rose creeping over it. It was said that a bell would be hung and having come from Cambridge where a peal of bells rang often of an evening, I was disappointed when a solitary bell was hung in what replaced the lovely rustic archway. The church was interdenominational and when I was a child the Anglican vicar was the Rev. Lord, who used to cycle up from New Lynn for his service on the first and third Sundays of the month. The Presbyterians held their service on the alternate Sunday. Miss McLay, who lived in Quamby (the big house which stands behind the kindergarten), took an interdenominational Sunday School each Sunday morning, with Beatrice Young as her assistant. Nola and I were not very enthusiastic pupils; I think because it was really quite a long walk, yet again, after our treks to school each weekday. Anyway, we had times of enthusiasm; I won a book for memorising the names of all the books of the Bible and at Christmas time, Nola and I used to sing with John and Edward Geddes (Andrew was then too young), *Jesus Bids us Shine with a Clear, Pure Light* and *Away in a Manger*.

My sisters and I had been baptised in St Andrew's Anglican Church, Cambridge and in about 1943 Rev. Lord decided we should be confirmed. There were very few buses on Sundays so every Sunday afternoon we walked down to St Thomas' church in New Lynn for confirmation classes and walked back again in the late afternoon. We were duly confirmed by the Bishop of Auckland. I felt very good for a while and became a dutiful member of the church, sometimes attending communion on the second Sunday of the month. Sometimes the Rev. Lord, Dr and Mrs Pope, who lived nearby in School Road, Mr Gus Bishop, who was the church warden, and I were the only ones there. When we sang hymns the Rev. Lord droned away in front, Mr Bishop droned away at the back, Mrs Pope warbled away to one side and I contributed my part too, although I don't remember how it sounded. The Bishop had been quite right to scold the very large congregation at our confirmation for their very poor attendance at church services.

My mother joined the Country Women's Institute and the Women's Christian Temperance Union, known as the WCTU, which was held at Miss McLay's house, Quamby. The WCTU had quite a bit of influence in Titirangi in those days; the area was 'dry' for many years. Anyway, it was at these meetings that my mother made her friends in Titirangi. Jill Barlow, who became prominent in the local drama group, was her good friend, and so was Mrs MacFarlane, who lived on top of the hill opposite Lopdell House. She later bequeathed her house to the Presbyterian Church. She had a croquet lawn with a little pavilion where the Presbyterian carpark at the top of Atkinson Road is today. My mother often played croquet there and when we went to meet her after school Nola and I were allowed to knock a ball around too.

On the hill next to Mrs MacFarlane's house was the Soldiers' Memorial. It was a lovely, peaceful place to go, with a view out over the Manukau, to sit on the park seats and contemplate the names of the local soldiers who had gone to the First World War. There was a small cannon pointing to the west that was removed once the Japanese war in the Pacific started. No one seems to know now what happened to it. There was no pathway around the road, so children always walked to school over the little pathway that wound up around the Soldiers' Memorial and down to Atkinson Road. A large ground orchid grew on the side of the path near the entrance to Mrs MacFarlane's house. We once saw a waxeye feeding her two little wee chicks on a branch of a small red matipo tree by the pathway.

Nola and I were noticed, I suppose, because we were twins. There were in fact five sets of twins at Titirangi School during our last year there. Anyway, when anything needed to be done in the community they thought of 'Mrs Bray's twins'. During the war Kitty Clark, who we believed had been a nurse and had driven an ambulance during the First World War, gave home nursing lessons in Macandrew Hall to the Country Women's Institute. She needed a patient to be washed and of course they thought of Mrs Bray's twins. Neither of us wanted to. Then, I am ashamed to admit, I chickened out, walked away and left Nola to it. She was duly washed and was commended on her 'clean tummy button'! (I carried my shame up until a couple of years ago when I apologised to Nola for leaving her alone; she couldn't even remember it!) The last straw came when we were asked to collect donations for the Bible Society. It went all right until we came to a little house, 'Pooh Corner' in Westridge Road. A child came to the door and when we told her why we were there she turned and called out, 'Mum, there are a couple of religious kids at the door'. We fled home and said we were never going to do that again — and we didn't.

Not long after Macandrew Hall was built, sometime in the early 1940s, Mrs Peace put on a pageant. On such occasions Nola and I usually had to be angels or fairies when we would have much preferred to be the wicked witch or some such exciting character. However, this time we were Pierrot and Pierrette. I missed my call and after a long silence Nola came to my rescue and said my part, which jogged me out of my reverie, and I said her part. When a flower show was held in the hall (about 1942), Mr Joe Beveridge (Bill [Boysie] Beveridge's father), who lived along Exhibition Drive and was the local Forest Ranger, became very enthusiastic and gathered hundreds of specimens of native trees for my mother to take to the show. A lot of the specimens we knew but there were many which we had never seen before. It was a wonderful collection. As did a lot of other children, I made a dish garden of mosses and twigs. I also drew a poster of the Statue of Liberty. What the Statue of Liberty had to do with a flower show I don't know, but it earned me enough points to share a cup with another girl.

We had come to Titirangi during the May holidays so at the beginning of the new term Mum took us down to the old Tin Shed to enrol us for school. However, it was too crowded so we had correspondence lessons, sent to us in cardboard envelopes from the Correspondence School in Wellington, for the rest of that year until the new school opened at the beginning of 1939. When we started school Consuelo Foley and Mabel Sowery became our friends. We walked around View Road (Kohu Road) to school and in the ways of children, it was never a straight run. We fossicked in the bushes along the way. One morning some boys from Konini Road threw a human skull to us that they had found in the bush not far from the school. We tossed it around and threw it to someone else passing by. I remember thinking it was probably from the Maori Wars. We thought no more about it and it never occurred to us to report it anyone; a real round human skull! A lot of us would walk home together after school having fun, until Koromiko Road (Kopiko Road) divided off View Road and then we became enemies. View Road kids fired stones at the Koromiko Road kids and vice versa until a girl got injured on her face, which was of course reported to the school and that was the end of that.

Gibby Shaw's father cut the grass on the northern slope of Mt Atkinson. A track zigzagged up across the grass to the top of the hill and there were small pohutukawa, planted on Arbor Day, scattered here and there.

During the war young people gathered at the hillside to watch small planes (perhaps Kittyhawks) practising dogfights over the Whenuapai Aerodrome. If someone had a guitar or ukulele, and someone usually did, there would be a spontaneous sing-along; *Roll Out the Barrel*, *She'll be Coming Round the Mountain*, *Maori Battalion March to Victory* and so on.

The local dump was over the edge of View Road, opposite the junction of The Drive to the summit, but we were never tempted to fossick in it. We seldom went straight home from school. Sometimes we would stop off at Mabel's place and sometimes at Consuelo's. Our mother was very trustful of us but I don't suppose she would have been very pleased to know of the time when Consuelo went to measure the water level in the reservoir that is under the top of Mt Atkinson and we climbed down the iron ladder that hangs on the inside wall. It was dark and still and scary hanging above all that deep water and, I realise now, rather dangerous.

Mrs Foley kept a cow called Daisy. It was a cause for laughter when Mrs Foley called her cow for milking because my mother's name was also Daisy. Daisy the cow grazed in a paddock, now nearly all bush, which stretched, with only the driveway to Ken and Kitty Clark's house to interrupt it, all the way from the wash-water pond (wash-water from the filtration system used at the filters) over the bank at the top of Waima Road to the first sharp corner of Scenic Drive, just beyond the present Titirangi School. Mr Peace, who also worked at 'the filters', lived in a house on Huia Road that backed on to the Titirangi end of the paddock. When Daisy was grazing near Mr Peace's house sometimes, on our way home from school, we went with Consuelo to herd Daisy back to the cowshed by the wash water pond for the evening milking. In the days before pasteurisation we bought our milk from Mrs Foley. Albie Foley, then about five years old, used to bring us our milk in a sparkling billy and he would call out 'milk' in his little voice. There were lots of frogs in the wash-water pond and they croaked all day and night, which none of us seemed to mind. Sometimes after rain a few would wander and get run over on Scenic Drive. I have not seen nor heard a frog in Titirangi for years and years.

When the opportunity came in about 1940, my father started working at 'the filters'. They employed an electrician and a carpenter and Dad became the maintenance engineer, sharing shift work with the others: day shift, afternoon shift and night shift, filtering the water supply from the Upper Nihotupu Dam.

It was then that Tommy Belsh became our friend. With his older brother Harold and his mother he lived with Mr Potts, who also worked at the filters, and lived in the first house down Waima Road (now Woodlands Park Road). Tommy made wonderful things from three-plywood with his fret saw and he played a mouth organ. Sometimes in the summertime, when Dad was not working during the day and the tide was right, he would walk with Tommy, Nola and me and down the Zig-Zag Track to Titirangi Beach for a swim. Tommy would play his mouth organ all the way there and all the way home. We thought he was wonderful. There was a little open place in the bush near the top of the Zig-Zag and, in the summertime when the cicadas were singing, dozens of dragonflies used to hover there in the sunlight. I wonder what happened to the concrete trough and drinking tap at the top of the Zig-Zag? We always stopped there for a drink.

Dad found that Lou Woonton (Mrs Waite) was still living in Woonton's Bay (Davies Bay). She had been one of the girls at the Saturday night hops at the old Titirangi School during the days when Dad was working with his father on the building of the Upper Nihotupu Dam. When the tide was right, Mum and Dad would go down early in the morning to Lou's little house above the rocks in Woonton's Bay. Lou would wade out into the sea to spear a flounder or two for their breakfast together. In the forties Dad and Pam and a neighbour, Mr Westbury, became keen flounder fishermen. On the midnight tide they would go down to Little Muddy Creek with their handmade spears and carbide lamps and we would have flounder for breakfast, dinner and tea.

From Punga Slopes we could see the last part of View Road (Kohu Road) from Scenic Drive up to Westridge Road. There were no houses along that stretch of the road except for a little cottage by Scenic Drive and a little holiday house opposite, up on the ridge overlooking the Manukau Harbour. Charlie Foley owned most of the land on the northern side of the road, and much of the other side too. Mr Foley spent a lot of time working his land and we could hear the echo of his boots as he walked up the stony road; so quiet it was. He would clear a section of land, dig it over, plant potatoes and, after reaping the crop, put up a notice saying, 'For Sale Apply C. Foley near Filters', with a price of about £95 for a section. And so it was until all his sections on that stretch of View Road were sold.

When in about 1940 Mr Potts retired and moved away, his filters' house, then one of only two houses at the top of Waima Road, became vacant, and we went to live there. Mr Glass and his son Robin lived in the house next door. That was the beginning of a wonderful childhood friendship that both Nola and I cherish to this day. We were both going to marry him but neither of us did. During the week Robin was at boarding school, but the weekends were a lot of fun. He was two or three years older than us and taught us many things: our first French words, 'Comment allez vous?' He said if you push your fingers together you squash millions of germs; that acid in your stomach curdled milk, and so on. He was very generous with his beautiful, shiny bicycle and its resounding bell. He devised all sorts of difficult routes for us to follow on his bike, in and out and around the shrubs and trees in our garden, with our times measured by a sun dial that he had made with a stick stuck in the ground. Sometimes we were mechanics and took his beautiful bike to bits and put it together again, sometimes with a few washers left over. In the summer Robin used to double us both, turn and turn about, down to French Bay for a swim and, as I remember, we spent most of the day there swimming and sunbathing, always in our possie under the pohutukawa tree at the end of the beach. There were lots of boats anchored in the bay in those days and we would swim from one boat to another. We went out to *The Shark* when the tide was in, sunbathed on her decks until the tide went out, and then walked back up the beach. I don't think any of us knew who owned *The Shark*. Sometimes we played cricket on the footpath in our front garden and sometimes we played tennis on a big concrete area at the lower filter station further down Waima Road.

In the early 1940s prisoners escaped from Mt Eden jail, killing a warden. They were at large for quite a while and were then reported to have stolen a car. Then, one day while we were playing tennis down at the lower filters we saw a car go along Exhibition Drive and, being a bit cheeky, we called out if they were the escaped prisoners then thought no more about it. However, that night when Mr Westbury, who lived in a new house next door to us, was on shift at the lower filters, Dad heard Mrs Westbury calling for him. She said that someone was trying to get into her house. She was too afraid to leave her bedroom so Dad climbed through her bedroom window, grabbed a chair and went thump, thump, thumping through her house. He heard running footsteps on the back verandah. The lock had been chiselled all around and was ready to be knocked out. Dad ran back to our house and told me to run up to the filters and report that someone had tried to get into Mrs Westbury's house. But my knees went to jelly so Pam grabbed a spanner and ran to raise the alarm. Immediately police were everywhere. The prisoners were caught early the next morning sleeping underneath the big kauri known as Clark's Kauri. One of them was snoring, which gave their hiding place away. They had indeed been in the car we had seen earlier on the Exhibition Drive. Next day at school there were all sorts of stories. Robin was disappointed because he had slept all through the drama; and Dad received a commendation for his bravery in running through the house to disturb the escaped prisoners.

Mr Westbury had an old open tourer car. When the blackberries were ripe we would all pile into his car with billies and kerosene tins and drive out to the end of Exhibition Drive and then walk down along the pipeline into the Parau Valley, where the blackberries were huge. We would gather tins and tins of them for Mum to make blackberry jam and blackberry pies. Also, we used to go down to Mr McEldowney's at the bottom of School Road to pick sacks of plums from his orchard, where Grendon Road is now. We could eat as many plums as we liked at the orchard, but of course afterwards Mum had to cope with two sick kids. Each year Dad would chop down one of the tall teatrees that grew thickly at the bottom of our back garden. We would help him drag the branches up to a big chopping block on the back lawn.

Clark's kauri, c.1930. Mia Stein Collection

Estelle Bray

An axe was permanently stuck in the chopping block and whenever we felt inclined, which was often, we would chop up the branches for firewood, which was stored in a large cupboard by the wood stove in the dining/kitchen room. Wetas love teatree so of course very often they would creep out into the house. Living in Waima Road the bush around us became our playground. We knew where to find little ground orchids and mosses and the small *Metrosideros* creeper with very small leaves and little red berries, and where sundews grew in damp places; and we knew where to find good rata vines to swing on; all gone now with the development of housing in Waima.

Pam started work at John Court's in the city in about 1941 and earned 16 shillings per week. She was generous with her earnings and would take Nola and me to 'the flicks' at the Delta in New Lynn. Cinemas were called picture theatres in those days, such as the Civic Theatre, the Regent Theatre and the Majestic Theatre in Queen Street. It was not until we were well into our teens that we ever ventured alone into the city on a Saturday night. Mostly we caught the 10-to-7 bus at the filters down to the Delta, where pictures started at 7.30. There was always a double feature, very often a cowboy film and then such films as *Hold Back the Dawn* with Charles Boyer, *The Letter* with Bette Davis and of course Bing Crosby and Bob Hope with Dorothy Lamour in *The Road to Morocco*. A lot of people had permanently reserved seats upstairs. The bus home left the city at 10-to-11 so, rather than hang about in New Lynn, we would often walk home. There were very few cars on the roads those days but if one did come we would hide in the bushes until it had passed (a bit of natural self preservation I suppose). There were very few houses along Titirangi Road. Walking along the ridge between Pleasant Road and Golf Road there were no lights to be seen out towards the ranges. We often saw shooting stars and at times a comet.

After the puriri tree in the village had been cut down a string of shops were built. Pam had a workshop in one of them, making garden ornaments. She was very skilful and her work was sold all over New Zealand. However, as it was war time when she turned 18 she was man-powered to work first at Tom Clark's pottery in New Lynn putting handles on cups, which was then considered an essential industry, and then at Radio 1936 in the city, assembling radios for the Army.

Nola and I started at Auckland Girls' Grammar in 1943. We felt we were very much country girls. Our lives were certainly very different from those girls who lived in the more central suburbs. There was a bus shelter made of corrugated iron on the corner where the carpark at the filters is today. On rainy days people would leave their shoes and umbrellas in the shed for when they returned at the end of the day. They were never stolen and neither was the money left in kerosene tins for a butcher who used to come up from Glen Eden. We used to catch the ABC bus at about 10-to-8 each morning. It had come round Scenic Drive and went back along View Road, picking up passengers at Westridge Road and at a bus shelter at the top of Koromiko Road. Our weekly ticket cost 2 shillings and sixpence. The bus picked up passengers all along Great North Road until the convent in Avondale and then only dropped passengers off, along Great North Road through Avondale to the city. The buses were packed to standing room only and often the people to whom we had offered our seats would have us sit on their knees. They were always the same people on the buses and we came to know them, such as Professor Blaiklock, on whose knee I have often sat, and a very beautiful lady who used to get on at Park Road who we called Blondie for obvious reasons. We never did learn her real name. Coming home after school our bus left the city at 3.45 pm and mostly we were able to have a seat. During the war we girls would sit and knit scarves and mittens, balaclavas and socks for the Army, Navy and the Air Force. The boys from Mt Albert Grammar were always playing pranks and would wind our balls of wool around the luggage racks. The bus to Titirangi Hotel dropped us off at Mr Titchener's store, where we would pick up our mail from Vernon Titchener's little post office tucked in a back corner of the store. From there we would walk the mile home each afternoon. We were home by about a quarter to five; it was quite a long day. We learned our homework on our way home around Scenic Drive or else we would practise singing in two parts: *Twinkle Twinkle Little Star* or *The 23rd Psalm*, which we had learnt at Grammar. Only Ken and Kitty Clark could hear us as theirs was the only house on Scenic Drive from Titirangi to Charley Foley's house, with its great big macrocarpa trees where all their chooks used to roost at night. It was down over the bank at the junction of Scenic Drive and Woodlands Park Road. Consuelo Foley, who had been born on the same day as Nola and I, often gave us a bantam to put in Dad's hen run for our birthday.

Sometimes, girls from Grammar who lived in the city would come out on a Sunday and we would hike out along Exhibition Drive to Mackie's Rest and down to the stream in the Parau Valley for a swim. Even in winter the valley was lovely and warm. That same stream now feeds the Lower Nihotupu Dam, (we always called it the Parau Dam).

At the end of 1947 Nola and I left school. Nola went to work in the Railway Engineers Draughting Room at the Auckland Railway Station and I had been given a job as a technician in the laboratory of J.R. Butland analysing cheese, on Great South Road near Rockfield Road. It was an awful long way to go from Titirangi, but such jobs then, for girls just out of school, were not easy to find.

Early in the morning I would cycle around Scenic Drive to catch the 10-to-6 bus which I could see coming up School Road (South Titirangi Road). I would throw my bike into the bushes at the entrance to Gibby Shaw's house and jump on the bus. As nearly everybody went to work in the buses, it was always full when I got on so I would have to stand all the way to Pitt Street, where I jumped off and ran along Karangahape Road to Grafton Bridge to catch the bus to Rockfield Road. If I missed that bus I took another to Ellerslie and walked through paddocks to the back of Butlands. Coming home I caught a 6 o'clock bus, known as the 'drunks bus', cycled home around Scenic Drive and got home just before 7 o'clock. I enjoyed the work but stayed for only a year as it was really too far to go each day. Then I got a job as Curator of the Insect Collection in the Entomology section of the DSIR in Mt Albert. Living in Titirangi stood me in good stead as on weekends I was able to collect plant galls caused by midges and tiny microscopic Eriophyid mites found mostly on putaputaweta trees, which were being studied by one of the men working in entomology who was doing a thesis on plant galls. Eventually I was given time off to attend botany lectures at the university and was able to make a wonderful collection of native plants that unfortunately was later destroyed.

I met my husband there and we were married in the Titirangi Soldiers' Memorial

Church in February 1955. We bought a section near the top of South Lynn Road.

There was a little stream running through the bush at the bottom of our section. When we first owned it, a lady came up through our bush walking her dog. She said that she had found a huge old rata tree so the bush, she thought, was of long standing. As it happened Bill and I went to live in Tonga and the Cook Islands and then in the Motueka area; it was 13 years before we returned. We came back ready to build on our section but, to our disappointment, it had all changed. The bush at the bottom of our section and across the valley, including the rata tree, was all gone. The stream had been replaced by a sewerage vent and pipes and, in the middle of our section, someone had dug a rubbish pit, full of rubbish; and there was the wreck of an old car lying on its side. We cleared it all away, sold the section and then bought one in the bush at 230 Atkinson Road and had a Lockwood house built. While our house was being built in 1969 we rented a flat in Wood Bay from Mrs Symes. Our daughter, Catherine, started at the Titirangi School, which was quite changed from the days I remembered. The banks were bare of trees and the playing fields bare of grass. Our son, Tarn, was three years old and, as I had been a Play Centre Supervisor in Lower Moutere, I became Assistant to Supervisor Heather Carter at the Titirangi Play Centre and Tarn was able to attend. When Heather left I became the Supervisor. When we first returned to Titirangi there were few old faces I knew in the street. However, after starting at the Play Centre there was always somebody to stop and chat to. I supervised at the Play Centre for a year or more until our son Carl was born in September 1971.

While at the Play Centre I offered to show someone how to make baskets. An arrangement was made to meet at my neighbour's house, Kath Smitherain, and when I got there, there were five women; and the next week nine, and so I had a class. Shortly after, when Heather Carter opened her bookshop in the new block of shops next to the hardware shop, Heather said she would like to sell baskets. So I made one and took it to her. When I returned home she rang to say it had already sold and would I make another. Then I shared a stall at the Anglican Craft Festival in the Memorial Hall and sold all 30 baskets I had made and got orders from five shops. Crafts were booming in Titirangi and I gave basketry lessons in the old Community House in Rangiwai Road and cane furniture classes at Green Bay High. It was through the Play Centre and my basketry classes that I have met most of my Titirangi friends.

There was a spinning group in Titirangi and a

Marriage of Estelle Bray to Tammerus Willem Canter Visscher at Titirangi Soldiers' Memorial Church, February 1955.
Estelle Canter Visscher (nee Bray) Collection

friend and I wanted to join them but they already had as many members as they could accommodate in their houses. So, with Elaine Ludwig, Raewyn Robinson and Ann Tildersley we formed our own group. We were very enthusiastic and became affiliated to the New Zealand Spinners and Weavers' Guild. As members of the Guild we had to give ourselves a name so we called our group 'The Yarn Spinners'. Spinners have come and gone over the 30 years or more but we still meet to spin yarns, although none of us spin much wool any more but we do tapestry and quilting and other needlework.

Ken Hanson

Ken Hanson lived in Titirangi for 32 years from 1949 to 1981. He was a teacher at Titirangi Primary School and in several other schools in the area. He was interviewed by Marc Bonny in 2004.

A teacher's story

Shortly before going to live at Titirangi, I remember going there to visit the Rev. Edwin Brace, known to all as 'Bracey'. He was from England, and besides being a man of the cloth he had been an architect. His place was about half-a-mile down Huia Road on the left. He had just finished building it. Building then was very difficult owing to shortage of materials because of the war. However, he had built a lovely cottage-like house with a slate roof. I believe the slates came off the pumphouse at Western Springs. He had made all the concrete wall blocks himself. He had had to ride miles to get up there each evening just to make a few more blocks. He couldn't buy a bath so had made an excellent one out of concrete and tiles. When the house was finished he encouraged young people to come and enjoy his home as a retreat, and often lots of us thoroughly enjoyed the company and the peace to be found there.

As one approached the Titirangi township, on the left in Rangiwai Road, opposite where the post office was then (now Masala restaurant), was the Atkinson family home and further on was Titchener's grocer shop (now The Hardware Café) and then a beautiful old puriri tree, which stood by Zella's Home Cookery, then came School Road and the old Titirangi Hotel, which later became the School for Deaf, known as Lopdell House. On the opposite side of the road was a service station and then Rod Shaw's house, next to where the supermarket is now.

Soon after the war, my wife Joyce and I purchased land from Mr T.A. (Gus) Bishop in the Waima block that was being opened up. This section was at the end of Manuka Road where it met Tainui Road, and was covered in bush. We set to work and cleared some of it and built a temporary bach to live in. For a little while there was no water or power.

When Taraire Road was put in bordering our property and meeting up with Manuka and Tainui roads, it made us into a corner block. The mail when it came was Rural Delivery.

When the water main was first put in I connected up to the meter and suddenly a fountain of water shot up about eight feet into the air. I rushed around to Rod Shaw's (he worked for the Council) and told him what was happening. He was unflappable and calmly said something like, 'Here hold on, which side of the meter is it?' (The road side.) 'Well, what are you worrying about, I'll get to it later,' and he did — about three hours later! I remember too that there were several wild pigs hanging up under his house. He was a pig hunter, and there were still a few wild pigs around the area then.

Nobody had much money and we young people found our own amusements. One was a New Year's Eve get-together held on the lawn in front of Sister Frazer's army hut, with lovely music supplied by Bill and Mary Bond. The music had been turned up to waft through the trees in the moonlight from their place over in the next road. It was an altogether delightful evening.

There was a great togetherness then, where the community went out of its way to help each other. For example, when Bill Bond's house burned down, the next morning everyone came and did the dirty work of cleaning up the site, making it ready to rebuild. The ladies also supplied beautiful cakes for the workers. Our fox terrier also helped with the clean-up. It found a well blackened roast of meat and smartly carried it away!

I became a teacher and for promotion had to do two years' service in the country. The first country school I went to was Oratia, where I loved the job as the people were wonderful. I travelled to and from Titirangi in an old Model A Ford ½-ton flat-top truck with 12-inch tray sides. One day, going home up Shaw Road with the children who lived up that way sitting on the tray, a stray bull loose on the road took to us. It ran behind and rammed the back of the truck time and time again. Of course the children screamed every time it rammed and on that hill the old truck just couldn't get away from that very angry bull — until eventually the beast got tired and gave up. I guess those children will always remember that!

One Saturday morning some boys took me to collect swarms of wild bees for my hives. All went well until coming home one of the boys said he knew of a swarm that was hanging on a tree under the road bridge, on the West Coast Road. We stopped, clambered down and stood working out how to get the swarm down and into a box. One boy, probably bored, picked up a stick, threw it and brought the whole lot down on top of us. I still don't know who won the race to get out of there!

The classroom was the Oratia Hall, over the road from the school, and had only a table, desks and blackboard, all of which had to be carted downstairs twice a week when the hall was needed at night for weekly bowls and Saturday night dances.

The next school I went to for country service was Hobsonville. Other West Auckland schools I taught at were Titirangi (three times), Glen Eden, Avondale, Point Chevalier, Blockhouse Bay Intermediate and Rutherford Primary, all of which have their own stories and happy memories.

In my earlier Titirangi days we found a 25-foot derelict launch lying on Cornwallis Beach, which we bought for £100. We got it floating and brought it back to Titirangi Beach using a Seagull outboard motor. All the ribs had to be replaced and this had to be done on the beach between tides, using a Primus making steam to pass through downpiping containing the new ribs. They had to be bent into shape and then riveted into place. Eventually we got the boat's old Rugby motor going too and so she was finished, only to be sold, as by then we needed the money to build our home. This was built with the last of the Glenburn bricks, made by the brickworks in Avondale. The drainage pipes were from Crum's pipeworks.

My father, Victor, was building a seaside bach on what is now a small road going off the end of the Titirangi Beach esplanade. There was only a narrow track around the cliff then and along this we took timber, blocks, cement, shingle, roofing materials; the lot, and what a job! Building there is certainly much easier now.

At Titirangi Beach there was a shop nearby up a side road and a little ice-cream kiosk right on the beach flat that opened only sometimes. Later, cars were not allowed along the beach unless you were a resident. Mr Shaw was the Beach Warden. He also kept the beach tidy. Often were the times we would see him there, busy with his rake.

I remember Gus Bishop talking about his father, who had seen baskets of human bones that had been hung in the trees there after a bloody battle had taken place. He also spoke of how in the early days, after dark, the flounder spearing was done using a frying pan full of burning kauri gum for a light. I wonder if they caught many?

On the road out to Huia is the Kakamatua Stream, where a long time ago a number of bodies were washed up following the wreck of HMS *Orpheus*. A local inhabitant told me a story about how one night he and a friend heard a dinghy load of people rowing up the stream. Someone in the dinghy was saying that the area was haunted! From onshore these two decided on a bit of fun to help things along and so cries and wails like 'Ooh, ooh, agghh!' were heard. The rowers took off with lightning speed, and probably still swear the place is haunted!

We had not long been living at Titirangi when we saw an advertisement offering a dinghy and outboard motor in exchange for a bicycle. Well, we made the exchange and felt like millionaires, for we now owned a boat! The first thing that happened was that when the weather blew up very rough the motor stopped at a time when we sorely needed it. Fortunately another fisherman saw our plight and towed us back ashore, badly shaken. That Christmas we got lifejackets for presents. Another time we were out fishing and a bloated and badly decomposing cow appeared alongside, coming down from Onehunga. On another occasion we were over by the South Channel and a cocker spaniel, just about on its last legs, came swimming down from Onehunga. We got it aboard and took it back to Titirangi Beach where it suddenly got a new lease of life and took off, to where we know not! On yet another occasion two intoxicated men were fishing in a dinghy not far from us, arguing loudly as one wanted to go ashore and the other didn't. Eventually, one who was immaculately dressed in a dark suit, just stood up, told the other one that he would walk ashore, and then stepped over the side. He was rescued in time — just!

There were a lot of fish in the Manukau Harbour then, and lots of piper in the piper grass growing on the beach. A true fishing story concerns a friend who one evening rowed out alone to the sandbanks by the South Channel to go flat-fishing. He would be one of the luckiest people I know. He anchored on to a sandbank, got out his spear and his light and as it was getting dark got out on the sandbank and commenced operations. He speared a number of flounder, putting them into a sugar bag on his shoulder, but when he had enough and with his light failing, he just couldn't find his boat, and the tide was rising. He didn't find the boat, the tide continued to come in, but in the small hours as he was standing on tiptoe with the water just lapping into his nose, another fishing boat came by, the owner heard him shouting and he was saved. What luck!

In the Titirangi area possums were a great problem. The first time I saw one was when I woke up to see a grey shape sitting on the open windowsill, uttering very loud and strange cries. In the dark I grabbed a broom to push this unknown horror away but it simply held on to the other end. A tug o'war ensued, very frightening when half asleep! Like other settlers I shot lots of possums after that, once killing three with one shot as the one I saw with its eyes glowing in the torchlight, had another one on the branch behind it with a baby in its pouch.

On Waima Road (now Woodlands Park) on the left where it meets Manuka Road, there is a large old kauri tree. Our daughter, rounding that corner on her way to school, heard a lot of commotion with birds and looking up saw a huge branch coming crashing down. She was very lucky for it narrowly missed her.

Some of the folk who came to live nearby in Taraire Road were Shirley and Howard Wilson, Mr Isaacson, Sister Frazer and her mother, Mr and Mrs Faithful, Bill and Mavis Penny, Mr and Mrs Curtis, Graham and Loma Smith, and a retired gentleman, Jack Hodinott, who came from Rhodesia and had been in a position of responsibility in the Police Force there. When there was trouble with the Mau Mau uprisings he decided to go back and help, and was killed.

Sometimes when we were entertaining visitors we would walk up Mt Atkinson to see the monument and the extensive view from up there, or sometimes go to the massive kauri tree off Tainui Road. Before the land was subdivided we would go and see the waterfall, which is in the bush somewhere near and below the Waima Store, but now it is on privately owned land.

Our friend Bill Bishop once took us on a day tramp, starting at the Titirangi upper filters and then along Exhibition Drive, which originally had been put in to build and to service the water pipeline bringing water from the dam to the filters. The bush along there is beautiful, but Bill had also borrowed keys that allowed him to unlock gates for us so we could go through the pipeline tunnels. The thousands of glow worms there were a sight never to be forgotten. I think we walked out to the Nihotupu Dam and back. It was most impressive; the absolute silence except for the birdsong, and with the beauty of the day and of the place — it was just so wonderful, I have never forgotten it.

Fog could sometimes be a problem on Scenic Drive. Some nights coming home on a motor-bike we were periodically enveloped in unexpected patches of fog. It was quite frightening as visibility was suddenly nil! On a later occasion, when coming home in our old truck at night along Scenic Drive from Shaw Road towards Titirangi, the fog was so thick that my wife got out and walked the white line just in front, for that was the only way we could keep on the road and find our way home.

Teaching at Titirangi Primary School

Just below the end of the lowest classroom there stood an interesting large kohukohu tree. The flowers on this tree grow straight out from the trunk, and it was a beautiful tree. Once my class and I walked around to the end of Tainui Road to see the magnificent old kauri tree there. We had just started marching off in two lines to come back when a very agitated, unkempt man sprang out of the bushes wanting to fight me, saying he was going to knock my block off! The children didn't know whether to run, stay and help, or what to do. Eventually the man cooled down. He was something of a recluse, and one of the boys apparently had removed from a teatree at the side of the road a small piece of cardboard from a cigarette packet, which had the words, 'Keep out' pencilled on it. With teaching there's never a dull day!

Then there was the time when I had a sinus problem and had to stay in bed for a week. After a few days my class decided that they would all come and visit me. One lunch hour they got themselves into orderly lines and walked the mile around to my home. That was great, except they hadn't told anybody so when they returned late they found both the headmaster and the relief teacher not very happy at all.

We had a piano accordion band at school. Some of the children had learned to play, so once a month we used to have musical evenings, and later these were held in the local RSA hall. There were about 25 children who played, sometimes solo, sometimes together and all parents who wished to attend were welcome. The children took turns playing for their

Staff at Titirangi School, 1954. Back row, from left: Mr Hanson, Mr Pound, unknown, Mr Rankin, unknown. Front row: Mrs M. Bond, third from left; Mrs Singh, third from right.
Titirangi Primary School 125th Jubilee Committee

Ken Hanson

dances, as they did also for the musical games. 'Musical chairs' was always very popular. Once a year at Christmas we all entertained the old folk at Sunset Home. At all the functions it was always a joy to see the children at their best. The boys would hand around plates of food to the girls and to the adults without getting in first. I sometimes wondered if they were the same boys I knew in daily life!

Another memory is of a lady who used to come weekly for religious studies, which I think was done in most schools. Well, this lady was very intense and put great fear into the children, departing somewhat from the official syllabus, so it wasn't long before there were lots of complaints about children having nightmares and she was asked to leave. However, she was so dedicated that she would wait outside the gate and gather the children up as they left school, and take them over the road to where the war memorial stood to continue her endeavours to save them from the devil. It was quite a worry for everybody.

I also remember a school bottle drive in South Titirangi Road. The children called in to peoples' houses and politely asked if the people had any old bottles that the school could have for their bottle drive. All went well until at the home of a well-known gentleman one boy was taken by the owner and shown a very large stack of bottles. This was too much for that small boy, so as the man turned to go inside he excitedly shouted back up to us, 'Hey, bring down plenty of boxes because there's a real hop-head living here!' Oh dear!

Eventually I had to take early retirement due to deteriorating health, so we sold our Titirangi home and went to live at our beach property on Waiheke Island, leaving behind a lovely area, lovely memories, and a lifestyle that had given us so much happiness.

Ken Hanson's 1955 Standard 1–2 class at Titirangi School. Author Marc Bonny is third from right in the front row. The classroom was one of two prefabs with a coal stove. *Titirangi Primary School 125th Jubilee Committee*

Hendrina Sluiters

Hendrina Sluiters was a Dutch migrant to New Zealand during the 1950s. She lived in Godley Road when she arrived in Titirangi. The following interview with Hendrina was recorded by Marc Bonny on 26 July 2005.

From Holland to New Zealand

My husband was a structural engineer and carpenter and always wanted to have his own business. After the war in Holland there was a lot of work. My husband started his own business and we purchased furniture from some friends going to Indonesia and lived in their flat. But we couldn't stay in the flat. A lot of people were going overseas to America, Canada, Australia. We thought of going to Australia, but my husband's brother, who also wanted to come, had a friend in New Zealand who said that you are better off to come to here as it is a bit more refined. This friend made sure someone was waiting for us when we arrived by ship in Auckland.

We told our parents we were going. My only brother had already gone to Venezuela. We came in 1950 and then my parents came in 1952. We just took a desk and a few bikes and a sewing machine. At first we were staying at the top end of Mt Eden Road, opposite the road that leads to the hilltop. It was very beautiful and we loved it. We didn't want to go back to Holland. We were so happy here. There was no pension in Holland in those days, so there was no reason my parents couldn't come, although they had to be 20 years here before they were entitled to stay. We started to look around for a big section because our parents were coming, and we loved Titirangi and its kauris. We didn't have much English, only school English. In Holland we had learned English, we had taken three foreign languages: French, German and English. English has easy grammar. Coming to New Zealand was like heaven then. There was plenty of work, you could leave your house open, and there was one murder a year, whereas now there is one a day!

So, in 1950 in Titirangi there was Titcheners and Zellas Home Cookery; over the road was Shaw's Petrol Station and the dairy. I remember the deaf school and the post office in front of it. May Dyers was in it, and I was a bit nervous of her as she was so abrupt, and my English was so poor, so I dreaded going there. I also remember Mrs Carter's bookshop, under Dr Jacobs' medical rooms.

Under the present Catholic Church in Rangiwai Road there was the Plunket. I went there with my baby and it was slippery and I fell down and hurt myself with quite a bit of blood! The roads were terrible and slippery. The grader didn't come often enough we thought. The road was like a country lane and down below was the La Rosa farm and we could see all the sheep and horses. I once picked up a pair of shoes at the bus stop and thinking they were abandoned I thought finders keepers! So I took them home, and then someone told me that they probably belong to a lady who had to go to town and changed into another new pair until she got back to the bus stop later. When I learned this I put them back. These little things happen when you are new in the country. It was not unusual, this change-of-shoe episode out here, as the roads were so rough. Then we started to complain because it was so very dusty in the dry weather. We had a petition going with all the neighbours for the road to be sealed. They tarsealed it around 1959, but then it became a speedway and the traffic increased.

I used to push my little baby up to the 'Top' (Titirangi shops) to do my shopping. The telephone was a bit different then, there was a party line, but I could ring the grocer and he would deliver the order.

I have been always involved with the Presbyterian Church opposite the Titirangi School. It was built maybe 25 years ago. The manse was the old MacFarlane house by the old memorial site behind the present church on the top of the hill. The MacFarlanes gave the house to the church, so we had the land to build this church.

The first house we lived in was built during the Depression. The windows were all a bit different because it was built from demolition material. The place was used as a holiday cottage for people living in the city. We went to Titirangi Beach or French Bay for picnics.

I remember the Titirangi Light Opera Club, we saw *Pygmalion*, and I also remember going to the Women's Institute meetings in the daytime. They were very friendly to newcomers. There was also a women's group down at the hall at Titirangi Beach.

I remember Mr Bower who had the first house at the top of the road. I know they used Crum Park for the pottery clay.

My daughter went to Titirangi School about 1958. She could speak Dutch also. In those days we had a privately run playcentre in the Macandrew Hall. My daughter's children also went to Titirangi School. I was in the choir many years ago. It started off as the League of Mothers, a Christian-based friendship group at the Macandrew Hall. Out of that came the choir and the Titirangi Singers, which is still going, although we all have grey hair now. We sing for the oldies and go to the retirement villages.

The food in New Zealand to us was really strange at first. At the butcher we saw these big pieces of meat, whereas where we had come from we could buy only tiny pieces of meat, but 'nicely' presented. Back in Holland we had more choice to put on our bread but when we came here it was different. We had 'black pudding' and brawn in New Zealand but it was all new to us. Everything was so big, like a big piece of topside; it looked rough. Of course we would finely slice it and fry it. Our cooking was so different but I learned. I never knew what a roast dinner was before, but I loved to learn that. We never had butter in Holland because all the butter was exported away. I loved the butter and creamy milk here. Scones and pikelets were new to us. When we were asked to bring a plate I brought a plate, until you realise you have to put something on it from home! Another thing that was new was the tram. I stood on the wrong side to get on it, because in Holland you get aboard on the right side. And to get a cup of coffee back then, well, forget it! In those dairy milkbars you had to slide into narrow column seats and maybe have a cup of strong tea and scones. We never had hot pies before either. We did get Reizensteins bread here, and of course now it's called Vogels. It was the Dutch here that introduced the coffee habit really.

Another hard thing was the slang. When I rang my husband at work for the first time and the phone was on the wall, they said, 'Hang on,' I hung up! When TV came it was lovely, twice a week and no advertising and all those innocent things like *Mr Ed* and *My*

Three Sons, but when the other stuff came my husband didn't like our child watching all that. My husband was too busy doing calculations at home and so on to take much interest in TV.

Of course you couldn't buy a car unless you had some pounds sterling or overseas money. I had a little Austin 7 and before this my husband had this old Ford V8. So when my mother and father were coming out my husband said, 'You have to learn to drive'. And so I learned in the V8. But when our parents came out he sold it and we kept the Austin 7, and kept the motor-bike as well. I had to look after my parents, drive them; interpret for them, take them to doctors and everything. This was 1952. We had to be a guarantee for them, as the government wasn't going to pay for them. A doctor also stood guarantee for them, and we got someone else for my husband's parents. It was really a big risk for us, but we were young and it turned out very well because our fathers were bricklayers and there was plenty of work. My husband took them to work, so it was that we never had to give them any money as they worked and saved.

My father and mother lived with us for four years and my husband's parents rented a place in Golf Road and also kept two boarders to help pay the rent. Then my husband started to build houses for them.

He worked very hard and when my parents had been here for four years, he built a house for them and then two years later a house for his parents. I didn't go back to Holland until two years ago. My husband had no other relations to see there, only cousins, so he didn't want to go back. My brother in Venezuela had come to visit us here, and he wanted to live here very much but his wife wanted to go back to her mum in Holland so my brother went back to Holland. Two years ago, aged nearly 80, I visited my brother in Holland. I was so glad I did and saw my lovely country. It is so beautiful. I didn't recognise so much of the cities, but outside the cities I could see the old country.

I remember the fish and chip shop starting in Titirangi. Miss Baildon in haberdashery was in that shop later for many years. She lived next door. Mrs Carter had the bookshop and was there a long time but when the New Lynn shopping centre began it took away all that business and Mrs Carter had to close.

Of course we had limited money. Once we bought a caravan and that enabled our parents to see the country, one lot at a time. We bought our first new car, a Ford Zephyr, with money from my brother in Venezuela when he came to see his father and mother here. We arranged that we paid for everything for them here and we would swap the overseas funds he had, so we could buy the car for the caravan. My daughter had piano music lessons from a lady up the road. I wanted to learn the piano in Holland but you had to be rich to do that then. I also worked very hard during those years.

I am a committed Christian in the Presbyterian Church and I go every Sunday and take part in everything. When I joined this church, the Rev. Gunn had an operatic group going to reach out into the community and in no time I was in that as well and have many photos. We had the Sunday School next to the fire station in Titirangi and we rented the Memorial Church before building our own.

Dr Mary Hamilton

Dr Mary Hamilton practiced medicine at Titirangi for 23 years, from 1950 to 1973. She was interviewed by Marc Bonny for the West Auckland Historical Society in January 2006.

I came to Titirangi in December 1951 at the recommendation of the Health Department. My parents had arrived in New Zealand at the end of November and were met with the news that I had resigned from my job as assistant to the GP on Waiheke Island and that I proposed to move to this 'fringe of heaven' on the western side of Auckland. The nearest practitioners were in New Lynn and, although some of them lived in Titirangi, most of them welcomed my arrival, seeing it as relieving them from any need to respond to calls from Titirangi/Laingholm/Huia area.

The 'village' at that time was literally a village with a hardware shop next to the Four Square grocery store run by Bill Chermside on the left side of the road. The garage (Shell station) opposite was run by Rod Shaw, who lived in a house behind the garage. The post office was housed in a small wooden building on the corner of School Road, next to what is now called Lopdell House, but at the time was known as the Hotel and housed the School for the Deaf. Cyril Allen was headmaster of the deaf school and lived with his family in a house on the other side of School Road. May Dyer was the Postmistress and remained in that job for many years, even after the post office was moved to the swanky new building in Rangiwai Road in the 1970s. The local dentist, Keith Plowman, had a surgery next to the garage, but there was no accommodation available to rent for a doctor's surgery.

Most of the houses were hidden in the bush, but by counting the letterboxes I was able to make a rough estimate of how many people lived in the area and I concluded that a practice there might be a viable proposition; it would certainly be semi-rural in character, for which I had a personal preference. The Health Department was extremely helpful in offering me a locum post at Whenuapai Airport, which was then the civil airport for Auckland. The usual Port Medical Officer was a serving Air Force officer who was due to go on leave for the month of January, so filling in for him in clearing all the overseas arrivals would tide me over financially through the initial stages of establishing myself in the area. The locum job was something of a farce as my job consisted of watching people disembarking from the newly arrived overseas plane and walking into the reception building. If anyone sported an obvious rash I could stop them, otherwise there was nothing to do. However, it was not my place to criticise the arrangements.

I favoured practising from rooms at my home rather than a lock-up surgery. We had found a house in Titirangi Road between Golf and Godley roads on a large section with a stand of pohutakawas around the entrance. The section sloped away from the road but the entrance was set back and the flat area north of the pohutakawas could be cleaned off and metalled to provide off-street parking for patients attending the surgery, a very important consideration. The house was large enough to serve both as a residence and temporary

RSA interior, April 2010. Bruce Harvey Collection

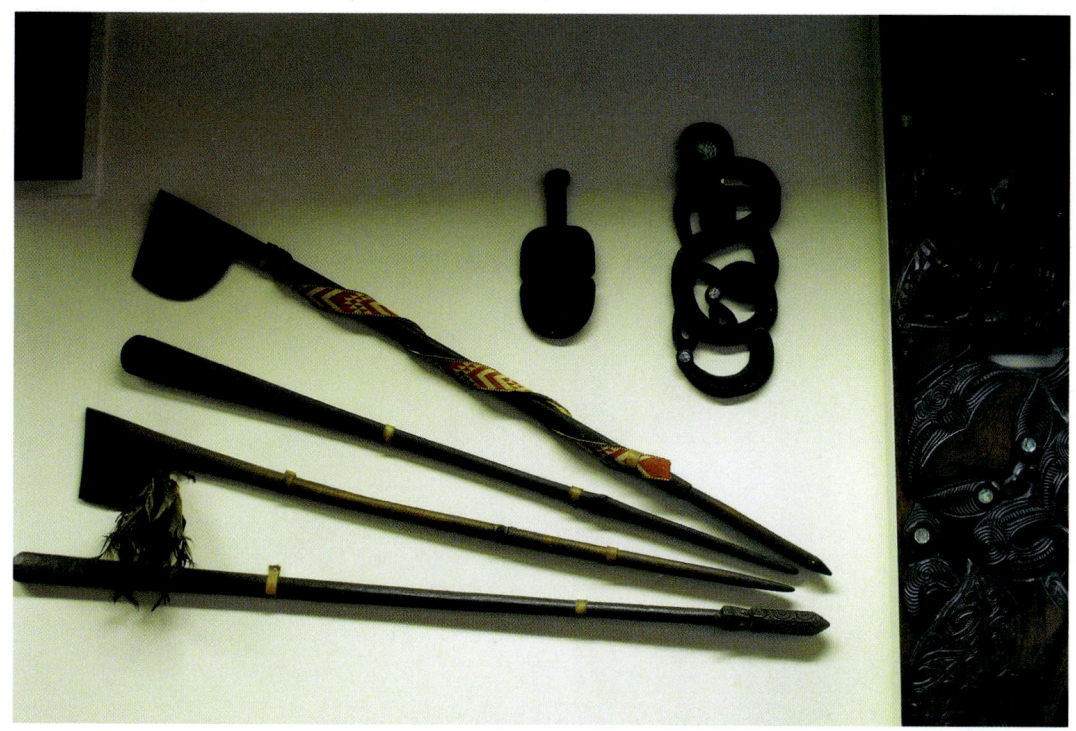

Artefacts on display at the RSA, April 2010. Bruce Harvey Collection

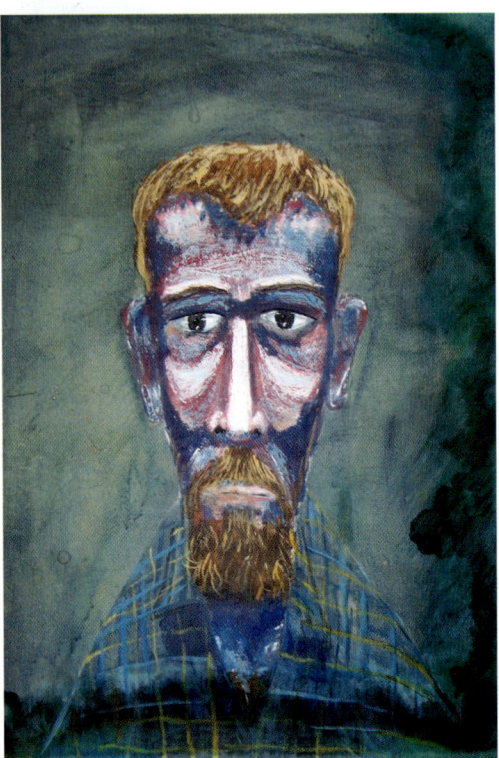

(Above) David Kennedy with his painting of the interior of a New Lynn kiln during the firing process, February 1956. Kennedy worked the nightshift at the kiln.
Photographer: George Bonny, Marc Bonny Collection

(Left) David Kennedy's Antarctic paintings. These resulted from a trip on USS *Glacier*, and were done during the years 1957–59.
Photographer: George Bonny, Marc Bonny Collection

(Far left) David Kennedy, self portrait, 1958.
Photographer: George Bonny, Marc Bonny Collection

Lois McIvor and her painting *Western Waters*. Canvas, 1993. Lois McIvor Collection

Lois McIvor's *Millennium*. Oil on canvas, 1999. Lois McIvor Collection

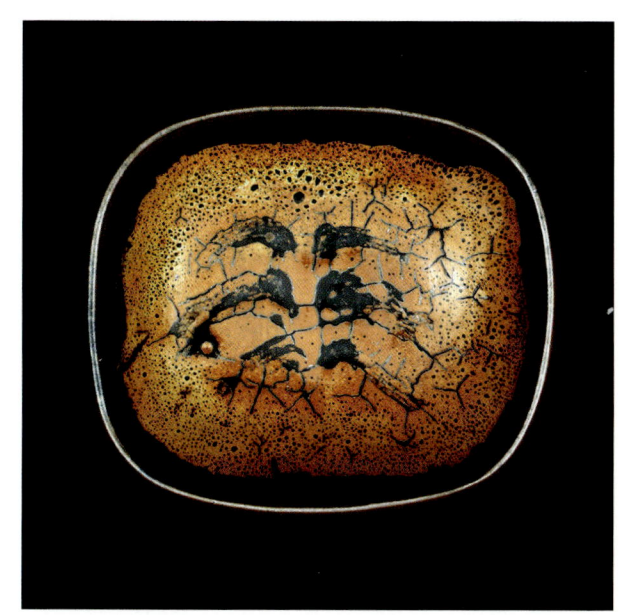

(Above) Len Castle, press-moulded dish, 31 cm. Iron containing glazes, Paturoa period, 1970. Len Castle Collection

(Right) Len Castle at the Montana New Zealand Book Awards ceremony, 2008. Booksellers New Zealand/Geoff Dale

French Bay-inspired paintings by Colin McCahon.
Photographer: George Bonny, Marc Bonny Collection

Colin McCahon's *French Bay*, 1954. Gouache on paper, 740 mm x 867 mm.
Auckland Art Gallery Toi o Tamaki, cm000086

Colin McCahon with his oil on canvas, *French Bay*, 1956. The size of the canvas is 1268 mm x 965 mm. Photographer: George Bonny, Marc Bonny Collection

A group at a McCahon cottage viewing-day during the 1950s.
Photographer: George Bonny, Marc Bonny Collection

Marc Bonny and friends on the swings at Titirangi Beach, c.1956. From left: Jenny Irving, Lesley Brook, Marc Bonny and Anthony Brook.
Photographer: George Bonny, Marc Bonny Collection

High tide and a hot day at French Bay, c.1955.
Photographer: George Bonny, Marc Bonny Collection

Saturday tennis on the asphalt court at the Clark property, mid-1950s. Bruce Henderson is serving and is partnered by Harry Makin; at the opposite end are Stephanie Bonny and Ian Cumming. Bill Webb is walking off the court. Marc Bonny standing at right and Lincoln Lee sitting (partly obscured by bushes on right).
Photographer: George Bonny, Marc Bonny Collection

View from Okewa Road, the Bonny house at right. Cape Horn at left in the background, c.1955. Photographer: George Bonny, Marc Bonny Collection

French Bay Yacht Club. Bruce Harvey Collection

The Davis brothers' boat shed on Tanekaha Road, 2007. Marc Bonny Collection

surgery until my father could build consulting rooms for me; the only real problem I encountered was in getting a telephone connection.

There were no available lines in the old telephone exchange and the Post Office wanted me to wait until the new exchange was built. That was to be several years but fortunately Alec Bishop, who was the Riding Member in the Council, came to my rescue and persuaded the Post Office to run a special line from the Whau Bridge to my home. This was an Auckland number so patients had to make a toll call to contact me, but it was better than no phone at all and it did mean that I could contact the hospital directly as necessary.

The residential situation in Titirangi itself was a remarkable mixture of very elegant homes and small baches. Most of the latter were, in fact, either holiday homes near the beaches or temporary cottages occupied by people who were building new and more substantial homes. It was an area still under development. The most prosperous homes were situated on Rangiwai and View roads (Kohu Road).

Harry and Edna Atkinson lived with their family in the house later to become the Community House on the left corner of Rangiwai Road. This house was designed by Tibor Donner, a rather volatile Hungarian who was then city architect for Auckland City Council. The Atkinson house was a very modern home for that period. Harry was regarded as the squire and Edna was a motivating force behind the Beautifying Society.

Their immediate neighbours were Ethelwyn and Mac Geddes. Ethelwyn was the force behind the Titirangi Drama Group, producing most of their plays performed in the Macandrew Hall in Titirangi Road. This hall was located almost opposite the end of Godley Road and was the headquarters for the Country Women's Institute, but there was another hall in Rangiwai Road on the right-hand side, opposite the drive into Harry Atkinson's home, which also housed the public library and was used for public meetings. Still further up Rangiwai Road and above the Geddes lived John and Pat Odlin on the left side, and Thayer Fairburn and his family across the road. Tibor Donner with his wife Madge and daughter Margaret lived in another house of outstanding design in View Road, demonstrating Tibor's ability as an architect.

The roads were something else. The only sealed roads were Titirangi Road and Scenic Drive. All the rest were metalled tracks, which were commonly dubbed 'goat-tracks'. I arrived with a brand new motorcar that took terrible punishment and within two years the front suspension had to be totally replaced. The worst road was the one to Laingholm, but those to French Bay and Titirangi Beach were only marginally better. There were two routes to Laingholm, one via Woodlands Park and another known as Laingholm Drive. Both were equally appalling.

Laingholm itself was a small settlement with a store on the beach and a hall nearby. A few months after I hung up my shingle in Titirangi, I was approached with the request that I should set up a branch surgery there using a room in the hall as a consulting room. They wanted me to come there every day but since it took me nearly an hour to get there and the same time to return I felt unwilling to make that commitment. However, I agreed to run a clinic there two days a week for a few months to see how it worked out. The properties in Laingholm were very cheap, with sections available for £50 compared to the

£300 or more in Titirangi. Many of the Laingholm residents did not run cars but used the scanty bus services, and consequently they preferred to go right into Auckland for their routine medical services rather than get off the bus in Titirangi or New Lynn and have to spend some time waiting there for the return service. I would go out there to find requests for house calls waiting for me, only too often for matters which could (and should) have been dealt with in a normal surgery situation, and the very small number of patients presenting themselves at the hall did not justify the amount of time which I had to spend away. The hall was poorly equipped and I felt that the situation was unsatisfactory, so after the initial trial period I advised the people there that I would be discontinuing this service.

This resulted in a letter of complaint being sent to the Auckland branch of the British Medical Association, citing the withdrawal of the service as 'unfair'. Fortunately I was at the meeting when this letter was read out and was able to explain precisely what had happened. Several of the New Lynn practitioners were also at the meeting and backed me up, stating that the Laingholm people were over-demanding and bad payers. At that time the recognised fee for a consultation at the surgery was 10 shillings and sixpence, of which the Health Department paid 7 shillings and sixpence. Knowing that and being aware that the Laingholm people were probably the least affluent of my patients, I never pressured people into paying the extra 3 shillings, so even with the Health Department paying 1 shilling per mile for my car expenses, it was undoubtedly an uneconomic service from my point of view.

The area further west posed fewer problems because there were not many people living in Parau and 'the Huia', but the road out there was equally appalling. As the years passed Titirangi itself became more heavily settled and most of the small baches disappeared, replaced by substantial homes, so the area gradually became suburban and lost its semi-rural aspect. Simultaneously my practice, which had been a general practice with a bias towards paediatrics, began to change into one with a bias towards geriatrics.

David Kennedy

David Kennedy was representative of the many artists who made Titirangi their home in the 1950s. In this piece, Marc Bonny remembers his early association with David and his family.

Artists in Titirangi

Around 1955/6 at Titirangi I became very aware of my parents' friends. Especially if they had a nice car! My father was a structural engineer and worked in his office in town usually, but he had many outside interests other than visiting his building sites during the pouring of concrete and setting steel structures. Visiting him in his office before he took us out often meant listening to endless phone conversations between himself and the building site foreman or architect, discussing precise details of his plans. Mother's job was deputy editor of *Home and Building* magazine. Conversation at the table was invariably of the personalities around housing and commercial architecture. Dad was clearly involved with the same group of people. Perhaps the only person I have ever seen lift my father into genuine laughter and amusement was artist David Kennedy and sometimes his wife, Phyllis. When David was primed up a bit he could imitate Dylan Thomas and make amusing quotes from *Under Milk Wood*.

Because we had two cliffside sections between French Bay and Titirangi Beach, I became unwittingly involved with their children on their visits to my parents' house at Okewa Road. In 1957 I was 10, Garth Kennedy was about four and Gianna was around two or three. Both Gianna and Garth were very energetic children, and Phyllis was fairly particular about them. I seem to remember that my older brother took off smartly on hearing the Kennedys were coming and disappeared to Shag Point, perhaps with his rod to catch fish. He was into doing things that resulted in things that you could eat; he kept hens for the eggs and he trapped possums.

As the chief attraction of our house for older children was the steep and rough cliff cutting down to the beach, and nobody had fallen directly over the cliff to date, it was my choice in a way to become their baby-minder when the adults got down to some serious discussions and lighthearted banter about their lives and the arty talk that went with it. David Kennedy used to always wear the same garb, a good-looking tall, strongly-built man, blondish hair and strong beard and features, wearing green or brown corduroy trousers and a green or red tartan shirt; suitable wear for fine or rough work in the artist's studio or casual socialising. Phyllis had a lively Italian background and was very perceptive.

Thus, my job on these afternoons was to use all reasonable force but not to excess to wear out these two children to exhaustion and distract them from their obvious interest in careering over the bank into the sea. Distractions included playing with toys, bikes, a goat and cats. A trip under the house to my two little model aero-engines to start them up noisily on the bench and sniff the lovely castor oil and ether fuel was usually enough to distract the children from any further trouble. No TV came to our street until around 1959/60, when some of us neighbours tiptoed into Griersons next door to watch those early transmissions.

While I deposited my charges back to their owners in suitably worn out condition, I then developed my next curiosity and went up the drive to check out this fantastic twin-carb red leather, bucket-seated TF1500 MG parked quite close to our old 52 or later 56 Ford Prefect that I loathed to be seen in, especially too close to Titirangi School.

David saw my fascination with the car fairly early on and must have inwardly taken note of this. So lo and behold within a short time the phone would ring on Saturday afternoons and he would ask, 'Could Marc

Phyllis Kennedy, c.1962.
Marc Bonny Collection

make his way over to Park Bay Road (now Paturoa Road) around 5 or 6 to babysit for Garth and Gianna?' Arriving on time I was surprised at how quiet everything was and how quickly the children settled down. Not a sound. Staring down at the coffee table in the lounge there were many up-to-date copies of *Punch* magazine and maybe *The Listener*. Around 2 a.m. they would arrive home and my first ride back home in the MG with David came about. With half a crown in my pocket (or was it five shillings?) I calculated my enormous wealth accruing for doing next to nothing. The money I got sometimes was spent by going to the dairy opposite Lopdell House and pretending to buy cigarettes 'for my mother' after school. David almost chain-smoked Pall Mall Kingsize plain cigarettes from an Elastoplast tin he used as a cigarette case at the time.

The new fish and chip shop in Titirangi combined to make the walk home as good as it could get, spending our bus fare, combined with any extra money, there, although we also often biked to school. Around 1958 or 1959 David talked of getting a berth on the USS icebreaker *Glacier* to Antarctica and this he did, producing sketches and fantastic paintings of penguins, helicopters, and icebergs.

My brother Richard and I received personal postcards stamped from the ship's post office. David and Phyllis loved Dad's 8 mm Charlie Chaplin films. Dad's favourites were *The Cure*, *The Prisoner* and *Easy Street*. When films came out with sound I remember David saying he loathed Charlie Chaplin's voice-over referring to himself as the 'little fellow did this and that and so on'.

My birthday present from Phyllis was a hand-sketched black-and-white framed picture she did of Charlie Chaplin. Then I got a painted nikau palm frond from an exhibition that Phyllis put on at the Titirangi Coffee Bar.

David offered to take me to town on business one day and we finished with a trip over the bridge to the north side. With my hair flying all over the place and holding on to the dashboard handle, David pointed to the speedo when it reached 100 mph for me to view.

David also did a lot of woodcarving for a while, and at his studio we viewed some magnificent work. Most of his work was snapped up fairly smartly and he never appeared to have large amounts to view or consider buying. My father got in quick a few times and occasionally bought a piece of his work.

Around 1960 our family went to Rotorua and we visited the Kennedys at their father's bach at Hotwater Bay, Rotoiti. David arrived to pick us up in their little launch, standing high on top of it looking over and operating the throttle and steering wheel with one foot. As we sped along he drew a pencil sketch of something to interest us at the same time. We enjoyed the cold lake and the bracing warmth of the hot puddles all afternoon. Sometime later, David and Phyllis talked seriously of a trip to Greece. Around 1961 or 1962 they left for a trip. Letters to us suggested Phyllis found the place different from what she was used to. She described bargaining with the butcher over a piece of meat almost leading to a tug of war, the hopelessly thin drainpipes and the dirty Acropolis. David decided Greece was the place for him and Phyllis came back with the children. Although separated, I believe they remained lifelong friends. In the meantime, we had shifted to Parnell in 1961 and the Titirangi era was relegated in my memory until the 1990s, when I came back and West Auckland Historical Society and local Titirangi oral histories became important.

Dr David Blaiklock

This piece about Titirangi in the 1940s is taken from the recollections about his school days by Dr David Blaiklock, son of Professor E.M. Blaiklock. The memoir was collected by Marc Bonny in December 2007.

I was at Titirangi School from 11 October 1945 and right through 1946. About the beginning of March 1946 we had a change of headmaster to a chap named McGrail, a bit of a wild Irishman. The story goes he didn't like being at Titirangi because he didn't want to leave Panmure School. He was a bit cross and bad tempered with us.

I remember very clearly the day after he had had a run in with a boy in Standard Four. This boy had had his arm up in a crooked fashion and McGrail had come along and remonstrated angrily with him to hold it straight. Apparently the boy had hurt his arm working 'cow bales'. The next day he arrived about three minutes late and was going to be told off by McGrail, but his mother came in and really yelled loudly at McGrail in front of the whole class.

McGrail wasn't going to take any nonsense from her. He shouted, 'Get out, get out', to her so loudly that my parents over the valley could hear and wondered what on earth was going on. This made a deep impression on me. McGrail 'won' the dispute, forcing her out of the room, and he banged the doors right next to where we were sitting. She was outside kicking the closed doors with her high-heel shoes. The rights of parents were much less in those days!

The war had ended when our family built a new house at Koromiko Road (now Kopiko Road) in 1945. I liked the house, the view and the bush, the beautiful birds singing and the newness of the house. Myna birds from India came about 1947, a very aggressive bird that we didn't like. Kopiko Road today is a lot more bushy than it used to be. Photographs taken in the 1920s show it to be quite barren then.

Our milk delivery at Kopiko Road was brought by horse and cart in 1945 and early 1946. It was a husband and wife job, and Milly Brown was the name of the lady. Often the delivery was late, and for a long time Milly used to say, 'They have new stands at New Lynn and have been cemented in and they were not yet set hard enough'. Milly would empty into one of our billies enough milk for us and put it at the bottom of our drive. We had a fridge at home. I remember our Irish Terrier, Kerry, when he saw the horse at the bottom of our drive. He backed off for a minute, but then wanted to strain at the chain and attack the 'big dog'.

I remember Titchener, the grocer, and Shaw's across the road, where there was a dairy. Further down the road from Titcheners was the big puriri tree, and next to that was Zellas teashop and Home Cookery. Zella was quite an attractive woman who had a daughter. Titirangi was a place where everyone knew everyone else. Mrs Luckens was a character and people said she was a Communist, which was a bad word in those days.

I went to Avondale Intermediate in 1947, and my diary recalls that was not a happy year because I used to be bullied by one fellow in particular. People in those days didn't realise that active bullying was taking place regularly and that it can ruin a boy's life. I got a name for having a 'Woolworths bladder' because at 10-to-12 I always got up and went to the toilet, but nothing was wrong with me. I just figured by doing this I wouldn't have to meet the bully in the toilet later at lunchtime. I welcomed the long break, because of the polio epidemic, that occurred. By the time we resumed school the bully guy had forgotten about me.

In 1945 our family got to know Horace and Freda Holt. Freda was more forceful, Horace a more gentle type. She was a member of the Titirangi Beautifying Society and she helped me that first spring in Titirangi in 1945 with some dish arrangement of flowers to enter the competition for the Cutlers Cup. I actually won the cup thanks to Mrs Holt. I agreed with my father in his conservation efforts. The Beautifying Society's meetings were at Macandrew Hall. I remember the first year we were in Titirangi there was a garden party for the whole of Titirangi in the grounds of the Geddes house at Rangiwai Road.

In 1910, E.M. Blaiklock's parents bought 30 acres 'of hard clay' at £10 an acre, 'somewhere in the manuka beyond New Lynn', between Golf and Godley roads, about halfway down. The young Blaiklock, later to become Prof. Blaiklock, eventually settled in Titirangi's Koromiko (now Kopiko) Road.

(Above) A young Eddie (E.M. Blaiklock, b. 1903) with his father Edward, sitting on a fence near the top of today's South Titirangi Road.

(Left) Eddie Blaiklock and his mother.

(Right) Mrs Blaiklock milking the house cow. Eddie and family dog waiting patiently alongside, c.1914.
All Blaiklock Family Collection

Walking to Whatipu

The walk to Whatipu was 16 miles from Titirangi and I was fairly tired by the time I got there. I had some great walks with Dad. We went out to Whatipu with Thayer Fairburn one time, and he told us all about the *Orpheus*. He said that Hetherington's book on the *Orpheus* was wrong in parts. Thayer's book was so painstaking it very nearly didn't get written. We walked down to Mackies Rest and then down to Huia Road on the way to Whatipu. We had lunch at Cornwallis or Mill Bay. We started early, sometimes 6 a.m. or earlier. Getting near Whatipu was like going to another world, we felt so isolated when there. We liked that isolation and stayed four or five days at Whatipu Lodge. One of the most interesting trips was in 1946 when we got the bus to Huia and old Con Brian was on the bus. The whole bus was dominated by Con, who had obviously been drinking a bit, sitting at the back of the bus. Con got off at Huia and the bus went on to Little Huia. Then we walked over to Whatipu with the moonlight showing on the waves, and had a magnificent time. We heard a crashing sound that my father said was wild pigs. We rested the next day or went for a walk up to the Pararaha Valley towards Karekare. Then we'd have a bonfire to boil a billy and cook some sausages. Afterwards we would walk along Gibbons Track and look to the sunset. My father would talk about all his Greek and Roman interests. It was great. We walked home about three or four days later.

Dr David Blaiklock with his father on an overseas trip in 1977. Blaiklock Family Collection

Edward Musgrave Blaiklock and Kathleen Blaiklock. Blaiklock Family Collection

The lodge at Whatipu was shut down in the early fifties for a while. I remember Gibson, quite a pompous Englishman, who tried to make the place a bit more posh and put the price up to 30 shillings per day to stay. My father wasn't happy about the price rise so that was the end of going to Whatipu for a while, and I felt devastated. The Lodge shut down for some years until Phil Sharp arrived, and in 1970 I took my son down for his first trip on a wild day. We were never allowed to swim there I remember. We visited the other West Coast beaches occasionally by day. Once we went to Bethells to stay but my father wasn't well and so we had to come home. We had walked in from Scenic Drive. I was fascinated by all these areas and wrote about them in my diary. When I was 15, the English master forbade me to write again on the subject of the Waitakeres for 12 months as he considered I had written 'too often' about this subject.

Wallie Titchener

Wallie Titchener is a descendant of the Bishop family and was the owner of Titirangi's first grocery shop. He was raised in the village and has retained strong links with the area all his life. Wallie wrote this memoir in 2010.

From very early age I was aware that we were part of the Bishop family, the original inhabitants of Titirangi. My grandmother, Bertha Peat, who I was very close to, would often tell me stories of the old days; of how John and Christina McLeod came to New Zealand and landed in Russell in the 1830s. Their daughter Elizabeth had met John Bishop from Kent on the boat, and they were married after their arrival in New Zealand. They all left Russell following Hone Heke's sacking of the town in 1845 and, having arrived in Freeman's Bay, John Bishop in partnership with Mr Canty, had taken over the land that is the present Titirangi and began their farm. They milled the timber and planted vegetables.

I recall a number of things that my grandmother told me, including that in 1863 the family could hear the cries of the wind of the storm raging down the Manukau. They knew that something terrible had happened; of course it was the wreck of the *Orpheus*. [It is also recorded that it was a calm and sunny summer's day — Ed.] My grandmother always said that land in those days was passed to a son; as a consequence the remnants of the original holdings were held by Gus Bishop because he was a surviving son of Chappie Bishop. [William Bishop inherited the majority of the land, some went to Chappie from his mother, but the girls of the family were certainly excluded — Ed.] I believe there was a level of soreness by various members of the Bishop family that these holdings of land had been focused through one offspring.

John and Elizabeth Bishop had a family of eight children. One of them, Euphemia, married Robert Betts Peat. Another daughter, Sarah, married Thomas Robert Speer. Robert and Euphemia's son, Frank, married his cousin, Bertha Speer. Frank and Bertha Peat were my grandparents.

A son of Henrietta Bishop and Thomas Coulter married a daughter of Euphemia and Robert Betts Peat. Jack and Lillian Coulter lived just down South Titirangi Road when we were kids. My mother and grandmother would often point out various people and families in the area to whom we were related as descendants of the Bishops. They have largely drifted away today.

Frank and Bertha Peat raised their family in Dargaville. They had two boys and a girl. One boy, Kiri, died of whooping cough when he was five. Frank Peat was a very successful jeweller but devoted his life to collecting Maori artifacts. They had a very large home in Dargaville, which ultimately became so cluttered he decided to sell the business and home and move to Titirangi and build the Treasure House. This occurred in 1925 and he said the only other business in Titirangi Village then was the Tea Kiosk, owned by his first cousin, Alec Bishop.

Following the construction of the Treasure House, Alec Bishop floated a company to build the hotel. The marketing would include bringing passengers from the ships out to

The Treasure House and gift shop, South Titirangi Road, c.1926.
W. Titchener Collection

Titirangi to stay at the hotel and visit the Treasure House. The Treasure House was a great success and I still have the visitor's books, which have glowing comments throughout. The first entry is by Dame Nellie Melba, the opera singer, and there were entries from governors-general, including Lord Bledisloe, and many prominent people of the times.

As is explored elsewhere in this book, the hotel failed to get a licence and subsequently floundered. As a consequence, Frank Peat sold his collection to the Dominion Museum and the Rotorua Museum and set up a new tourist operation at what was then the main gate at Whakarewarewa. The premises are still there and are still used as a tourist gallery.

The road to Titirangi was concreted during the Depression; if only the liquor licence had been obtained then probably the Treasure House and hotel would have remained in Titirangi. Most tourist brochures of that era in Auckland include a visit to the beautiful Treasure House in Titirangi.

Frank Peat was responsible for some high quality, innovative and successful souvenirs. In particular, he commissioned a beautiful porcelain from England called 'Maoriland' by Grimwades. Today specimens are rare, but there are pieces on display in the Auckland War Memorial Museum. Parts of the collection that were never sold have been kept together in the family and these would form the base, even today, for a similar 'Treasure House'.

In the late 1920s my paternal grandfather, Walter Titchener, built Titirangi Groceries, a Four Square brand, in the premises now occupied by The Hardware Café. My grandfather was joined in the business by his two sons: my father Arthur and his brother Vernon. Walter was active in the establishment of the Four Square grocery co-op and was its chairman for seven years in the 1940s. Arthur was a carpenter by trade, but joined his father in retailing. Vernon was disabled at birth and older residents would recall him moving about Titirangi with his limited mobility. He ran the plug-in telephone exchange and post office at the back of the shop. Vernon worked at the telephone exchange until he was 70 and never at any time took a government benefit, despite his disability.

Titirangi Groceries seemed to thrive at this stage, being the only grocery outlet west of New Lynn. During the course of his work, my father met my mother. She lived at 1 Huia Road, in the two-storied house known as Quambi, which was beside the Treasure House. They were married in 1938 and set up home in Titirangi Road, where they both lived until their deaths in 1988 and 1996 respectively.

The Soldiers' Memorial Church, in Park Road, was instigated by the Bishop family in memory of the two sons lost in the First World War. My mother, who was a very good pianist, was the original organist when the church was built. My wife Adrienne and I were married there in 1966. At that time the minister, Jim Gunn, and the neighbour, Mr Hawkins, were in disagreement. People were advised not to be married there because Mr Hawkins would turn up his radio on the open windowsill and drown out the proceedings. However, my mother, who knew Mr Hawkins, solved the problem during a visit and, sure enough, for our wedding and into the future there was no loud radio to mar proceedings!

The first shop at Hotel Titirangi (now Lopdell House), c.1930. Unknown child in the foreground.
W. Titchener Collection

Frank Peat was a businessman clearly ahead of his time. His art objects were sought after by clients from far afield. I still have packets of letters, particularly from America, seeking high quality souvenirs. His negotiations to sell the collection caused debate in parliament, as many MPs, including Gordon Coates the prime minister, were thrilled and thankful that this collection, frequently described by experts as the finest in the world, was being retained in New Zealand and was not sold to USA for the considerably higher sum that was nearly negotiated. Despite the obvious benefit to this country, there were still some MPs who thought the owner should not profit from his lifetime's efforts, presumably assuming the state should just take it.

My paternal grandfather and namesake, Walter Titchener, was born in Devonport and came to New Lynn in 1922. He built his home there, and also a bach named *Te Whare*, in Arapito Road. He had risen to the rank of major in the First World War and afterwards managed Tanfield Pottery in Queen Street, before opening Titirangi Groceries as a family business, which included my grandmother Elise-May, and their two sons. The shop had storage underneath and a ramp down the side to slide the bulk stock in. My dad was a carpenter by trade but took to groceries like a duck to water. Dad wrote articles on how to be efficient for the magazine of the fledgling Four Square (Foodstuffs) organisation in its early days. He would never burn cartons or packaging and when we were kids he would bring home bulk stock most nights. We would sit around the kitchen table weighing wheat, flour, sago, sugar, semolina and so on, and occasionally even broken biscuits. Back then bulk groceries could be bought pre-packaged, but my father would have none of it. It all helped the bottom line and those business lessons I learned then have always remained with me.

Delivering groceries in the early days of Titirangi gave my father a dislike of dogs. Many early residents, from Titirangi to Huia, had a dog. My dad used to say he would be handing over the cartons of groceries while the owner's dog bit his legs. Maybe the dogs sensed his extreme dislike of them. He used to tell the story of a house in Park Road where the dog would bite him without fail, while the owner watched. Finding the owner out on one occasion he chased the dog round and round outside the house until they were both exhausted. Subsequently, when he delivered the groceries the dog would not emerge from under the hedge.

An additional advantage of starting Titirangi Groceries was that it provided work for my disabled uncle, Vernon, who always required walking assistance. Vernon ran the manual plug-in telephone exchange in the shop and became very well-known. When the exchange moved in the 1950s to South Titirangi Road, Vernon was employed there until it was automated in the 1970s. Vernon knew every number in Titirangi and all the customers on party lines. Residents received a great service from him, including his advising callers and sometimes phoning customers to tell them a call had come in while they were out.

A common sight in the 1920s and 1930s was my father carrying Vernon around on his back. With Vernon being very slow in movement and my father being of impatient nature, it was easier for Vernon to be hooked around my father's neck and be carried. This was a frequent sight and probably built my father a fitness and strength that lasted throughout his life. My mother's earliest recollection of my father was seeing him with my uncle on his back at the bottom of the steps beside Lopdell House on his way to the bach at Arapito Road.

My maternal grandfather, Frank Peat, built the house called Quambi at 1 Huia Road. At the time he was building the house there was a corrupt inspector at the County Council who would not approve the position of septic tanks unless offered money. My grandfather played dumb until, as my grandmother recalled, the inspector said, 'For Gods sake, £5 will do it'. My grandfather was a personal friend of Gordon Coates, the prime minister, and passed the information to him. Subsequently, the County Council had one less staff member!

My father told me how they rowed the clinker dingy from the foot of the section at Te Whare and often came across sharks in the Manukau. He always recalled the day off Jenkins Bay when a shark was drifting under the rowing boat end to end. It was larger than the 14-foot dingy, he assured us — I don't think it was a 'fish story'!

Graham and Vivienne Shaw

These stories are from an interview by Marc Bonny with Graham and Vivienne Shaw in November 2008.

We lived in New Lynn till I was about nine. The property in Titirangi, where the supermarket is, belonged to my grandmother. There were two houses on the property; the old house down the back of the property and another at the front, originally a cafeteria or tearoom. They added pieces around it and it became the second house on the property. My father, Frederick Shaw, was the only member of his family who went to the First World War. He was a prisoner for two years in Germany. When he returned he found that other members of the family had taken over the place. At this stage we were living in the old house at the back. Uncle Gilbert, my father's brother, and my grandmother were living in the front house nearer the road. Uncle Gilbert eventually built a house in Pleasant Road and shifted there, so our family moved into the front house. Over the road was the Four Square grocery belonging to Mr Titchener, and in the back corner on the right of the shop was the post office. On the left-hand side of our house was a Council house, where my Uncle Arthur, my father's brother who worked with him, lived. It was the house on the left-hand side looking west across the main road.

Rod Shaw, my father's cousin, and his sons, Bob and Bill, eventually lived there, and Millie, his wife, turned it into a shop. I think it may have been a dairy, and they lived in the back half of it. Bob ran the petrol station about 1945/6. Then Titirangi started to grow and developments occurred.

A fruit shop started up between Rangiwai Road and Titcheners. The dairy on our side stayed the same but eventually I think it might have closed down. Bill Shaw ran his taxi business from there. Bill was Rod's son and he started the taxis in Titirangi. A chemist shop was built straight across the road from the supermarket, and the post office was down near the Hotel. Under the Hotel there was a big garage; when I was a kid, there was a trucking firm in there. I went to New Lynn School till I was about nine, then to Titirangi, the new 1939 school, on the present site. My mother went to the original 1873 Titirangi School that burned down. She was friendly with Ada Bishop.

Generally we walked home across the top of Monument Hill. The top field of the school was tarsealed and had a couple of tennis courts on it, which was great. The bottom field was pure clay, there was no topsoil or grass on it. The water used to flow down over the top ground and made a big trench right across the middle of the lower field. The new field had not been built then. The boys used to play on the muddy lower field, and we'd come back to the classroom each day covered in clay. We used to kick a football around down there, although we had no idea of the rules of the game. The headmaster, Mr R. Blennerhassett (1940–42), a really nice guy, was finally conned into coming down and playing with the boys. He kicked off the ball and about 10 of us pulled him down into the clay; he never came down to play with us again.

The boys' job was to get the firewood for the pot-belly stoves in the classrooms. This particular teacher, we called him 'old Pegleg' as he had a limp, was in charge of the boys. He'd say, 'Right, go into the bush and only cut down dried teatree. We had this kid in our class who would cut down a green one every time; old Pegleg would go berko! There was no swimming pool then, but there was a U-shaped tunnel or air raid shelter, which I think the men of Titirangi put in. It was always locked but when there was a practice air raid the girls would go in the left-hand side and the boys in the right-hand side. Of course it was dark in there and we'd meet in the middle. The tunnel was more or less underneath the drive that goes down to the school at the end near Atkinson Road. One year of the war we had something like 13 different teachers as there were not many teachers available. I don't remember any bombers or military aircraft roaring overhead or anything like that.

Where the supermarket is now was a hill with quite big kauris on it. I used to climb these and the bus stop was right outside there. In those days we had the ABC buses and 'Mad McCrae'. The stop was about 20 metres to the right of our gate. The driver would come up the hill, stop the bus and toot the horn and we'd rush out. The drivers knew everybody. The Shaw bus, a Republic with solid tyres, was owned by my father. When he went to the war, his brother Gilbert ran the bus. He was running it when it had a crash and went through a bridge.

There were three Shaw families, my father and his two brothers, in Titirangi. The original Shaws landed in the Hokianga, and then they came down to Helensville and some finished up in Cabbage Tree Swamp, now Eden Park. The main branch that I remember came to Oratia, hence the name Shaw Road. There was Dad, his brothers Arthur and Gilbert, and a number of sisters who all lived on the farm on Shaw Road. Another branch

In the foreground, now the supermarket's carpark, are the three Shaw houses: two side-by-side and one behind, in the bush. The Hawkins' house is just beyond. On the road to the left (early South Titirangi Road) is the puriri tree. This picture was taken from Rangiwai Hill. Photographer James D. Richardson, 18 January 1920. Auckland City Libraries Special Collections, 4-4035

The old dairy (one of the original Shaw houses) with newer shops adjoining to the left and Rod Shaw's petrol station to the right. Photographer John T. Diamond. Waitakere Library & Information Services, J.T. Diamond Collection, 2406 (10A)

that lived also in Shaw Road was Rod Shaw and his sons, Bob and Bill. The Council built a house in Atkinson Road about 50 metres down from the school on the left, and my Uncle Arthur (Artie) and cousins lived there. Arthur had a multitude of kids, about 13, I think.

My sister married the son of Mr Thomas, who had the daffodil farm. When Arthur shifted to the council house, Rod came into that house that had been the dairy, and his son Bob had the petrol station. Later on Rod built another house, down behind the service station. I started the mechanic's garage business where the New World supermarket is now, around 1952/53. When I built it I understood that I could buy the property, which had two sections side by side. I approached my mum and dad about this, but because there were another three kids in the family it would be seen as favouritism. I was young and without any financial experience of running a business, so although I ran it for a while it seemed to be a pointless exercise to me as I couldn't own it, so I just bailed out.

Fred Shaw, my father, came back from the First World War and got a job with the Council. Titirangi Beach and Zig Zag Track became his special area. When he first came back he worked in the Parnell Rose Gardens and in the Domain, and eventually he and Arthur had the job of keeping Titirangi Beach and Mt Atkinson. They used to mow Titirangi Beach with handmowers! After mowing Titirangi Beach they would put the handmowers over their shoulders, walk up through the Zig Zag Track and up to Mt Atkinson and mow Mt Atkinson with the same handmowers! As kids we used to go to Mt Atkinson, put a rope on the front of the mowers and help pull them along.

When the Council had a function in the Town Hall in Auckland, they used to get my father to go out into the Waitakeres to get a sort of creeper fern that could only be found in certain places, to decorate the Town Hall. Another one of Dad's jobs as a Council worker was to get little rimu and kauri trees, around five inches high. He would get all these, put them in boxes or trays on the flat roof of the garage until they had stabilised, and then send them to some place for eventual planting out.

We had hundreds of American soldiers during the Second World War and they'd have about six big GMCs or big American trucks with six wheels and they would come down to Titirangi Beach during the weekends in the summer. It seemed like thousands of them and they would have all these girls with them with untold bottles of booze. All the car parks up Titirangi Beach were full. Cornwallis was too far out, so Titirangi Beach was the place. Up one side of the road were all these cars parked, allowing just enough space for another vehicle to pass. On the paddock towards the French Bay side was a mini kiosk shed, with a side that opened up to serve ice-cream, or hot water when large crowds were around. So there were thousands of people there in the summer. The beach itself was beautiful. There was a sandbank further out and the tide used to come round and then cover it, and between the sandbank and the shore was the place that we used to dig for pipis. In those days we could reach down when swimming and smash them together and eat them raw. Now it looks just like dead shells everywhere.

In 1949 Titirangi decided to have a voluntary fire brigade, so my friend Jim Rogers and me, aged about 18 at the time, put our names down, but we weren't successful, which annoyed us at the time. I was fit from pig hunting at the time, and I lived about 50 metres from where they put in the fire station. I was driving when I was 16 and got a heavy truck licence at 18. The Titirangi engine was a 1942 International crash tender, four-wheel drive fire engine, which I reckon I could have driven better than the guys who were driving it because I was driving heavy vehicles all the time.

Our family history is written in a book, *The Gardener and the Squire's Daughter*. Our ancestor worked in the Mission Station at Mangungu in the Hokianga Harbour in 1838 and then came to Dargaville. A branch of the family stayed in Dargaville but the others came down by boat and rivers to the Cabbage Tree Swamp and then to Oratia and Titirangi. Arthur McEldowney was a great fellow; he had been at school with my mother. In 1953 he divided up his land and sold some to us. As we didn't have any money he said just pay me so much a week or a month.

H. Morgan Lewis

Harry Morgan Lewis was born at Hawera in 1914. His family moved to Titirangi in 1931 and was there for 48 years. In 1945, Morgan co-founded the New Lynn Timber Company with his father. A builder by trade, Morgan took on the role of managing director for the company from 1954 to 1974, at which time the company was sold. Morgan married Betty in 1945 and they had two sons, Phillip and David. In 1961 Morgan became a justice of the peace and in 1989 he was awarded the Queen's Service Medal. He was a founder member, supporter and, from 1997, patron of the Titirangi Returned Services Association. His wife Betty passed away in 1992 and Morgan died in 2002. Marc Bonny interviewed Morgan in 2001.

The Village

Zella's tearoom was probably exactly where the chemist is now and Zella Rowell had a sort of home cookery there. Her brother went overseas during the Second World War. The famous puriri tree was near Titchener's shop. The original School Road (South Titirangi Road) never used to come straight up as it does now; the route was altered after the hotel was built. The original route was through the old fire station.

When we first came to Titirangi, Titchener's grocery shop used to be in the hotel. Vern Titchener ran the post office part of the shop. The shop was separate from the hotel and had been leased out for the purpose in the 1930s. The present Hardware Café building was the next permanent grocery prior to 1940. One of the Sowrey boys did deliveries for Chermsides, the grocer at Titirangi. The Sowreys won a lottery and built a house on the corner of View and Westridge roads with the proceeds, around the beginning of the Second World War.

Tanekaha Road

When we were in Tanekaha Road most people got their groceries from New Lynn, from Gillian and Bell. There was another old chap who used to run a shop next to where the Bank of New Zealand in New Lynn was but there was no delivery included. We used to cart stuff back on a bike sometimes with a 'pk'-type sugar bag over our shoulder.

There were not many living in Tanekaha Road in those days but after the war more people came. We used to go after flounder using a candle and half a kerosene tin. Tanekaha Road was just a mud road from 'The Forks'. The Forks were about 100 yards up the road from where it is now. A cutting was put in there from French Bay Road. We would leave our car there in bad weather and put on boots to get down Tanekaha Road by foot.

Titirangi Beach Road had no metal on it when we first came but French Bay was always metalled. Park Road was just scoria and not sealed until the 1950s. Our house in Tanekaha Road was originally a bach that we built.

We used to live at Mt Albert but during the Depression we lost the Mt Albert house and went to live in the Tanekaha Road bach. That bach had a terrazzo sink bench and a white tile bath that you stepped down in to but it cost rather too much in heating. My sister had the front bedroom and there was another bedroom that my brother built into the corner of a big verandah. When we first moved there we had no water supply or power or telephone. We got water off the roof and had a long-drop up the path. We were the first permanent residents in that part of Tanekaha Road, from the bus stop to the end of Okewa Road. The house was the end house on the left. Around 1950 we sold to Jack and Essie Jones. Bill Orr, an engineer for the New Lynn Borough Council, was living down Okewa Road, on the left-hand side near the end. Dentist Geoff Jenkins was down there

Wedding of Morgan and Betty Lewis, 1945.
Harvey Waite Collection

too. He worked at New Lynn, opposite the Bank of New Zealand. The other New Lynn dentist, Colquhoun, was an anti-fluoride campaigner.

Later, my father built the house on the corner of Okewa and Tanekaha roads and we sold that to the Horrocks family. When we built our original house I was about 16 and carted the timber out when I had just got my licence. That was the time they were doing the concrete road section between Golf and Godley roads and you had to make a detour up Godley Road. That didn't help the Titirangi Hotel business, which any way had no liquor licence.

I had my first vote at the 1935 general election. Only 130 people from all over the Titirangi district took part. The polling booth, the only one for miles, was in the garage under the Titirangi Hotel.

We used to deliver for the New Lynn Timber Co. and I often did it on my way home. I had a good business there but I retired in 1974. I sold to someone who was caught in the 1987 financial crash. The original timber company site was very rough and the Council used to drop all their rocks and rubbish there to fill the gully in. My father bought it for the rates that were owing on it, £48. It was three-quarters of an acre, with rates at £24 per year. Then we bought half an acre of land at the back. That area is now The Warehouse.

The Webber home at French Bay, c.1965. In the late 1940s the family operated a store out of the house. In the 1950s, Jack Webber also ran a grocery delivery service using his American station wagon.
Trevor Pollard Collection

My father's gang put the second room on the old Tin Shed School about 1931/32. They had a tennis court down below the road. My father was a good English tradesman builder.

There used to be a tennis court at the bottom of Opou Road. The court was right at the end of the road and the hall was on the left. It started about 1936, and we had it down in chips and then we sealed it.

Titirangi Road was cut off while it was being concreted in the late 1920s and early 1930s but they did one side at a time. When they were doing the hill down to New Lynn you had to go around Old Titirangi Road. I left school aged about 17 and then carried on at night school two days a week. I used to ride a pushbike from home where I was working, to New Lynn station and leave the bike there, then train to Mt Eden and walk to

Seddon Tech for the building construction course. When coming up Titirangi Road at night, if there was enough moonlight, I would disconnect my bike dynamo to make the going easier.

I was married in 1945, and my family were still living at our original Tanekaha Road home, so we went to live for two years with my mother-in-law in Arapito Road while I was building my own house at 15 Tanekaha Road. My father had built the house across the road (this became Horrocks' house later) and they went and lived there. Next door to us was Pickering, who had the fish shop in Sandringham. Arthur Thode, the land agent in New Lynn, was also there. He had a house made of glazed bricks. I built my house at number 15 on Tanekaha Road, not very far down from the French Bay Road corner. I bought two sections on Tanekaha Road and two sections on Titirangi Beach Road. We were on the edge of the reserve. Coleman, the fire chief, was on the other side of the reserve. The track that went down to Titirangi Beach went between the two properties.

French Bay

The Webber's house in French Bay was turned into a store in the front ground floor. Jack Thuell lived there before the Webbers. He had the ground floor part made into a shop, and there was a sort of dance floor. A couple of Webber boys, Robert and John, were good yachties. Jack Webber, the father, used a green American stationwagon for deliveries and supplying the store in the fifties.

We built another house at French Bay, for Mrs Wiles. She owned the whole property on the front next door to Webbers. She had a kiosk made of corrugated iron there, and later they shifted that across to the beach for the first French Bay Yacht Club.

The Yacht Club started in the early fifties I got involved in the sixties particularly. They made a nice job of the new Yacht Club. Wally Silva was the foreman for Downer Construction Company and he supervised it most carefully. He had foundations bored right through the sand to the papa rock and filled in with concrete. Eddie Bougher had a trimaran and I remember the Newbys. They used to have winter programmes building the Moth class yachts. They could be built cheaply and my boys had several of them. Before marine ply came in they used to build yachts of solid wood, although it was very thin and could be bent into shape. I remember Jack Newby built one out of pukatea, a greenish soft wood, before plywood came in. But the solid wood boats were heavy. Gordon Addis was commodore. The yacht races were held on a Sunday usually.

We had a big launch anchored down at French Bay that was put in the water about 1929–30, when I'd just left school. It was called *Ngaire*, which is my sister's name. It was anchored out of French Bay and on a big tide it used to go aground, being away out near the channel. We took the boat to the South channel for the best fishing at 'The Horseshoe'. There it was only about two metres deep at low tide. Sometimes we used to sleep overnight on our launch. We had a fishing licence, the first one after they brought the regulations in. The idea was you could only sell the fish, but you couldn't hawk it. My father knew some people in Mt Albert and we would take some of the fish there, where a young chap used to sell them.

The Lewis family launch, *Ngaire*, off French Bay, 1930s.
Keith Hewitt Collection

We had a bach at Cornwallis for 18 years on Council-leased land. The boats going into Onehunga from around New Zealand were the *Ronaki*, which used to go up to Hokianga, and *Hauturu* to New Plymouth, and *Honaki* also. The *Mamaku* was a good-looking black coaster that was seen in the fifties.

At Easter 1932, one night there was a fishing boat coming up the harbour after crossing the Manukau Bar. The bloke steering it had a master's certificate for the Manukau but he put the boat up on the rocks at Shag Point, with seven people on board. They came around to us for help about 9 o'clock at night. The only phone at French Bay was Hewitts', through the Avondale exchange, so we took the master over there to ring up Onehunga to his people to say what had happened. We had a car but we couldn't get seven people in it so we decided we would take them up to Onehunga in the launch. It was probably midnight before we got away and it was cold. Petrol was the big problem because you could only get it with coupons. We had to take all the petrol out of the car, but the master said he would get us more petrol at Onehunga to get us back again. We eventually got up there about 2 o'clock in the morning. He got some petrol and I set sail back on my own. I was as cold as a frog! They got the stricken 40-foot *Brittania* off the rocks by bringing in a barge. There used to be a lot of sand carted around the Manukau in those days and they brought a sand barge from Onehunga. At low tide they lashed the boat to it and as the tide came up it lifted it up enough for them to drag it up on to the beach. They just baled it out and at the next high tide towed it back home. It didn't damage the boat's hull. The captain had missed the buoy. They had about 500 snapper on board, and there were fish all over the place.

We used to support the Titirangi Country Women's Institute and go to their performances. Ron Gibbs did the lighting for the productions and his wife Vi also helped. They put on good shows. I used to know Ethelwyn Geddes quite well, and when they built the new War Memorial Hall in Titirangi it was going to be used for productions, they put in an acoustic system, but it wasn't used.

Titirangi has changed so much and of course the big problem is parking up there now. We used to practise cricket on the corner of Titirangi Road and Great North Road. I knew Nancy Lane quite well too, her husband was the manager of Westfield Freezing Works, and was tragically drowned with one of their children at Karekare. Nancy was one of Bert Atkinson's daughters and she originally lived in the old Atkinson house on the corner of View Road and the Scenic Drive with her sister and mother. I did a lot of work there during the Depression. I knew Jeff Thompson the builder, who built quite a few small houses in the area. My father built a place out at Woodlands Park for Booth, a milkman on a farm out there, before the road went through Waima about 1935. Wood Bay Road wasn't put in until after the Second World War.

I remember them putting in Rangiwai Road in the 1930s. All done by hand and wheelbarrow, and taking the cliff out and tipping the soil over the side. It was one of the first subdivisions in Titirangi. The Atkinson house, at the beginning of Rangiwai Road, was designed by Tibor Donner, and I knew him when he lived in View (Kohu) Road, just opposite Koromiko (Kopiko) Road. Jack Hunter, manager of Sweetacres, came up to live in the 'Butchers Alley' area. I remember Bill Webb also, and a family called Rogers, Secretary of the Ratepayers' Association.

I also did work for Dr Elias in Park Road. Mrs Elias had a sister who used to teach at Titirangi School. I think Sian Elias was not born then. Bill Carr-Rollett's father was the previous owner of the Elias' property. He was editor of the farming section of the *Herald*. Ted Frankham was Secretary of the Yacht Club. Howard MacDonald had a turning business in New Lynn, and he lived down Tanekaha Road where the Earllys used to be. Mr Ferris built and used to own the poultry farm at the end of Paturoa Road, Titirangi Beach.

Marc Bonny

Marc Bonny lived much of his young life in Titirangi and now lives in Laingholm. His parents were embedded in the Titirangi culture of music and arts in the fifties and sixties. Marc has a deep interest in the history of the area. He has been a committed member of the West Auckland Historical Society for many years and in 2010 was the Society's newsletter editor.

Titirangi in the 1950s

We came to Titirangi in 1951. My parents had spent six months or more in Melbourne in 1950. Possibly the two Titirangi sections were bought before going to Australia. My father, who was always interested in the Alpine Sports Club, decided to buy a couple of sections out at Okewa Road, Titirangi, right on the cliff between Shag Point and Little Beach, before French Bay.

Around 2005 some of the second section has succumbed to sliding into the sea in a slip of possibly 100 tons. The pohutukawa ended up at the cliff bottom, its leaves redirected and pointing optimally for survival toward the sun, roots happily readjusting to the sea floor: the story all around the Manukau. This section provided our access down the cliff, holding on to tree roots, to what was more or less our own private beach.

While the house was being finished we stayed in a bach a little way up on the right from the corner of Okewa and Tanekaha roads. Right outside this bach was possibly the worst section of potholes in the road, often with water filling them. Our section was a bit dangerous for younger children simply because there were practically no fenced sections down Tanekaha Road from about the French Bay turnoff. This posed problems for me when I had to walk home from the bus and get past a few dogs who seemed to own the road when I started school in 1952. The village itself had tarseal or concrete on the road but our areas were slow to be sealed. The last bit up from South Titirangi Road to the 'top' (Titirangi Village) was a gravelly grind in the early fifties. Potholes were just everywhere. The grader made the 'new' surface a bit spongy until the rain sorted everything out again. The Okewa Road metal surface was also very hard and flat in places. Trolleys made with pram wheels were the in-thing for us kids to get most of the way down Titirangi Beach or Tanekaha roads.

Around 1958, on a Friday night the weekend would began for my brother and me with a trip up to the 'top' around 8 o'clock at night. There were some large kauri trees beside the welcoming lamp-lit path that led down to the library building with its reeky smell of old books on a bright red-pink library dispensing table, contrasting memorably with the tarseal of Rangiwai Road. The Library was quite a meeting place for my parents and their friends. Jay Hoby was probably the librarian at the time. Dr Mary Hamilton was a friend and a fantastic trail-blazer in her day. I am told she would arrive in a house and sweep the contents of a table aside to properly place her bag. She waived most of her bill if she deemed the family in straightened circumstances and did not withhold further attention from anyone who was sick.

Lopdell House was really grey and dirty in those days. The dirt road going up the last steep bit to what Alwynne Broady called the 'rooting tooting shop' or post office, was quite hard on any vehicle. ABC's chief radiator repairer, George Mihaljevich, said any bus would be wrecked by those potholed roads.

Also worth mentioning was the endless search for redeemable soft drink bottles in the 1950s that were worth a penny or so if not too dirty. A collection of seven or eight was enough to come away with a fresh bottle of Coke or lemonade. Perhaps that redeemable value is what we need these days. Bottle drives were common back in the fifties for charities and very worthwhile, both to rid a house of refuse and give to a worthy cause. I still see the odd cart converted to a trolley being used to take a few redeemable bottles up to the nearest store.

Short and not so short electrical blackouts were common in the fifties in Titirangi, but I never remember any particular difficulty, in fact I thought it was quite cosy to have to get candles out.

Once every few weeks our grandfather, Emil Bonny, a music teacher and cellist, and his third wife, Betty, were picked up by Dad to be taken for tea at our place. There was just enough room in the Prefect for the cello in its fabric case. Dad got a taste for the cello and finally Emil gave Dad an instrument and he learned fairly quickly. Emil was a National Orchestra cellist in the early 1950s, and one time London Symphony cellist I believe, around 1914. We went to see him a few times at the Auckland Town Hall playing in the Orchestra. Whenever Dad spoke to him they started briefly in English then reverted fairly rapidly to French, especially over the phone.

Titirangi had a music circle from way back. Geoff Hole was in this. The Atkinsons and Fairburns had large selections of records and the group had alternative house visits to various members to play some classical music records. I remember it as a very dry affair, and one night our house was the venue. My brother and I disappeared under the house into the workshop where an old powerful chassis-only valve radio with 12-inch speaker, facedown on the table, was Dad's offering for those wanting to listen to 1ZB. So on this night I was listening in the basement to my usual 1ZB, maybe *Life With Dexter* or *The Drama of Medicine* or some such thing. The next thing down came an angry Geoff Hole to tell me to turn it down so they could listen and enjoy the upstairs classical music properly.

'Ring, ring, ring', went the bell around 9 a.m. in the morning at the Titirangi Soldiers' Memorial Church on a Saturday or Sunday. In earlier times the bullock horn used by the Bishops would call the men in. We heard the bell regularly at Okewa Road. Sadly the bell was stolen about 2006 and so far there is no sign of it.

Quite a short way out in the channel we saw many trawlers and smallish green and white coasters plying their way to the southern ports from Onehunga. We looked for the *Mamaku*, a proud, stocky and solid little black and white coaster that went to Mapua, Nelson, where Mum's sister and my cousins lived, so we had a special affection for it. Occasionally the boats would come into the Manukau Harbour in the fog or perhaps near dark or maybe when the tide was a bit far out. A mass of clanking could be heard and maybe cursing and swearing at having lost a day, while the boat, being temporarily wedged into the sandbank, anchored to wait for high tide.

At Titirangi the fire siren went off and you waited to hear how long the fire engine took to respond. Hopefully within a short time another siren could be heard somewhere in Titirangi, making its fitful way forward in time to save the house.

I remember the atmosphere of the plays the Titirangi Country Women's Institute put on. Jim Gunn had his Titirangi Light Opera also going from about 1957, and I think used Macandrew Hall for the *Mikado*, which was very good. Bruce Henderson was a great player and a fine actor. We were taken up to the hall one Saturday morning, us kids that is, and we got into the face makeup for fun.

I remember Edna Atkinson as the great organiser of Arbour Day at Titirangi School, and her appearance with a fashionable cigarette holder made her look very glamorous. She fitted the party extrovert life that her Tibor Donner house was known for. An article in *Home and Building* by Edna depicted the time capsule of landscape gardening in Titirangi around 1953, and particularly described her fruit trees while living at Rangiwai Road.

Trevor Pollard

Trevor Pollard has lived and worked in Titirangi all his life and is now President of the West Auckland Historical Society. In this section, Trevor remembers the Scarlett family, long time Titirangi residents.

The Scarlett family

I met Pop (Mr T.H. Scarlett) at Wood Bay Beach when I was only 9 years old, and he was 64. He was a quietly spoken man, and very deaf. He would row out in his clinker-built dinghy regularly to fish, as would many people in those days, including my parents. Fishing was good in those days, just off Fish Rock, or up on to the sandbanks at high tide, lining up the pine tree near Green Bay. Pop Scarlett had a section in Opou Road, next to the track that led down to Wood Bay. There was no road access there until 1941. My folks bought the first two sections there off Grand Daddy Hieatt in 1941. The old gentleman's son, Gordon Scarlett, and his mate Ron Minnett, had a yacht called *Vagabond*. It was a mullet class boat with a retractable centerboard; ideal for the Manukau Harbour with all its sandbanks. They belonged at that time to the Onehunga Yacht Club.

Some years later, in 1948, Gordon was building his first home in Opou Road and the mullety had been sold. At that time there was a cement strike and my parents were building their home too and needed cement. Gordon had a Model A truck, and we found we could buy cement directly from the works at Whangarei at a price of eight shillings a bag with our own transport. He offered to do a load for us too.

Unfortunately my parents did not take up the offer, thinking it was expensive, but later the price of all building materials went up anyway. Gordon was a good builder, and gave us lots of good advice. As with most people in the area at that time, my parents were 'do it yourself' builders. In 1950 we moved permanently to Wood Bay, but our house was not really finished and we lived for a while in a small bach. We saw a lot of Gordon, who had now finished his house and married a nice lady called Jo. They were a happy light-hearted couple who drove an unusual large Austin car with square windows.

At that time I was looking at buying some land and looked at another of old Pop Scarlett's properties, five acres in Golf Road opposite Ava Avenue, but I couldn't afford to buy it on an apprentice's wages. Soon after that old Pop Scarlett died. Gordon sold his Opou Road property and moved to Golf Road and built another house down a long driveway.

Gordon and Jo had a son, Brett, who was introduced to yachting at the new French Bay Yacht Club. Gordon helped to build the Club building. He used to speculate in property a bit and bought an old house in French Bay from the Fletcher family. They would renovate; Jo was a very artistic person at interior decoration and she would 'do it up' inside, and then they would move on, so they lived in several houses; in Takahe Road and then in Otitori Bay Road.

We remained friends and they gave us references in 1972 when we adopted our daughter Trish. After Trish's christening, Jo gave us a beautiful painting that she had done of the Soldiers' Memorial Church in Park Road, Titirangi. Jo and Gordon passed away in the 1970s, but their son Brett and his family came to live in his parents' house at 3 Otitori Bay Road. Afterwards I often worked with him on many bathroom and kitchen renovations and extensions. They were a grand family.

In 1941 my parents and I visited a Titirangi bach owned by the Knight family in Opou Road, French Bay. With other local folk we would walk down a steep bush track to Wood Bay at low tide. I remember a friend, Mrs Aitken, would sing. She had a beautiful voice and in that amphitheatre with bush from the water's edge uninterrupted to the sky, it would bring tears of joy to my mother's eyes.

The bays had no roads, subdivision was in the future. When a proposal was made to subdivide part of Wood Bay, my parents put their deposit on two sections. There was no power; we used kerosene lamps and we drew our water from a freshwater spring, but we thought it was heaven. Almost every weekend and holidays we spent there, first in an army hut, then in a bach, and finally in 1951 we went to live there permanently in a newly built large home.

I started my plumbing apprenticeship at age 16. My interest in the West really started then as I was seeing into many homes, nooks and crannies, and talking to the older generation of people who had links with the earliest settlers. The Bishops, the McEldowneys, the Geddes family, the Clarks, Sir Tom Clark's father, John Grierson, founder of the Titirangi Fire Brigade, the Hewitts and the Hieatts, Morgan Lewis and his father of the New Lynn Timber Co., Alwynne Broady and her uncle Mr Parish, and my dear friend and mentor Professor Blaiklock, and his son Peter and wife Jean.

The Fire Brigade has been a continuing interest for many years, and three fire brigade foundation members — Lyn Coleman, Harry Lawrence and Tom Johnston — were friends. They gave me the inspiration to write about the 50 years of the Titirangi Volunteer Fire Brigade, and my Scottish friends inspired the book about the 70 years of the St Andrew's Society of New Lynn. I have always lived in Titirangi and three or four generations of the families have passed before my eyes. I guess some of the changes would surprise the pioneers, as future changes will surprise us, but it has been an evolving community and a great place to live.

In 1995 the Queen's Fire Service Medal was presented to Trevor Pollard. He had led the brigade through trying times during the restructuring of the NZ Fire Service.
Trevor Pollard Collection

Appendices

1. The Bishop family

First generation

John Bishop
m. Elizabeth McLeod

- Christiana 1842–1937
  - m. 1. John Porter ———— 2 sons
  - 2. Archibald Wilson ———— 1 daughter
  - 3. Adam Henry Winder ———— 2 daughters

- Hannah 1844–1931
  - m. William Pugh ———— 5 sons, 3 daughters

- Sarah 1851–1923
  - m. Thomas Robert Speer ———— 5 sons, 4 daughters

- Eliza Jane 1853–1933
  - m. Leonard John Armstrong ———— 3 sons, 2 daughters

- Elizabeth Euphemia 1856–1911
  - m. Robert Betts Peat ———— 6 sons, 2 daughters

- Henrietta 1858–1941
  - m. Thomas William Coulter ———— 2 sons, 3 daughters

- William 1860–1943
  - m. Alexandrina Tinling ———— 2 sons, 3 daughters

- John (Chappie) Joseph 1865–1933
  - m. Emily Surman ———— 3 sons, 3 daughters

Third generation

Parents	Children
Christiana Bishop / John Porter	Joseph m. Ann Lightfoot John (Jock)
Archibald Wilson	Sarah m. 1. A.M. Atwood m. 2. W. Meredith
Adam Winder	Agnes m. G. Malam Margarette Eliza m. A.J. Thom
Hannah Bishop / William Pugh	Christina John William m. Jessie Smith Richard m. Thirza Tregidga Mary Elizabeth m. W. Hughes Evan Thomas John David
Sarah Bishop / Thomas Robert Speer	Richard m. Margaret Broomfield John Bishop m. 1. Alice Moull m. 2. Nora Evans m. 3. Letitia Rowena Christina m. Edmund Lowe Laura m. Henry Scelly Bertha* m. Frank O. Peat William m. Ethel White Thomas m. Marie Evans Rebecca Dora m. William Wright Norman m. Elsie May Preston
Eliza Jane Bishop / Leonard Armstrong	Leonard m. Janet Higham Maud Percy Christina m. J.M.C. Barker Sydney m. Vera Barker
Elizabeth Euphemia Bishop / Robert B. Peat	Robert Frank Oscar* m. Bertha Speer Herbert m. Maude Baker Mark Bishop m. Ethel Wilson Elizabeth* m. J.J. Coulter John Trevor Cris Albert m. Ida Carr Rose Evelyn m. Lawrence Wilson
Henrietta Bishop / Thomas W.H. Coulter	William Henry* m. Elizabeth Bishop John Joseph* m. Elizabeth Peat Laura Maud
William Thomas Bishop / Alexandrina Tinling	William Alexander (Alec) m. May Louisa You Elizabeth* m. William H. Coulter Elsie Margaret Herbert John Dorothy (Dora) m. (?) Jones
John Joseph (Chappie) Bishop / Emily Surman	John Thomas Augustus (Gus) m. Lilian Lusty William Norman Emily Elizabeth (Essie) m. Robert Hodge Ada Charlotte Christina (Cricket)

2. Crown grants and landholders in Titirangi

This table shows the initial grantee and major landholders mentioned in this book. It does not show the many transactions and conveyances.

Lot No.	Year	Crown grantee	Conveyed to/purchased by
12	1862	Ellis	
	1896		Attwood to Hoffman
	1916		McQuoid to Wallace (part)
18	1853	Cox	
	1858		Cox to Laing
	1923		Laing to Warner
20	1856	Norman	
	1882		Connell
	1882		Laing
	1923		Laing to Warner
	1923		Warner to Laing
21	1853	Meed	
	1858		Meed to Porter
	1859		Russell to Cochrane
	1879		Samuel Jackson
22	1853	Murdoch	
	1854		Ralph
	1895		Pugh
	1897		Brabandere
	1929		Ellis
23	1855	McCauley	
	1893		Pugh
24	1856	Bremner	
	1857		Porter
	1890		de Brabandere
25	1855	Brimner	
	1856		Canty and Bishop
	1931		Bishop to Bond and Bond Ltd
	1936		Downey
26	1855	Mahon	
			Nixon
	1890		Nixon to Bishop
	1929		Bishop to Auckland City Council
27	1855	Hibernia Smyth	
	1855		Henry
	1865		Smyth to Bishop

Lot No.	Year	Crown grantee	Conveyed to/purchased by
28	1854	Henry	
	1874		Gittos
	1906		Atkinson
	1929		Auckland City Council
29	1855	Greenwood	
	1904		York
	1941		Hoffman
30	1855	Mahon	
	1878		Armstrong
	1936		Booth
32	1854	Fleming	
	1886		Armstrong
	1929		To Crown
37	1855	Crowther	
	1901		Crowther to Woonton
	1921		Anderson
38	1858	Greenwood	
	1888		Moore
	1901		Merrett to Auckland City Council
39	1855	Haslip	
	1885		McEldowney
	1939		McEldowney
44	1853	Langford	
	1853		Canty and Bishop
	1916		Bishop to Malane
	1925		Bishop to Bishop
45	1853	Langford	
	1853		Canty and Bishop
	1925		Bishop to Bishop
46	1853	Langford	
	1853		Canty and Bishop
	1925		Bishop to Bishop (part)
47	1855	Denyer	
	1901		Hoffman to Crown (Hetana Hamlet)
48	1855	Henry	
	1874		Gittos
	1885		Atkinson
49	1855	Henry	
	1885		Phillips to Atkinson
	1902		Atkinson to Auckland City (part)
	1920		Atkinson to Godley (part)

Lot No.	Year	Crown grantee	Conveyed to/purchased by
53	1854	Greenwood	
	1878		Greenwood to Woonton
	1958		Eye and others
54	1856	Laing	
	1891		Eastwood to Woonton
	1902		Shaw
92	1861	Porter	
	1881		Hall
	1927		Viskovich
	1927		Hayes Motors Ltd
242A	1886		Henry Atkinson
	1900		Phillip John Woonton
244	1886		Henry Atkinson
	1900		Phillip John Woonton
281	1882		Elizabeth Brown
	1882		George Thomas Hogg
	1886		Henry Dieterien
292	1956		Gwladys Sarah Gardner
	1966		M.R. Griersen and B.M. Griersen
	1978		City of Waitemata

3. Map of lots

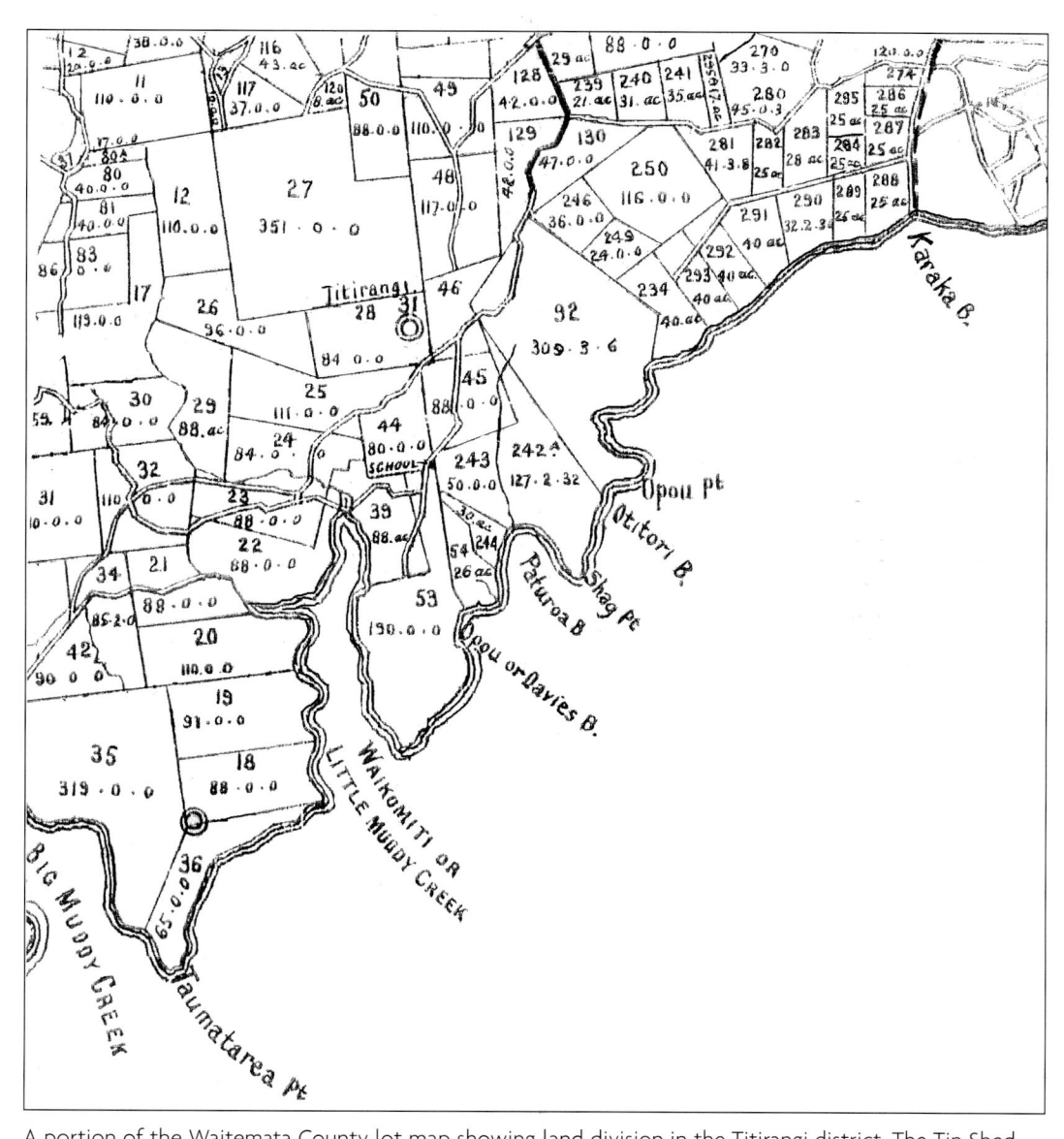

A portion of the Waitemata County lot map showing land division in the Titirangi district. The Tin Shed School is marked at the northern tip of Lot 53. New Zealand Survey, Index Map of Waitemata County, NZ Maps Sheet 2, 1895–1906 (No.4788)

4. Electoral Roll for Northern Division 1855

(*Auckland Provincial Journal*, Auckland City Library)

Robert Austin, Titirangi, Labourer
John Beechin, Muddy Creek, Labourer
Henry Bishop, Muddy Creek, Splitter
Michael Bourke, Muddy Creek, Sawyer
James Brien, Big Muddy Creek, Sawyer
David Cable, Titirangi, Farmer
Henry Carr, Little Muddy Creek, Sawyer
John Cartwright, Little Muddy Creek, Sawyer
Magnus Clark, Big Muddy Creek, Sawyer
James Coley, Big Muddy Creek, Settler
James Cox Jnr, Big Muddy Creek, Farmer
William Crouch, Titirangi, Sawyer
George Denyer Henry, Titirangi, Farmer
Terence Donnelly, Titirangi, Settler
William Filmer, Little Muddy Creek, Sawyer
John Gibbons, Huia, Prop. Of Mill
Edward Hamilton, Titirangi, Sawyer
William Harrop, Muddy Creek, Wood Cutter
Reuben Haslep, Little Muddy Creek, Sawyer
Hugh Henry, Titirangi, Sawyer
William Horne, Muddy Creek, Wood Cutter
George Jay, Titirangi, Sawyer
George Johnson, Titirangi, Sawyer
Henry Jones, Muddy Creek, Sawyer
Thomas Kaine, Big Muddy Creek, Bullock Driver
James Kelly, Titirangi, Sawyer
John Laing, Muddy Creek, Sawyer
John Laing, Big Muddy Creek, Shoe Maker
Peter Laverty, Titirangi, Sawyer
Cuthbeart Leathart, Muddy Creek, Boat Builder
Richard Lee, Muddy Creek, Sawyer
William Lucas, Big Muddy Creek, Sawyer
Richard McGraham, Titirangi, Sawyer

John McPiker Snr, Little Muddy Creek, Sawyer
John McPiker Jnr, Little Muddy Creek, Sawyer
Charles Moore, Little Muddy Creek, Carpenter
Charles Moore Jnr, Little Muddy Creek, Carpenter
Edward Murdock, Big Muddy Creek, Sawyer
James Nixon, Big Muddy Creek, Sawyer
William O'Brien, Titirangi, Sawyer
Francis O'Neil, Muddy Creek, Sawyer
Samuel Oulsen, Muddy Creek, Sawyer
Richard Parsons, Titirangi, Sawyer
Clement Partridge, Titirangi, Farmer
John Pearce, Big Muddy Creek, Sawyer
William Prior, Titirangi, Foreman
Patrick Purcell, Muddy Creek, Gardner/Shingler
John Reece Snr, Big Muddy Creek, Sawyer
John Reece Jnr, Big Muddy Creek, Sawyer
Christopher Rich, Muddy Creek, Sawyer
Thomas Riley, Titirangi, Sawyer
John Robertson, Titirangi, Farmer
James Robinson, Muddy Creek, Sawyer
Hugh Robinson, Titirangi, Farmer
John Shaw, Titirangi, Sawyer
William Sheldrake, Big Muddy Creek, Sawyer
Richard Skinner, Little Muddy Creek, Sawyer
Thomas Smith, Muddy Creek, Splitter
Joseph Smith, Titirangi, Sawyer
William Soaper, Muddy Creek, Wood Cutter
Reuben Stokers, Muddy Creek, Labourer
William Swanson, Whau, Timber Merchant
James Thurston, Titirangi, Sawyer
John Turner, Muddy Creek, Sawyer
John Wade, Huia, Settler
William Watts, Titirangi, Sawyer
Charles Williams, Muddy Creek, Sawyer
Benjamin John Wooten, Big Muddy Creek, Settler

5. Waitemata Electoral Roll, 1881

Armstrong, Leonard John, Freehold, Titirangi, Part 32, 55 acres

Armstrong, Thomas S, Freehold, Titirangi, Part 32, 55 acres

Bishop, William, Residential, Titirangi, Farmer

Boyd, John, Residential, Titirangi, Bushman

Carroll, Benjamin, Residential, Titirangi, Settler

Crown, John Moorehouse, Residential, Titirangi, Farmer

Holloway, Henry, Residential, Titirangi, Teacher

Lennox, Neilson Gordon, Freehold, Titirangi, Stationer

Mack, Thomas, Freehold, Titirangi, Farmer, Part 53, Waikomiti

Maioha, Honana, Freehold, Titirangi, Settler, 243 Waikomiti, 50 acres

Matheson, John Thomas, Freehold, Titirangi, Farmer, Part 54, Waikomiti, 13 acres

Matheson, Thomas, Freehold, Titirangi, Farmer, Part 54, Waikomiti, 13 acres and dwelling

McKee, Edward, Residential, Titirangi, Settler

McKee, Richard, Residential, Titirangi, Settler

Meade, Robert, Freehold, Titirangi, Farmer, Part 24, Waikomiti

Morrison, James, Freehold, Titirangi, Farmer, 252–255, Waikomiti, 96 acres and dwelling

Nelson, John, Residential, Titirangi, Bushman

Porter, John, Freehold, Titirangi, Settler, Part 53, Waikomiti, 31 acres and dwelling

Pugh, William, Freehold, Titirangi, Farmer, Part 24 and 45 Waikomiti, 92 acres and dwelling

Rigby, John, Residential, Titirangi, Farmer

Smith, William John, Freehold, Titirangi, Settler, Part 53, Waikomiti, 33 acres and dwelling

Woonton, Edward, Freehold, Titirangi, Farmer, Part 53, 33 acres and dwelling

Yorke, Joseph Owen, Freehold, Titirangi, Farmer, Part 24, Waikomiti, 36 acres

Spanz, Charles, Residential, Titirangi, Farm Labourer

6. Titirangi women enrolled to vote in the Eden electorate, 1893

Adams, Hannah, Titirangi, Domestic Duties

Armstrong, Eliza Jane, Titirangi, Domestic Duties

Armstrong, Louisa Linda, Titirangi, Domestic Duties

Austin, Emma, Titirangi, Domestic Duties

Austin, Marie, Titirangi, Domestic Duties

Bishop, Alexandrina, Titirangi, Domestic Duties

Duncan, Kate, Titirangi, Teacher

Hogg, Hannah Elizabeth, Titirangi, Domestic Duties

Kilgour, Matilda, Titirangi, Domestic Duties

McEldowney, Lydia, Titirangi, Domestic Duties

Sheffield, Jessie, Titirangi, Domestic Duties

Yorke, Mary, Titirangi, Domestic Duties

7. The Titirangi Post Office

1 Mar. 1873	Post Office opened. Mr James Pugh appointed Post Master.
1877	Thomas Coulter appointed Post Master. Post Office moved from Pugh's house to old Bishop house in Huia Road.
1878	H. Carrol appointed Post Master.
1878	Henry Halloway appointed Post Master.
1883	J. Porter appointed Post Master.
1913	Mrs A.J. Bishop appointed Post Mistress.
1931	Mr W.A. Bishop appointed Post Master.
1931	Post Office moved to Tea Kiosk (in newly built Lopdell House).
1935–47	Post Office held at Titchener's grocery.
1939	Telephone facilities added (private).
1947–68	Army Hut Post Office with public telephone facility from 1946.
Oct. 1961	First Post Office Little Muddy Creek. John Porter appointed Post Master. (Porter died by drowning in 1862.)
June 1962	Post Office closed.
May 1862	New Post Office opened in Big Muddy Creek. William Filmer appointed Post Master.

1862	John Wood appointed Post Master.
1864	John Jones appointed Post Master (salary £1 per year).
1884	Alexander Hackie appointed Post Master.
Oct. 1885	Name changed to Brook Lynn.
Jan. 1913	Name changed to Nihotupu.
Dec. 1914	Name changed to Parau.
April 1916	Closed.
5 Nov. 1921	Reopened as Parau.

8. The Titirangi Drama Group

1935	Institute Room built (Macandrew Hall).
1942	First Christmas play.
1944	Prizewinner North Auckland Federation of Women's Institutes.
1951	Men appearing in casts (other than the pantomime).
1956	In New Zealand finals British Drama League.
1959	£1000 pounds to enlarge stage and improve seating.
1964	Last programme with title Titirangi CWI Drama Circle.

Titirangi Drama Group

1966	More funds needed to upgrade hall fire safety regulations and toilets.
1967	Garden Party at Rangiwai to raise funds for hall upgrade.
1969	First of a series of fundraising costume balls.
1973	Another fundraising Garden Party.
1976	Became an incorporated society.
1982	Three-year lease taken out on Paturoa Beach Hall. Backed Titirangi Community Arts Council to persuade Waitemata City Council to buy Lopdell House.
1984	Brian Keys, architect, instructed to go ahead with preliminary plans for new theatre. $10,000 loan from Waitemata City Council. Negotiations with council.
1984	Plans to move to Lopdell Theatre. Delays, but *The Visit* put on in April. Promotional evenings. Loans from Waitemata City Council, grants from Lotteries, Portage Trust, Northern Regional Arts Council enabled theatre to be finished. Brian Berg is President during this year.

Further reading

Architecture

Clark, Justine and Walker, Paul, *Looking for the local: Architecture and the New Zealand Modern*. Victoria University Press, Wellington, 2000.

Gatley, Julia (ed.), *Long Live the Modern, New Zealand's New Architecture 1904–1984*. Auckland University Press, Auckland, 2008.

Lloyd Jenkins, Douglas, *At Home: A Century of New Zealand Design*. Random House, Auckland, 2004.

McKay, Bill, 'Modern Houses in the West' in *Block: The Broadsheet of the Auckland Branch of the New Zealand Institute of Architects*. Itinerary n. 13, 2008–4.

McKay, Bill, 'A Possum in the Kiwi Bush' in *R. Blythe & R. Spense (eds.), Thresholds*. SAHANZ, 1999, pp. 209–212.

Norton, Peter, *The New Zealand Pole House*. Hickson's Timber Impregnation Co. (NZ) Ltd, Auckland, 1976.

Pound, Francis, *The Invention of New Zealand: Art & National Identity, 1930–1970*. Auckland University Press, Auckland, 2010.

Shaw, Peter, *A History of New Zealand Architecture*. Hodder Moa Beckett, Auckland, 1997.

Shaw, Peter, 'Modernism in New Zealand Architecture' in Daley, Debra (ed.), *New Zealand Home and Building*: The Newstalk 1ZB 1950s Show. Robin Beckett, Auckland, 1992, pp. 22–31.

Arts

Coney, Sandra, *Cameron Johnson: First artist of the West Coast of Auckland*. Keyhole Press, Auckland, 2010.

McIvor, Lois, *Memoir of the Sixties*. Remuera Gallery, Auckland, 2008.

Simpson, Peter, *Colin McCahon, The Titirangi Years 1953–1959*. Auckland University Press, Auckland, 2007.

West Auckland History

Diamond, John T., *Once the Wilderness*. The Lodestar Press (3rd ed.), Auckland, 1977.

Harvey, Bruce and Trixie (eds), *Waitakere Ranges: Nature, History, Culture*. Waitakere Ranges Protection Society Inc., Auckland, 2006.

MacDonald, Finlay and Ruth Kerr (eds), *West: The History of Waitakere*. Random House, Auckland, 2009.

Northcote-Bade, James (ed.), *West Auckland Remembers*. West Auckland Historical Society Inc., Auckland, 1990.

Northcote-Bade, James (ed.), *West Auckland Remembers: Volume 2*. West Auckland Historical Society Inc., Auckland, 1992.

O'Grady, Alison, *West Lynn Garden: A Place of Beauty*. West Lynn Garden Society Inc., Auckland, 2010.

Scott, Dick, *Fire on the Clay*. Southern Cross Books, Auckland, 1979.

Index

Roman numerals refer to colour sections.

Abbott, Zena   102
Addis, Gordon   218
'Aid-ee-s Canoe'   140
Aimer, Kenny   154, 155
Akitai   15, 16, 17
Alice Glen   13
Allen, Cyril   76, 79, 200
Allen, Miss   171
Anzac Day services   52
Arataki Visitors' Centre   64, 124, 160
Arlingtons   84
Armstrong, John   29
Armstrong, Tom   46, 145
Atkin, William   20
Atkinson family   55
Atkinson, Henry   55, 57, 58, 81, 122
statue   vi
Atkinson House   107
Atkinson Paddock   147
Atkinson Park   64
Atkinson Road   148, 154, 159
Atkinson, Edna   57, 201, 202
Atkinson, Harry (Henry)   29, 30
Atkinson, Harry and Edna   50, 79, 80, 201
Atkinson, Henry Jr   57
Atkinson, Hubert James (Bert)   56, 65, 149, 220
Atkinson, Jean and Nancy   58, 149
Atkinson Valley Road   157, 214
Auckland Automobile Association   61
Auckland Bus Company   68, 69, 70, 174, 179, 188, 214, 221
Auckland Centennial Memorial Park   125
Aunt Countess   145
Avonleigh Road   153

Baildon, Miss   199
Baker, Charles   24
Banks, Margaretha   51
Bates, Edward   122
Belsh, Tommy   185
Bethell, Pa   156, 176
Beveridge, Bill   49, 184
Beveridge, Joe   41, 63, 163, 164, 184
Big Muddy Creek   20
Bishop, Ada   143, 145, 164, 165, 168, 213

Bishop, Alec   34, 65, 72, 80, 83, 170, 201, 209
tea rooms   38
Bishop, Bill   39, 194
Bishop, Christina (Cricket, Aunty Winder, Aunty Crister)   33, 137, 164, 165, 168
Bishop, Emily Elizabeth (Essie)   37, 91, 142, 168
Bishop, Euphemia   209
Bishop family tree   225
Bishop, Gus (T.A.)   139, 168, 178, 191, 193, 208
Bishop, Henrietta   209
Bishop Kiosk   38
Bishop, John   19, 24, 27, 136, 141, 142, 179, 208
Bishop, John (Jack)   139, 167
Bishop, John Joseph (Chappie)   12, 29, 32, 34, 136, 139, 142, 167, 208
Bishop, Mary Katherine (Mrs Fraser/Garbeley)   36, 169
Bishop reunion 1965   39
Bishop, Sarah   209
Bishop, Thomas Augustus   32, 35, 36, 37, 90
Bishop, W.C.N.   34
Bishop, William Norman   37, 38, 51, 52, 91, 92, 166
Bishop, William Thomas   30, 34
Bishop's Gate   26, 87
Bishop's Hill   136
Blaicklock, Dr David   128, 205
Blaicklock, Professor E.M.   15, 85, 127, 128, 129, 160, 188, 205, 206, 208, 224
Blaicklock, Jean   224
Blaicklock, Peter   224
Bledisloe, Governor-General Lord Charles   129, 209
Blockhouse Bay   13, 14, 152, 153
Bloomfield and Partners   73
Boer War   51
Bond, Bill and Mary   192
Bonny, Emil   221
Bonny, Marc   86, xxx, xxxi
Boots family   160
Bougher, Eddie   218
Bown, Milly   206
Bowness Bay   161
Boyd, Reverend   158
Boyes, Neville   149
Boylan Road   169

Brace, Reverend Edwin 191
Brake, Brian 102, xvii
Bray, Alan 178, 179
Bray, Charles 178, 184
Bray, Estelle 178
Bray, Thomas 20
Bray, Wilemina Mary 178
Bright, Ellen 161
Bright, George 161
Bright, Harry 161, 162
Bright, Margaret 161, 162
Brimner, William 25, 41
Brittania 219
Broady, Alwynne 53, 157, 163, 221, 224
Broady, Paris 224
Brooklyn (Parau) 50, 137
Brown, Barrett 122
Brown, Vernon 123
Buffett, Peter 65, 71
Burbery, Arthur 148
Burbery, George 147
Burbery, Jane 148, 16
Butchers Alley 155, 156, 220
Butler, Mike 147

Campbell, A.M. 128, 171
Campbell, Rod 83
Canty, Thomas 25, 208
Canty's Creek (Oratia Stream) 25, 56
Carpay, Frank 104, 119
Carrol, Ben 27, 46, 71, 142
Carr-Rollett, Bill 88, 220
Carter Road 61
Carter, Heather 190, 198, 199
Caselberg, John 103
Casey, Jack 172, 173, 174
Cashmore family 172
Castle, Len 101, 109, 110, xxvii
Catholic Church 80, 84, 89, 198
Chant family 165
Chapman, Dr G.U.P. 97, 170, 171
Chermside, Bill 200, 216
Clark, Geoffrey 165
Clark, Ken 185, 188
Clark, Kitty 184, 185, 188
Clark, Tom 84, 165, 188, 224
Clark's Bush 125, 128
Clark's kauri 136, 187
Coates, Gordon 177, 211, 212
Coleman, Linden 97, 218
Coleman, Lyn 224
Commercial Buses 68
Conlon, Captain Sydney 85, 86

Conlon, Thora 85
Cottingham, Lynn 171
Coulter, Jack and Lillian 209
Coulter, Thomas 29, 46, 209
Country Women's Institute 183, 184, 219, 222
Crown grants 226
Crum Park 147
Curnow, Allen 106
Cumming, Professor Ian xxxi

Daffodil Farm 53, 148, 159, 214
Daffodil Street 53, 158
Davies Bay 45
de Brabandere family 43, 130
de Brabandere, Robert 137, 139
Denyer, George Henry 21, 43
Denyer, Henrietta 43
Diamond, Jack (John) 133
Diana 24
Diggle, Edith xi
Donner, Tibor 57, 105, 201, 220, 222, xviii, xix
Dorset 17
Drama Club 77
Dunvegan 26, 33, 168
Dyer, May 197, 200

Eden Garden 131, 132
electoral rolls 230
Elias, Dr 220
Elias, Sian 220
Ellis, Mr 151
Endt, Dick 165
Eureka 148
Exhibition Drive 59, 60, 62, 67, 141, 164, 168, 169, 184, 187, 188, 194

Fairburn, Geoff 149, 150
Fairburn, Thayer 15, 149, 156, 201, 222
Ferris, Mr 220
First World War see World War, First
Fitzroy, Governor Robert 17
Foley, Charlie 186, 188
Foley, Consuelo 184, 185, 188
Folk Music Club 121
Ford, Mr 156
Foster, Bob 95
Frank Lopdell House 76
Franklin, Ted 220
Fraser, Bruce 169
Frazer, Sister 194

French Bay   93, 94 171, 182, 202, 203, 214, 218, 219, xxx
French Bay Sporting Association 1938   93
French Bay Yacht Club   93, 95, 172, 218, 223, xxxii

garden party   33
Gardner Brothers   152
Gardner, Charles Fisher   85, 149, 154
Geddes family   57, 122, 123, 224
Geddes, Andrew   122
Geddes, Claire   122
Geddes, Edward   122, 174, 183
Geddes, Ethelwyn   58, 100, 122, 201, 219, xiv
Geddes, Janet   122
Geddes, John   122, 123, 174, 183, xv
Geddes, John McKail   50, 122, 123, 207
Geddes, Mac   201
Gibbs, Ron   219
Gillies, Colin   122
Godley Road   14, 147, 152, 153, 197
Godley, Lena   84
Golf Road   152, 188, 199, 222
Gordon, Esme   163
Gordon, Glenis   164
Gordon, Graham   163, 164, 165
Gordon, Ian   165
Gordon, Ken   163, 164, 165
Gordon, Richard and Melanie   164
Gordon, Sam   164
Gray, Murray   121
Green Bay   13, 149
Green, Miss   46
Greenwood, Mr   45
Gregg, Logan   81, 83, 86
Grendon Road   41, 154, 187
'Grey Ghost'   97, 98
Grey, Governor George   17
Grierson Amer and Draffin   66, 154, 203
Grierson, John   130, 149, 224
Grinter Brothers   66
Group Architects   109
Groves, Pauline   171
Guernsey Valley Farm 52
Gunn, Reverend Jim   158, 200, 210, 222

Hackshaw, James   109
Hamilton, Dr Mary   200, 221
Hanson, Ken   191, 195
Hanson, Victor   193
Happy Valley   148
Hardware Café, The   39, 87, 88, 117, 170, 191, 209, 216, xi

Haresnape, Bill   104, 107
Haresnape, Isobel   156
Haresnape House   xxii
Harre, Bill   175, 176
Harvey, Mayor Bob   77
Haslep, Reuben   26
Hawkins, N.G.   128, 210, 211
Hay, Wally   148
Haywood, Rudall   131, 169
Hazlett   21
Hebe bishopiana   35, iv
Helenslea   164
Henderson House   109
Henderson Mill   18
Henderson, Bruce   100, 107, 108, xii, xxxi
Henry, Hugh   21, 42
Henry, John   42
Henry's (Bishop's) Hill   42
Hetana Hamlet   43
Hewitt, Captain   172
Hewitt, Norm   98, 172, 173, 219, 224
Hieatt, Brett   223
Hieatt, Gordon Scarlett   224
Hikurangi Purchase   17
Hoby, Jay   149, 221
Hobson, Governor William   17
Hodge, Essie   92, 136, 141
Hodinott, Jack   194
Hodson   151, 152
Hoffman, Herman   63, 168, 169
Hole, Geoff   78, 79, 100, 221, xiv, xvi
Holibar, Bernard   83, 169
Holt, Horace and Freda   7, 20, 128
Home and Building   106, 109, 203, 222
Honaki   219
Hongi Hika   14, 15, 16
Horrocks family   218
Hotel Titirangi   71, 73, 74, 75
Huia   202
Huia Dam   141
Huia Filter Station   165
Hunter, Jack   220
Hunter, Mr   75
Hyam, Joseph   19

Isaacson, Mr   194
Island Creek   167

Jacobs, Dr   198
Jacobsen Brothers   141
Jacobsen's Depot   61
Jacobsen's Tunnel   168
Jenkin, Arthur   152

Jenkin, David   121
Jenkins, Geoff   216
Jess   24
Johnston, J.S.   30
Johnston, Cameron   31
Johnston, Tom   224
Jones, Mrs   182
Jones, Dora   34
Jones, Jack and Essie   216

Karangahape Pa   15, 16
Karaka Pa   14
kauri   124, 150
Kauri Timber Company   136
Kearney, Fane   57, 58
Keller, Helen   76
Kelly, John   20
Kennedy, David   86, 102, 108, 203, xxvi
Kennedy, Garth   203
Kennedy, Gianna   203
Kennedy, Phylis   203
Kilgours   158
Kiln Hill   31, 139
Kiwi Tamaki   15
Knight family   15
Kohu Road   201
Konini Road   181
Kopiko Road   160, 184, 205, 206
Koromiko Road   205
Kororareka   24
Kotuitanga   13
Kurtz, Edmund   155

Laing, Duff   137
Laing, Les   137
Laing, Marshall   65, 150
Laingholm   13, 68, 202
Laishley, Reverend Richard   14
Landing Road   133
Lane, John Vernon   220
Langford, John Alfred   25
Langlands, Mr   179
Law Society Dixieland Band   123
Lawrence, Dave   90
Lawrence, Harry   97, 224
Leathart, Cuthbert   42
Lee, Lincoln   xxxi
Lewis, Betty   216
Lewis, Harry Morgan   83, 84, 88, 89, 95, 171, 215, 219, 224
Library Trustees Interim Committee   47
Links Road   153

Little Muddy Creek   13, 136, 141, 154, 180, 186, v
Little Muddy Creek Post Office   41
Little Muddy Bridge   v
Little Muddy Landing   17
Lopdell House   76, 98, 105, 191, 200, 212, 221, vi
Lopdell House Gallery   77, 131
Lord, Reverend   183
Lott, Letitia   171
Lower Nihotupu Dam   160, 188
Luckens, Mrs   69, 158, 157, 205
Ludwig, Elaine   191
Lunn, Mr   158
Lusty, Lillian   38

Macandrew, Arthur   78, 222
Macandrew, Jennie   78
MacFarlane   149
Mackies Rest   62, 63, 141, 168, 188, 207
Maddison, Dr Peter   132
Mamaku   219, 221
Manukau Harbour   144, 153, 177, 180, 181, 182, 194, 219, 220, 223
Manukau View   24
Manukau Volunteer Coast Guard   96
Martin, Reverend   158
Masala restaurant   191
Mason, Honorable H.G.R.   89, 177
Mason, J.R.   49, 177
Matheson, Thomas   42
Mathew, Felton   17
Maungakieke   14
Macandrew Hall   79, 100, 147, 149, 157, 158, 184, 198, 201, 207
McCahon, Colin   77, 100, xxviii, xxix
McCrae, Bob   159, 213
McEldowney family   42, 136, 137, 187, 224
McEldowney Road   41
McEldowney, Arthur   215
McGrail, Mr   205
McHardy, Mayor I.G.   123
McIvor, Lois   100, xxvii
McKenzie Road   169
McLay, Miss   183
McLeod, Christina   208
McLeod, Elizabeth   24, 25
McLeod, John   24, 208
McNaughton, Bruce   131
McPherson, Isabel   164
McPike, J.   26
McQuoid family   67, 68
Mead, Arthur   97, 178

Mealing, Mr   147
Mellars, Judith and Lyndell   171
Mihaljevich, George   221
Millet family   172
Mitchell House   107
Mitchell, John   16
Mitchinson family   171
Monument Hill   213
Moore, Charlie   21
Morepork Hill   169
Mount Atkinson   61, 136, 180, 184, 185, 214
Murch, George and Katie   149
Murdoch, Graeme   16

Navarina   22
Nelson, Jack   28, 138, 167
New Lynn   14
New Lynn Borough Council   131
New Lynn School   151, 155, 213
New Lynn Timber Company   217
New Vision Gallery   101
New World Supermarket   214
Newby, Jack   172, 218
New Zealand Land Wars   8
Nga Oho   15
Ngapuhi   16, 122
Ngaire   218
Ngati Ata   15, 16, 17
Ngati Awa   15
Ngati Poutukeka   16
Ngati Whatua   15, 16, 17
Nihotupu Dam   56, 59, 60, 97
Nihotupu Filter Station   62
Nixon's Paddock   138
Norton, Peter   xxiv
North, Murray   130
Northcott, Martin   93

O'Grady, Alison   131
Odlin, Jim   50
Odlin, Joan and Pat   201
Ogier, Tom   52
Okewa Road   170, 171, 217, 220, 221, xxxi
Old Tin Shed   184
Old Titirangi Road   218
Onehunga   144
Onslow, Lord   30
Opou Point   16, 93
Opou Road   218
Oratia   156, 166, 170, 175, 176, 192, 213, 215
Oratia Stream   25, 56
Orpheus   156, 193, 207, 208

Orr-Walker House   112, xxiii

Parau   157, 160, 178, 202
Park Drive Kiosk   81
Park Road   170
Parkers Brickworks   152
Parr, C.J.   36, 59, 61, 64, 141
Parr, Jack   28, 138, 167
Patterson, Mr   27, 46, 142
Paturoa Beach   204
Paturoa Road   182, 220
Peace, Mrs   185
Pearl   45
Peat, Bertha   208
Peat, Frank Oscar   29, 71, 72, 149, 208, 210, 211
Peate, P.W.   73
Peat, Robert Betts   209, iii
Perrin, Patricia   101
Pinesong   84, 86
Pleasant Road   188
Plowman, Keith   200
Pollard House   109, 111, xx, xxi
Pollard, Trevor   6, 97, 99, 223
Pollard, Trish   223
Pope, Reverend   183
Porsolt, Imi   109, xxi
Portage Road   149
Porter   18
Porter, Alice   17
Porter, Captain William Field   17, 19, 20
Porter, John   28, 41
Poutukeka   16
Prebyterian church   198, 200
Presbyterian Women's Union   92, 160
Pugh Farm   47, 48, 56
Pugh, William   27, 46, 47, 142, 166
Puketutu Island   16
punky tree   31, ii
Puponga   15
puriri tree   124, 216

Quamby/Quambi   72, 149, 183, 210, 211

Rahui Kahika   125
Rakataura   13
Rangiwai   122, 127, 220
Rangiwai Hill   213
Rangiwai Road   191, 201, 220
Rankin, Jim   141
Rarawa   143
Rau, Mr   148
Rawling family   168

Reckie, R.   81, 83
Reckies/Reekies   81, 89, 160, 170, 174, 182
Reeves, Sir Paul   132
Reid, Robert   122
Renown, H.M.S.   140
Rewi's Last Stand   131, 169
Ridge Road   171
Rigby, John   71
Rigby's (Rangiwai) Hill   41
Robinson, Raewyn   191
Roche, Lieutenant Colonel   30
Rogers, Tommy   151
Rollett, F. Carr   62
Ronaki   219
Rouell, Zella   216
Royal Forest and Bird Society   130
Rudolph Steiner School   133
Ruru Hill   38, 169

Sage, Mr   158
Sang, Ron   110, xvii
Scarlett, Brett   223
Scarlett, Gordon   223
Scarlett, Jo   223
Scarlett, T.H.   222
Scarlett, William   43, 70
Scenic Drive   62, 163, 182, 188, 194
School Road   136, 142, 170, 180
Scott, Dick   103
Seddon, Richard John   43
Shadbolt, Maurice   102, 121
Shadbolt, Tim   131
Shag Point   219, 220
Shaw family   xi
Shaw Road   63, 163, 192, 194, 214
Shaw, Arthur   213
Shaw, Bob and Bill   212
Shaw Fred   212, 214
Shaw, Gilbert   67, 68, 184, 188, 197, 213
Shaw, Graham and Vivienne   212
Shaw, John   163
Shaw, Rod   124, 178, 180, 192, 200, 212
Shears, Bill   69
Shrubsall family   73, 75, 174
Silich, Mrs   174
Silva, Wally   218
Simcock, Derek   174
Sluiters, Hendrina   194
Smeele, Peter   86, 87, 102, vii
Smith, Frank   145
Smith, Graham   194
Smyth, Hibernia   22, 23, 138, 148
Soutar family   89

South Lynn Road   190
South Titirangi Road   17, 92, 154, 209, 213, 221
Sowery family   181, 216
Sowery, Mabel   184
Speer, Bertha   208
Speer, Thomas Robert   208
Speer, William   29
Stack, Frederick Rice   i
St Andrews Society of New Lynn   224
St Francis Hall   92
St Louis   25
Staniland, John   128
Strewe, Odo   102, 109, 165
Strid, Bill   88
Surman, Mr and Mrs   177
Surman, Emily   29

Tamaki isthmus   13, 17
Tamaki Makau-Rau   14
Tamaki River   15
Tanekaha Road   170, 216, 221, xxxii
Tangiwai Reserve   130
Taplin, Mrs and Lorraine   172
Tarlin, Clarrie   139
Taylor, Ned   141
Te Kai o Poutukeka   16
Te Karaka   15
Te Kawerau a Maki   14, 15, 16, 17
Te Keene, Chief   17
Te Whau Point   14
Thode, Arthur   218
Thomas family   158, 214
Thomas, Albert Peter   53, 148
Thomas, Martin   148
Thompson, Jeff   220
Thuell, Jack   172
Thursby, Fred   148
Tildersley, Ann   181
Timmins family   150
Tin Shed School   49, 51, 167, 217
Tinling, Alexandrina   29, 46
Titchener, Mr   157
Titchener, Adrienne   210
Titchener, Arthur   39, 170, 180, 182, 191, 205, 212, 216
Titchener, Vernon   29, 170, 188, 210, 211, 216
Titchener, Wallie   39, 208, 210, 212
Titchener, Walter   39, 209
Titirangi Beach   153, 161, 170, 193, 202, 203, 214, 217, 221
Titirangi Beach Hall   104

Index   243

Titirangi Beautification Society 79, 217
Titirangi bus 68
Titirangi Bush Preservation Society 9, 126, 128, 129, 130
Titirangi Community House 133
Titirangi Country Women's Institute 78
Titirangi Drama 116
Titirangi Drama Group 201, 233
Titirangi Filters Ratepayers and Residents Association 130
Titirangi Fire Brigade 224
Titirangi Folk Club 104
Titirangi Highway Board members 44
Titirangi Highway District 20, 44
Titirangi Hotel 66, 179, 180, 188, 217
Titirangi Kiosk 37, 67
Titirangi Light Opera Company 198
Titirangi Music Festival 121
Titirangi Painters 133, xiii
Titirangi Post Office 197, 200, 232
Titirangi Primary School 191
Titirangi Ratepayers' and Residents' Association 130, 132
Titirangi Ratepayers Association 37, 77, 89, 104
Titirangi Road 37, 160, 182, 188, 218
Titirangi Returned Servicemen's Association 9, 35, 80, 88, 89, 90
Titirangi School 38, 46, 50, 57, 159, 179, iii, x
Titirangi School Committee 34, 38, 42, 50, 58, 89
Titirangi School for the Deaf 76, 160, 197, 200
Titirangi Soldiers' Memorial Church 91, 158, 182, 189, 210, 221, 224, ii
Titirangi Tatler 132
Titirangi Village puriri tree 129
Titirangi Volunteer Fire Brigade 98, 99, 97, 215, vii
Titirangi War Memorial 52, 58, 76, 90, 219, viii
Titirangi War Memorial Hall 35, 78, 133, 191
Toby Jug 81, 154
Tobys 81, 84, 170, x
Tokoroa Point 13
Transport Bus Service 159
Treasure House 71, 73, 208, 209, 210
turehu 14

Upper Nihotupu Dam 56, 140, 160, 178, 185

Vagabond 223
van der Voort, Pim 130

Vischer, Estelle Canter 178
Vulinovich, Mattie 174

Waikomiti Hotel 7
Waima 166, 194, 220
Waima Crescent/Road 167, 167, 181, 188, 194
Waima Stone 131
Waiohua 8, 14, 15, 16 17
Waitakere City Council 131, 132
Waitakere Ranges Protection Society 130
Waite, Harvey 45
Ward, Maurice 151
Watercare Services Limited 63
Wattle Bay 171, 177
Webb, Bill 220, xxxi
Webber, Robert and John 172, 173, 216, 218
West Lynn Garden 131
Westbury, Mr 186, 187
Whatipu 207, 208
Whau (River) 13, 15, 16-20, 27, 44, 155
Whau Bridge 43, 149, 156, 201
Whau canal 56
whau (plant) iv
Whau portage 14, 15, 18, 56
Whau Portage Sculpture 14, iv
Whiteoak, Cyril 102, xi
Wiles, Mrs 218
Wilson, Bill 109
Wilson, Howard and Shirley 194
Winder, Adam 28
Windust, Patience 145, 146
Witten, Lily 47, 49
Witten Hannah family 149
Wood Bay 101, 153, 177, 190, 222
Woodfern Crescent 157
Woodmans Rest 16, 42
Woonton, Edward 45
Woonton, Lou (Mrs Waite) 186
Woonton, Phillip John 45
Woontons Bay (Davies) 186
World War, First 35, 51, 72, 83, 88, 89, 91, 140, 179, 183, 184, 210, 212, 214, 215
World War, Second 49, 68, 69, 75, 88, 90, 106, 216, 220
Worley House 108
Worley family 86, 87

Young, Beatrice 183

Zellas Home Cookery and Tea Room 157, 191, 197, 205, 215
Zig-Zag Track 58, 162, 172, 185, 214